China

AS A GREAT POWER

MYTHS, REALITIES
AND CHALLENGES
IN THE
ASIA-PACIFIC
REGION

EDITED BY STUART HARRIS &
GARY KLINTWORTH

China

AS A GREAT POWER

MYTHS, REALITIES AND
CHALLENGES
IN THE
ASIA-PACIFIC
REGION

EDITED BY STUART HARRIS &
GARY KLINTWORTH

 LONGMAN

St. Martin's Press
New York

Longman Australia Pty Ltd
Longman House
Kings Gardens
95 Coventry Street
Melbourne 3205 Australia

Offices in Sydney, Brisbane, Perth, and associated companies throughout the world.

Cover Design by Rob Cowpe
Typeset by Kimberly Ellen
Set in Palatino 10/12 pt
Printed in Singapore
through Longman Singapore

The
publisher's
policy is to use
paper manufactured
from sustainable forests

National Library of Australia
Cataloguing-in-Publication data

China as a great power: myths, realities and challenges in the Asia-Pacific region.

Includes index.
ISBN 0 582 80320 9

1. Great powers. 2. China - Foreign relations - Asia. 3. Asia -Foreign relations - China. 4. China - Foreign relations - Pacific Area. 5. Pacific Area - Foreign relations - China. I. Harris, Stuart, 1931– . II. Klintworth, Gary, 1945- . (Series : Topics in Asian history, politics and international relations).

327.5105

CHINA AS A GREAT POWER: MYTHS, REALITIES AND CHALLENGES IN THE ASIA-PACIFIC REGION

St Martin's Press, Scholarly and Reference Division, 175 Fifth Avenue, New York, N.Y. 10010

Printed in Singapore

ISBN 0-312-1206-7

Library of Congress Cataloging-in-Publications Data

China as a great power: myths, realities, and challenges in the Asia-Pacific region/ [edited] by Stuart Harris & Gary Klintworth.--1st ed.
    p.   , 23.4cm x 15.6cm
    Includes bibliographical references and index.
    ISBN 0-312-12106-7 : $39.95
1. Asia--Foreign relations--China. 2. China--Foreign relations--Asia. 3. China--Politics and government--1976- 4. China--Economic conditions--1976-   I. Harris, Stuart, 1931- . II. Klintworth, Gary, 1945-   .
DS33.4.C5C46 1995
327.5103--dc20   95-10897

CIP
First edition 1995
First published in the United States of America 1995 by
Scholarly and Reference Division,
ST. MARTIN'S PRESS, INC.,
175 Fifth Avenue,
New York, N.Y. 10010

Contents

Tables

Figures

Acronyms and Abbreviations

ACD	arms control and disarmament
ADB	Asian Development Bank
AMM	Annual Ministerial Meeting (ASEAN)
APEC	Asia-Pacific Economic Co-operation
ARF	ASEAN Regional Forum
ASEAN	Association of Southeast Asian Nations
BAKIN	National Intelligence Co-ordinating Board (Indonesia)
BCP	Burmese Communist Party
CBMs	confidence-building measures
CCP	Chinese Communist Party
CCPIT	China Council for the Promotion of International Trade
CNS	comprehensive national strength
COCOM	Co-ordinating Committee for Export to Communist Areas
COSCO	Chinese Ocean Shipping Company
CPM	Communist Party of Malaya
CPT	Communist Party of Thailand
CSCAP	Conference on Security and Co-operation in the Asia-Pacific
CSCE	Conference on Security and Co-operation in Europe

DPRK	Democratic People's Republic of Korea
EAEC	East Asian Economic Caucus
EC	European Community
EDI	Electronic Data Exchange
EEZ	Exclusive Economic Zone
FDI	foreign direct investment
GATT	General Agreement on Tariffs and Trade
GDP	gross domestic product
GNP	gross national product
GSP	Generalised System of Preferences
IAEA	International Atomic Energy Agency
IDA	International Development Agency
IDSA	Institute for Defence Studies and Analyses
IMF	International Monetary Fund
IPR	intellectual property rights
ISIS	Institute of Strategic and International Studies
KADIN	Indonesian Chamber of Commerce and Industry
KMT	Guomindang (Kuomintang)
LAC	Line of Actual Control
LDP	Liberal Democratic Party
MFN	Most Favoured Nation
MIA	missing in action
MITI	Ministry of International Trade and Industry
MOU	Memorandum of Understanding
MPT	Ministry of Posts and Telecommunications
MTCR	Missile Technology Control Regime
NAFTA	North America Free Trade Agreement
NEPA	National Environmental Protection Agency
NGO	non-governmental organisation
NIEs	newly industrialising economies

NIEO	New International Economic Order
NPT	Non-Proliferation Treaty
ODA	Overseas Development Assistance
OOCL	Orient Overseas Container Line
PBEC	Pacific Basin Economic Committee
PECC	Pacific Economic Co-operation Council
PLA	People's Liberation Army
PPP	purchasing power parities
PRC	People's Republic of China
RMB	Renminbi
SALT	Strategic Arms Limitation Talks
START	Strategic Arms Reduction Treaty
TAC	Treaty of Amity and Cooperation (ASEAN)
TCR	Trans-China Railway
TEUs	Twenty-foot Equivalent Units
TKR	Trans-Korean Railway
TMGR	Trans-Mongolian Railway
TMR	Trans-Manchurian Railway
TSR	Trans-Siberian Railway
UNCED	United Nations Conference on Environment and Development
UNDP	United Nations Development Program
UNEP	United Nations Environmental Program
USSR	Union of Soviet Socialist Republics
VCP	Vietnamese Communist Party
VPA	Vietnamese People's Army
WMD	weapons of mass destruction

Contributors

Greg Austin, Research Fellow, Northeast Asia Program, Research School of Pacific and Asian Studies, Australian National University, Canberra

Des Ball, Professor, Strategic and Defence Studies Centre, Research School of Pacific and Asian Studies, Australian National University, Canberra

Leszek Buszynski, formerly Senior Research Fellow, Strategic and Defence Studies Centre, Research School of Pacific and Asian Studies, Australian National University, Canberra

James Cotton, Professor of Political Science, University of Tasmania, Hobart

Rafe De Crespigny, Reader, Faculty of Asian Studies, Australian National University, Canberra

Christopher Findlay, Director of the Chinese Economy Research Unit, University of Adelaide, Adelaide

David S.G. Goodman, Institute for International Studies, University of Technology, Sydney

Stuart Harris, Convenor, Northeast Asia Program, Research School of Pacific and Asian Studies, Australian National University, Canberra

Hong Lijian, Department of Asian Languages and Studies, Monash University, Melbourne

Hu Angang, Research Fellow, Research Centre of Eco-Environmental Sciences, Chinese Academy of Sciences, Beijing, People's Republic of China

J. Bruce Jacobs, Chairman, Department of Asian Languages and Studies, Monash University, Melbourne

Samuel S. Kim, Professor, Woodrow Wilson School of Public and International Affairs, Princeton University, Princeton, USA

Gary Klintworth, formerly Senior Research Fellow, Northeast Asia Program, Research School of Pacific and Asian Studies, Australian National University, Canberra

Murray McLean, Assistant Secretary, East Asia Branch, Department of Foreign Affairs and Trade, Canberra

J. Mohan Malik, Lecturer in Defence Studies, Faculty of Arts, Deakin University, Geelong

Peter Rimmer, Head, Department of Human Geography, Research School of Pacific and Asian Studies, Australian National University, Canberra

Sha Zukang, Deputy Director, Department of International Organisations, Ministry of Foreign Affairs, Beijing, People's Republic of China

Carlyle Thayer, Associate Professor, Department of Politics, University of New South Wales, Australian Defence Force Academy, Canberra

Ian Wilson, Senior Lecturer, Department of Politics, Faculty of Arts, Australian National University, Canberra

You Ji, Lecturer, Department of Political Science, University of Canterbury, Christchurch, New Zealand

Preface

In considering the challenges that the dynamic development in Asia is offering to the world, global attention is belatedly turning away from the presumed pre-eminence of Japan to the future role of China.

China's size and geographic location, along with its capacity to sustain economic growth under difficult conditions, have brought into focus the potentiality of China not just in economic competition terms but in political and strategic terms as well. This potentially has been reinforced by China's permanent membership of the United Nations Security Council. Moreover, China's well-publicised military modernisation, disputes over various ocean boundaries and island sovereignties in the South and East China Seas, as well as its relations with North Korea, have raised China's profile on the international agenda.

Whereas domestic developments in China have long been studied in depth by experts from various countries, China's foreign relations, and particularly the range of its actual and potential impacts on its own region, have been examined less intensively.

Although the question of global interaction is already raising apprehension in the West, it is in the more immediate region that China's actions will have the greatest impact. Whether these meet the expectations of those fearful of China or of those optimistic that China — although seeking greater involvement and influence in the region — will be a co-operative international actor, is a matter of more immediate concern to China's regional neighbours.

In trying to clarify some of these issues, a wide range of questions suggest themselves. Can China maintain its political integrity? Can it continue to overcome the enormous problems of economic development in the future and maintain anything like the current growth rates that provide much of the basis for concern? Will China in future seek to be expansionist, settle old scores left over from the last century or be satisfied with its current borders, content to exercise influence in non-military ways? What does China's history indicate as to its future attitudes and responses internationally — in general and with respect to specific neighbours? Assuming that China can become a strong power economically, could it evolve into a democratic market-based society such as that of Taiwan? What does China's military modernisation portend? And how will the post-Deng Xiaoping changes affect China's regional policies?

These are the kind of questions increasingly being asked in the region and more widely, and which this volume addresses. The contributors to the volume focus in particular on the myths, realities and challenges of China and their implications for the Asia-Pacific region. Because what happens in the region will increasingly impinge on the West as a whole, however, this analysis has an obvious significance for the global community.

The draft chapters were originally presented at a workshop organised by the Northeast Asia Program in the Research School of Pacific and Asian Studies at the Australian National University (ANU) (in conjunction with the Asia Research Centre of Murdoch University) and held at the ANU. Three additional chapters were subsequently added to fill gaps dealing with Russia, India and the transport and communications aspects of China's integration with the region. Each draft chapter was revised and updated in the light of discussion by expert commentators including Paul Dibb, Peter Drysdale, Mark Elvin, Andrew Mack, James Mackie, Peter Polomka and Peter Van Ness of the ANU, Tim Dunk of the Department of Defence, David Mannett (formerly Department of Defence), David Kelly of the Australian Defence Force Academy, Richard Rigby, Peter Rowe and Roger Uren of the Department of Foreign Affairs and Trade (Canberra), Senior Colonel Pan Zhenqiang of the National Defence University (Beijing), General Yu Jianzhong, Defence Attache of the Peoples Republic of China (Canberra), Ian Pfennigworth (previously Australian Defence Attache in Beijing), Andrew Yang, Chinese Council for Advanced Policy Studies (Taipei), and An-Chia Wu, Institute for International Relations (Taipei). The trouble they, and others at the workshop, took to make thoughtful and constructive contributions to the discussion of the chapter drafts is greatly appreciated.

In addition, the assistance of Ian Hayward, Bruce Major, Barbara Owen-Jones, Lynne Payne, Marylin Popp, Robin Ward and David Sullivan in organising the workshop and assisting with the production of this volume is gratefully acknowledged.

Stuart Harris
Gary Klintworth
Canberra, February 1995

1 Introduction: Reading the Chinese Tea Leaves

Stuart Harris

Given its size, geographical position and the consequential implications for political and strategic influence, China's sustained economic growth has great regional and ultimately global significance. This has increasingly impinged upon the thinking of countries in the Asia-Pacific region. Where China's policies will take the Asia-Pacific region, and how Chinese policies will affect the region in the future are of growing interest and the source of some apprehension to China's near and not so near neighbours.

There is a critical need to put some balance into our judgments of China's future role and approach in the region. Yet the basis for making such judgments of China's future policies is limited. The reading of the tea leaves in Beijing continues to provide much of the basis for determining Chinese objectives or methods for achieving particular international, as well as domestic, aims. Tea leaf reading may be unavoidable, but it needs to be put into some kind of context. The purpose of this volume is to provide such a context. It is directed not to the immediate future, despite the likely impacts of the inevitable early leadership succession, but to the more fundamental issues of the future.

Allen Whiting has made the point that ten years is probably the limit of sensible debate about the future on this subject. In accordance with that, this volume is concerned primarily with how China's interaction with the region will have developed by the turn of the century. This introduction is designed to suggest an overall perspective and to raise some questions pertinent to furthering our understanding of likely future developments.

The difficulty of making judgments about China's likely approach is partly due to the still less than adequate understanding of China that exists in the region and partly to the rapidity of change in Chinese society, as well as in its external environment. The making of judgments has not been helped by the relatively limited attention given in the West to many of the general aspects of China's international policies.

For a long period, the world was concerned with, first, the Cold War and then — following the fall of the Berlin Wall and the disintegration of the Soviet Union — the various aspects of a new post-Cold War world order. The Western world seemed to pay less attention to some of the underlying changes in the Asia-Pacific region, with such attention as was directed to the region being focused for a long period predominantly on Japan. Only recently has China been seen as central to consideration rather than a peripheral influence in regional and global terms.

In a sense, China's broader significance — as a permanent Security Council member and a nuclear weapon state — has been substantial for some time. More recently, China has developed significance in other contexts: it is a major international trader; it is an important arms exporter; the potential for substantial cross-border population movements has grown; and any global solution to important international environmental problems, such as those of the ozone layer or of global climate change, will require China's co-operation.

Despite the growing shift in focus, many assessments, even when not based on outdated stereotypes (or even myths), rely on a conventional wisdom that is often misleading. Consequently, a statement by a Chinese leader, or a contract to buy or sell arms, often leads to hasty judgments, rather than to considered views of Chinese international objectives and of the associated constraints.

Historically, the external response to China has ranged from the romantic through the fearful to the dismissive — the latter less so in recent years — but in other respects the change has not been great. Differences of interpretation now range from those who see China 'as an irredentist power'[1] and read in Chinese history of a country that has been at war relatively recently with almost all its neighbours (and has fought both superpowers), to those who see little in the historical record to suggest any imperialist or expansionist motivations by Chinese governments but see, rather, China as a 'relatively satisfied power', not seeking territorial aggrandisement.[2] In part, the difference is semantic: whether recovering Taiwan, Hong Kong, Macau, the Paracels and the Spratlys is regaining territorial integrity or territorial expansion is at least in part a matter of perspective. It is not entirely so, however.

The Chinese are often represented as being two-dimensional, responding particularly to Chinese historical acculturation, and being compliant to leadership views. Many observers argue that cultural factors — shared values that legitimate social and political practices — have particular importance in China's case, whether arising from their Confucian, Taoist or Buddhist inheritance or from the carry-over of Marxist-Leninist ideology and organisational and administrative structure. Fairbank argued, for example, that United States–Chinese relations are best seen in light of cultural differences.[3]

Again, it is commonly argued that in China, the leader as a great man has been (and remains) a more important factor in political relationships than in most countries. This reflects both major ideological influences — the Marxist-Leninist ideology of the leadership of the Party reinforcing what Pye terms the Confucian tradition of rule by men rather than by law.[4] In addition, the lack of developed and mature governmental institutions is seen as giving the leaders more importance.

Looking at how such factors influence Chinese international policies is made difficult, however, by the Chinese reticence about introspection. In contrast to other Asian countries, such as Japan, the Chinese 'have opened few doors into their collective subjective realm'.[5] It would be strange, however, if as well as culture and leadership, China's international approach did not also reflect various other domestic factors, with ideology, politics and social and economic development also being critical. Consequently, we need to keep the role of these domestic influences generally in mind, and subsequent chapters in this volume will address them directly.

While some observers would see those domestic factors as the more important, such influences are unlikely to be independent of other relationships. Like that of most countries, China's international approach can be expected to reflect not just domestic factors, but China's position in the international system and its responses to the dynamics of that system as well. Given that those dynamics now reflect a new world order — however that may be defined — how will China respond?

The change in the international system has a number of characteristics particularly relevant to China:

- the decline of superpower conflict with, in consequence, a view that China's importance and international influence had diminished with the 'China card' having become irrelevant to the West;[6]
- a world with only one superpower, a superpower whose capacity is diminished but not necessarily to China's advantage since Japan, in particular, previously an 'ally' (in the united front against the Soviet Union), may now be a rival for regional power;
- a shift to a degree of multipolarity and considerable strategic uncertainty and volatility, with problems for China, whose international relations were substantially based previously on balance of power considerations;
- peaceful relations between Russia and others including China, judged by some observers as of overwhelming importance: 'No single event

has had as much impact on the People's Republic of China as the disintegration of the Soviet Union';[7] and

- the substantial reduction of the importance of ideology as understood in traditional terms, a greater emphasis on realist interpretations of international developments and, at the same time, an increased sense of a global community.

Given these and other changes, what constitutes the new world order in this context is unclear for a number of reasons, including the following:

- It was often thought that politics would give way to economic concerns, yet, while economic competition has become more critical a feature of international relations, politics remain central.
- Despite hopes that peace would be widespread around the world, the scope for localised conflicts, where ethnic, racial or religious factors seem to have replaced ideology as the basis of conflict, has increased.
- Global interdependencies are growing, however, and structural changes in the international market framework impinge increasingly upon political frameworks — a particularly important factor in China.
- the United Nations is also assumed to have a more important role, but as one of five permanent members of the Security Council, China is likely to have a critical involvement in anything coming before the United Nations which affects the Asia-Pacific region.
- In the region, the dominance of the United States has been replaced by a more complex balance of power, with a major role for China.

Consequently, since what constitutes the new world order is itself unclear, where China fits is not easily determined. An important question, moreover, is how China perceives the new world order. To some observers, despite the importance of the leader, 'by and large, Chinese leaders' perceptions of the world are still a mystery'.[8] Not only is it open to question whether the Chinese know with any precision where their view of the world order fits but, more importantly, there is not just one set of views. Particular sectors or groups among China's leadership and intellectual elites have different views and do not see the situation in the same light.

On the other hand, that 'Beijing is unsure of its place in a world no longer dominated by superpower rivalry'[9] is presumably true of a number of countries in the Asia-Pacific region, and none more so than Japan. Given this, the question might instead be whether it can be said that China has a view of an appropriate world order that it will seek to impose, or whether it will respond flexibly to changes as they occur.

The Chinese in the Cold War period responded to a variety of overriding motivations, particularly in their approach to the problems of the United States and of the Soviet Union. The opening to the world, or economic interdependence approach, may also be seen in part, if not wholly, as bending to international conditions rather than following an independent decision-making process. But there is the more general question of the broader or longer term national attitudes and collective expectations — the larger patterns that will be influential even with Deng's successors, whoever might eventually emerge as dominant.

In one sense, China's formulation of its international policy statements has reflected a number of uniformities. It has been consistently opposed to hegemony and, as well as arguing for peace and independence, has continued to press the Five Principles of Peaceful Coexistence outlined by Zhou Enlai in 1954: mutual respect for each other's territorial integrity and sovereignty; non-aggression; no interference in each other's internal affairs; equality and mutual benefit; and peaceful coexistence. Yet the unpredictability of Chinese international policies has been a noteworthy characteristic, particularly in its strategic triangle relations with the two superpowers. Of course, for most countries, their external policies are neither fully consistent nor predictable. China, presumably like other countries, has often had to put national security ahead of ideology, domestic politics and other considerations. In China's case, however, it has been argued that it has been particularly unstable.[10]

Before looking at some of the factors that may influence how China will relate to the region in the future, we start by looking at how China has responded, and is responding, to changes in the international environment. This, in part, is what the following chapters attempt to do.

Most countries have four broad international objectives which can be very generally described as: national security, economic welfare, a predictable international framework and an improved world order.[11]

National security

In the new context, China can be seen as more secure, in the traditional sense, than perhaps at any time in its history.[12] Since, compared with China, few other major powers 'have felt as threatened, for such a long period of time, and by such powerful adversaries',[13] this is a major change.

China's security concerns for a long time centred on the Soviet Union, the United States, Japan, India and, in part because of the involvement of major powers, Indochina. For many Chinese, Russia now seems to have become a 'friend' in the short term at least, Indochina has ceased to be a major problem, and a degree of accommodation has been achieved with India.

China is not, however, without longer term security concerns: 'the changes in the world situation have put China on the defensive',[14] in part because of fears of domination by a United States-led hegemony. One argument is that in part, China's concerns are less over individual countries, such as Japan or even the United States, than over alliances such as one between the United States and Japan against China.[15]

A particular formulation of that argument stems from the three worlds theory of Mao, articulated by Deng in 1974. While that formulation is not now central to mainstream discussions of its international policies, China tends not to discard rhetorical concepts, and it is still at least a rhetorical factor to some involved.[16] The concern is domination by 'First World Countries', with Japan part of a United States hegemony in the region. In that formulation, the United States itself is currently only a second-level threat and Japan is the major threat, with a stronger navy than China, expanding military expenditures and a capacity for developing smart weapons, including space weapons. A Chinese think tank reported in 1990 that Japan 'will likely be China's major enemy in the next thirty years'.[17]

An alternative view is that China's rapid deployment forces are still predominantly located in northern China, 'to defend the capital and be prepared for a possible attack from Russia'[18] and there is undoubtedly considerable caution about Russia's future military potential.[19] As well as wary eyes being kept on Vietnam and India, and the attention on Japan, some Chinese analysts are becoming especially concerned about the United States, notably regarding its relationship with Taiwan.

On the other hand, China's official position, increasingly based on a more systematic and professional process of policy formulation, is essentially moderate. For example, it contributed helpfully to the settlement in Cambodia, was far from obstructive in the United Nations over the Gulf War, has been flexible in its policy towards North Korea,[20] has agreed to abide by the terms of the Missile Technology Control Regime and, despite its various concerns about relations with the United States and its oft-repeated general opposition to the stationing of troops on foreign soil, it is not pressing strongly for United States withdrawal from Asia.

A further view would see the relationship with the United States as China's major security preoccupation, although in a broader sense than simply that of territorial integrity. The relationship between the United States and China has been and remains an ambivalent one. Historically, influences have been both favourable (the United States open door policy of the late nineteenth century) and unfavourable (the bitterness of the Cold War period including Korea and Vietnam, as well as many subsequent disputes). Ideological concerns have also stemmed from China's perception of the United States as an imperialist power and the United States' perception of China as proselytising communism.

More recently, the ambivalence has taken on two new dimensions. A 'normalised' relationship with the United States emerged as a counter to China's preoccupation with the threat from the Soviet Union and, more recently, its 'open to the world' policy reflected its concern to gain United States capital, technology and markets. This 'opening to the world' poses problems for China at two levels. The first is how it can maintain the economic relationship with the United States without sacrificing its independence or limiting its self-reliance, something that it faced and overcame effectively in the case of retention of most favoured nation access to the United States market. The second is how it can continue to argue internationally against what it sees as United States imperialism and the United States monopoly of power.

The latter aspect has increased in importance since the breakup of the Soviet Union and since Tiananmen Square. China has been concerned at the willingness of the United States, as the sole remaining superpower, to intervene in international events militarily, to continue stationing troops overseas, to maintain a large nuclear arsenal and, despite its own large arms exports, to criticise (and take action) on China's arms sales. It is also concerned that there has been a change in United States policy since Tiananmen Square. This has moved from the past policy norms of 'encouraging Chinese domestic political and socio-economic reforms but not making United States policy contingent upon Chinese domestic practices'[21] to a much greater emphasis on imposing conditions regarding China's domestic policies.

Both dimensions come together in a major political concern of the Chinese, the United States policy towards Taiwan — particularly its sales of arms. An earlier crisis in United States–China relations over Taiwan had been resolved by the 1982 joint communiqué dealing with limiting United States arms sales. This communiqué was sufficiently imprecise to leave grounds for considerable uncertainty.[22] The seeming breach of this understanding is part of the continuing concern, despite the shift in policy of the Clinton administration, which contributes to what the Chinese see as an imperialistic United States approach to China's internal affairs, with an ambiguous United States policy being driven increasingly by the reassertion by the United States Congress of a role in determining United States relations with China.

This may be especially significant if, as some argue, China's leaders are increasingly concerned about what they describe as 'splittism'. This refers to the pressures on the internal stability of the country — whether over Tibet, the new central Asian republics, Mongolia or elsewhere — and is reflected in the policies of economic interlinking they have been developing to minimise the potential political threats.

China sees the moves within Taiwan to speak more openly of independence as being encouraged by the United States, with its arms sales reinforcing that attitude. This poses a difficulty for China and for the Taiwanese government, both of which have been pursuing a peaceful approach of encouraging economic contacts. Taiwan could become more politically central in the competition for power in the post-Deng period and Whiting's earlier concern that United States policy needed to be finely calibrated to enable Chinese abilities to tolerate ambiguity to be maintained may be once again relevant.[23]

Similarly, China is concerned about the international pressure over Tibet, and fears that Hong Kong could become a base for destabilising political activity within China. Its more traditional concerns about borders revolve around shared land borders with fourteen countries (including three new central Asian republics) and six ocean borders. Obviously, problems exist along the central Asian republics' borders, but there are disputes in a number of areas, notably including those in the South China Sea. One might read its new strategic doctrine, emphasising rapid deployment, as reflecting its standard approach of being able to deliver effective 'lessons', or 'coercive diplomacy' regarding border violations rather than conducting major wars.[24] It may also suggest that it sees military force as an important diplomatic instrument.

China's concerns with the developments on the Korean peninsula are partly the fear of the United States' reaction should a nuclear capacity be established in the North, as well as the instabilities and uncertainties that might come from a change in the North's regime, a united (possibly nuclear) Korea, problems of refugees should a collapse occur, regional responses (including a nuclear program in Japan) and underlying concerns that South Korea should become more tied in with Japan or be part of a United States-led regional hegemony directed at China.

China is committed to military modernisation, but then presumably so are most countries. Given the attention directed to China's policies, however, a question increasingly asked is how significant, actually or potentially, is China's current military expansion? If the answer is that the buildup is seen in the region as at least potentially significant, the next question is whether it is taking place because China's leaders want China to achieve the accoutrements of a major regional and perhaps global power; because its leaders accept what has been said to be its military strategists' view that defence is best achieved by preparing for war; because it simply wants to catch up with the superior technologies available to most of its major neighbours (a factor given emphasis by the demonstration effect of the Gulf War); or because of other reasons, such as China responding to military, and particularly naval, buildups in the region.

Chinese leaders, for their part, are aware of the concerns, and their spokespersons have responded strongly to the 'absurd argument, to the effect that a strong China will pose a threat to other countries by seeing it as either an utterly groundless rumour reflecting a lack of understanding or an attempt to sow discord'.[25] Nevertheless, even if this is so, while the regional concerns exist, there could be pressures for regional responses and the arms race spiral could accelerate.

China's approach to international issues has put a lot of weight on its territorial security, but its security concerns are wider, since security has a broader sense than just territorial integrity. One such concern for China's leadership is security in the sense of 'political stability', or what China's government judges that to be — hence its view, shared in part by its Asian neighbours, that human rights of the individual cannot be at the expense of the overall stability of the nation. The question of China's concerns about security in this wider sense — particularly sensitive in a country which, for the first time, has both a stable and a modernising government — relates directly to its concerns about the consequences of its economic interdependence.

Economic welfare

In looking at China's objectives in the field of economic welfare, it is relevant that China's economic policy changes predated the developments leading to a new post-Soviet world order. China adopted its open foreign economic policy in 1978, developing its Four Modernisations policy. This remarkable change in approach poses a major challenge to China's international position, because interdependence impinges on sovereignty (or at least effective autonomy).

It also poses a particular domestic challenge. Chinese governments in the past have been dependent upon economic prosperity for the implied moral consent of the governed (the so-called Mandate of Heaven). If there was an economic problem, it was the government's fault. Now not only has economic growth come from relaxing government involvement, but it is to a degree not within the government's control because of the interdependence with the global economy.

China has to accept the internationally set conditions for trade, foreign investment and technology transfer and it faces pressures on its domestic policies that, in consequence, it can ignore only at a substantial cost. Consequently, it is likely that the interplay between interdependence and independence will continue as a feature of China's policy. Indeed, this aspect might grow in importance if Chinese nationalism also becomes increasingly important, particularly in response to United States pressures.

Questions about the links between modernisation and Chinese national identity have been reflected in the debate among Chinese leaders, and they may recur. Some Chinese leaders are concerned that too high a degree of interdependence will undermine China's culture and that the associated 'contamination' of Western cultures and values will affect the moral basis of the government. While wanting modernisation, they would want a less rapid process and a less open approach internationally.

The presently prevailing reformist view is seemingly more tolerant of the interaction with foreign cultures, perhaps accepting them as inevitable. The question is whether this will weaken the government's (and party's) position in managing its domestic politics with, consequently, implications for future foreign relations.

Deng's 'economics in command' approach — the adoption of market measures in the all-out pursuit of economic development — even if it meant depending upon foreign investment and technology, and even if it led to inequalities in the pace of regional development, therefore raises important questions.

It is commonplace to describe China's open door policy as pragmatic. Undoubtedly, its external policies have been less ideological, less personal, less radical, more flexible and related more to China's immediate national interests. The question, however, is what is the meaning of pragmatism when used to describe Chinese external relations under the leadership of Deng Xiaoping.

Another question is whether it is seen as pragmatism by the Chinese leaders. This is not just that they normally argue from high principles based on the morality of their approach, but — because if by pragmatism we mean the end of ideology — they would not necessarily accept that ideology had ceased to be relevant. At least it may not be seen as pragmatism in simple Western terms (even assuming it means the same thing in all Western societies).

Critics within China argue that the reforms in their present form are simply adapting Western ideas and Western capitalism, perhaps forgetting that Marxism-Leninism (like the ideas of Sun Yatsen) is itself Western in origin. Linked with these arguments are Chinese concerns about 'peaceful evolution' (a concept apparently developed by John Foster Dulles in the 1950s), articulated by many Chinese leaders as a conspiracy by the West to undermine socialism and restore United States-style capitalism in China.[26] Although the issue dropped into the background with the resurgence of the reformers, after Tiananmen Square warnings resurfaced that the United States was in fact conspiring through 'peaceful evolution' to restore capitalism in China.

The counter-argument of those supporting the continuation of Deng's reforms is that, through the 'socialist market economy', they are 'building socialism with Chinese characteristics', seeing China, in the current process, as at 'a primary stage' of socialism. What this means is far from clear; whether it is merely a means of legitimising a new policy approach to the domestic constituency in a context where a moral or principled basis is needed for policy, or where Western ideas may only gain significance if imbued with Chinese characteristics, rather than reflecting a basic qualification of the concept of pragmatism, or whether it stems from a belief in the essential superiority of Chineseness[27] is open to question. Undoubtedly, peaceful evolution is the hope of many in the West, although not necessarily based on strictly American values, but it raises related questions as to how far peaceful evolution is inevitable and what the end result of such evolution is.

Moreover, given that 'pragmatic policies' can in fact change frequently and quickly, another question can be posed: whether a further change in a different direction could easily occur. To some extent, where a 'pragmatic' approach may go in the future may be more difficult to assess than one based on ideology.

Again some counter-perspective is needed. Although modernisation makes China more powerful, it gives China an interest in good relations with the major economic powers and with its neighbours in the region, as well as an interest in a strong international economy. It also gives it a strong interest in a peaceful international environment.

A predictable international framework

The major component of this third international objective has been the multilateral system. During the Mao period, China was disparaging of the United Nations, but it subsequently joined most significant international organisations and has been constructive and active in its participation. China has now sought to join the World Trade Organisation (incorporating the General Agreement on Tariffs and Trade) and is making substantial internal changes to facilitate its acceptance.

Although its moderate international policies have meant that in general it has been content to follow and accept what has been happening, that has not always been the case as, for example, with arms control. There it has been pressing for an international regime, particularly in respect of nuclear weapons.

China has substantially improved its relations with all of its neighbours in the region. As well as giving it the peaceful environment it needs to facilitate its modernisation program, this may also be to offset the concerns about United States hegemony, or to counter the emergence of an idea of a China threat in the region, with the aim of encouraging better economic relations or to limit arms expenditures.

Regional co-operation is also an important component of maintaining international order and stability. The Association of Southeast Asian Nations (ASEAN) has been endeavouring to find ways in which to engage China constructively in regional affairs and, increasingly, to create a framework for multilateral security discussions in which China could participate — in part to contribute to confidence building with China, but also to balance the influence of other regional powers, such as Japan. For a similar reason, China may also have a particular interest in multilateral security discussions, and statements in support of broader regional security arrangements have been made by Chinese spokespersons.[28] China is participating in the ASEAN Regional Forum.

For its part, China has moved back from supporting insurgencies in the region, and its interest in regional economic co-operation in recent years has been constructive and flexible as part of its general effort to develop its science and technology base for its modernisation. Cross-currents do exist, however. For example, it expressed full support for Prime Minister Mahathir's East Asian Economic Caucus, in part perhaps to offset United States regional influence.[29]

It has, however, participated since 1991 in the ASEAN foreign ministers' meetings. At the same time, ASEAN countries are still nervous about the Spratly Islands as the Chinese have built up their military presence and reasserted China's sovereignty. Chinese leaders have emphasised that they will not use force and will settle differences peacefully, including those over joint exploration and development of resources. Many countries enter into negotiations not always intending to reach agreement, however, and the Spratlys will remain a centre of concern to ASEAN countries if negotiations achieve no progress while the military buildup and China's creeping expansionism in the South China Sea continue.

The issue of Hong Kong falls within the context of international order, not because it is an international issue from China's perspective, but because parts of the region would see it as particularly destabilising if, subsequent to the 1997 transfer of power, things do not go smoothly. Perceptions seem to be especially relevant here. Views on the original agreement themselves differ markedly. One judgment is that 'in negotiations with Britain over the future of Hong Kong, Peking entered into a joint declaration that was more generous, more explicit, and more binding than most observers had believed to be possible'.[30] Others take a different view — often strongly. Yet in the same circumstances, how many other countries would have taken China's approach?

Foreign Minister Qian Qichen has repeated what Deng said in 1982, that 'if there is serious chaos in Hong Kong, the Chinese government would be forced to reconsider the date and method in resuming Hong Kong'.[31] This is presumably being used to apply pressure, although China would have to be concerned at any impact on its internal stability from an uncontrolled Hong Kong.

Governor Patten's dispute with China can be seen as concern by Britain to ensure a reasonably representative government in post-1997 Hong Kong, or as a continuation of a British–Chinese conflict having little to do with either Hong Kong governance or democracy. While Britain may underestimate the support for China's position in Hong Kong, China may underestimate the impact on the region — and on Hong Kong's economic viability — of a serious breakdown in a smooth transition in 1997, as well as its impact on Taiwan. The debate on the issue is almost certainly confused by the cultural differences noted by Fairbank, as well as by the uncertainties of leadership manoeuvring. A tremendous amount of distrust between the two governments does not help.[32]

Part of the regional interest in China's world view concerns the ethnic Chinese. According to Wang Gungwu, writing in 1958, the consciousness of the ethnic Chinese in Southeast Asia remained Chinese, and they understood politics 'to be something that was of China'.[33] The ethnic Chinese can hinder or help regional relationships. In the past, they suffered by commonly being assumed to be associated with Chinese support for communist parties in Southeast Asia. While this aspect has largely disappeared, their advantages in economic links with China may be helpful unless they come to be seen in their home countries as unduly favouring China in their business development or unduly controlling bilateral trade.

An improved world order

Among other things, China seems not to have given up its earlier stated objective of establishing a new international order, although it now sees this as being achieved peacefully. In considering how China perceives that the international system can be improved and what its position in that changed system would be, it is necessary to look at how China perceives the world, what its objectives are, how those perceptions and objectives have changed over time, and how they differ from those of others in the international community.

A number of simple conclusions have been drawn over time about the nature of China's international objectives — from the Mao view of 'global revolution' to a 'Middle Kingdom' complex to an aggressive imperialistic approach. At times additional perspectives are derived from the tribute system, a pattern of ritual relations in which states bordering China accepted a kind of Chinese suzerainty, which at the time (usually that of the Ch'ing dynasty) was 'thought of as having given Asia a framework of political order'.[34] Again, scholars often refer to China's sense of an East Asian hierarchy, in which China's history and civilisation claim that it was and should be the leader.

Another perspective is that China's international approach is based on a moral perspective and the Chinese advocacy of the Five Principles is, in a sense, a statement of moral principle. A form of moral perspective probably exists in most countries' approach to foreign policy, so the question is how that moral perspective differs in the case of China. Most countries have a perception of how they would like to see the world work. Although it could be argued that most Western democracies are relatively status quo or gradualist countries, Western countries largely see international standards underlying the world community's actions and attitudes being advanced by the extension of Western-style institutions. These underlie Western democracy and capitalism, or at least the liberal market system, seen as the principal means through which international standards can be raised. Moving through the multilateral system to gain acceptance of rules that improve international co-operation within these institutional arrangements is consistent with this objective.

According to some observers, China judges its strength not from its institutions but from its Chineseness. Others cannot become Chinese, but can at least be brought to recognise the value of the Chinese. On this view, the Chinese seem obliged to envision international politics as fashioned of some sort of (Confucian) 'moral hierarchy'.[35]

Since it has long been accepted that what China says and what it does are commonly substantially different (even more than is the case for countries generally) this may perhaps be explained in terms of its use of polemics as a weapon to an extent not done in the West. On the other hand, it may provide a basis for a 'shaming' approach which extends a domestic process internationally, in a way that may be seen as especially useful when economically or strategically weak.

An objective of China's modernisation is to overcome such weakness and to build a more powerful China which will be more influential in international affairs. Deng said in 1984 that China needed at least twenty years of peace to concentrate on modernisation; reflecting on that, China has seemingly accepted for the time being the legitimacy of the existing international system. Subsequently, Deng was more optimistic about China's progress, saying that China will be truly powerful and exert a much greater influence in the world by the turn of the century.[36] In particular, China expects to play a major role in the politics and economics of the Asia-Pacific region. The answer to our earlier question, as to how far China's view of the world order differs from what it currently is, then becomes important, since this will be a starting point to understanding what Chinese regional objectives will then be — even if this does not reflect the methods of achieving them. If it is true that China's government is based upon the rule of people rather than that of law, this would also have important implications for policy analysis. For those who relate changes in Chinese international policies to leadership preferences and responses, this not only gives special importance to the problems of leadership succession, but it also means that China's approach to the world may change substantially with changes in the leadership.

This, of course, has been seen with the change from the radical ideological approach of Mao to what has been termed the pragmatic approach of Deng. Although an immediate question then is whether and how China's policies will change with the Deng succession, this is not the important question. There are limits to how much China can effectively implement any major changes at the present time. The important questions concern how the situation might develop after another decade or so of Chinese modernisation when those limits will be substantially reduced.

Conclusion

Barring massive upheavals in China, Deng was basically correct in saying that by the turn of the century, China would have the resources to be powerful, with much greater strategic influence, not just in the region but globally; and much more influence economically. Hong Kong will have come within its jurisdiction and relations with Taiwan will have moved to a different level. It would be surprising if China's approach did not change significantly, reflecting its increased international stature and power. The ends to which it might address itself as a consequence, as well as how it relates to individual countries in the region, are therefore crucial.

The kinds of factors that are important are how far China's growing trading and economic relations with the region will condition its approach. While, as with most large countries, external economic relations may be less important than its internal economic dynamism, a buoyant international economy and a stable regional environment will continue to be important in maintaining its internal dynamism.

This also depends, presumably, upon how far the 'open to the world' policy continues, and whether the economic and administrative reforms are sustained — or, indeed, how far they can in fact effectively change course even if that were desired. In particular, domestic political developments — the tolerance, voluntary or involuntary, of the effects of 'peaceful evolution', and the extent to which Chinese nationalism, and the concern at the impact of Western ideas on Chinese culture become important — will influence significantly how China's attitudes internationally might develop.

Also important, presumably, will be how other countries react to China — this reaction, in the case of the China's entry to the GATT and the World Trade Organisation, also depending, to a considerable degree, upon progress in domestic reform. China will also become a more important economic competitor on world markets. In these, as well as in other areas, tensions and disputes of various kinds might be expected from time to time, without necessarily implying more fundamental conflicts.

For those who put great weight on China's cultural inheritance and the extent to which culture reinforces power,[37] how far will its historic sense of an East Asian hierarchy with China at its head influence its judgments of 'proper' relations among the countries in the region? How far will that lead it to re-establish not just its centrality in the region (which, it could perhaps be argued, it has already done), but lead it, as many in the region fear, to seek to re-establish the political and cultural hegemony of the past?

Relations with the United States and Japan will presumably be the major features of relations at the turn of the century. To some extent, perhaps, with Japan, but particularly in the case of the United States, Taiwan may become substantially more important. How far the question of human rights increases or diminishes in importance will depend upon progress in domestic political reform, but it could also be influenced by how far Chinese nationalism becomes an important factor. Indeed, there is a more general question about how far, given the decline in ideology in Chinese politics, nationalism will be a substitute to bolster the government's (and the party's) legitimacy. While the question of nationalism — whether cultural, ethnic or state — is a contested one, and substantially beyond the scope of this volume, in some form it could have 'profound implications for unresolved territorial claims and how a modernised China might use its power'.[38]

Uncertainties then exist about the use to which China will put its increased power and influence in the region in a decade or so's time. It is possible for those changed circumstances to be worrying to the region. Since great powers are commonly difficult to live with, especially at times of great change, difficulties and tensions in regional relationships are likely in any case. The lesson of China's early 1980s links with the United States against the Soviet Union is that China, in alliance with any other sizeable power, would have a particularly substantial impact on the strategic balance.

On the other hand, from China's perspective, its security and economic concerns may seem substantial, to be countered by achieving that increased power and influence. Its potential security threats, minimal in the next decade or so, look more worrying over a longer (20- or 30-year) time perspective — whether from a revitalised Russia, a more assertive Japan, perhaps a less accommodating India, a greater Pan-Turkish or Islamic push in central Asia, or a gradually weakening United States seeking to contain China through alliances with other regional powers.

Its economic concerns — a need to continue to grow to maintain political legitimacy, to cope with and raise the living standards of its increasing population, and to prevent the 'splittism' and internal instability which it still substantially fears — are in the longer term at risk from the rise of competitors on world markets such as Russia and Eastern Europe, or from protective actions by the West, notably the United States and Japan.

Presumably, it will address these various concerns not only directly but also indirectly through the existing international system and by looking for changes in that system that give it more influence on and control of international events and its international environment. The questions, then, are whether the mixed signals from a reading of China's past or current approaches, and from reading the Chinese tea leaves, lead to optimism or pessimism about China's exercise of that influence and control in its future interactions with the region.

Notes

1 Gerald Segal, 'The Challenge to Chinese Foreign Policy' in Stuart Harris and James Cotton (eds), *The End Of the Cold War in Northeast Asia*, Longman Cheshire and Lynne Rienner, Melbourne and Boulder, Col., 1991, and 'China and the Disintegration of the Soviet Union', *Asian Survey*, vol. 32, no. 9, September 1992, pp. 848–68.

2 Harry Harding, *China's Second Revolution: Reform After Mao*, Brookings, Washington, 1987, p. 261.

3 Paul Evans, *John Fairbank and the American Understanding of Modern China*, Blackwell, New York, 1988, p. 339.

4 Lucian Pye, *The Mandarin and the Cadre*, Center for Chinese Studies, University of Michigan, Ann Arbor, Mich., 1988, p. 135.

5 ibid., p. 5.

6 Michael Yahuda, 'The People's Republic of China at 40: Foreign Relations', *China Quarterly*, no. 119, September 1989, pp. 519–39.

7 Segal, 'China and the Disintegration of the Soviet Union', p. 848.

8 Yufan Hao and Guocan Huan, 'Introduction: Chinese Foreign Policy in Transition', in Yufan Hao and Guocan Huan (eds), *The Chinese View of the World*, Pantheon Books, New York, 1989, p. xv.

9 Samuel Kim, 'China as a Regional Power', *Current History*, vol. 91, no. 566, September 1992, p. 247.

10 Chih-Yu Shih, 'A Markov Model of Diplomatic Change and Continuity in Mainland China', *Issues and Studies*, vol. 28, no. 6, June 1992, pp. 1–15.

11 Stuart Harris, *Review of Australia's Overseas Representation*, Australian Government Publishing Service, Canberra, 1986.

12 Des Ball, 'Forword', in Gary Klintworth, *China's Modernisation: The Strategic Implications for the Asia-Pacific Region*, Australian Government Publishing Service, Canberra, 1989, p. iii; and Segal, 'The Challenge to Chinese Foreign Policy', p. 79.

13 Harding, *China's Second Revolution*, p. 210.

14 Euchul Choi, 'China's New Round of Economic Reforms and Sino-Korean Relations', *Korean Journal of National Reunification*, vol. 1, 1992, p. 36.

15 Stuart Harris, 'Implications for Regional Security and Cooperation', in *Proceedings of Symposium: Australia–Korea to the Year 2000; Prospects for Change and Cooperation*, Seoul, November 1992.

16 Lai Sing Lam, 'From Mikhail Gorbachev's Policy to China's Regional Role', *Journal of East Asian Affairs*, vol. 7, no. 2, Summer/Fall 1993, p. 600.

17 ibid., pp. 600–601.

18 *Far Eastern Economic Review*, 14 January 1993, p. 19.

19 Bonnie Glaser, 'China's Security Perceptions', *Asian Survey*, vol. 33, no. 3, March 1993, p. 256.

20 Jia Hao and Zhuang Qubing, 'China's Policy Toward the Korean Peninsula', *Asian Survey*, vol. 32, no. 2, December 1992, pp. 1144–45.

21 Qingshan Tan, *The Making of US China Policy: From Normalisation to the Post-Cold War Era*, Lynne Rienner, Boulder, Col., 1992.

22 Allen Whiting, 'Sino-American Relations: The Decade Ahead', *Orbis*, vol. 26, no. 3, Fall 1982, pp. 708–9.

23 ibid., p. 718.

24 Steve Chan, 'Chinese Conflict Calculus and Behaviour: Assessment from a Perspective of Conflict Management', *World Politics*, vol. 30, no. 3, April 1978, pp. 391–410.

25 Shugin Liu, 'China's Reform and Opening Up and Foreign Policy', *Foreign Affairs Journal* (Beijing), vol. 28, June 1993, p. 4.

26 Ian Wilson, 'Commentary', in Stuart Harris and James Cotton (eds), *The End of the Cold War in Northeast Asia*, Longman Cheshire and Lynne Rienner, Melbourne and Boulder, Col., 1991, pp. 105–6; and Glaser, 'China's Security Perceptions', p. 260.

27 Chih-Yu Shih, *China's Just World: the Morality of Chinese Foreign Policy*, Lynne Rienner, Boulder, Col., 1993, pp. 126–27.

28 Tony Walker reports that in an interview with Senior Colonel Pan Zhenqiang, Colonel Pan said that China should press hard for multi-

lateral security arrangements like the Conference on Security and Cooperation in Europe, to lessen regional tensions and overcome longstanding mistrust: *Age* (Melbourne), 30 May 1994.

29   *South China Morning Post*, 12 January 1992.

30   Harding, *China's Second Revolution*, p. 244.

31   *Far Eastern Economic Review*, 30 September 1993, p. 29.

32   ibid., 22 July 1993, p. 13.

33   Gungwu Wang, *Community and Nation: China, Southeast Asia and Australia*, Allen & Unwin, Sydney, 1992, p. 36.

34   Arthur Waldron, *The Great Wall of China: From History to Myth*, Cambridge University Press, Cambridge, 1990, p. 31.

35   Shih, 'A Markov Model of Diplomatic Change and Continuity in Mainland China', p. 3.

36   Harding, *China's Second Revolution*, p. 245.

37   Akira Iriye, 'Culture and Power: International Relations as Inter-cultural Relations', *Diplomatic History*, vol. 3, no. 2, 1979, pp. 115–28.

38   James Townsend, 'Chinese Nationalism', *Australian Journal of Chinese Affairs*, no. 27, January 1992, p. 101.

2 A Chinese View of the World Situation and the New International Order

Sha Zukang

The disintegration of the former Soviet Union has brought to an end the international bipolar structure and the world is now in a transitional period, moving towards multipolarity. Recent developments have presented us with a better chance of avoiding a new world war, thus making a lasting peace more attainable. Contrary to popular expectations that the end of the Cold War would bring peace and prosperity to the world, however, many contradictions that were submerged have come out into the open. One does not need to look far to find countries and regions being torn apart by ethnic or religious feuds or by territorial disputes and armed clashes, due to exacerbating political and socio-economic crises. Some of these crises have given rise to internal turmoil, sometimes to local wars. A case in point is the Eurasian area between the Asian and European continent. In the meantime, economic factors have become even more important in international relations, with economic regionalisation and grouping becoming the order of the day. The current international economy, moreover, remains a most daunting challenge. The developed countries are caught up in an economic recession in varying degrees; difficulties faced by the developing countries are yet to be solved; and the gap between the North and the South has continued to widen in recent years. Peace and development remain the two most grave challenges facing us today.

To achieve peace and development, China has on many occasions called for the establishment of a new international political and economic order of peace, stability, justice and rationality, based on the Five Principles of Peaceful Coexistence and on the recognition of the diversity of the world and differences between states. The Chinese government is willing to co-operate extensively with other countries and will continue with its unremitting efforts for the establishment of such a new order, for achieving peace and development in the world.

The situation in the Asia-Pacific region

The disintegration of the bipolar structure was apparently less significant in the Asia-Pacific region, in which countries enjoy the benefits of political stability — in relative terms, of course — and economic prosperity. In general terms, the regional hot issues in the Cold War period have been more or less resolved; the problems left over from history have been or are being solved, or brought under control. With the majority of countries following a good-neighbour policy, relations between them have largely improved, which in turn has helped to boost relative political stability.

In addition, the economic performance of the region has never been better. East and Southeast Asia have taken the lead in economic growth for several years running. It is estimated that an upturn trend has carried on to 1994 with an average growth rate of some 7 per cent, demonstrating extraordinary economic vitality and adaptability. Ever-increasing economic cooperation in all forms has contributed once again to regional stability by offering a strong economic base.

By and large, I believe the end of the Cold War and bipolarity mean for those of us in the region more opportunities than challenges. For a rather long period in the future, peace, stability and economic development can be expected to be mainstream. This being said, we should not lose sight of the destabilising elements in the region, such as hegemonism, power politics, acts of interference with others' internal affairs and infringements upon countries' sovereignty. For that reason, arduous efforts by states concerned are required to safeguard the relative stability and to maintain the rapid economic growth rate in the latter half of the 1990s and perhaps the next century.

China's status in the Asia-Pacific region

The Five Principles of Peaceful Coexistence are the very basis on which China establishes and develops relations with all states, especially those in the Asia-Pacific. It is on this basis that China is prepared to work hard with other countries interested in preserving peace and stability in the Asia-Pacific region and in achieving common development. Indeed, China is a big country in the Asia-Pacific. It possesses nuclear weapons and is a permanent member of the United Nations Security Council. But this does not mean that China should enjoy privileges or, for that matter, special rights over others in handling world or Asia-Pacific regional affairs. If China wants to make due contributions to the international community, it has, first and foremost, to manage its own internal affairs well by, for example, improving its economy. It is our conviction that international affairs should be dealt with by all the members of the world community, whether they are large or small, rich or poor, strong or weak, through discussion and consultation on an equal footing and with mutual respect. So far as China is concerned, it always considers itself an equal member of the international community. It goes without saying, of course, that China has its own national interests to protect. As has been proven by history, the Chinese government and people never allow its internal affairs or sovereignty to be interfered with or infringed upon. The only difference between China and certain states is we never pursue our national interests at the expense of other countries and peoples. China's call for the establishment of a new world order based on the Five Principles of Peaceful Coexistence and the principles enshrined in the United Nations Charter, in the final analysis, stems from the belief that the establishment of such a world order will bring secure peace and opportunities for socio-economic progress for all members of the international community, while their national identities and cultural traditions are preserved and developed.

Like any other Asia-Pacific country, China wishes just as much to have a peaceful, stable and secure international environment in its neighbourhood and in the world — something which is needed for domestic development and improving the well-being of the population. China is convinced that the maintenance of peace and stability in the region is in its own interests and conducive to the economic development and social stability of other Asia-Pacific countries. China is a staunch force for security and stability in the Asia-Pacific.

Relations between China and the Asian-Pacific states

China has followed the policy of good neighbourliness and is committed to extensive friendly co-operation with its neighbours. Such efforts have in recent years yielded notable results.

Exchanges and co-operation between China and the Association of Southeast Asian Nations (ASEAN) states in the fields of politics, economics and culture have been strengthened and expanded. China appreciates and supports the efforts of ASEAN in safeguarding peace and stability in this region. China has taken part in the Post-Ministerial-Conference (PMC) and the ASEAN Regional Forum (ARF). China attaches importance to ASEAN'S role in preserving regional peace and development, has increased dialogue and consultations with ASEAN countries, and has reached a common understanding on many important regional and international issues. China will continue with its friendly co-operation and dialogue with ASEAN countries in this respect.

The Sino-Japanese relationship is developing soundly and steadily. Constant contacts between the two states have been carried out at different levels and in all fields. President Jiang Zemin's visit to Japan in April 1992 and the Emperor Akihito's visit to China in October the same year ushered in a new phase of development in Sino-Japanese relations. Chinese Foreign Minister Qian Qichen made a trip to Japan in May 1993. Successful co-operation has brought about encouraging results in the fields of politics, economics, science and technology, and culture. Japan is an important country with a highly developed economy and China's hope is that Japan remains on the road to development and peace so as to make an active contribution to peace, stability and development in the Asia-Pacific and the world.

Relations between China and India have been improved and further developed since Premier Li Peng's visit to India in 1991. The two sides have maintained high-level exchanges and have been engaged in co-operation in the fields of politics, economics, science and technology and culture. China and India have also been co-operating closely in international affairs. In September 1993, Indian Prime Minister Rao paid a visit to China, during which the leaders of the two sides further exchanged views and agreed to develop good-neighbourly relations on the basis of the Five Principles of Peaceful Coexistence. The border disputes are the only major outstanding issues between the two sides and these are problems left over from history. The two countries have signed an agreement on the maintenance of peace and tranquillity along the line of actual control in the China–India border areas. The signing and implementation of this agreement will be conducive to tranquillity along the line of actual control in the China–India border areas, create a favourable atmosphere and conditions for the eventual settlement of the border question, help increase mutual trust, promote bilateral friendly relations and thus produce positive effects on regional peace and stability.

Sino-Russian relations have been developing rapidly. China and Russia have reached agreement in principle on troop reductions along the borders. The prospect for mutual co-operation in the fields of economics, trade and culture is very broad indeed. The Russian Defence Minister's recent trip to China reflected normal contacts between the two armies. It had nothing to do with any military alliance or arms transfers.

Co-operation between China and Korea in the fields of economics, trade, and science and technology has been further strengthened and expanded since the establishment of diplomatic relations between the two countries.

Since the normalisation of Sino-Vietnamese relations, the two countries have resumed and further developed their overall relations, which is satisfying. As to the territorial disputes between China and Vietnam, the leaders of the two sides have promised to settle them by peaceful means through negotiations. In October 1993, the two countries signed an agreement on basic principles governing the settling of the territorial disputes. This document, the first important agreement reached since the beginning of Sino-Vietnamese territorial negotiations in 1974, marked a positive development. In addition, the two sides also agreed not to do anything that would further complicate the matter, nor let the issue hinder the normal development of the Sino-Vietnamese relationship.

In our relations with Asian-Pacific countries, Sino-American relations represents an important aspect. I believe a normal Sino-American relationship is helpful to peace and stability in the Asia-Pacific region under the new international circumstances. Not long ago, there was some friction between China and the United States, such as arms sales to Taiwan, the Yinhe incident and various kinds of unreasonable sanctions, all of which were manifestations of power politics, in violation of China's sovereignty and interfering with China's internal affairs. With regard to Sino-American relations, China maintains that the two sides should enhance confidence, reduce troubles in accordance with the three communiqués, iron out differences through dialogue and, when problems cannot be solved for the time being, seek common ground while reserving differences. Imposition of sanctions causes damage to the interests of China and the United States alike and cannot solve any problem.

The leaders of China and the United States held a formal meeting in Seattle in 1993, which turned out to be very successful. Although we do not think all the problems in Sino-American relations can be solved through one or two meetings, we do believe that ways can be found so long as the two countries, given the overall situation, recognise the importance of a better Sino-American relationship for the interests of both China and the United States and for stability and prosperity in the Asia-Pacific region.

The modernisation of China

Great achievements have taken place in China's economy since the adoption of the policy of reform and opening-up to the outside world. China's economy has now entered into a phase of fast growth. The GNP rose by almost 13 per cent in 1992 and the growth rate in 1993 was again a double-digit one. China's foreign trade and economic co-operation have been expanding rapidly. Total trade volume in 1992 represented a 5.2-fold increase over 1978, the year before the start of the economic reform and opening-up, representing an annual growth rate of 13.9 per cent. China's high-gear economy has not only helped to meet the basic needs for food and clothing of over 1.1 billion people, pushing the Chinese people on to a relatively comfortable livelihood, but it also promoted economic exchanges and co-operation between China and other countries. It is a good thing both for China and for the world.

China has encountered some problems in the course of rapid development, which will be resolved by hastening and deepening the reform. The Third Plenary Session of the Fourteenth Central Committee of the Chinese Communist Party (CCP) adopted a number of decisions on certain issues relating to the establishment of a socialist market economy in China. The main objective of the document is to systemise and specify the goals and fundamental principles guiding economic reform as set out in the Fourteenth Central Committee of the CCP. This is a very important document in that it is the program of action for speeding up of the reform and opening-up, for quickening the pace of socialist modernisation and construction and for building a socialist market economy.

China's defence strategy and armaments

The military strategy of China has always been a defensive one, with its primary task being to provide reliable security safeguards for reform and opening-up, and economic construction. It does not constitute a threat to any country.

Recently, there has been a saying that if China becomes stronger militarily, it will upset the military balance in Asia. This kind of saying is utterly groundless. China is a developing country with a large population, low level of development, and a low GNP per capita. The primary task for China is to raise productivity and develop the economy. China does not seek an armament level beyond its legitimate defensive needs, nor does it engage in an arms race with any other state. Our national defence budget is very small. The military budget for 1993 was around US$7.3 billion, which is only 2.66 per cent of American military spending of US$274.3 billion. China's military spending is US$6 per head, one of the lowest in the world, compared with US$1100 for the United States. China has neither troops nor military bases on foreign territory, does not seek hegemony, and will not do so even when its economy is highly developed in the future. As distance tests a horse's strength, so time reveals the truth. Without any intention of aggression and expansion, China constitutes an important force for peace in the Asia-Pacific region.

The question of the security mechanism in the Asia-Pacific region

In recent years, a number of countries have put forward proposals for the establishment of a security mechanism and confidence-building measures for the preservation of the relatively stable situation in the Asia-Pacific region. As these proposals are different from one another in their content, geographical scope and approaches for implementation, it is difficult to reach agreement at present. Nonetheless, the fact that these proposals have been put forward testifies to the common aspiration of all countries for the maintenance of regional peace and stability.

Geographically located in Asia, China naturally attaches importance to the security of the region. We believe that Asia is different from Europe. The impact of the end of the Cold War on the Asia-Pacific region was a minor one, which is why the region has maintained a relatively high degree of political stability and a fast economic growth rate. We believe that the most prominent feature of the Asia-Pacific region is its diversity, as evidenced in the variety of its ethnic groups, religions, political systems and cultural traditions, as well as the differences in the level of economic development. Consequently, any discussions on security mechanism should proceed from the actual conditions and characteristics of the region. China is willing to discuss with all the other countries in the region, including Australia, questions relating to this subject and will be open-minded with regard to any proposal that is conducive to peace, security and stability in the Asia-Pacific region.

Some basic guiding principles need to be followed when discussing the question of a security mechanism in the Asia-Pacific region:

- The Five Principles of Peaceful Coexistence and the principles enshrined in the UN Charter are the most fundamental principles, the core of which is mutual respect for each other's sovereignty and non-interference in each other's internal affairs.
- The settlement of international disputes by peaceful means should be the norm for countries in this region in resolving their problems, whether left over from history or cropping up in the future. As for some outstanding problems that cannot be solved immediately, they should be shelved for the time being until such time is ripe for a negotiated solution, so that these would not obstruct the normal development of international relations and economic co-operation.
- No country in the Asia-Pacific region should seek hegemony in the region, join or set up military blocs or political alliances against other countries.
- Countries in Asia and the Pacific should not seek armament levels beyond legitimate defensive needs. The United States and Russia should start reducing their large naval presence in the region, while cutting down on their nuclear and conventional arsenals. Furthermore, all countries should exercise restraint in conventional arms transfers. Arms transfers should not be used to interfere in others' internal affairs.
- The nuclear-weapon states in Asia and the Pacific should undertake not to be the first to use nuclear weapons and not to use or threaten to use nuclear weapons against non-nuclear-weapon states and nuclear weapon-free zones. Nuclear-weapon states should recognise the status of the South Pacific as a nuclear weapon-free zone, undertake corresponding obligations and support the establishment of nuclear weapon-free zones in their own region and in other regions.
- At present, economic co-operation in the Asia-Pacific region has, to a large extent, transcended difficulties posed by differences in social, political and economic systems, and has become a major factor for stability in the region. Countries in this region should continue to strengthen their economic co-operation and trade relations, promote scientific and technological exchanges and co-operation, and support such regional economic organisations as APEC and the United Nations Economic and Social Commission for Asia and the Pacific (ESCAP) for even greater

roles. The developed countries should help their less developed neighbours, for the goal of common security can only be achieved through common economic prosperity.

- Any discussions on a security mechanism must take into account regional characteristics (i.e. diversity and complexity). Only when the future mechanism suits the specific conditions and is conducive to the maintenance of peace, security and stability of the region and to the promotion of friendly co-operation in the region can it be expected to receive wide-ranging support from all countries in the region.

Countries in Asia and the Pacific should continue bilateral, regional, multi-tiered and multi-channelled dialogues on the security of the Asia-Pacific region. China is ready to participate extensively in the discussion and dialogue on a security mechanism in the Asia-Pacific region.

China's position on the Taiwan question

Taiwan is an inalienable part of China. Of the more than 100 countries with which China has diplomatic relations, all recognise that there is only one China and that the government of the People's Republic of China is the sole legitimate government of China.

I believe that every Chinese without exception would like to see the Taiwan question solved and China reunified. China has consistently held that there is only one China in the world and that Taiwan is an inalienable part of China. China opposes policies such as 'two Chinas', 'one China, one Taiwan', or 'one country, two governments'. On the premise of one China, with different social systems on the mainland and Taiwan, we can coexist and develop side by side for a long time without one swallowing up the other. This approach has taken into account the actual situation in Taiwan and the practical interests of our compatriots there. After reunification, Taiwan will become a special administrative region. Unlike other provinces or regions in China, Taiwan will have a higher degree of autonomy.

People on both sides of the Straits are all Chinese. It would be a great tragedy for all if China's territorial integrity and sovereignty were to be split and its people were to be drawn into war. We therefore call for the peaceful reunification of China — an aspiration shared by all Chinese. I think any subject could be discussed on the premise of one China. So long as the two sides sit down and talk, they will always be able to find a mutually acceptable solution. For years, China has been working hard to push forward economic co-operation and exchanges in various fields on the basis of mutual respect, complementarity and mutual benefit and to realise direct trade, postal, air and shipping services.

The reunification of China will not only bolster the stability and development of the country itself, but also enhance friendly relations and co-operation between China and other countries and promote peace and development in the Asia-Pacific region and the world as a whole.

Sino-Australian relations

Sino-Australian relations have developed rather smoothly since the establishment of diplomatic ties between the two countries. In 1992 there was a boost in bilateral relations and an apparent increase in high-level exchanges. In his trip to China in June 1993, Prime Minister Keating stressed the need to further revise Australia's foreign policy and to develop its relations with China and other Asian countries. Co-operation and consultation on international affairs between China and Australia have been enhanced. During the three meetings between the foreign ministers of China and Australia in 1993, views were exchanged on such issues of common concern as the Cambodian question, the situation in Myanmar, the nuclear problem on the Korean peninsula and security in the Asia-Pacific region.

Since the first regular consultation on disarmament at deputy foreign ministerial level in 1985, seven rounds of such consultations have been conducted and the eighth round is about to start. In addition to trade and economic relations, exchanges and co-operation between China and Australia in the fields of culture, education, and science and technology are being strengthened constantly.

I believe that the relations and contacts between the two states and peoples will be further improved and enhanced if we adhere to the principles of peaceful coexistence, equality and mutual benefit.

3 Tradition and Chinese Foreign Policy

Rafe de Crespigny

Introduction

The present-day People's Republic of China has inherited, and recognises, a long historical and cultural tradition of Han Chinese people in the heartland of East Asia. It is appropriate, therefore, to consider some of the influences which that history and culture, and the physical facts of geography and demography, may have upon the Chinese government's view of the world and upon its approach to and conduct of foreign policy.

Such a subject, of course, is both large and complex, and this chapter can present no more than a summary of some possible approaches. My concern here is to outline the geographical and historical background to the Chinese tradition of unified imperial government, to consider the involvement of the Han people with the lands to their north, south and west, their experience of the maritime frontier, and their dealings with the peoples they have encountered in those regions. This should reveal substantial continuities both in general outlook and in practical policy, so that the models from the past may be found to have echoes in the answers to present-day questions.

The very nature of China as an international entity is affected by the contrast between the dominant and unifying force of central government — based upon the north — and the expanding, potentially fragmentary economic prosperity of the south. The internal tensions which can now be observed between the government at Beijing and the regions of the southeastern seaboard can thus be traced for two thousand years into the past. In similar fashion, the dealings of the People's Republic with the former Soviet

Union, and now Russia, with modern Mongolia and with central Asia and Tibet mirror the difficulties which the earliest imperial governments of China found in dealing with non-Chinese peoples of different cultures and economic concerns. In the north, there is the long defensive tradition symbolised by the Great Wall. In the west, there is a parallel drive for expansion and control of smaller states which might give opportunity for exploitation by more powerful and dangerous rivals.

The northern and western frontiers have long been a cause of concern to the Chinese, but in the south, until modern times, there had been no alien threat. The peoples south of the Yangzi and beyond the Nan Ling to the region of present-day Guangzhou were politically weak, strongly influenced by the literate civilisation of the north and quite easily assimilated or taken over. Trade with southeast Asia was maintained without difficulty, whether in Chinese or foreign ships, and the proud record of the Ming voyages to the Indian Ocean and Africa appeared to confirm the security of Chinese interests in the region.

By the nineteenth century, however, this comfortable tradition was all but overthrown. On the one hand, the military and technological power of the West had turned the safe frontier of the south into a region of open concern, while at the same time the southern expansion of the Chinese people had now developed beyond the seas, largely out of the control of the imperial government. There was a challenge to Chinese tradition from both the West and from overseas Chinese, along with a separation of the Chinese people themselves from the established patterns of authority and ideology. For more than a hundred years, successive rulers of China have sought to deal with both the moral and the physical implications of this change, and none has yet found a stable solution.

The basis of the state

In the human geography of east Asia, the North China Plain is of central importance, and its occupation and control have been critical to the history of China. Topographically, the Plain may be viewed as a vast delta of the Yellow River, opening at the south of the Taihang mountains near present-day Kaifeng and extending eastwards over hundreds of kilometres to the sea-coast north and south of the Shandong hills and peninsula. North of Beijing, the plain is bounded by the high ground of the Badaling, the line of the Great Wall, and in the south it extends across the basin of the Huai to the lower course of the Yangzi.

This vast expanse of open ground is now inhabited by some 400 million people, and since ancient times it has been a centre of population large enough to dominate the region. Whichever political authority has been able to command the North China Plain has naturally taken a leading role in eastern Asia, and in favourable circumstances has extended its dominance far to the north, south and west. The sheer numbers of people, and the resources of their enterprise, bring great power to the government which controls them, and no other area can match this potential.

The economic strength of the plain, and of the hill country in present-day Shanxi and Shaanxi provinces to the west, is traditionally based upon peasant agriculture. The soil is wind-blown loess or water-borne silt, easy to work using the most primitive tools. Moderate rainfall and temperature allow the cultivation of corn, millet, wheat and bean crops, while the Yellow River and its major tributaries such as the Fen and the Wei provide opportunities for the construction of canals both for irrigation and for transport.

In the north, by contrast, the open lands of the Gobi desert, the Mongolian steppe and the hill country and plains of Manchuria are cold and dry. Just north of Beijing, the mean temperature in January is ten degrees Celsius below freezing, the growing season is barely seven months a year, and annual rainfall is under 500 millimetres. In traditional times, therefore, the peoples of these territories relied chiefly upon hunting or grazing, not settled agriculture, and they had no opportunity to develop the variety, the security or the prosperity of their neighbours on the North China Plain.

To the south, on the other hand, in the lands beyond the Yangzi, the temperature seldom falls below freezing, the growing season may extend throughout the year, and the climate supports paddy rice and catch crops of vegetables. The country itself, however, is broken into a medley of rivers and lakes, valleys and mountain divides, so that no one territory can establish ready dominance over another, and none has been able to match the concentrated power of the northern plain.

Quite appropriately, therefore, the founding legends of Chinese civilisation feature deities and heroes like Prince Millet, creator of agriculture, and the Great Yu, who tamed the floods of the open plain and brought all the world into submission. Similarly, the records of archaeology and history indicate that the origins of Chinese culture may be most readily traced to royal cities on the edge of the North China Plain: Anyang near the Taihang Mountains, Zhengzhou and Luoyang by the Yellow River, or present-day Xi'an in the loess country of the Wei valley. At one time or another, each of these was able to establish local power over its immediate surroundings and a loose hegemony across the plain, and in the third century BC the First Emperor of Qin completed the process by the conquest of all this heartland of China.

The power of Qin was short-lived, but it was succeeded by the 400-year dynasty of Han, which set the pattern for pre-modern China. Within the empire, central power was maintained by careful provincial administration, controlled by officials appointed directly from the court with no good opportunity to gain local connections or loyalties. These officers came naturally from families of landed wealth but, in contrast to the feudal system of Europe, each man was chosen for his quality as a literate clerk, not by hereditary right, and he owed public allegiance only to the emperor: in China there was no conflict between Church and State such as bedevilled the Holy Roman Empire and the Christian kingdoms of France, England and Spain.

The core of imperial power was based upon a peasant economy. Most of the revenues of the empire, collected in cash or in grain, were brought to the capital along the network of a Grand Canal, and these resources were devoted to the rituals of state, the maintenance of administration, the pleasures of the ruler and the requirements of war. Like most early states, this was government as exploitative industry, and the official doctrines of Confucianism did little to conceal the reality of power or ease the local oppression of the poor and weak by the prosperous and influential. At the grass roots of the state, there was clan and family feuding, with powerful men supported by retainers and banditry on the margins. The ultimate sanction, keeping disturbance within limits, was the threat of intervention by the imperial army.

Despite the frequent denigration of the soldier's trade in Chinese tradition, there is as much regard for physical courage, admiration of military prowess and lust for glory to be found in the literature of China as in any other civilised society. Classics and histories have frequent accounts of war, with praise for leading generals and strategists, and the ancient concept of the Mandate of Heaven, admired by Confucius and endorsed by Mencius, assumes as a matter of course that a righteous ruler will come to power through triumph in combat. Regardless of rituals and claims to moral virtue, each emperor held power because he was the recognised descendant of the man who won the last civil war, and each kept his throne for just so long as the most powerful army in the empire continued to obey him. Whether he sought merely to hold his position, to expand his territory, or just to deal with enemies on the border, force was the ultimate argument of each Chinese ruler.

The frontier of the Great Wall

There is a Chinese proverb that you may conquer the empire on horseback, but you cannot rule it from there. The rule certainly applied to the territories of China proper, where government over settled peasantry was maintained by regular administration, backed with the threat of force. To the north, however, the people could not be settled, for the climate does not allow grain to grow tall enough for harvest, and the economy of the steppe is based upon cycles of nomad herding. The various tribes and clans had identifiable grazing lands which they travelled through and would defend against others, and they accumulated property of cattle, sheep, camels, tents and chattels, but they did not remain in one place, and techniques of control which worked in China were inadequate to deal with them.

The lands of the north, moreover, provided only a poor living to their people, at the same time as prosperous, settled China had goods of interest and value, from additional grain to ironware, gold, silk and even wine. There was thus high demand for trade among the people of the north, but the items which they offered — horses and wool and furs — were marginal to Chinese interests. For much of traditional history, therefore, initiatives for trade were in Chinese hands, and a major duty of officials in the north of the empire was the control of markets with the non-Chinese, and the prevention of unauthorised contact between those within and those beyond the frontier line.[1]

So trade and blockade were a means to control the barbarians, but the weapons required reinforcement: the non-Chinese would not necessarily accept this position of economic and thus political dependence, and they had weapons and strategies of their own. Firstly, though nomad peoples normally travelled on established grazing routes, they could move fast and far when they needed to, and secondly the nature of their society, based upon small groups of campfires and tents, allowed hot-headed young men to gain a reputation by raiding and plundering the sedentary south. If the Chinese tried too hard to restrict trade with their neighbours of the north, those people might seek to fill their needs by force of arms or, indirectly, by the threat of such force.

It was these circumstances which tended to produce empires in the north to rival those of China. The Xiongnu state of the Han period, the Xianbi which succeeded them, the Uighurs of Tang, the Ruchen of Song and the Mongols who came afterwards were all founded on the core of a single tribe and clan, which gave its name to the federation it controlled.[2] To a considerable degree, these were warlord states or pirate kingdoms, and although their efficiency and success might vary from one time and territory to another, from pinpricks along the border to the conquest of China and all central Asia, the empires of the steppe were ultimately founded on a need for conquest and plunder, and their drive for expansion was often driven by poverty, misfortune and starvation at home.

Faced with such enemies, the government of China had two policies. One was that of bribery — in a sense no more than an extension of the trade-and-blockade method of control. Nomad leaders could be granted titles, subsidies and gifts, sometimes even alliance by marriage, both to enhance their power among their own people and to encourage them to keep firebrands in order. If a pirate king could be turned into a prosperous client or even a parasite, Chinese interests were served as well as if the emperor had exercised direct control.[3]

The second policy, of course, was that of war — commonly the last resort, for it was always expensive and fraught with difficulty. In such conflict, the Chinese had the advantage of administration, generally of well-trained infantry, and often superior weapons, such as the crossbow or the cannon. Their great disadvantage was mobility, for the farmlands of China were a poor place to breed horses, and the nomad horsemen could choose where to concentrate and strike at will.

Here was a major purpose of the Great Wall. Ten feet high or more, it was an immediate obstruction to any force of cavalry, which must either get its horses over by ramps and ropes, or seek to capture a gate in direct assault. For either event, the Wall was manned by pickets and scouts, with a system of signalling from watch-towers by flags and flares to a reserve army in the rear.[4] The defence therefore had warning of the attack, a force could be gathered to receive and repel it, and the invaders were only too aware that the Wall remained across their line of retreat. Properly garrisoned and supported, the Wall was all but impregnable, most enemies were wise enough not to try it, and this firm line of defence could be supplemented by punitive expeditions when the need arose or when a forward party at court sought glory for domestic purposes.

For civilian purposes, the Wall was the line of demarcation between subjects of the emperor and those without the law, while travel and trade in one direction or another was controlled by passports and customs. Politically, moreover, this barrier ensured that not only the subjects, but also the rulers and commanders of the frontier marches, were kept under tight control. In traditional China, one anxiety of rulers at the capital was the possibility of splinter states at the edge of the empire which might ally with aliens against them. Under the authority of central government, the Wall was as much a means of control over the people of China as a fence against the enemy.[5]

Indeed, in the two thousand years since its first completion, there have been few periods the Wall was fully guarded against the outside, and military options generally took second place to cheaper methods of control by trade, blockade and bribery. The farmers and the nomads, however, were never friends, for their ways of life were incompatible, and both sides had memories of ill-will. When the Chinese look north, they can see millennia of hostility, culminating in the conquests of the Mongols and the Manchus. When peoples of the steppe look south, they see an imperial state which has always sought to control them by economic or military means, while the last freedom of the grasslands and the desert has disappeared between the two great empires of China and Russia.

The western regions

The region known as Chinese Turkestan has been a source of interest and concern to governments of China since earliest times. During the Han, expansion was based upon two considerations: to compete with and outflank the Xiongnu empire on the west; and to obtain horses for the imperial army by trade with western Asia. As it happened, however, the lands of the Tarim basin and the Takla Makan desert, and of Zungaria and Turfan to the north, were susceptible to Chinese control. The desert trade routes leading to the west were punctuated by oasis cities, watered by rivers flowing from the snows of Tibet and the Tian Shan ranges, and these could be dominated by Chinese armies and resident officials. At one period or another through the centuries which followed, the forces of China were able to intervene in the quarrels of these city-states, and the history of Chinese involvement in the region extends over two thousand years.

Control, however, was not continuous, and Chinese government has been maintained effectively only for around a quarter of those two thousand years. From the time of Tang, moreover, when the Chinese were defeated by the forces of Islam at the battle of Talas River in 751, the cultural and religious history of central Asia followed a different pattern. The present government of Xinjiang, the 'New Territories', is based upon the conquests of the Chinese general, Zuo Zongtang, in the service of the Manchu Qing dynasty during the second half of the last century, but the people, of Turkish language and Muslim persuasion, have little in common with their modern overlords.

Traditionally, Chinese interest in these western regions has been military and political, not a matter for private citizens. From earliest times, when Zhang Qian and Gan Ying travelled west as agents of Han, to the celebrated journey of the monk Xuanzang of the Tang period, who journeyed to India in search of Buddhist scriptures,[6] Chinese in the west were primarily concerned with official or religious affairs, and trade along this silk route was largely in foreign hands. Many merchants settled in China itself, forming significant minorities of Muslims and even Jews.

South of this region, in the foothills of the Tibetan massif, tribes known variously as Qiang, Di, Ailao and by other names faced pressure from Chinese settlers and local officials in present-day Sichuan and Yunnan. Here there was no firm central policy, and Tibet itself was generally beyond imperial concern. Though the Tibetans were included with the Chinese as subjects of the Mongols in the fourteenth century, they had restored their independence by the time of the Ming, and they had no natural connection to the Chinese state.

During the eighteenth century, however, as the Manchu rulers of China extended authority over the Mongols, they inherited also a nominal suzerainty over Tibet, and for the balance of the Qing period a succession of *amban*, or 'protectors', were appointed to Lhasa, while the Lama government maintained representation at Beijing. The authority and influence of the *amban* varied, but it was not absolute, and in the late nineteenth and early twentieth century Tibet became part of the 'Great Game' played between the empires of Russia and of the British in India. Bayonets were sent to Lhasa, and the McMahon line was drawn at Simla, largely without involvement of the Qing, while the fall of the empire in 1911 saw the rulers of Tibet reassert their independence against the new Republic.

From this point of view, until the invasion of 1950–51, confirmed by the suppression of local rebellion in 1959, there had been no close connection between the Chinese government and the heartland of Tibet. The Lama government, however, had limited international recognition, and when the Chinese armies came, it commanded no firm position in the United Nations, and had no friends from whom it might seek effective support. Viewed from Beijing, Tibet under foreign influence was a potential threat, and the new communist regime had no desire to see the Great Game continued. Behind the rhetoric of liberation on the one hand and of genocide on the

other, control of Tibet is important to China — and it may be argued that
the war with India in 1962 was less about correct interpretation of the borders than about removing Indian interest in the ownership of Tibet as a
whole. For that purpose, it was most successful.

Both in central Asia and Tibet, therefore, the traditional pattern of Chinese
interest is that of an imperial power concerned with grand strategy and
dealing with a perceived threat from powerful neighbours, whether
Xiongnu, Mongols or Russians. In neither region is there close cultural connection, nor a sense among the subject peoples, Muslim Uighurs or Buddhist
Tibetans that they share the interests of their Chinese masters. From Beijing's
viewpoint, however, such concerns are irrelevant: in traditional imperial
style, these territories are in China's sphere of interest, and they cannot be
allowed to fall under the control of others.

Expansion in the south

If the origins of Chinese culture and central political power are to be found
in the region of the Yellow River and the North China Plain, the basins of
the Yangzi and the lands further south have been the area of their development and expansion. For this there are three main reasons. Firstly, the
favourable climate, with high rainfall, warm weather and a long growing
season, meant that techniques of agriculture developed in the dry fields of
the north, notably irrigation, were readily compatible with rice cultivation
in the south. Secondly, the broken terrain of rivers, hills and marshlands
prevented any single political entity from gathering sufficient power to rival
the concentration of people and resources under unified government in the
north. And thirdly, perhaps most critical for Chinese culture in the long
term, the written language developed in the north brought both the advantages of civilisation and the dominance of Chinese thought and administration across the south.

In the earliest history, the southern state of Chu, extending across the
Han and the Huai in present-day Hubei and Anhui provinces during the first
millennium BC, was a major rival to the future empire of Qin, and there is
evidence that the culture of Chu owed much to the influence of the Pacific
and southeast Asia. Later, in similar fashion, the local state of Shizhaishan,
near the Dali Lake in present-day Yunnan, was essentially Indo-Chinese
and had little in common with the empire of Han. In these and similar cases,
however, the indigenous culture of the south was largely overwhelmed by
the sophistication and imperial power of China.

The core of Chinese expansion, however, was less official than private.
Through the first millennium AD, as Chinese migrated across the Yangzi to
settle in the south, they took over and absorbed the earlier inhabitants by
force, intermarriage or example. Most commonly, the emigrés were escap-
ing from warfare or from the oppression of government, and they were not
anxious for the benefits of imperial administration. Over time, however,

one regime or another established counties to control them, and the pioneers in their isolated valleys were absorbed without great difficulty into the centralised empire.

The process was irregular and often confused, with rival clans and groups intermingled among neighbouring villages, and a hierarchy between those who arrived at different times, such as the Hakka, and remnant groups which kept some semblance of their original non-Chinese culture and are now categorised as national minorities. The process, however, has been continuous, and the colonisation has not yet stopped: whether in the hill country of Taiwan, the regions of Guangxi, Guizhou and Yunnan in the far southwest, or even Tibet and Mongolia in the west and north, Chinese official control over its neighbouring territories has been encouraged and enforced by the steady spread of its people over two millennia.

The very success of this colonisation, however, produced problems within the world of China itself. From earliest times, Chinese colonists were prepared to seek independence: both the kingdom of Nanyue in Guangdong during the second century BC and the rebellion of the Trung sisters in Vietnam during the first century AD were led by clans of Chinese origin, and by the end of Han in the third century the lands south of the Yangzi were sufficiently colonised and prosperous for separate Chinese states to maintain themselves against the dominant powers of the north over almost four centuries. Despite the long unity of Tang, and the overwhelming conquest of the Mongols, both the Northern and Southern Song dynasties, and the early Ming, may be taken as demonstration that the heartland of China was moving south from the Yellow River to the lower Yangzi.

So even after the Mongol conquest, Marco Polo could describe Hangzhou as the greatest city of the world, and throughout Ming and Qing the cities of Yangzhou and Suzhou and the territory about them were centres of education and the breeding ground for the bureaucrats who governed the empire. Though nineteenth-century Shanghai was developed by foreigners, the intellectual energy and prosperity of the modern city was based upon a hinterland which had been of major importance in the culture of China for hundreds of years.

At the end of the fourteenth century, therefore, after the restoration of Chinese government from the Mongols, it was appropriate that Zhu Yuanzhang, founding Xuanwu Emperor of Ming, should establish his capital at Nanjing. One generation later, however, when his younger son the future Yongle Emperor seized power, the seat of government was transferred to Beijing, recently a capital of the Mongols. For the internal politics of the dynasty, the move was sensible: Beijing was the centre of the new ruler's military power, but it had far-reaching influence on the subsequent history of China.

From the perspective of a government based upon Nanjing, the lands of the south and the seaways beyond are interesting and important, while the northern frontier on the line of the Great Wall is a matter of more limited, though still substantial, concern. A government at Beijing, however, has a different perspective: not only is it closely concerned with defence against the north, it is inevitably interested in Manchuria, Mongolia and the territories of central Asia. At the same time, moreover, to a yet greater extent than in former times, the imperial court must rely upon supplies from the south, so the Grand Canal, from Hangzhou across the Yangzi, the Huai and the North China Plain, became an enormous drain, bearing the wealth of the south to serve imperial ambitions in the north.

China and the sea

Besides this internal tension between the prosperous south and the powerful north, one may also observe different attitudes towards the world of the sea. For northern China, communication by sea is difficult and uncertain: much of the shoreline, often including the port at Tianjin, is ice-bound in winter, and the alluvial coastline created by the Yellow River and other streams across the plain produces few secure anchorages. The tip of the Liaodong peninsula, ice-free by a chance of the currents, is in frontier territory,[7] and though there are harbours along the rocky shores of Shandong,[8] the peninsula itself has treacherous seas and is a danger to coastal shipping. From ancient times, travel to Manchuria and even Korea was better by land than by sea, while the islands of Japan were never a matter of imperial interest.[9]

South of the Yangzi, however, the view of the sea is quite different. Most Chinese water transport and naval warfare took place on rivers, lakes and along canals, but from earliest times there was trade along the coast from Hangzhou past Fujian, Guangdong and Vietnam, supported by the regularity of the monsoon and the security of harbours along the indented coast. Though Chinese citizens were frequently involved, however, and there was a strong tradition of shipbuilding and navigation to southeast Asia, it was largely a matter of private enterprise, and the traffic was shared with merchants from the islands of the south and the Indian Ocean.

During the time of the Yongle Emperor himself, the official view from the north was less restrictive. At the same time as he dealt with Manchuria, Mongolia, central Asia and Tibet, the emperor was interested in contact with Japan through the southern ports of Ningbo, Quanzhou and Guangzhou, and also with Annam and the further lands of southeast Asia. From 1405 the official voyages of the eunuch Zheng He, based upon the technology and experience of the seamen of the southern coastline, established authority as far as Java and Malacca, and a presence across the Indian Ocean to the coast of Africa.

In practical terms, however, this seaborne initiative was of brief duration. After the death of the Yongle Emperor in 1424, Annam was lost to the empire, and Zheng He's seventh voyage in the early 1430s was little more than an epilogue. A strong party at court opposed such ventures, government policy was consistently concerned with more pressing matters in the north, and in 1435 the Ming government reversed the policy of naval expansion. About 1477, the detailed records of Zheng He's voyages were deliberately burnt, and no further activity in the southern seas was ordered, or indeed permitted.

The official expeditions, moreover, had been combined with prohibition against private enterprise,[10] and even after they were ended, Chinese citizens were forbidden to trade or travel beyond the frontiers or across the seas. All commerce was to be carried out under the auspices of the tribute system so that no exchange of goods was permitted unless a country was formally in tributary relationship with China, and the restrictions upon overseas trade were later extended even to the coast.

Apart from the resentment overseas, the restrictive official policy brought a steady growth in the incidence of smuggling and the ravages of pirates. In 1567, after major disturbances and an almost complete breakdown of control along the coast, the prohibitions were abandoned, and in the last century of Ming the development of commerce with Portuguese, Spaniards and then the Dutch brought substantial contact between south China and the countries across the sea, while contemporary records describe how great migrations of Chinese people into southeast Asia at this time were carried, at least in part, by Chinese ships. The local Chinese community became a major factor in the Spanish Philippines, exchanging silver for silk and other luxuries borne on the Manila galleon. When the Dutch established their position in the East Indies, a Chinese fleet arriving at Batavia each northern monsoon presented opportunity for trade and brought a supply of coolie labour for the plantations.

When Ming fell to the Manchu Qing in the mid-seventeenth century, the 'loyalist' state of Zheng Chenggong (Koxinga) and his successors on the southeastern coast and Taiwan, driving out the Dutch and defying the new imperial power until 1683, showed the capacity of Chinese on the coast to match the power both of the foreigners and of the government in the north. In their struggle with the Zheng, the Qing forbade all seaborne trade, but late in the seventeenth century the ban was lifted, and Chinese ships competed profitably in the export market of tea and porcelain to the Netherlands East Indies and elsewhere in southeast Asia.

Official attitude towards such enterprise, however, was never enthusiastic. At one time or another, various edicts restricted private ships and fishing vessels, prohibited commercial voyages to the south, and opposed Chinese travel or residence overseas. In 1740, when Beijing ordered a trade embargo because Chinese had been massacred in Java, southern officials argued that the traffic was too valuable and that in any case people of Chinese stock born outside the empire deserved no more consideration than barbarians. Finally, in 1757, Canton was declared the sole legal port for overseas trade, with foreign traders controlled by local groups of merchants under official licence, and a government-sponsored monopoly which transferred profits to the imperial household. So matters of foreign trade were kept outside the mainstream of administration, and the emperor embezzled revenue from his own government.

Throughout this history, whether the imperial government hindered or accepted overseas and coastal economic activity in the south, it was always concerned with the advantage of the state, rarely with the interests of private merchants or citizens, and still less those of foreigners. Regardless of the effects of its policies, initiative was in the hands of the north, and despite argument, protest and emigration there was no challenge from the south of China against the authority of the capital, nor serious concern that traders from overseas might have policies or capacities of their own. Nothing in the experience of the past could have prepared the Qing dynasty for the incursions of seaborne power into the heart and structure of imperial power which began with the Opium War and continued into the present century.

China and the foreigners

At the most obvious level, the military and mercantile invasion from the West presented a political and economic challenge to the government of the empire which had never been mounted by any power from the south. In fact, the depredations of the European powers and the Americans were of less importance than the internal troubles which afflicted the Qing dynasty, from the explosion of population and its pressure against limited resources of land and technology to the physical threat of the great rebellions which culminated in the risings of the Taiping, the Nian, the Muslims and the Boxers. But the record of foreign arrogance and Chinese humiliation cut deep into the memory of a proud tradition.

The challenge of the West, moreover, was more serious and longer lasting than the century of aggression itself. China had been invaded and conquered by alien powers in the past, but never before had its people been faced with an alternative philosophy and culture which could stand comparison to the Chinese tradition and appeared in many respects to be superior. Not only did foreigners defeat Chinese troops with superior discipline and increasingly powerful weapons, but such civil innovations as steamships, railroads and telegraphs were far ahead of any Chinese technology, while the foreigners themselves, secure in their own tradition, showed little interest in that of China, and still less inclination to adopt it.

On the contrary, the influence of foreign ideas, whether actively propounded by Christian missions, or less ostentatiously by commercial and diplomatic negotiation and example, pressed against the core of China at a time when the natural weakness of the alien Qing dynasty was at its most vulnerable. On the one hand, the misery of over-population and the disorders of rebellion made the traditional Confucian creed, energetically adopted and sponsored by the Manchus throughout their three centuries of government, appear discredited and increasingly irrelevant. And at the same time the apparent success of Western techniques, whether in technology and science, or in political structure and civil law, brought increasing interest in foreign ways among intelligent Chinese.

By the end of the nineteenth century, the traditions of imperial China had been shaken by the growing acceptance of Western ideas, and they were ultimately destroyed by the arguments of Kang Youwei and his school, which claimed the whole apparatus of Confucian teaching had been falsely interpreted. Despite rearguard arguments, once the question was raised so baldly, the Western-based alternatives presented by reformers and revolutionaries such as Sun Yatsen destroyed not only the empire, but also the ideology with which it had become so closely identified.

It is hard to comprehend the full effect of this loss of faith, but it is surely unwise to neglect its influence on China during the present century. We can observe, from our own experience in Australia, the need for some concept of community and nationhood. Early twentieth century China, with weak government structures and massive political and economic pressure at home and abroad, was under far greater strain. Some patterns in society, from centralised government by an educated elite to the importance of clan, family and local connections, continued from the past, but the people were faced with a failure of moral and philosophical tradition that had formerly been admired and unquestioned. Moreover, just as the formal structure of Confucianism was overthrown, the development of popularised *baihua* writing meant that the classical language, which had linked all educated men with their mentors of the past, ceased to be the normal medium of intellectual debate. As Confucian temples were seized by reformers and turned into schools for Western learning, the politicians, philosophers, teachers and students of the new China began the search for some ideal to put in place of the discredited indigenous tradition.

Among a multitude of alternatives, Sun Yatsen called for Nationalism, Democracy and Socialism, liberals discussed Democracy and Science, Chiang Kai-shek flirted with Fascism, and the Communist Party under Mao Zedong (though it exchanged proletarian for rural revolution) claimed to follow Marx and Lenin. The search was eclectic, but the ideals which justified the new revolutionary state were drawn predominantly from the West. For a short time, the excitement of revolutionary Maoism, accepted with interest by many in the West and in the Third World, gave promise of a new world leadership, but the failure of those ideals at home and abroad removed that claim to authority.

In that sense, the traditional Chinese view of their national identity, their place in the region and in the world at large has been replaced at every level by alien concepts, and though the pragmatic policies of recent years may bring a level of prosperity, they also mark China as just one more developing country, very large and potentially very powerful, but currently dependent upon trade and investment from former enemies, Japan, South Korea, Taiwan and the United States. In similar fashion, in international affairs, it is hardly possible for China to claim a position of ideological authority or even regional dominance. The country's role at present is largely determined by Western-based concepts of international law, by the practice of Western-style diplomacy, and by the structures of the new world order composed from Western initiatives.

Within China itself, moreover, besides the direct effects of foreign intervention, developments in the twentieth century have enhanced those tensions between north and south which had been, to some extent, controlled during the last centuries of the empire. Just as the regions and people closest to the foreigners, from the compradores of Shanghai to the revolutionaries based upon Guangzhou and Japan, became leaders of the new republic, so the modern development of the 1980s and 1990s is heavily dependent upon the entrepreneurial skills of the seaboard. This economic power can occasionally show itself in practical terms: at the time of the Boxers in 1900, when the imperial government declared war against the foreigners, the governors of the south declared neutrality; during the early Republic, provincial warlords maintained practical independence behind a facade of national identity; and the Nationalist unification of the late 1920s, albeit ephemeral, was the first occasion in Chinese history that the empire was conquered from the south. All these precedents could make any northern-based government wary of committing military or naval force to commanders in the south, and give cause for concern about pressure for economic independence among the southern provinces and regions.

Further afield, though the overseas Chinese had been often rejected and all but disregarded by the traditional empire, the people themselves still retained their interest and extended their patronage to the communities and the country they had left. At the same time, they used their skills to acquire wealth under the commercial and legal protection of Western colonialism. In the late nineteenth century, as Sun Yatsen and other revolutionaries sought their political and financial support for change within China, the overseas Chinese developed factions and interests in favour of one party or another, and the tensions within China during the twentieth century, particularly those of the Nationalists and the Communists, were reflected in local debates and rivalries.

In this respect, the overseas Chinese have a complex relationship with the People's Republic and Taiwan. Though there have been pan-Chinese movements by both the Nationalists and (with unfortunate effects) by the Communists dealing with Malaya and Indonesia, both governments formally regard overseas Chinese as citizens of the states in which they live. At the same time, the ties of sentiment are strong, so that much foreign investment in present-day China is directed by old associations and local connections. Politically and culturally, however, the opinions overseas are not necessarily those of the regime in power, and the influence of overseas interest on the mainland in particular, both in such traditional forms as the construction of city temples and ancestral shrines, or by the import of foreign ideals of democracy and government accountability, has a capacity for low-level grassroots disruption. Most recently, of course, the aftermath of the Tiananmen incident of 1989 has seen increased opposition to the present government, both among established communities and naturally among those who have been forced, or made their escape, into exile. A hundred years after Sun Yatsen sought the support of overseas communities for his bid to overthrow the empire, similar interests are at work against the regime of the Chinese Communists.

Tradition and the view from Beijing

The present regime in China inherits two broad perspectives from tradition and history: the long record of power and authority in its region of east Asia, and the more recent humiliation and oppression at the hands of Western imperialists. In argument with foreigners, Chinese officials refer often enough to both of these, each time with justification. On the other hand, there are few countries in the world which cannot claim some comparable experience of glory and defeat, and most of them, like the Germans and the French, or even the Australians and the Japanese, seek to overlay the past with the practicalities of the present: the alternative, as in former Yugoslavia, is rather too horrible for most people to contemplate.

So there are questions about the attitude of the present Chinese government. How deeply does a sense of past humiliation affect attitudes and policies — as opposed to forming a useful device for rhetoric? What does it mean to depend upon access to a Western-dominated market — with constant debate on Most-Favoured-Nation status with the United States, and regular criticism from liberals concerned about human rights? One thing that has happened is that the tradition of China as a centre of dominant culture has largely been destroyed: since the collapse of formal Confucianism and the failure of the Cultural Revolution, few people home or abroad give credit to ideas or ideals from China. And while the People's Republic may have a great economic future, its prospects for success are closely linked with investment from its former oppressor, Japan, its separatist rival, Taiwan, and markets among its old imperialist enemies.

On the broader world stage, with a permanent seat on the Security Council, China plays its role as an independent great power with no substantial influence of ideology. If there is one major concern which may be related to experience from the past, it is the issue of state sovereignty and the insistence on non-interference with internal affairs. Here, on the one hand, the history of foreign intervention during the nineteenth and early twentieth centuries may afford real or apparent justification, while the traditional pride of China, as the centre of an empire which had no match for centuries, adds to the theme.

Unfortunately, however, this separatist approach can bring difficulty and embarrassment in major world forums. Apart from the constant irritation of human rights and an awkward approach to free international trade, the Chinese position on the environment, whether it be a question of atomic tests at Lop Nor, coal pollution spreading across Japan, or the destruction of species at home and abroad, must be a matter of concern for any world policy.[11] At the same time, the traditional Chinese attitude to the family and to maintenance of the male line, with implications for the pressure of China's population against possibilities of technology and investment, holds the seeds of disaster for the country itself, for its neighbours and, through increased legal or illegal migration, for further parts of the world.

More immediately, however, it is in China's dealings with the region that the patterns and perceptions of the past appear most obvious, and provide contradictions and conflicts for the present and future.

Firstly, in contrast to the theory of equal sovereign states developed by the West, the traditional Chinese concept of international relations was based upon concentric circles, from the imperial capital outwards through variously dependent states to the barbarians beyond the pale. So governments in the region owe tribute and subservience to the central power at Beijing. The relationships may be described in intimate style, as father and mother, elder and younger brother, or even lips and teeth, but there is a hierarchy, and the relationship may be confirmed by force. In this respect, natural Chinese interest in East and Southeast Asia is influenced not only by a sense of good order but also by expectations of control and guidance. North Korea may still receive support as a natural dependent, and when the Vietnamese turned recalcitrant in the late 1970s, the Chinese army, with limited success, sought to 'teach them a lesson'.

Secondly, as successor state to the former empires of Qing and Ming, the government of the People's Republic is faced with the requirement to draw and maintain borders, recognisable in modern Western-style international law, upon a traditional map which possessed no such strict demarcations. Where the Qing dynasty, moreover, controlled a multinational empire, with Chinese and non-Chinese alike subservient to their Manchu rulers, the concept of Nationalism, proclaimed by Sun Yatsen and maintained by his Communist and Guomindang successors, restored and confirmed the dominance of Han Chinese over their neighbours. So Tibetans, Muslims, Mongols and other national minorities are judged as part of extended China, but must accept their status as subordinate citizens; while regions such as Taiwan and the South China Sea are subject to claims of sovereignty which could be resolved quite differently elsewhere in the world.[12] Regardless of ideology, and certainly transcending the ideals of Marxism, here is a strong tradition of racial and national power.

Finally, we should observe that, since earliest times, whether expressed in the restrictions of the Great Wall or on more open frontiers to the west and south, the interests of central government have been those of official control, while private enterprise, initiative and profit were of minimal concern. And at present, within China itself, one should not underestimate the pressure for disunity. The long tension between north and south is not yet resolved, and is only increasing as economic development enhances the prosperity of Shanghai, Guangzhou and the southern seaboard. In terms of Beijing's view, therefore, guided by such traditional concern, it is intolerable that Hong Kong should present an alternative form of government or become the heart of a rival economic system, while the ideals of human rights and self-determination must take second place to the demands of national sovereignty. Waiting in the immediate future, I would suggest, is a critical influence of China's tradition.

Notes

1 Predictably, most historical literature and interpretation is based upon Chinese sources and reflects Chinese opinion. Yü Ying-shih, *Trade and Expansion in Han China: A Study in the Structure of Sino-Barbarian Economic Relations*, University of California Press, Berkeley, 1967, pp. 99–105, gives a clear presentation of this traditional perspective. For a discussion of the northern frontier from the less common point of view of the non-Chinese peoples, see Sechin Jagchid, 'Trade, Peace and War Between the Nomad Altaics and the Agricultural Chinese' and 'Objectives of Warfare in Inner Asia', in *Bulletin of the Institute of China Border Area Studies*, vol. 1, July 1970, pp. 35–80, and vol. 4, July 1973, pp. 11–23, and also Denis Sinor, 'The Inner Asian Warriors', in *Journal of the American Oriental Society*, vol. 101, no. 2, 1981, pp. 133–44.

2 See, for example, Rafe de Crespigny, *Northern Frontier, the Policies and Strategy of the Later Han Empire*, Faculty of Asian Studies, Australian National University, Canberra, 1984, pp. 174–76, with notes at pp. 504–5 citing De Groot, Maenchen-Helfen, Pulleyblank, Barfield and Pritsak.

3 In modern Chinese scholarship and propaganda, this policy of *heqin* is often described as a sign of traditional Chinese benevolence towards their neighbours. Like any such agreement, however, it was maintained as long as each side found it convenient. One of the most celebrated examples of this policy is the story of the beautiful Lady Wang Zhaojun, said to have been a concubine of the emperor of Han sent to live among the Xiongnu despite the monarch's love for her. A tomb claimed to be hers is shown to tourists near Hohhot in Inner Mongolia (though it is probably from the Tang period, 700 years later), and her story is now told as a symbol of Sino-Mongolian friendship. In traditional literature, the story of the Lady Wang is seen as the tragedy of the lost love of the emperor languishing amongst barbarians. In history, the Lady Wang was a useful ally of Han, and sponsor of a pro-Chinese faction at the nomad court.

4 On the structure and military organisation of the Wall, see, for example, Arthur Waldron, *The Great Wall of China: From History to Myth*, Cambridge University Press, New York, 1990/1992, and Michael Loewe, *Records of Han Administration*, Cambridge University Press, Cambridge, 1967.

5 On this, see the classic work of Owen Lattimore, *Inner Asian Frontiers of China*, 2nd edn, Capital Publishers, New York, 1951, pp. 477–83.

6 The travels of Xuanzang in the seventh century formed the basis of the celebrated Chinese novel *Journey to the West*, or *Monkey*, and the sutras he brought back with him were stored in the Great Goose Pagoda still to be seen in present-day Xi'an.

7 For this reason, at the beginning of the century, the Russians sought to hold Port Arthur, now part of Lüda, and the Russo-Japanese war was fought to determine its ownership.

8 The two major harbours of Shandong are Weihai on the north, the nineteenth century base of the Chinese Northern Fleet, later held by the British, and Qingdao on the south, occupied by the Germans and then by Japan.

9 The only serious attempts at invasion of Japan from an empire based on China were the two expeditions mounted by the Mongol Kubilai Khan in 1274 and 1281; the second was destroyed by a typhoon — the miraculous *kamikaze* of Japanese tradition. During the Ming dynasty, in reverse, Japanese pirates were a serious nuisance along the China coast, but they were no threat to the empire itself.

10 See, for example, Hok-lam Chan, *The Cambridge History of China: Volume 7; The Ming Dynasty Part 1*, Cambridge University Press, Cambridge, 1988, p. 302 ('The Chien-wen, Yung-lo, Hung-hsi, and Hsüan-te reigns, 1399–1435') and citations in his footnote 2.

11 It is now generally accepted that the pressure of cultivation is bringing deforestation, erosion and environmental degradation to every part of China, with implications as varied as silting of the Gulf of Zhili, decline of the water table in the North China Plain, long-term effects upon climate, and the extinction of the Giant Panda through the destruction of its western forest habitat. Further afield, moreover, traditional east Asian or Chinese medicine, supported by the prosperity of Japan, Taiwan, Singapore and other communities in southeast Asia, has already had devastating effect upon tigers in Asia and the rhinoceros population in Africa, and the effect can only be magnified as Chinese become wealthy enough to afford the costs of poaching such increasingly rare species.

12 Chinese claims to the South China Sea are extremely broad: they encompass the whole region and they are accompanied by rhetoric about integral national sovereignty. There is, however, no evidence that any state, including China, has ever controlled the scattered islands and reefs with constant authority, while occasional seasonal settlements by fishermen, or the passage of Zheng He's fleet (later repudiated by the Ming court), do not seem sufficient to establish a claim.

4 China in the Post-Cold War World

Samuel S. Kim

Introduction

What can we say about 'China as a great power' — and its global role — in the transition from a bipolar to a multipolar world? The question seems elementary enough yet the answer is far from obvious. In world politics, the perception and credibility of national 'power' matters — and changes — as much as the reality of it. Of course, there is no 'scientific' way of assessing national power. Embedded in an interactive and interdependent world are multiple power centres of a wide variety of material and non-material resources keyed to an increasing number of transnational problems. In a rapidly changing international environment, the very notion of 'great power' is subject to continuing redefinition and reassessment. The ending of the Cold War has shattered the illusion of a consensus on what constitutes a 'great power' or 'superpower' in 'post-international relations'.

Assessing Chinese capabilities — and intentions — at this critical juncture in world history is all the more complicated by the profound domestic social, economic and ecological transformation that China is experiencing even as the global system in which it is now embedded undergoes a structural and political metamorphosis. The rise-of-China question highlights several paradoxes. The habitual pronouncement for state equality and antihegemonism is belied by the belief, shared by Chinese of all political persuasions and tacitly acknowledged by most countries, that China, through the sheer size of its population and geography, its United Nations Security Council permanent seat, its nuclear weapons and the greatness of its civilisation, has a natural entitlement to great power status in the international community.

Part of the problem is that the West in general — and the United States in particular — has often defined the complex and changing Chinese realities in terms of its own self-images and interests. During the Cold War, assessments of China's national power or power potential have become legion, ranging from a 'sleeping dragon' to a 'superpower candidate' to an actual great power balancing the relationship between the two superpowers. Only a few years ago, many portended, in the wake of the Tiananmen tragedy, a declining if not collapsing China. And yet today it is common to hear, and increasingly faddish to say, that the rise of China as a superpower — with the fastest growing economy in the world — is as certain as anything can be in post-Cold War international relations.

To muddy the waters, paradoxically, Beijing touts that it now enjoys the best external security environment and the deepest peace ever since the founding of the People's Republic while at the same time beefing up military power projecting capabilities with all deliberate speed. The revealing paradox of the capitalist world economy is that Leninist China, with the fastest growing economy and the fastest growing military budget in the world — China's military spending increased by 13.8 per cent in 1992 even as global military spending fell steeply by about 15 per cent in the same year — is at the same time the fastest-growing emitter of greenhouse gases and the largest recipient of largesse from the World Bank. The great irony of all this is that the West began to sing the rise-of-China chorus at a time when China's leaders, bereft of their vaunted swing value in superpower rivalry in a post-Cold War world, were shifting from the pretence of being a global power to asserting China's status as the dominant military power in East Asia.

Defining the state of the post-Cold War world

It was not until April 1991 that the idea of 'world order', though still set in quotation marks, began to receive serious consideration. Apparently George Bush, through his invocation of 'a new world order', provoked Beijing's reactions to what was perceived to be an imminent danger of a unipolar/hegemonic world order. For the first time in PRC history, a flurry of programmatic essays on 'new world order' found their way into the mass media with official imprimatur. What emerge, if only in rudimentary form, are Chinese notions of world order. If world structure is an empirical and objective reality — presumably referring to the 'correlation of global forces' — world order is apparently a subjective and aspirational condition some Western states strive to achieve. Nevertheless, world order and world structure are said to be closely interrelated and interdependent. At the same time, global debate on the new world order is symptomatic of the emerging neo-Darwinian contest for an all-out struggle for power in which every major state actor jockeys for a favorable position during the process of tumultuous global change.

Embedded in the Chinese agonising reappraisal of the changing global situation is a concern for drawing distinctions between *world* order on the one hand, and *regional* or *international* orders on the other. Whereas a world order is basically a set of world regulations — hence a potential threat to state sovereignty — an international order is a more benign notion, embodying certain statist norms needed to facilitate transactions in the absence of a supranational Leviathan. Although, theoretically, new world order and new regional orders may develop in tandem, the former is dismissed as a wish list of abstract values, while the latter have become more feasible. In actuality, the major powers are said to have concentrated their efforts on the establishment of new regional orders.

Against this background, the primary mission of the Chinese debate on world order has been to legitimise the government's call for a new international order. Despite the twists and turns in Chinese foreign policy over the years, the Westphalian sovereignty-centred notion remains dominant in the Chinese image of world order. In the wake of the Tiananmen carnage, state sovereignty acquired special resonance in Beijing's multilateral diplomacy with its repeated calls for a 'new international political and economic order' based on the Five Principles of Peaceful Coexistence. The principle of state sovereignty and the principle of state equality — the two core principles of the Westphalian world order system — are declared to be the cornerstone for the existing international order as well as the chrysalis of a new international order. There is no alternative to the sovereignty-centred international order, we are told, given the structural reality that two social systems (capitalism and socialism) and three categories of countries (modern capitalist countries, socialist countries and nationalist countries) will coexist and compete over a fairly long period and that none of them can replace or eliminate the other. Indeed, the most basic characteristic of post-Tiananmen Chinese multilateral diplomacy is the supremacy of state sovereignty: *no state sovereignty, no world order*.

There is much irony in all of this so-called *new* China constantly invoking the *old* Westphalian principle of state sovereignty in the name of establishing a new international order. It seems equally paradoxical that China has had to rely on the Western principles of state sovereignty and state equality to define and project its own conception of world order. The concept of sovereignty — essentially Western in origin — entered relatively late in China's long and well-chronicled history. It took nothing less than a traumatic encounter with Western — and Japanese — imperialism in the nineteenth century to finally catalyse the disintegrating empire to latch on to state sovereignty with a vengeance. As in the Western realist image of world order, sovereignty in Chinese foreign policy thinking seems to serve as a theory of limits, prescribing the statist parameters of international order. Although Marxism was important in the shaping and legitimation of a PRC political identity, it provided no lasting guide to seeking China's proper place in the state-centric world. Lenin, in contrast, updated and rescued Marxism by fusing it with the concept of the nation-state. It is hardly surprising, then, that after the First World War and the Bolshevik Revolution, Lenin had much greater appeal in China than Marx, although the differences between the two were blurred in the Marxism-Leninism that eventually merged with Mao Zedong Thought in the official ideology of the People's Republic.

Indeed, in the course of its international relations, the People's Republic has succumbed to wild national identity mood swings, acting out a series of dramatically diverse roles on the international stage. Although recovered in 1949 with Mao's 'standing up' proclamation of the founding of the People's Republic, state sovereignty and control has remained the *leitmotif* of Chinese foreign policy thinking. Even during the heyday of the Sino-Soviet alliance in the 1950s, China was constantly testing the twin alliance dilemmas of abandonment and entrapment while at the same time rejecting Soviet proposals for joint military forces. During the post-Mao era, especially in the period 1979–89, the rhetoric of state sovereignty was attenuated as the central foreign policy challenge was redefined as one of keeping the outside world safe and congenial for China's born-again modernisation-cum-status drive. The logic of the post-Mao opening is simple enough: China would now have to engage in international co-operation for the enhancement of a so-called 'comprehensive national strength' (CNS or *zhonghe guoli*) — national security and economic prosperity — with little trade-off in sovereignty. This neorealist logic clothed in the rhetoric of global interdependence seemed anchored in confident nationalism that China can still extract maximum payoffs from the capitalist world economic system with minimum penalties for its state sovereignty.

Despite the Western origin, the traditional concept of state sovereignty is of special appeal to the Chinese communist state with a serious legitimation crisis. For this theory has had two rather distinct meanings — the two sides of a same dialectical scissor so to speak, recognising on the one hand a supreme authority within a state while at the same time rejecting any superior world authority in international (interstate) relations. In the post-Tiananmen Chinese case, the so-called People's Republic has seized state sovereignty as a sword with which to cut down people sovereignty at home and a shield with which to ward off external criticism of human rights abuses. Of course, what makes state sovereignty all the more compelling and problematic in the post-Cold War setting is the unresolved unification problem. The question of how state sovereignty would actually protect the rights of the people and bring power and plenty in this post-modern age of global communications and interdependence is seldom directly addressed in the Chinese definition of the world situation.

Obviously, Beijing wants to make sovereignty *de rigueur* for its foreign policy. The most noticeable consequence of the sovereignty-bound definition of the changing global situation in recent years has been the acceleration of the process of decoupling local and regional conflicts from global superpower rivalry. The new foreign policy line — as confirmed by Jiang Zemin's political report to the 14th Party Congress in 1992 — may be characterised as the CNS line. The Congress seemed to have signalled an official closure to the decade-long cost–benefit debate about the bipolarity versus multi-polarity question. Bipolarity is now pronounced to have ended as the international system is heading rapidly towards multipolarity. Multipolarity is cast in a new light as giving China more geo-economic leverage opportunities and more geopolitical space than could be realistically considered if the predominant definition of the world situation was bipolar.

In Beijing's view, then, a multipolarising world is seen as giving rise to new geopolitical alignments in the Asia-Pacific region and, concomitantly, intensified rivalry for the enhancement of comprehensive national strength. The broader point is that the CNS interpretation of the world situation comes much closer to a realist-nationalist rather than a Marxist interpretation of uneven development and international conflict formation. The central challenge of post-Cold War Chinese foreign policy is said to be threefold: 'We must especially take advantage of confrontations among Western nations, strengthen ourselves, and consolidate the neighboring region by giving priority to our maneuvers in Asia and the Pacific region'.[1]

Coping with the post-Cold War challenges

Of particular concern to China as a multinational state is that local and regional ethno-national conflicts, previously overshadowed and repressed by the global superpower contention, are breaking out in many parts of the world. Very few of the 82 armed conflicts in the four-year period 1989–92 were classic inter-state conflicts befitting the traditional definition of 'war'. The overwhelming majority of armed conflicts are 'internal conflicts' and 'state-formation conflicts'. Wars of national identity mobilisation have emerged as the primary species of regional conflict in the post-Cold War setting.[2]

A dramatic increase of United Nations peacekeeping — and peacemaking and state-making — operations in 1991–92 prompted Beijing to redefine its stand in a contingent manner. It is now argued that peacekeeping operations can only be established and conducted in compliance with the principle of non-interference in internal affairs as the United Nations Charter does not authorise involvement in the internal disputes of its member states.[3] In China's foreign policy thinking and behaviour, the Security Council is an important *arena* to demonstrate its status as a global power and as a Third World champion while at the same pursuing its maxi/mini Realpolitik, but not a world order *actor* in the promotion of collective security. In the post-Tiananmen period, the Security Council has become the surest and cheapest way to China's international forum, with shopping and showmanship used as a way of compensating for domestic legitimation deficits. This was manifest in all the hype surrounding Premier Li Peng's participation in the United Nations Security Council Summit in January 1992.

There is, deep down in Chinese world order thinking, little commitment to revitalising the United Nations Security Council as the principal instrument for preventing, abating or even managing regional conflicts. Of the

Permanent Five, China has jumped the gun by projecting the most sceptical posture toward Secretary-General Boutros Boutros-Ghali's *Agenda for
Peace*, proposing the revitalisation of the global collective security system
envisioned in the United Nations Charter itself.[4] Apparently, the Secretary-
General's report contained too many sovereignty-diluting features thus provoking Beijing's public opposition: 'UN reform should contribute to
maintaining the sovereignty of its member states. Sovereign states are the
subjects of international law and the foundation for the formation of the
United Nations. The maintenance of state sovereignty serves as the basis
for the establishment of a new international order.'[5] In actuality, it is not so
much China's defence of state sovereignty anywhere or anytime as fear of
a precedent being made to order for possible use against the multinational
Chinese state that seems to serve as the unstated code of conduct. The
Chinese press at home and representatives in the Security Council repeatedly issued warnings about the danger of shift from Chapter VI (non-
mandatory pacific settlement provisions) to Chapter VII (mandatory
enforcement measures) of the UN Charter.

The general silence and passivity on regional arms control and disarmament issues, in contrast to its activism in global arms control and disarmament (ACD) forums, bespeak Beijing's acute concern that the
establishment of a multilateral arms control regime would cut too close to
China's expansive regional security zone. A real if unstated code of conduct guiding China's consecutive and simultaneous participation in multiple security games on the global, regional, and bilateral chessboards is a
maxi/mini axiom — maximising narrowly construed security interests while
minimising normative costs by projecting China as part of the global solution. This is a two-eyed policy, giving moral and rhetorical support to global ACD negotiations — and free-riding off superpower arms control
processes — while at the same time taking selective unilateral disarmament
measures in a few 'safe' areas (e.g. the demobilisation of one million PLA
troops). China's stand is framed in terms of differentiated responsibilities
in the global ACD processes. Since the two superpowers account for 95–97
per cent of all nuclear warheads in the world, we are told, it is they who
must bear the primary responsibility by drastically reducing their nuclear
arsenals before other nuclear weapons states can join the disarmament
process. Not surprisingly, the Third World's longstanding demand to halt
all nuclear tests has fallen on China's deaf ears; China remained in recent
years the only nuclear-weapons state not to pledge or follow a moratorium
on nuclear testing. Since a comprehensive nuclear test ban and nuclear disarmament are linked, the United States and Russia 'have the obligation to
take the lead in halting all nuclear tests *and* carrying out drastic nuclear disarmament so as to create conditions for a comprehensive ban on nuclear
tests'.[6]

The Strategic Arms Reduction Treaty (START-I and START-II) that will
reduce each nuclear superpower's strategic arsenal by about three-quarters
(to fewer than 3500 warheads) seems to have no discernable impact on

China's ACD behaviour. While acknowledging and characterising these treaties as 'some initial progress', China insists that such progress is still limited and that the two nuclear superpowers still have a long way go in the process of nuclear disarmament. Pending the realisation of 'complete prohibition and thorough destruction of nuclear weapons', however, all nuclear-weapon states should undertake the following commitments:

- not to be the first to use nuclear weapons and conclude an international agreement on the no-first-use principle;
- not to use or threaten to use nuclear weapons against non-nuclear-weapon states and nuclear weapon-free zones and conclude an international agreement in this regard; and
- to support the proposals for the establishment of nuclear-weapon-free zones, and undertake the corresponding obligations.[7]

Thus China asks others to follow what it says, not what it actually does.

With the collapse of the strategic triangle, the temptation to use, by way of substitution, whatever other instrumentalities Beijing possessed became well-nigh irresistible. The Chinese leadership found that arms sales, especially in the nuclear and missile field, were another way of demonstrating its status as a great power, and that festering regional conflicts in the Third World, especially in the Middle East, could not be resolved without China's participation and tacit cooperation. The conventional view that Chinese arms sales patterns and directions follow the logic of market demand factor — and that economic power in post-Mao China grows out of cash sales on the arms barrelhead — is not so much wrong as it is incomplete. China's missile sales to Saudi Arabia earned not only hard currency but also a much-sought-after diplomatic switch from Taipei to Beijing (21 July 1990). Despite its long sustained refusal to recognise Israel until the Palestinian question was solved, Beijing maintained covert military ties with that country since 1980 and finally recognised and established official diplomatic relations in early 1992. Since Tiananmen, Israel has emerged as China's leading foreign conduit supplier of advanced technology, becoming in effect China's secret channel to United States technology. Remarkably, Beijing seems to have recovered rather quickly from the reality shock of the collapse of the Soviet Union, turning Russia into a wholesale arms bazaar for advanced weapons systems (e.g. China bought $1.8 billion of weaponry from Russia in 1992, including 24 advanced SU-27 fighters).

On the question of a post-Cold War collective security system in the Asia-Pacific region, the Chinese leadership has, at least until recently, expressed a preference for a unilateral approach in bilateral clothing. The dogged determination to define national identity in terms of state sovereignty, state status and state security stands in the way of responding positively to any proposal for a regional collective security system. Soviet President Mikhail Gorbachev's Pacific overtures in 1986–88 for a comprehensive security system for the entire Asia-Pacific region were countermanded and scaled back to the bilateral negotiating level in order to pressure the Soviets to meet

China's three security demands as the price for renormalising Sino-Soviet relations. Beijing quashed all other similar Australian, Canadian and Japanese proposals for a multilateral Asian-Pacific security conference — a sort of Conference on Security and Cooperation in Asia (CSCA).[8] Likewise, Beijing rejected any international conference, let alone the establishment of a multilateral regime, for handling territorial disputes. It maintained instead that disputes should be resolved by the countries directly involved on a bilateral basis. China opposes the 'internationalisation' (multilateralism) of disputes since the Paracel and Spratly islands have been Chinese territory over the centuries. This is not to say that Beijing would refuse to participate in any regional multilateral security dialogue — and Beijing is a participant in the ASEAN Regional Forum (ARF) discussions on regional security — but participation is not the same as commitment to the idea of collective security.

A series of assertive unilateral moves in recent years gave rise to the 'China threat theory' (*zhongguo weixie lun*). Since 1988 Beijing has pursued a strategy of attacking the weakest link by occupying ten islets and atolls in the disputed Spratlys, mostly at the expense of Vietnam, while ignoring territories claimed or occupied by Taiwan, the Philippines (at least until February 1995), Malaysia and Brunei. As if such a strategy of establishing *de facto* control of the South China Sea were insufficient, the National People's Congress, on 25 February 1992, adopted 'The Law of the People's Republic of China on its Territorial Waters and Contiguous Areas', 'in order to enable the People's Republic of China to exercise its sovereignty over its territorial waters and its rights to exercise control over their adjacent areas, and to safeguard state security as well as its maritime rights and interests' (Article 1). It was the first time China had claimed direct sovereignty through such unilateral legislative sleight of hand.[9]

In short, China's strategic behaviour seems anchored in and driven by the conflation of state sovereignty, state security, state status and 'lateral pressure'. The dogged determination to define and act upon its national identity in such a nationalistic fashion stands in the way of responding positively to the challenge of establishing a collective security system for the Asia-Pacific region.

Gradually, post-Mao China seemed to have shifted from *dependencia* theory to neorealist theory of global interdependence — that all countries, North and South, East and West, are becoming increasingly interdependent and interpenetrable in the context of one world market. The two *bêtes noires* of the Maoist era — global interdependence and the division of labour and specialisation — were embraced as integral parts of the new open policy. In line with its growing enmeshment with the capitalist world economy, post-Mao China abandoned its model projection in Third World policy and drastically downgraded its system-transforming role in the global political economy. One might be tempted to believe that Tiananmen dealt the concept of global economic interdependence a lethal theoretical blow. But it has become apparent that the return of Stalinist fundamentalism, as far as

Chinese foreign economic policy is concerned, proved to be more domestic smoke than external fire.

In practice, the post-Mao leadership has followed neither a classical Marxist, nor a neo-Marxist *dependencia* theory, nor has it followed a Western liberal global interdependence model. Rather, its development strategy reflects a neomercantilist model. The concept of global interdependence is narrowly construed and confined to the global political economy. Post-Mao China turned the *dependencia* view of interdependence on its head — *dependencia* theory reversed, as it were — viewing it as a one-way street, with the West now supposed to provide the benefits of China-specific entitlement without imposing any political and ecological conditions. China's neomercantilism — or what has come to be known as 'market Leninism' or 'Leninist capitalism' — is constructed around state interventionism to maximise a trade surplus, bilateral and multilateral aid, technology transfers and foreign investment.

The implications of China's Leninist-capitalist road are rather unsettling. Advertised or not, Maoist China commanded appeal as Third World champion of the NIEO, which led many *dependencia* theorists to commit the fallacy of premature optimism embracing Beijing as the centre of anti-centre self-reliant development. Still, Mao's China stood out as the only Third World country that gave but never received any bilateral and multilateral aid. This alone vested Beijing with a measure of moral authority in global developmental politics. In making a dramatic U-turn from aid giving to aid seeking in 1978, China began to enmesh its political economy in the capitalist world system. In the process, China somehow managed to establish an all-time global record in doubling per capita output in the shortest time period (1977–87).[10] If China continues to thrive in the global marketplace, and if South Korea's economy continues to decline in tandem with its remarkable democratisation process, the Chinese Leninist capitalist model will present a challenge to the development theorists and policy makers that they may find most troublesome.

China has been exceptionally successful in securing World Bank financial assistance to fuel its modernisation/status drive without too many strings. For the period 1981–93, the World Bank has approved loans and credits to China valued at $16.5 billion. Tiananmen had only short-term consequences (a modest interval of less than eighteen months), but no significant long-term repercussions, as the World Bank has allowed China to reassert its claim to even more than its previous share of the total multilateral pie for the Third World. For the most recent fiscal year, 1993, China received from the World Bank loans worth US$3.2 billion or 13.4 per cent of total multilateral aid, once again becoming top recipient. In striking contrast, China's assessment for the United Nations budget — which applies to all the organs and specialised agencies of the United Nations system — is only 0.77 per cent, not even the largest Third World contributor, as Brazil (1.59 per cent), Saudi Arabia (0.96 per cent) and Mexico (0.88 per cent) have all surpassed China's contribution.

Foreign trade made a great leap forward and outward in the post-Mao era, playing a crucial role in the modernisation/status drive. It has been growing at an average annual rate of 12.9 per cent — exports at an average rate of 15.1 per cent in 1979–92. The share of foreign trade as a percentage of GNP rose from less than 10 per cent in 1978 to 27.3 per cent in 1988. Tiananmen had only a slight and temporary faltering effect, with the foreign trade share of GNP dropping to 26.3 per cent, then rapidly rising to 31.4 per cent in 1990, 36.7 per cent in 1991, and 38.5 per cent in 1992. The post-Tiananmen years, paradoxically enough, have witnessed an unprecedented rise in foreign trade, foreign direct investment, foreign exchange reserves and economic growth rate.

In foreign direct investment (FDI), too, China stands out as an exceptional Third World country. 1992 was declared a vintage year with $11.3 billion (implemented) representing 49 per cent of all FDIs invested in China in 1979–91 — and almost the same amount as was lured by the United States, the world's biggest economy, only to be surpassed by a staggering $20 billion-worth actually invested ($100 billion contracted) in 1993. No Third World country comes anywhere near such figures and no Third World country can ever expect to reach this magnitude of FDI inflow since about 80 per cent is coming from sovereignty-free overseas Chinese in Hong Kong, Taiwan and Macau.

Against the backdrop of such an economic boom, a new way of measuring the world's economies by the so-called purchasing-power parities (PPP) of each state's own currency rather than by its dollar exchange value has catapulted China from the ranks of Third World states to those of economic powerhouses. Under PPP calculations introduced by the International Monetary Fund (IMF) in May 1993, China's economy at $1.7 trillion for 1992 (instead of about $400 billion) comes out four times bigger than most previous estimates, making it the world's third largest, after the United States and Japan.[11] By the year 2002, according to World Bank forecasts, the gross domestic product of 'Greater China' (consisting of mainland China, Hong Kong and Taiwan) is projected to rise to $9.8 trillion, surpassing the United States ($9.7 trillion) as the world's largest economy.

One would have expected a national 'rise-of-China' celebration, yet all top leaders — Jiang Zemin, Qiao Shi, Zhu Rongji and Qian Qichen — have lost no time in speaking against the IMF conclusion.[12] The multilateral diplomacy of China-specific exemption and China-specific entitlement came to the fore with particular clarity. If the PPP-based estimation of Chinese per capita GNP ($1600 as against $370) is accepted, Beijing would immediately be disqualified from IDA soft loans for poor developing countries with the $765 per capita income threshold. Like a true believer suddenly caught exposed in a red-light district, the official reaction highlighted the true colour of China's posturing as Third World champion in global development politics. Post-Mao China has more or less disqualified itself as a Third World country by what it *is* and what it *does*. To be 'third world' is to acknowledge the reality of 'global apartheid' symbolised and structured by extreme unevenness, hierarchy and deprivation in the capitalist world economic system and to promote global system transformation for a just and equitable world economic order.

With unprecedented clarity, Tiananmen dramatised to the global audience — and in global prime time — the widening chasm between people sovereignty and state sovereignty. The most basic, recurring theme in Chinese human rights thinking is that communities come before individuals, duties and obligations before rights and privileges; hence, human rights inhere not so much in individuals as in collectivities. Even the much-touted 'right to development', one of the central themes in post-Mao China, inheres in the state, not in the individual. This theme of collective human rights-cum-state rights — and the theory of cultural and economic relativism — was somewhat tempered in the 1980s as China began to participate in UN human rights politics only to come back with greater vigour in post-Tiananmen foreign relations. The proposition that individuals have finally become subjects of international law in the post-Holocaust and post-Nuremberg era is ruled out of court on all counts in the Chinese international law literature and policy pronouncements. To take human rights as the basis of international relations is to reject the essence of the international order. Inconsistent with the claim that the international community can only intervene in the situations of 'large-scale human rights violations', the right to *national* self-determination has been nullified by the first principle of *state* sovereignty. If a nation within a state demands independence or self-government, this is also a matter of domestic jurisdiction of that state and the principle of national self-determination is not applicable in such a case.[13]

In the normative domain of global human rights politics, China has unabashedly positioned itself as the Third World's most vociferous human rights 'champion'. Paradoxically, North–South tensions have sharply increased as East–West conflicts over human rights have suddenly waned with the end of the Cold War. Tiananmen made it possible, even if temporarily, for the United Nations to censure China for its human rights abuses at home. Since 1990, China has managed to piggyback on the Third World's power of numbers to escape international censure. Vote on a draft resolution to 'take no action' on the human rights situation in China has not changed much between 1990 (17 for, 15 against and 11 abstentions) and 1993 (21, 17 and 12 respectively). The worst has thus been avoided (though only just), due to a combination of several factors — the Iraqi invasion of Kuwait that suddenly pre-empted centre stage; China's putative support for — or at least refusal to veto — Security Council Resolution 678 in the Gulf crisis, pro forma motion of Western powers; and abstention by a dozen or so democratic Third World states in the United Nations Human Rights Commission.

Against this backdrop, China has pursued a 'divide and conquer' strategy in its global human rights diplomacy with mixed results. The first-ever 'White Paper' on human rights released in late 1991 'accepted' international human rights principles by redefining them in terms of state sovereignty, the right to development, and cultural, economic and social relativism.

The bottom line of China's 'right to development as an inalienable human right' seems simple enough: 'If one really intends to promote and protect human rights ... then the first thing for him to do is to help remove obstacles to the development of developing countries, lessen their external debt burden, provide them with unconditional assistance'.[14] It is precisely this proposition of unconditional aid that is sweet music to the Third World, even if China has always received special treatment in getting the lion's share of bilateral and multilateral aid with virtually no strings attached.

The logic of China's human rights diplomacy is to slice up the concept of universality little by little, region to region, to the point where there is little left of the United Nations human rights monitoring and implementation regime. China has led the way on behalf of some of the most oppressive Third World countries to keep the United Nations human rights regime small, fragmented (regionalised), ineffective and abstract. The efforts to alter the structure and terms of reference of a World Conference on Human Rights (WCHR '93), held in Vienna in June 1993 to conform with its own minimalist view, received little support. However, China pressed successfully for the General Assembly to include the relationship between development and human rights as one of the priority topics at the WCHR '93 as well as to hold regional preparatory conferences.

As a result, Asia's first regional human rights conference was held in Bangkok (29 March–2 April 1993) and attended by governmental delegates from 40 countries stretching from the Middle East to the South Pacific. The 30-point Bangkok Declaration that emerged from the conference is full of contradictions and ambiguities papering over some serious intraregional cleavages among several groups of countries. That the chief delegates from China, Burma and Iran, three notorious human rights offenders, made up the drafting committee speaks volumes about China's 'leadership' role in this first-ever Asian human rights conference. The Declaration, sharply criticised by nearly 250 representatives of 110 Asian non-governmental organisations (NGOs) for the governments' transparent attempt to avoid accountability for their failures to protect human rights, urged that states be allowed to set up their own human rights mechanisms and discouraged Western countries from making progress on human rights a conditionality for extending development aid.

At WCHR '93, China uncharacteristically assumed an aggressive active role in leading a pack of worst Third World offenders to attack the core principle of *universal* human rights so as to dilute a final declaration with multiple standards and meanings. The Chinese divide-and-conquer strategy framed in cultural and developmental relativism theory — that human rights should be applied differently keyed to different national, cultural and developmental stages and conditions — failed in the end as the final Declaration affirms the universality of human rights — the international community 'must treat human rights globally in a fair and equal manner, on the same footing and with the same emphasis'. Although the Chinese push for multiple human rights standards was actively supported by several Asian states (Malaysia, Indonesia, Pakistan and Singapore), Japan and South Korea (as a newly democratising country) made it clear (much to their credit) that the Chinese line is not the Asian perspective by whole-heartedly embracing the concept of universal human rights.

The Chinese government's continuing political oppression of nearly a quarter of humanity within its porous borders — some 3000–10 000 people have been executed every year since 1983 — has already become a clear and continuing global human rights challenge and certainly one of the most vexing problems taxing Beijing's precious global time and diplomatic resources. It is true that there were not many teeth in the international sanctions imposed in the wake of the Tiananmen massacre. Yet the greatest damage of all is not so much from the content or duration of the sanctions themselves as from the collapse of international reputation and credibility of the make-believe moral regime in global idealpolitik that the sanctions reflected and effected. That China has managed to piggyback on the Third World's power of numbers to wriggle off the hit list of the United Nations Human Rights Commission since 1990 has a lot to do with the new Sino-Third World partnership of human rights misery against the Western linkage politics in international institutions — linking multilateral aid to democratisation and environmental protection.

The greening of world politics in recent years and the universal awareness of China's status as an environmental giant afforded Chinese leaders another opportunity to apply their maxi/mini code of conduct in foreign policy. A close fit between Chinese and Third World interests on eco-development — and the shared fear about environmental conditionalities in aid and trade — allowed Beijing to reassert its Third World leadership role in this quintessentially functional domain. China's green diplomacy was aimed at maximising foreign aid and technology transfers and minimising the international normative and material costs of the Tiananmen crackdown.

The maxi/mini strategy has led Beijing to adopt a 'cash first, co-operate later' posture in its global environmental diplomacy. Yet its 'principled stand' on the global campaign to protect the ozone layer was framed in quid pro quo terms: China refused to sign the 1987 Montreal Protocol without a promise of big cash and greater 'flexibility' on the use and production of chlorofluorocarbons. In June 1991, Beijing finally signed the amended Montreal Protocol. Apparently, a series of amendments adopted by the June 1990 London Conference satisfied the maxi/mini principle of differentiated responsibilities and rights. At the Chantilley Conference in February 1991, Chinese representatives openly opposed any international action to set emission ceilings with the claim that such ceilings would violate the principle of state sovereignty. Yet it was announced in late April 1993 that the United Nations Development Program (UNDP) would assist China in developing a $2.1 billion program to phase out the use of ozone-depleting substances by the year 2010, drawing upon the multilateral fund set up under the Montreal Protocol.

In preparation for a more serious challenge ahead at the first-ever Earth Summit — the United Nations Conference on Environment and Development or UNCED — in mid-1992, the Chinese government sponsored a two-day Ministerial Conference of Developing Countries on Environment and Development in Beijing in June 1991. Although only 41 developing countries participated, China seems to have realised, with the adoption of the Beijing Declaration, its main objective of projecting its own party line as the united principled stand of the Third World. China's commitment to the global effort for environmental protection and sustainable development is keyed to various preconditions stated as 'principles':

- the principle of differentiated responsibilities;
- the principle of differentiated obligations;
- the principle of state sovereignty and equality;
- the principle of untied aid;
- the principle of differentiated capabilities; and
- the principle of preferential treatment.[15]

Once again, in 1992, Premier Li Peng headed a huge 77-member delegation in a bid for Third World leadership at the Earth Summit in June, presenting over a million characters' worth of position papers and documentation for negotiation in the name of 'the Group of 77 plus China' — a '77 plus-one' doctrine on eco-development.

In this quintessentially functional domain, China has framed its stand in maxi/mini terms: what is good for China's own (eco)development is also good for the global environment. And yet, the gaps between environmental policy pronouncements and environmental policy performance continue to widen unchecked. So much of China's eco-politics is more show than substance. For instance, Beijingers were banned from burning coal in order to reduce pollution during a visit by the International Olympic Commission in early 1993. Today China is the world's fastest-growing polluter and the third-largest contributor of greenhouse gases, only behind the United States and the former Soviet Union. Although environmental protection is a heavily legislated issue area, its enforcement is devolved to local environmental protection bureaus which tend to protect the extensive business interests of the local government organs that supervise and fund them.

There can be little chance of stabilising world demographic pressure unless the Chinese improve their family planning programs and services. Although the success of Chinese family planning efforts is widely recognised, their effectiveness has been greatly exaggerated. The much touted one-child policy is a 1.6 child policy even if existing provincial regulations with so many exceptions on family size were fully implemented. In actuality, Chinese women today have an average of about 2.5 children. The long Deng decade of some fourteen years witnessed a demographic explosion of nearly 200 million additional people — the equivalent of ten Taiwans — and China is projected to add another 160 million people during the 1990s — the equivalent of the current population of Brazil.

The implications of these enormous numbers and of the accompanying social, economic, political and even international pressures are staggering in the context of China's accelerated industrialisation and shrinking ecological carrying capacity. Without a real economic growth rate of 8–9 per cent a year, there is no hope of absorbing an expected additional 180 million people into the labour market in the remainder of the 1990s. The projections of major indicators of environmental change in China suggest that there is no realistic hope for a reversal of China's environmental degradation during the coming two decades (1990–2010): a 25 per cent decline in per capita availability of arable land; a 30 per cent decrease in forest reserves; a 40 per cent higher demand for water; and a 50 per cent higher need for commercial energy; such increases in pollution rates as a nearly triple release of waste water and a 50 per cent rise in SO_2 emissions. Indeed, China can be said to have already crossed critical thresholds of environmental sustainability, presaging new local, regional and even international conflicts of a seriousness unprecedented in recent history.[16]

Conclusion

China, according to Lucian Pye, is 'a civilization pretending to be a state'.[17] The most paradoxical conclusion of the present chapter is the Pye image reversed — China is a weak state pretending to be a strong state. Post-Tiananmen China is a repressive state propped up by the four state institutions of violence, power and coercive control — the People's Armed Police, the Ministry of Public Security, the Ministry of State Security and the People's Liberation Army. The principal defining feature of a weak state is the lack of a unifying and legitimating value system and the correspondingly high level of internal threats to regime security. The Tiananmen massacre and the collapse of global communism have joined and conflated China's legitimation and identity crises in a dramaturgical way. The post-Cold War global situation is defined and acted upon in terms of how it affects the state's internal security. As a result, post-Tiananmen foreign policy has been highly conflicted with the danger of being overwhelmed by pressures to reconcile the irreconcilable.

The problem of the strong state thesis embedded in the rise-of-China global chorus today is that it does not sufficiently take into account deepening legitimation and ecological crises. The post-Tiananmen government is paralysed by a mega-crisis — multiple and interlocking crises of authority, identity, motivation and ideology. 'Market-Leninism' is said to be the answer to the legitimation crisis — the only way to protect the inviolability of one-party communist rule by improving the people's livelihood. Yet post-Mao corruption and clientelism from cities to the countryside are not only much worse today than they ever were under the Nationalists. Such phenomena are an intrinsic part of the economy and the necessary grease to keep the Leninist capitalist system running, giving rise to the perceptions of relative deprivation, distributive injustice and socialist/capitalist alienation.

The rise-of-China chorus seems like another phase of the long cycles in America's perennial overestimation of Chinese 'power', only a half-truth that tends to obscure rather than clarify the underlying structures of the Chinese state. The PPP-based confirmation of China's new 'first world' economic status skates over the rise of a two-tier economy that is rapidly widening the gap between rich coastal China and poor interior China. With income disparities and class differences between the two Chinas, one highly visible and the other hidden, rising rapidly — per capita income in the former is already sixteen times that of the latter — many Chinese refer to the latter (four-fifths of the country) as 'China's third world'.

Additionally, China's seeming economic boom, resting on decades of anti-ecological policies and practices, has proceeded apace as if there were no limits to environmental deficit financing. At stake is nothing less than the ecological underpinning of Chinese society. Already some 15 per cent of China's GNP is being lost due to environmental degradation and damage. The National Environmental Protection Agency has an annual budget of 10 million yuan, equivalent to 1 yuan for about every 8600 that are lost annually due to environmental damage. A study by World Bank scientists in 1992 warned that 'the increasing pressure on this limited resource base to feed, house and meet the energy needs' of the Chinese was rapidly destroying 'whole ecosystems' and threatening to put the brakes on China's current economic boom. Even under the best of circumstances, the eco-developmental challenge is more often met in promise than in performance as 'what has posterity ever done for me?' is the unstated norm of eco-politics everywhere, including democratic societies. For the post-Tiananmen regime with a serious legitimation crisis and preoccupied with the question of its political survival, these social and eco-developmental challenges are daunting, to say the least.

There is irony that the post-Tiananmen outburst of state sovereignty has occurred even as the gap between claims and realities of Chinese state capacity has continued to widen unabated. State sovereignty and control are substantially eroded due to the pressures both of unprecedentedly strong resistance from the local forces and of unprecedentedly strong penetration from the transnational forces. One of the most significant and paradoxical consequences of post-Mao reform has been the substantial degrading of the level of coherence of the state itself. The trend toward a more fragmented state system and increasing autonomy at the local levels of the state has resulted in serious erosion of China's state capacity. With the growing globalisation of the Chinese political economy, the devolution of power at home, and the fragmentation of authority and decision-making structures at the apex during the post-Mao era, the centre has been forced to make a series of decentralising compromises enabling the party-state's central planners to maintain the appearance that they were still controlling the economic reforms and opening to the outside world. By the end of 1993, central planning accounts for about 6 per cent, down from 10 per cent in 1992 and from 30 per cent just four years ago. Ironically, the centre relaxed its control to cause such an unprecedented economic growth only to lose, by instalments, its sovereign power over the economy. As economic empowerment slips out of the centre's hands, so too does political control.

At the same time, contemporary global information has broken down the exclusive control over information that the centre once enjoyed. The announcement of State Council Proclamation No. 129 in October 1993, banning the purchase or possession of satellite dishes by ordinary Chinese, has merely underscored the extent to which the state has lost control over information. There are today in China some fifteen million subscribers to multi-channel systems wired to some 500 000 satellite dishes ('heavenly threads') that import English-language programs. This revolution reflects the globalisation of increasingly intertwined political, economic, social and normative structures and values and as well fosters the rapid mobilisation of people's needs, demands, frustration and intolerance. In a sense, China has lost its sovereign control over global human rights politics. With increasing PRC participation in global human rights politics, the shrinkage of social and geographical distances, the emergence of global human rights standards and norms, and the proliferation of human rights NGOs providing a steady flow of information on human rights violations, it is becoming increasingly difficult for China to maintain a policy of 'do as I say, not as I do'.

This weak, insecure and fragmented China is more unpredictable and hence more dangerous than a strong, confident and cohesive China and as such one of the major factors fuelling the uncertainty-driven arms racing in Asia, posing a major challenge to the establishment of a more peaceful and humane regional and global order in the years to come. The search for external enemies to unite an insecure state is favourite sport for desperate despotic rulers losing their grip on power. A weak state may well perceive and/or manufacture external threats to state interests and might then employ its military power to protect those interests. It now seems virtually certain that a substantial portion of China's economic resources will be used for the qualitative improvement of Chinese military power, especially blue-water naval, air and nuclear power, as a way of enhancing China's comprehensive national strength. As well, Chinese leaders will continue to cultivate the perception and credibility of assertive negative power (spoil value) that an engaged and strong China with special exemption and special entitlement is an irreducible prerequisite to any legitimate and viable world order. It seems safe to project that the immediate future will be more or less like the immediate past as the Kennedyesque premise persists in the conduct of foreign relations — that is, ask not what China can do for a more peaceful, equitable and democratic world order; ask rather what the global community can do to make China a rich, powerful, and reunified country.

Notes

1 See Tokyo KYODO in English, in Foreign Broadcast Information Service, *Daily Report: China* [hereafter cited as FBIS-*China*], 27 February 1992, pp. 24–25.

2 Peter Wallensteen and Karin Axell, 'Armed Conflict at the End of the Cold War, 1989–92', *Journal of Peace Research*, vol. 30, no. 3, August 1993, pp. 331–46.

3 Hu Yumin, 'UN's Role in a New World Order', *Beijing Review* [hereafter cited as *BR*], vol. 34, no. 23, 10–16 June 1991, pp. 12–14.

4 See An *Agenda for Peace: Preventive Diplomacy, Peacemaking and Peace-Keeping*, UN Doc. S/24111, 17 June 1992, and Paul Lewis, 'U.N. Set To Debate Peacemaking Role', *New York Times*, 6 September 1992, p. 7.

5 This point is made in Foreign Minister Qian Qichen's major speech at the 46th Session of the United Nations General Assembly, which comes close to being China's annual state of the world report. For an English text of the speech, see FBIS-*China*, 1 October 1992, pp. 4–8, at p. 7.

6 See 'Working Paper: China's Basic Position on the Process of Nuclear Disarmament in the Framework of International Peace and Security, with the Objective of the Elimination of Nuclear Weapons', UN Doc. A/CN.10/166, 24 April 1992, p. 3; emphasis added.

7 ibid., p. 4.

8 See Li Luye, 'The Current Situation in Northeast Asia: A Chinese View', *Journal of Northeast Asian Studies*, vol. 10, no. 1, Spring 1991, pp. 78–81.

9 A recent internal document states that these island groups could provide *lebensraum* (*shengcun kongjian* — literally 'survival space' — in Chinese) for the Chinese people: 'In terms of resources, the South China Sea holds reserves worth $1 trillion. Once Xinjiang has been developed, this will be the sole area for replacement of resources, and it is a main fallback position for *lebensraum* for the Chinese people in the coming century'. See *Far Eastern Economic Review*, 13 August 1992, pp. 14–20, at p. 16.

10 See World Bank, *World Development Report 1991: The Challenge of Development*, Oxford University Press, New York, 1991, Figure 1.1, p. 12.

11 International Monetary Fund, *World Economic Outlook*, IMF, Washington, DC, 1993, pp. 116–19. Calculations using World Bank data suggest higher figures: $2.2 trillion and $545 billion respectively. See *World Bank, World Development Report 1994: Infrastructure for Development*, Oxford University Press, New York, 1994, Tables 1, 30.

12 See *Renmin ribao* (People's Daily), 7 July 1993, p. 2 and *Guoji shangbao* (International Commercial Daily), 24 June 1993, p. 1.

13 Wei Min, et al. (eds), *Guojifa gailun* [Introduction to International Law], Guangmin ribao chubanshe, Beijing, 1986, p. 247.

14 'The Right to Development: An Inalienable Human Right', *BR*, vol. 35, no. 51, 21–27 December 1992, p. 13.

15 For the full text of the Beijing Declaration embodying these principles and preconditions, see *BR*, vol. 34, no. 27, 8–14 July 1991, pp. 10–14.

16 He Bochuan, *China on the Edge: The Crisis of Ecology and Development*, China Books and Periodicals, San Francisco, 1991; Vaclav Smil, *China's Environmental Crisis: An Inquiry into the Limits of National Development*, M.E. Sharpe, Armonk, NY, 1993; Vaclav Smil, 'Environmental Change as a Source of Conflict and Economic Losses in China', and Jack A. Goldstone, 'Imminent Political Conflict Arising from China's Environ-

mental Crises', in *Occasional Paper Series of the Project on Environmental Change and Acute Conflict*, No. 2, International Security Studies Program, American Academy of Arts and Sciences, Cambridge, Mass., December 1992; and Shanti R. Conly and Sharon L. Camp, *China's Family Planning Program: Challenging the Myths*, Country Study Series no. 1, Population Crisis Committee, Washington, DC, 1992.

17 Lucian Pye, 'China: Erratic State, Frustrated Society', *Foreign Affairs*, vol. 69, no. 4, Fall 1990, p. 58.

5 China and the United States: Neither Friends nor Enemies

Gary Klintworth and Murray McLean

Introduction

Strategically, the United States–China relationship has been one of the most important of all great power relationships in the Asia-Pacific region since the Second World War. It has contributed to more confrontation, threats of war and military posturing than the relationship between any other two Pacific powers. But it has also included periods of great power accord and co-operation in conflict resolution. Over time, the relationship could become part of a system of co-operative security between the great powers in the Asia-Pacific region. As President Clinton told Chinese President Jiang Zemin at the Asia-Pacific Economic Co-operation (APEC) meeting in Seattle in November 1993, when the United States and China worked together, they were a 'powerful force for security and economic progress'.[1]

Yet, of all the relationships between states that comprise the Asia-Pacific community, it is the relationship between China and the United States that generates most apprehension and uncertainty about the future stability of the Asia-Pacific region. The United States, the richest economy in the world, is currently the world's number one military power (although, in relative terms at least, it may be in a period of slow decline).[2]

Realist theory posits that unipolarity inevitably stimulates the rise of new powers seeking to challenge the dominance of the state that is number one.[3] Samuel Huntington argues that the United States must, therefore, strive to hold on to its power and primacy or risk losing its ability to protect its interests, promote its values and defeat its enemies.[4] Perhaps intuitively mindful of this imperative, the United States Defense Department argued that America ought to prevent other states from aspiring to a larger regional or global role that challenged United States leadership and its values or overturned the established world order.[5]

Meanwhile, China is often seen as the world's next great power: it has over a fifth of the global population, is centrally located in East Asia and is the fastest growing major economy in the world. It is proud, sometimes xenophobic, and is conscious of its history as the Middle Kingdom that was once number one. It is also the world's third-ranked nuclear power. China's modernisation trajectory — if sustainable — means that it could overtake the United States in terms of GNP at some time in the first half of the next century. Some believe that, as a rising power, China, like Bismarck's Germany and Tojo's Japan, will be ambitious.[6] For many analysts with a pessimistic nostalgia for the black and white simplicities of the Cold War, China is perceived to be a dissatisfied state with the resolve and the potential to challenge United States interests and change the status quo.[7] Articles portraying China in this light, as a new, ambitious, non-democratic, chauvinistic state threatening stability in East Asia and challenging United States core values have found a receptive audience in United States academic journals.[8]

Some realists argue, therefore, that in the long term, the outlook for Sino-United States relations is one of growing rivalry with instability and disequilibrium its most likely regional and global consequence.[9] For such analysts it follows that the United States has a long-term strategic interest in seeking to postpone the day of reckoning by containing China as best it can — for example, by encouraging China's neighbours to do more to defend themselves, safeguarding Taiwan's *de facto* independence and preserving Hong Kong's autonomy. Further, such analysts would argue that, at the very least, the United States should aim, and is aiming, to promote an 'open society and democratic values' in China on the rationale that, as democracies do not attack each other, a democratic China will not threaten United States security.[10]

Assumptions

The prognosis of Sino-United States relations as prospectively a clash of the giants is based on several assumptions, the validity of which is open to some question. They include the following:

- If China became a superpower, it would not only want to challenge the United States for global supremacy, but it would also not share United States interests in global stability, in preservation of the United Nations system or find common cause with the United States — for example, to contain a rising Japan or Russia in ten to fifteen years' time.[11]
- China can become a superpower, and can keep up its present rates of rapid economic growth and remain intact despite profound demographic,

environmental and resource constraints and its fragile authoritarian state that is no more capable of harnessing the productive capacity of a huge sprawling society than its predecessors.[12]

- China's reform of its economic, financial and legal infrastructure may not follow, as Ramon Myers suggests it might, the Taiwanese or South Korean model of soft authoritarianism and, eventually, a democratising society.[13] Some would indeed argue that communism in China is already long dead and that, increasingly, what we see in China is capitalism with Chinese characteristics.[14]
- The fact that China that can both feed, and restrict the rate of population increase of, 1.2 billion people, and provide expanding export opportunities for the United States and other members of the Asia-Pacific community is a less attractive possibility for the United States or China's neighbours than an impoverished China beset by warlordism and unable to control mass emigration.

Without going into detail on all these assumptions, let us just look at one or two. China will take at least five or more decades before it is in a position to be compared with the United States. China is still a developing country, whatever the measure, and in per capita terms, it is still a low-income country like Kenya, Burma, Pakistan, Gambia and Rwanda. In 1994, it was ranked 143rd in per capita terms in the world according to calculations by the United Nations Development Program.[15] Assuming that China can quadruple GNP by the year 2050, it will be at the same point approximately that the United States was at in 1990 (US$5.5 trillion).[16] Richard Betts suggests that if China was able to achieve a per capita income that was just a quarter that of the United States, it would have a total GNP greater than the United States.[17] That is, if China's GNP per capita was US$5000–6000, then with a population of over one billion, it would have a GNP of more than US$6 trillion compared with United States GNP in 1990 of just over US$5 trillion.[18] For that to happen, however, would require a tenfold increase in China's GNP per capita. Even assuming that China presently has a per capita income of about US$1200, or three times the official figure (using International Monetary Fund calculations based on purchasing power parity), there would need to be an enormous burst of sustained economic growth for China to reach a per capita income of US$6000 per head by the year 2050. By then, of course, the United States, with a present per capita income of over US$20 000, would also have advanced.

China, however, may never catch up to the United States, even assuming that it remains intact as one China. It faces enormous problems from a growing but aging population, declining agricultural resources, a shortage of fuel and water, desertification, the rapid expansion of environmental pollution, the degradation of the ecosystem and periodic natural disasters such as floods, earthquakes and droughts.[19] China's forest cover, to take one example, has dropped 30 per cent since 1949 and is now less than 12 per cent compared with 33 per cent in the United States.[20] Since 1949, the area of soil erosion has increased by 32 per cent and the annual loss of surface soil is more than five billion tonnes, compared with 1.6 billion tonnes in the United States.[21]

On present trends, China will have a population approaching 1.5 billion by the year 2020.[22] By then, China will need an estimated total of 900 million tonnes of grain to feed itself, yet under optimal conditions it will be able to provide only 615 million tonnes from within China.[23] This leaves a grain deficit of about 285 million tonnes, which is more than all the grain currently produced in the United States, Europe, Australia, Canada and Japan.[24] At the same time, China, which generates 70 per cent of Asia's sulphur dioxides, will come under enormous pressure from the United States and the rest of the world to curb its emission of greenhouse gases.[25] The implication is that China will need the help of countries like the United States if it is to feed itself and preserve the regional and global environment.

Table 5.1   China and the United States: A comparison

	China	USA
Nuclear tests	40	950
Arms sales 1992 US$m	100	13600
Defence expenditure 1993 (1990 constant US$bn)*	8.8	256.5
Defence expenditure as a percentage of GDP (1993)	1.4	4.5
Armed forces (million)	3.0	1.9
Troops overseas	nil	200000
Principal surface combatants	54	188
Carriers	nil	12
Submarines	46	110
SSBNs	1	25
ICBMs	8	1000
Combat aircraft	4970	3485
Population (million)	1200	252
Land area 000 sq km	9597	9373
GDP** US$bn	420	5674
GDP growth 1980–90 constant 1987 (%)	9.81	3.35
GDP/per capita 1990 constant 1987 US$	328	19316

Notes

*   Note that some estimates, using purchasing power parity, put China's defence expenditure at US$51.6 bn.

**   The IMF's *World Economic Outlook*, May 1993, suggests China's GDP is closer to $1260 billion, using purchasing power parities.

Sources: *World Bank Tables*, International Economic Data Bank, Australian National University, Canberra, for Growth in GNP per Capita; *World Military Expenditure and Arms Transfers 1991–92*, United States Arms Control and Disarmament Agency, Washington, 1994; R.F. Grimmett, *Trends in Government Arms Transfers to the Third World by Major Supplier 1984–92*, Library of Congress, Washington, 1993; International Institute of Strategic Studies, *The Military Balance*, IISS, London, for all other data.

Any expectation of China being in a position to challenge the United States in strategic terms therefore needs to be weighed against its palpable lack of economic development relative to that of the United States. One could argue, indeed, that there is no proper comparison between China and the United States (see Table 5.1). China is physically large, but is relatively poorly endowed. It has over 100 million very poor people whose living conditions and health and education status are described by the World Bank as deplorable.[26] By the year 2000 it will have an estimated 200 million unemployed peasants and 68 million unemployed in the cities, according to a Chinese Ministry of Labour report.[27]

Militarily, China is simply no match for the United States. It lags 20–30 years behind the United States technologically in areas such as electronics, aircraft engine design, missile propulsion, metallurgy, communications, space technology, fire control and automated systems, lasers and infra-red technology. It has a serious shortage of scientific, technical and managerial personnel and its defence industries have 'numerous weaknesses'.[28] It lacks the command, control and communications systems. It has nothing to compare with or protect itself from America's surveillance, targeting and fire control systems. Its best ships are of a technology standard left behind by developed countries in the early 1970s while its aircraft, with the exception of a handful of Russian fighter aircraft, are derived from aircraft that first flew in the 1950s and 1960s. China has been unable to design and build an operational fighter aircraft of its own and it is still trying to build an airframe around Rolls Royce Spey jet engines that were purchased from Britain in 1975.[29]

Furthermore, the United States, after having spent five decades preparing for a war with the Soviet Union, the world's second superpower until its recent demise, has an overwhelming advantage in terms of training and readiness. China's armed forces have not fought a major war since the Korean War, with the last major military exercise (that against Vietnam in 1979) an embarrassment for the People's Liberation Army (PLA). Most informed observers of China's PLA give it little chance of being able to successfully invade Taiwan let alone defend itself against the capabilities of the United States. The United States is a superpower with modern weapon systems that have much more lethality than China can hope to possess, even in the next two or three decades, notwithstanding their hopes and aspirations to become a high-tech armed force with everything that the United States has in its inventory.[30]

Judging from reports about the quality and capabilities of Chinese missiles, tanks, aircraft and ships sold to countries such as Iran, Iraq, Thailand, Pakistan, Sri Lanka and Myanmar over the last decade or so, the United States faces no foreseeable threat from Chinese armed forces.[31] China has no carriers and no troops deployed overseas, whereas the United States has huge forces available in its Pacific Command alone. China has no marines or long-range airlift capability that compares with the United States' ability to mount an operation like the Gulf War's Desert Storm against Iraq.

As Geoffrey Blainey points out, wars often begin because nations disagree on their relative strength.[32] China can be in no doubt as to its relative inferiority. The piecemeal destruction of the Iraqi army (one that 'looks an awful lot like the Chinese army' according to a senior CIA official)[33] reminded China of the United States's precision firepower, its advanced weapons systems and its huge lead in critical military technologies, especially micro-electronics, electronic systems, surveillance, precision-guided missile technology and all-weather air attack capabilities.[34] The demonstration of United States firepower during the 1990 Gulf War did more than anything else to force a turnaround in China's otherwise declining defence expenditure.[35] The Gulf War, where control of the air was the key to the stunning destruction of the Iraqi army and its mainly Chinese-built T-69s, made China realise that its biggest weakness was air defence. Speaking after an evaluation of the results of the Gulf War, the Chairman of China's Central Military Commission, Jiang Zemin, said China had to devote its research and development resources to air defence for the next five years.[36] Not surprisingly, the first items that China sought from Russia after the Gulf War were a few SA-10 Grumble air defence systems and a handful of Su-27 fighter interceptors. Against a superpower like the United States, however, they are of little operational significance, and the technology gap between China and the United States is likely to widen over the next decade or so.

China and the United States: Natural rivals?

Nonetheless, even taking into account the marked imbalance between the strategic capability of the United States and China, many strategists look at China and the United States as the two obviously dominant powers in the Asia-Pacific region, particularly now that there is no Soviet threat for their strategic framework. Russia is a marginal player for the moment; Japan, despite its economic might, has a peace constitution, United States security guarantees, no nuclear weapons and a defence budget of just 1 per cent of its GNP. China, on the other hand, has geopolitical overhang because of its size, location, history, cultural reach, the overseas Chinese, its nuclear weapons and its long-term potential, as well as the absence of other candidates for superpower status.

On the other hand, most countries in Pacific Asia, including China, depend on the United States as an export market and none can match the military might of the United States Seventh Fleet. At the same time, China and the United States are divergent societies with vastly different cultural traditions that contrast the ideals of individual striving and collective harmony.[37] The United States is essentially Christian, democratic, materialistic and strongly influenced by television images and public opinion polls. It is, as Henry Kissinger said, a society extensively populated by refugees and deeply motivated by the protection of individual human rights.[38] It moralises about its foreign policy and has always wanted the Chinese to become like the Americans — Christian, capitalist and democratic. As one American missionary wrote regarding China in 1832: '... we have it, they lack it, we ought to give it to them so that they can be more like us and pursue our ideals'.[39]

This view of China does not seem to have changed very much: one of the constant United States demands made of China is the right of Voice of America to broadcast its message into the remotest parts of China, while CNN television footage of Chinese demonstrators fleeing from tanks and the polystyrene 'Goddess of Democracy' being toppled by the PLA was seen as a brutal assault on core American values.[40] As Robert Manning observed, Tiananmen ensured that China's behaviour was 'judged harshly as reflecting the thuggery of a repressive Stalinist regime at home and a rogue, outlaw state abroad'.[41]

Chinese views of the United States are just as prone to subjectivism. They are refracted through the lens of China's 5000 years of civilisation and its more recent experience at the hands of the European powers. China still smarts from the humiliations it endured between the first Opium War in 1839–42 and the time when China 'stood up' under Mao Zedong in 1949. As Harold Hinton observes, 'next to security, sovereign dignity is probably Beijing's most important concern in its external relations'.[42] This has left China hypersensitive to anything that smacks of interference in its internal affairs. China has, says Henry Kissinger, a 'prickly insistence' on the principle of state sovereignty.[43] This 'prickliness', revealed in unguarded moments, is manifest in China's annoyance when pressed over Tibet, Hong Kong, Taiwan and human rights. The West in general may criticise China in these and other areas but it is the United States that China identifies as its leading critic.

Since 1945, it has been the United States that has threatened China on more occasions and for longer periods than any other European power. Currently, no other great power irritates China as much as the United States, although equally, there is no other great power that is more important to China than the United States. China has not had problems of national security significance with Japan since the end of the Second World War. It neutralised any threat from the former Soviet Union with the rapprochement with Moscow that began in the early 1980s.[44] It has achieved a similar improvement in its relations with India in the southwest.[45] The United States had pulled out of Indochina by 1975 and abrogated its Mutual Defence Treaty with the Republic of China (Taiwan) in 1980.

The Taiwan issue

The United States is the only state, however, that can exercise critical influence over the direction of Chinese foreign policy. The United States maintains the equivalent of a defence relationship with Taiwan through the provisions of the 1979 *Taiwan Relations Act*. The Act, as an Act of Congress, has proved to be very close to the spirit and intent of the 1954 United States–Republic of China Mutual Defence Treaty. The Act states *inter alia* that it is United States policy:

> to make clear that the United States decision to establish diplomatic relations with the PRC rests upon the expectation that the future of Taiwan will be determined by peaceful means; – to consider any effort

to determine the future of Taiwan by other than peaceful means — a threat to the peace and security of the Western Pacific area and of grave concern to the United States; to provide Taiwan with arms of a defensive character; [and] to maintain the capacity of the United States to resist any resort to force or other forms of coercion that would jeopardise the security or social or economic system of the people of Taiwan.[46]

Section 2(c) of the Act provides that:

The preservation and enhancement of the human rights of all the people on Taiwan are hereby reaffirmed as objectives of the United States.[47]

Section 3 provides that the United States:

... will make available to Taiwan such defense articles and defense services as may be necessary to enable Taiwan to maintain a sufficient self-defense capability [and that the] President is directed to inform Congress promptly of any threat to the security of the social or economic system of the people on Taiwan, and any danger to the interests of the United States arising therefrom ... The President and the Congress shall determine the nature and quantity of such defence articles and services based solely upon their judgement of the needs of Taiwan.[48]

The Act was intended to be part of a transitional mechanism pending the settlement of the mainland–Taiwan unification issue. It was to become 'a relic of the past' as contacts between Taiwan and the mainland developed.[49] Read literally, however, the Act left open the possibility of renewed United States military protection and assistance to safeguard Taiwan's interests and deter mainland China if and when deemed necessary.[50] That was how the Act was interpreted at the time by the Japanese.[51] It is how the Act was interpreted by the United States in September 1992 when President Bush announced his decision to sell F-16 fighter aircraft to Taiwan.

Taiwan thus is the most important issue with the potential to sour Sino-United States relations.[52] Handled badly, 'the Taiwan issue might trigger an explosive crisis in Sino-American relations'.[53] Since 1972, however, both sides have been fairly pragmatic and relatively restrained in dealing with what could otherwise become Asia's most serious flashpoint. In view of their common interest in preventing conflict over Taiwan, China and the United States have developed a tacit agreement to abide by four basic rules regarding Taiwan:

- There is to be no use of force against Taiwan by China.
- The United States is not to recognise two Chinas, or one China and one Taiwan.
- The United States can continue to have 'unofficial' relations with Taiwan.
- Taiwan cannot declare itself independent.[54]

In September 1994, when the United States made the first significant adjustments to the nature of its dealings with Taiwan since 1979, it affirmed that its 'one China' policy remained intact and that any adjustments in its policy towards Taiwan were merely refinements, not changes to that policy.[55] For its part, China, while reaffirming its right to use force against Taiwan, has avoided any provocative military buildup or military activity in the area adjacent to Taiwan. China has, however, become increasingly concerned and strident about Taiwan's active pursuit of a greater international role that is more commensurate with its position as the world's fourteenth largest trading state. Furthermore, it sees the United States as acquiescing in, or even actively supporting, Taiwan's campaign for greater international respectability.

Spheres of influence

Generally speaking, China adheres to a basically non-provocative policy that eschews challenging the United States in areas that are sensitive to Washington, but of marginal strategic or political importance to China. This approach can be seen in China's abstention on votes for United Nations Security Council resolutions that have pushed back the limits on United Nations intervention in the domestic affairs of states. Given its strong opposition to conceding such a right, Beijing might have been expected to exercise its power of veto.[56] Instead, it has consistently abstained.[57] In August 1994, it abstained on Security Council Resolution 940 on Haiti which endowed the United States with United Nations authority to use 'all necessary means to facilitate the departure from Haiti of the military leadership and the prompt return of the legitimately elected president ...'[58]

Non-interference by China and the United States in their respective spheres of geographic influence clearly has its limitations. But for the moment, both sides seem to understand the parameters and are striving to maintain a good working relationship within those limits.

Arms sales

Another possible issue in Sino-United States relations concerns Chinese sales of weapons and technology to so-called pariah states. In particular, alleged Chinese sales of materials and technology that could lead to the proliferation of weapons of mass destruction (WMD) are seen in Washington as 'a significant and serious threat to American security interests'.[59] China, for example, sold CSS-2 MRBMs (range 3500 kilometres) to Saudi Arabia in 1986–87, Silkworm anti-ship missiles to both Iran and Iraq in the mid-1980s and other missiles including the M-9 (range 600 kilometres) to Iran and Syria in the late 1980s.[60] Acrimonious exchanges came to the surface after

Tiananmen, with the Yinhe affair in August 1993, involving alleged shipments to Iran of thiodiglycol and thionyl chloride (used in chemical weapons); there were also accusations that China was supplying nuclear weapons technology to Iran and Pakistan and was continuing to supply the M-11 short-range missile to Pakistan after it had pledged compliance with the Missile Technology Control Regime (MTCR).[61] In these areas, it is claimed that China has been 'indisputably irresponsible' and sanctions were imposed.[62]

However, according to a senior Chinese Foreign Ministry official, there is no unambiguously concrete evidence that China has reneged on its obligations under the MTCR or the Nuclear Non-Proliferation Treaty.[63] Missile proliferation was resolved as an issue in China–United States relations on 4 October 1994. In a joint declaration signed by Chinese Foreign Minister Qian Qichen and United States Secretary of State Warren Christopher, the United States agreed to lift sanctions it had imposed in August 1993, while China agreed that it would not export missiles covered by the MTCR.[64] China also signed an agreement on the eventual cessation of production of fissile materials used in nuclear weapons.[65]

There are other differences between China and the United States that flare up from time to time, such as the issue of free emigration, prison labour, political prisoners, Tibet, birth control, the right of the United States to broadcast its values into China, trade and IPR. But, as David Shambaugh observes, there are few concrete grievances between China and the United States.[66] Indeed, in some respects China has adopted positions which have effectively removed possible causes of strain in its relations with the United States. China supported United States policy on Afghanistan and Vietnam (after 1979), albeit because they shared a common foe: the former Soviet Union. Further, in the final analysis, China played a constructive role in the peace settlement in Cambodia and helped ease misunderstanding and tension on the Korean peninsula, pressing North Korea to abide by its commitments under the Non-Proliferation Treaty (NPT) and International Atomic Energy Agency safeguards. China signed the MTCR (February 1992), the NPT (March 1992) and the Chemical Weapons Convention (January 1993). Its releases of prominent Chinese political and religious dissidents have been much more cynical, usually occurring when its broader interests are under pressure, such as the most favoured nation renewal debate.[67] Trade is a particularly tense area of dispute. There is no doubt that China is undergoing major reforms of its trading regime as part of its desire to accede to the General Agreement on Tariffs and Trade, but its actions have not so far been adequate to alleviate the concerns of the United States and other countries about its institutionalising of a higly protective regime.

Nonetheless, it signed a memorandum of understanding (MOU) on intellectual property rights in January 1992, an MOU on the non-export of products made by prison labour in June 1992 and an MOU on market access in October 1992.[68] It has despatched several 'Buy American' trade missions to the United States to help ease the imbalance in bilateral trade, reduced tariffs on many products and eliminated quotas and other non-tariff measures, and granted market access concessions to United States companies.[69]

Chinese strategists, nurtured on Sun Tzu's *The Art of War*, believe a war should not be fought unless absolutely necessary and the country is really in great danger.[70] This principle was paramount in 1950 when Mao Zedong reportedly spent three days pacing up and down before deciding (in the face of strong opposition from leaders like Chen Yun) to intervene in Korea.[71] Today, and for the foreseeable future, there is little reason for China to become involved in conflict with the United States, provided it abides by its tacit agreement with the United States on Taiwan.

The United States is of a similar view as far as China is concerned. It has always been reluctant to go to war with China although General Douglas MacArthur was an exception until he was dismissed from office in 1951 after pressing for a larger war with China. The United States might complain about human rights in Tibet or Hong Kong and it might give support to Taiwan but it does not want to get involved in a confrontation with a country the size of China. Today, it seems clear that the United States would seek to avoid disputation with China over the latter's claims to Taiwan (provided force was not used) and it would not become involved physically in the event of a clash between China and other claimants to the Spratly Islands in the South China Sea.

Despite forecasts of great conflict between China and the United States, the remarkable fact is that, with the exception of the Korean War, the United States has never been involved in a war with China. It has contained China but it has also helped China enormously. The United States was always sympathetic to China's plight in the face of the depredations it suffered at the hands of the Europeans and Japanese in the period between 1839 and 1939.[72] Both China and the United States distrusted the Europeans and the Japanese.[73] They fought on the same side during the First World War and, during the Second World War, China helped the United States contain and then defeat Japan. After the war, Mao's China would probably have gone on to normalise relations with the United States for Mao had argued in favour of establishing a constructive relationship with the United States. He said, with some prescience, that:

> China's greatest postwar need is economic development ... America and China complement each other economically ... America needs an export market [and] an outlet for capital investment ... America is not only the most suitable country to assist this economic development; she is the only country fully able to participate.[74]

For its part, the United States was similarly inclined to recognise the reality of Mao's China. By 1949, the United States had written off the 'helpless and hopeless' Chiang Kai-shek and concluded that it had no strategic interest in Taiwan.[75] On 5 January 1950, President Truman announced that the United States would not become involved in China's civil war.[76]

If China had normalised relations with the United States in 1949, then the subsequent misperception that plagued Sino-United States relations and generated tension in East Asia for the next 25 years might have been avoided. Instead, China chose to 'lean to one side' (towards the Soviet Union) in reaction to what it felt was a negative United States attitude and a threatening United States posture in East Asia.[77] Any softening of Washington's disposition to recognise China was dispelled by Kim Il-sung's invasion of South Korea and American concern about the threat of monolithic communism that loomed with the formation of the Sino-Soviet alliance in February 1950.

With the outbreak of the Korean War on 25 June 1950, the United States reversed its hands-off policy. Taiwan became 'an important anchor in the United States defensive chain in the Western Pacific and President Truman ordered the Seventh Fleet to prevent a mainland attack on the Nationalists'.[78] These developments, the Korean War, the defeat of France in Indochina and crises over the offshore islands in the Taiwan Straits in 1954–55 and 1958 fuelled a Sino-United States Cold War. The United States' fear of China, in turn, sucked the United States into a strategy of containment against China and, ultimately, a decade of war in Vietnam.

According to Michael Oksenberg, the wars fought between China and the United States in Korea and, indirectly, in Vietnam were avoidable contests that flowed in large part from a United States failure to appreciate China's insecurity and engage in a constructive relationship.[79] Once the United States signalled its willingness to negotiate with China, Chinese fear of the United States eased and a co-operative relationship subsequently developed, with positive consequences for global and regional security. China became a responsible member of the United Nations. It stopped supporting revolutionary movement in Southeast Asia and it ceased shelling Taiwan's offshore islands. Sino-United States rapprochement in 1971–72 facilitated the United States' withdrawal from Indochina, helped contain the Soviet Union, and contributed to the eventual collapse of the Soviet Union. Indeed, Strobe Talbott describes the triangular dynamic involving China, the United States and the former Soviet Union as 'the most important development in global politics since World War II'.[80] Today, the strategic triangle no longer exists and, instead, the United States–China relationship is determined by bilateral perspectives based on domestic political and economic interests.

The lessons from this first 25 years of People's Republic of China–United States relations can be summarised as follows: when the United States pursued an aggressive forward-deployed posture aimed at confronting or containing China, the result was tension and conflict in Korea, in the Taiwan Straits and in Indochina. On the other hand, when the United States pulled back from China's doorstep and engaged in a dialogue as between equals, or joined with China to neutralise the Soviet Union, one of the results was to hasten the end of the Cold War and induce an easing of tension, increased co-operation and greater regional and global stability.

Put another way, tension in East Asia eased when the United States accepted China as a legitimate major power in East Asia, as President Richard Nixon did when he travelled to Beijing in 1972. Nixon acknowledged China's claims to Taiwan and announced the United States withdrawal from Indochina. In 1974, the United States chose to remain uninvolved when China used force to recover the Paracel Islands from South Vietnam. In 1979, the United States formally recognised Beijing and in the following year, it terminated its Mutual Defence Treaty with Taiwan and withdrew its remaining military personnel from the island. In effect, the United States had acknowledged the reality of a new China that was too big and too strong to be easily contained. China, after all, had fought the United States to a standstill in the Korean War and withstood isolation from the West for two decades in the 1950s and 1960s.

Unlike Russia, the United States does not share a common border with China. They are separated by the Pacific Ocean. They have worked out a *modus vivendi* on Taiwan, the only issue of any strategic significance, and they have similar views about Japan. They are also in the same regional clubs — the ASEAN Regional Forum, APEC and the Pacific Economic Co-operation Council. There are many grounds for disagreement between China and the United States, but it is hard to see a cause for war. One might reasonably conclude, therefore, as the Chinese have done, that there is little possibility of a direct conflict between China and the United States.[81]

Most countries on China's borders, including Taiwan, realise that they have to live with China, whereas the United States is located on the other side of the Pacific Ocean, notwithstanding its possession of a powerful Pacific Fleet. In these broad circumstances, there is a growing perception that in the long term, the United States influence and its military presence in East Asia will contract whereas China's power and influence is likely to grow. Countries in the region have adapted to these geo-economic realities with Thailand, Burma, South Korea, Taiwan and even Vietnam accommodating China in their respective foreign and trade policies.

This places China in an advantageous geopolitical situation in East Asia and has led to predictions that China might seek to fill the power vacuum left by any retreat of the United States. China, after all, is not challenged by any European power. Its northern borders are secure. It has strong cultural and economic links throughout the region via Hong Kong, Taiwan, Macau and, through the overseas Chinese, in every business capital of Southeast Asia as well as the west coast of the United States. It has an airstrip in the Paracels, holds islands in the Spratlys and is reportedly helping Burma build naval facilities in the Andaman Sea. Once the North Korean nuclear issue is resolved, the Koreans will probably not want such a large United States presence on the Korean peninsula.

It is this prospect of an ascendant China dominating East Asia that worries many American analysts. The realist response would be for the United States to try to contain China and prevent it from gathering power and influence. However, the lessons from the first two or three decades of Sino-

United States relations after 1949 is that containment is a recipe for tension and conflict. China, moreover, is simply too big and too important for a containment policy to be sensible or viable. Militarily, China is Asia's only nuclear power; it is of critical importance to the Asian regional economy and the Asia-Pacific economic community; and it has veto rights as a Permanent Member of the UN Security Council.

Generally, the Clinton administration has adopted a policy of constructive engagement with China, aimed at building a broad long-term framework to take the Sino-United States relationship into the twenty-first century, and to cater for the emergence of a strong China in the Asia-Pacific region.[82] In May 1994, President Bill Clinton formally abandoned America's linkage of China's human rights record to the renewal of China's most favoured nation trading status. His decision may have been helped by the fact that it was the United States, not China, that risked isolation over the human rights issue.[83] The United States' tendency to indulge in harsh, overbearing criticism of China on human rights is not supported by Asian countries.[84] Such considerations, of course, would be unlikely to constrain the United States and the West from once again linking trade restrictions with improvement of China's human rights record, in the event that there was another catastrophe of the order of the 1989 Tiananmen massacre.

Nonetheless, the Clinton decision reflects United States acceptance of the view that strategic, economic and cultural engagement with China is the best vehicle for bringing about gradual political and economic change in China. As United States Secretary of Commerce Ron Brown explained, a commercially based China diplomacy was more sensible and more profitable than harping on human rights.[85] Rather than confronting China over human rights, it was better for the United States to compete with other countries and win contracts in China to sell, for example, a power plant that would bring light to the 100 million Chinese who were currently without electric power.[86] Brown said they could then read at night or watch television and absorb Western ideas and ideals.[87] Withholding trade benefits as a means to try to pressure China over sensitive domestic issues, such as human rights and Tibet, would only reinforce China's suspicion of the West, and rebound to the disadvantage of American companies seeking to do business in the fastest growing economy in the world.

Economically, China's rapid growth and its location at the centre of a greater Chinese economic community give it considerable regional influence in East Asia, a fact recognised by Japanese, French and German corporations that have already stolen a march over their American competitors in areas such as telecommunications, transportation, power and financial services. As United States Undersecretary of State for Economic Affairs, Joan Spero, remarked, with economic considerations now a major focus of United States foreign policy, no region was more important to the United States for jobs than the Asia-Pacific region, including the fast growing Chinese economic conglomerate.[88] With national security inextricably linked to economic security, and over 150 000 American jobs dependent on United States exports to China, the Clinton decision on China to separate trade from human rights was inevitable. The perception of China as a vast, fast growing market and the interests of the American corporations like Westinghouse, Bell, Boeing, IBM, General Electric, Chrysler, AT & T and Kodak for a share in the US$250 billion in infrastructure projects that are expected to come on stream in China before the year 2000 demanded 'business as usual'.[89] For the United States, China is 'the biggest of the Big Emerging Markets and would provide much of the growth in demand for American exports in the years ahead'.[90]

China is growing four times as fast as the rest of the world as a United States export market, with the prospect that it will become one of the most important commercial relationships for the United States in the twenty-first century.[91] In 1992–93, America's exports to China grew three times faster than its overall exports.[92] United States exports to China/Hong Kong increased from US$5.3 billion in 1982 to US$18.6 billion in 1993, making China/Hong Kong the fifth largest export destination for the United States (see Table 5.2), compared with tenth in 1982.[93] The three Chinas combined (China, Hong Kong and Taiwan) comprised the second largest United States export market in Asia and the fourth in the world after Canada, Japan and Mexico. In terms of United States imports, China/Hong Kong ranked fifth in 1993 (see Table 5.3), after being seventh in 1983. The United States, meanwhile, has become the largest export market for China/Hong Kong (see Table 5.4), although in terms of total trade, it is second after Japan. This growth, however, brings with it serious problems which will certainly exercise the United States administration and Congress in the foreseeable future. The huge, and rapidly growing, trade deficit which the United States has with China will be a constant source of tension as long as China maintains highly protective trade barriers.

Table 5.2 United States' leading sources of imports (US$million)

	1993
Canada	112 966
Japan	108 992
Mexico	40 744
Germany	29 461
China/Hong Kong	26 976
Taiwan	23 373
United Kingdom	22 392
Korea	17 779
France	15 694
Italy	13 829

Source: International Monetary Fund, September 1994 and International Economic Data Bank, Australian National University, Canberra.

Table 5.3 United States' leading export markets (US$ million)

	1993
Canada	96 534
Japan	47 949
Mexico	41 635
United Kingdom	26 375
Germany	18 956
China/Hong Kong	18 640
Taiwan	16 616
Korea	14 776
France	13 272
Netherlands	12 839
Singapore	11 675
Belgium/Luxemborg	9 437
Australia	8 271
Saudi Arabia (1992)	7 163
Italy	6 460

Source: International Monetary Fund, September 1994 and International Economic Data Bank, Australian National University, Canberra.

Table 5.4 China/Hong Kong: Trading partners (US$ million)

To/from	Exports	Imports	Total
United States	26 976	18 640	45 617
Japan	22 648	40 181	62 829
Taiwan	2 772	18 347	21 119
Korea	4 863	11 581	16 445
Singapore	5 093	8 329	13 422
Australia	2 756	3 371	6 128

Source: International Monetary Fund, 1994, and International Economic Data Bank, Australian National University, Canberra.

Insofar as the United States' strategy for its relationship with China has changed, it will be strategically defensible and potentially very profitable. It aims to make a profit whilst simultaneously pushing China in the direction that Taiwan has taken — that is, democratic, capitalist, enmeshed in the global trading system and supportive of United States interests. Hence the United States has resumed an 'active engagement policy with the Chinese leadership in a vigorous high-level dialogue'.[94] According to Charles Freeman, Assistant Secretary of Defense, the great challenge for the United States is to promote the 'responsible integration of China into the Asia-Pacific community' so that with an increasing stake in the global system, it would be less likely to behave in an aggressive or unpredictable way when it became a global power.[95] This challenge, said Freeman, required United States engagement with China across all fronts, including military contacts.[96]

High-level United States military compacts with China, suspended after Tiananmen in 1989, resumed in June 1994 with the visit to China of the retiring United States Commander in Chief of the Pacific Command, Admiral Charles Larson. Xu Huizi, Deputy Chief of Staff of the PLA, then reciprocated with a visit to Honolulu and Washington in August 1994. Xu's visit was the first by a senior Chinese leader since 1989 and marked the restoration of full bilateral military relations between China and the United States.

Another reason for the shift in America's China strategy is concern that China might come to rely on Russia for military technology. Unchecked, this could result in lost arms sales, weakening leverage over the pace and direction of China's defence modernisation, and lost opportunities to develop personal relationships with key members of the Chinese government at a time of leadership transition. The United States, in China's view, has always been concerned that a closer Sino-Russian military relationship would undermine United States strategic interests in Asia.[97]

The United States shares many important strategic interests with China, including a denuclearised Korean peninsula, avoidance of conflict between the mainland and Taiwan, the containment of Russia, preservation of the United Nations system and the maintenance of a regional balance and global stability. The United States needs China's co-operation in the Security Council, on proliferation issues, in dealing with Malaysia and its East Asian Economic Caucus and in building an inclusive Asia-Pacific regional security forum.

For China, the United States is an important contributor to its long-term modernisation, and hence its survival as a society and a state. China needs the United States for its technology and as a market for its labour-intensive manufactured goods. Without the United States and its allies, China's entire modernisation strategy could be undermined. For the United States, on the other hand, China has one-fifth of the world's population that, uncontrolled and underfed, could cause a refugee problem that would eclipse anything the world has experienced in Rwanda or Somalia. As a rapidly industrialising economy, China's co-operation is also critical for the protection of the global environment. So, as Richard Betts asks, do we want China to be moderately well off, or do we prefer that China should remain on the edge of bare survival, always concerned about the impact of a natural disaster and starvation, on the verge of civil war, perhaps breaking up and precipitating masses of boat people?[98] As Barber Conable and David Lampton conclude, it is better for the United States to face the problems of success in China than the crises that would inevitably accompany failure.[99] Regional stability in the Asia-Pacific — for the mutual benefit of both China and the United States — requires co-operative Sino-United States relations.[100] This is in fact the conclusion that most Asian countries near China, including Taiwan, have already reached.

If both China and the United States can co-operate on this 'rich strategic agenda', and its economic and environmental dimensions, China should not become an adversary of the United States, at least not by default or because of miscalculation and misperception.[101] Instead, we could see a period of great peace and prosperity in the Asia-Pacific region. On the other hand, if China and the United States cannot work together, the Asia-Pacific region is likely to become tense, divided and unstable. This would overturn the favourable strategic environment China needs to restrain defence expenditure, relax its relations with neighbouring states, co-operate with other great powers and concentrate on economic modernisation.[102] Both China and the United States, therefore, have a common interest in preventing such an outcome. As Chinese Foreign Minister Qian Qichen has often reaffirmed, China wants to increase co-operation and minimise confrontation with the United States.[103]

Outlook

There is a certain appealing simplicity about the notion of a great contest between China and the United States, two distinctly different cultures. But just as possible is the notion that the Sino-United States relationship could be one of the cornerstones underpinning security and economic growth in the Asia-Pacific region.

Robert Gilpin suggests that an international system is stable (that is, in a state of equilibrium) if no state believes it is profitable to attempt to change the system.[104] A state will attempt to change the international system if the expected benefits exceed the expected costs (that is, if there is an expected net gain).[105] In the case of Sino-United States relations, China does not believe it can change the present system, and perceives that any attempt to do so — by, for example, challenging the United States — would cost China dearly. China would risk military defeat, diplomatic humiliation and huge economic loss for little or no gain. China, on the contrary, gains enormously from present international arrangements, hence its interest in joining the World Trade Organisation, APEC, the ASEAN Regional Forum and other regional and international organisations, and in maintaining continued access to the United States. Even if its communist party leadership finds it hard to accept, the fact is that China is gradually being Taiwanised and Westernised. There is, moreover, little possibility of its present open door policy being reversed. While there is residual dissatisfaction over the future of Taiwan and islands in the South China Sea, China is, on the whole, satisfied with the existing international system. It might seek change in certain other areas and it might like to hasten the recovery of Taiwan and islands in the South China Sea, but it is not interested in revolution or in a war. Indeed, all the trends on which one might base a forecast about China and its future point in the opposite direction. China has become something of a status quo power. It has given up supporting revolution in Southeast Asia, Africa and Latin America. It has a reasonable record in abiding by United Nations procedures and international law. It has settled boundary disputes with many of its neighbours and it has abstained or voted in favour of key United Nations Security Council Resolutions. In addition, one might point to the fact that gains in China do not necessarily mean losses for America. Sustained growth in China, provided it is accompanied by pro- gressive liberation of its trade regime, will lead to a bigger export market for the United States. With more opportunities to bring about peaceful eco- nomic and political change in China and a more relaxed and self-confident China, that country might be more willing to co-operate with the United States instead of feeling threatened and insecure.

While one cannot by any means dismiss the possibility that deep ten- sions will continue to dog United States–China relations and cause instability in the Asia-Pacific region, the potential exists for the relationship between China and the United States to be one of the most positive factors con- tributing to regional security in the Asia-Pacific in the twenty-first century. At the moment, therefore, as the United States Commander of Pacific Command, Richard C. Macke, remarked, the chief objective as far as China is concerned, is 'to reassure and engage China so that it will work with us to maintain regional stability'.[106]

Notes

1 USIS Wireless File, Canberra, 19 November 1993.

2 Paul Kennedy, *The Rise and Fall of the Great Powers*, Unwin and Hyman, London, 1988, p. 514.

3 Christopher Layne, 'The Unipolar Illusion, Why New Great Powers will Rise', *International Security*, vol. 17, no. 4, Spring 1993, p. 7.

4 Samuel P. Huntington, 'Why International Primacy Matters', *Inter- national Security*, vol. 17, no. 4, Spring 1993, p. 70.

5 Robert Jervis, 'International Primacy, Is the Game Worth the Candle?', *International Security*, vol. 17, no. 4, Spring 1993, p. 54, suggests that although the Pentagon plan was subsequently revised, the original state- ment of its objectives may still best represent the thrust of American policy.

6 Robert Gilpin, *War and Change in World Politics*, Cambridge University Press, Cambridge, 1981, pp. 94–95.

7 See, for example, Richard K. Betts, 'Wealth, Power and Instability: East Asia and the United States after the Cold War', *International Security*, vol. 18, no. 3, Winter 1993–94, p. 36; Nicholas D. Kristof, 'The Rise of China', *Foreign Affairs*, vol. 72, no. 5, November/December 1993, p. 59; Michael T. Klare, 'The Next Great Arms Race', *Foreign Affairs*, vol. 72, no. 3, Summer 1993, p. 141; Samuel Huntington, 'The Clash of Civilizations?' *Foreign Affairs*, vol. 72, no. 3, Summer 1993, p. 47; Larry M. Wortzel, 'China Pursues Great Power Status', *Orbis*, vol. 38, no. 2, Spring 1994, p. 157; Denny Roy, 'Hegemon on the Horizon, China's Threat to East Asian Security', *International Security*, vol. 19, no. 1, Summer 1994, p. 149 and Gerald Segal, 'China's Changing Shape',

Foreign Affairs, vol. 73, no. 3, May/June 1994, p. 43. On the other hand, for some it is a resurgent Russia, Japan or Germany that is potentially America's chief opponent: Edward Olsen, 'Target Japan as America's Economic Foe', *Orbis*, vol. 36, no. 4, Fall 1992, p. 491; and Samuel Huntington, 'America's Changing Strategic Interests', *Survival*, vol. 23, no. 1, January/February 1991, p. 8. If so, China might again prove to be an invaluable ally for the United States.

8 Remarks of Harry Harding, Brookings Institution, at a seminar at the Australian Defence Force Academy, Canberra, 20 May 1994.

9 Kristof, 'The Rise of China', p. 72.

10 Remarks of Harding, at the Australian Defence Force Academy.

11 There are many equally plausible scenarios for the future of China. Harry Harding, 'On the Four Great Relationships: The Prospects for China', *Survival*, vol. 36, no. 2, Summer 1994, pp. 22–41, concludes that, along with the forecast of a more aggressive China, equally likely are a China that continues to choose peaceful and mutually beneficial relations with its neighbours, and a China that falls victim to internal political and economic decay. See also Harry Harding, *A Fragile Relationship: The United States and China Since 1972*, Brookings Institution, Washington, 1992.

12 Richard Hornik, 'Bursting China's Bubble', *Foreign Affairs*, vol. 73, no. 3, May/June 1994, p. 28. If it is to become a modern creative society, China has to permit more individual freedom and consider some form of federal political structure with less centralised control: Wenyuan Qian, *The Great Inertia: Scientific Stagnation in Traditional China*, Croom Helm, London, 1985, p. 26.

13 Ramon H. Myers, *Thoughts on US Foreign Policy Toward the People's Republic of China*, Essays in Public Policy no. 47, Hoover Institution, Stanford University, 1994.

14 James T. Myers, 'Mainland China and the Ordeal of Change', in Bihjaw Lin and James T. Myers (eds), *Forces for Change in Contemporary China*, University of South Carolina Press, Columbia, 1993, p. 7.

15 United Nations Development Program, *Human Development Report 1994*, Oxford University Press, New York, 1994, p. 94. Even in fashionable purchasing power parity terms, China's per capita income leaves it as one of the poorest developing countries in the world.

16 Colonel Xu Xiaojun, 'China's Grand Strategy for the 21st Century', paper for the 1994 Pacific Symposium, Asia in the 21st Century: Evolving Strategic Priorities, Washington, 15–16 February 1994.

17 Betts, 'Wealth, Power and Instability', p. 52.

18 See Kennedy, *The Rise and Fall of the Great Powers*, p. 164.

19 *China: Environmental Strategy Paper*, volume 1, World Bank, Report no. 9669-CHA, Washington, 1992.

20 Luo Zhuchong, Ministry of Forestry, warning of China's impending ecological crisis, reported in the *Age*, 2 February 1989.

21 ibid.

22 Hu Angang and Zou Ping, *China's Population Development*, China's Science and Technology Press, Beijing, 1991, p. 182.

23 Hu Angang, et al., *Survival and Development*, Science Press, Beijing, 1992, pp. 49–50. See also Hu Angang, Chapter 17, this volume.

24 Table 1, Ross Garnaut and Guonan Ma, *Grain in China*, East Asia Analytical Unit, Department of Foreign Affairs and Trade, Canberra, 1992, p. 4.

25 Vaclav Smil, *China's Environmental Crisis*, M.E. Sharpe Inc., Armonk, New York, 1993, p. 136.

26 *China's Strategies for Reducing Poverty in the 1990s*, World Bank Report no. 10409-CHA, Washington, 1992, p. vi.

27 *South China Morning Post*, 28 August 1994.

28 'The Chinese Army Speaks', *Defence and Armament*, Heracles International, no. 70, February 1988, p. 57.

29 Chong K. Yoon, 'Problems of Modernizing the PLA: Domestic Constraints', in Larry M. Wortzel (ed.), *China's Military Modernisation — International Implications*, Greenwood Press, New York, p. 14.

30 For a slightly more optimistic assessment of China's military capabilities, see You Ji, Chapter 13, of this volume.

31 R. Bates Gill, *The Challenge of Chinese Arms Proliferation: US Policy for the 1990s*, Strategic Studies Institute, US Army War College, Carlisle Barracks, Pennsylvania, 1993, p. 29; Nazir Kamal, 'China's Arms Export Policy and Responses to Multilateral Restraints', *Contemporary Southeast Asia*, vol. 14, no. 2, September 1992, p. 124.

32 Geoffrey Blainey, *The Causes of War*, 3rd edn, Macmillan, Melbourne, 1988, p. 293.

33 Transcript, remarks by Martin Petersen, Director, Office of East Asian Analysis, Central Intelligence Agency, in *Hearings of the Joint Economic Committee on China's Economy*, US Congress, Washington, 30 July 1993.

34 Zhongguo Keji Luntan, *Forum on Science and Technology* (translated from the Chinese), no. 4, Beijing, 18 July 1991. According to the US Department of Defense, America leads the world in nineteen out of 22 critical military technologies, including microelectronic circuitry, gallium arsenide technology, software producibility, high-speed computers, machine intelligence and robotics, simulation and modelling, integrated optics, fiber optics, sensitive sensors, passive sensors, automatic target recognition, phased arrays, data fusion, signature control, computational fluid dynamics, air breathing propulsion, new composite materials, superconductivity and biotechnology materials and processing: George P. Milburn, 'New Technologies. An Overview', in

Desmond Ball and Helen Wilson (eds), *New Technology: Implications for Regional and Australian Security*, Canberra Papers on Strategy and Defence no. 76, Strategic and Defence Studies Centre, Research School of Pacific Studies, Australian National University, Canberra, 1991, p. 17.

35 See Table 14.2 in Chapter 14, this volume.

36 Reported in *South China Morning Post*, 14 June 1991.

37 John King Fairbank, *China Watch*, Harvard University Press, Cambridge, 1987, p. 1.

38 Henry Kissinger, 'China: The Deadlock Can Be Broken', *Washington Post*, 28 March 1994, p. 8.

39 Fairbank, *China Watch*, p. 4.

40 David Shambaugh, 'Patterns of Interaction in Sino-American Relations', in Thomas W. Robinson and David Shambaugh (eds), *Chinese Foreign Policy: Theory and Practice*, Clarendon Press, Oxford, 1994, pp. 210–12.

41 Robert A. Manning, 'Clinton and China: Beyond Human Rights', *Orbis*, vol. 38, no. 2, Spring 1994, p. 195.

42 Harold C. Hinton, 'China as an Asian Power', in Hinton and Shambaugh, *Chinese Foreign Policy*, pp. 348–49.

43 ibid.

44 See Gary Klintworth, 'Mr Gorbachev's China Diplomacy', in Ramesh Thakur and Carlyle Thayer (eds), *The Soviet Union as an Asia Pacific Power*, Westview, Colorado, 1987, p. 39.

45 Gary Klintworth, *The Practice of Common Security: China's Borders with Russia and India*, Working Paper no. 93/1, Department of International Relations, Research School of Pacific Studies, Australian National University, January 1993.

46 *Taiwan Relations Act*, Congressional Record — House 125, no. 38, 16 March 1979: H1668-70.

47 ibid.

48 ibid.

49 Lori Fisler Damrosch, *The Taiwan Relations Act After Ten Years*, Occasional Papers no 4, School of Law, University of Maryland, 1990, p. 2.

50 See Lin Bih-jaw, 'Taipei-Washington Relations: Moving Towards Institutionalisation', in Chang King-yuh (ed.), *ROC-US Relations Under the Taiwan Relations Act: Practice and Prospects*, Institute of International Relations, Taipei, 1989, p. 40.

51 Japanese sources, cited by A. James Gregor, 'US Interests in Northeast Asia and the Security of Taiwan', *Strategic Review*, vol. 13, no. 1, Winter 1985, pp. 52, 54.

52 Bonnie S. Glaser, 'China's Security Perceptions: Interests and Ambitions', *Asian Survey*, vol. 33, no. 3, March 1993, pp. 259ff; and Betts, 'Wealth, Power and Instability', p. 37.

53 Colonel Xu Xiaojun, 'China's Grand Strategy for the 21st Century'.

54 See Richard H. Solomon, 'The China Factor in America's Foreign Relations', in Richard H. Solomon (ed.), *The China Factor: Sino-American Relations and the Global Scene*, Prentice Hall, Englewood Cliffs, New Jersey, 1981, pp. 34ff; and generally Min Chen, *The Strategic Triangle and Regional Conflicts: Lessons from the Indochina Wars*, Lynne Rienner, Boulder, Col., 1992.

55 State Department Background Briefing, Washington, 7 September 1994, in USIS Wireless File, Canberra, 8 September 1994. This does not fully explain the US decision to sell F-16 fighter aircraft to Taiwan, contrary to the 1982 Joint Communiqué, in which 'the United States government states that it does not seek to carry out a long-term policy of arms sales to Taiwan, that its arms sales to Taiwan will not exceed, either in qualitative or in quantitative terms, the level of those supplied in recent years since [1979] and that it intends to gradually reduce its sales of arms to Taiwan, leading over a period of time to a final resolution'. Jawling Joanne Chang, 'Negotiation of the 17 August 1982 US-PRC Communique: Beijing's Negotiating Tactics', in Steven W. Mosher (ed.), *The United States and the Republic of China*, Transaction Publishers, New Brunswick, 1992, p. 129.

56 See, for example, Yi Ding, 'Opposing Interference in Other Countries' Internal Affairs Through Human Rights', *Beijing Review*, 6–12 November 1989, p. 10.

57 UN Security Council Resolution 688 permitted the use of force to protect Kurds in Iraq (1991); UNSCR770 permitted use of force to help civilians in Bosnia-Herzegovina (1992) and UNSCR918 allowed the French to use force to rescue civilians in Rwanda (1994).

58 UN Security Council Resolution 940, 31 July 1994, text in USIS Wireless File, Canberra, 2 August 1994.

59 Gill, *The Challenge of Chinese Arms Proliferation*, p. ix.

60 ibid., pp 30–36.

61 ibid., p. 36 and fn. 23, p. 51. The M-11 is claimed by the Chinese to be a short-range tactical missile with a range under the 300 kilometre limit of the MTCR. A Chinese Foreign Ministry spokesman said that China had supplied 'a very small number of short-range tactical misiles to Pakistan' but declined to say whether they were M-11 missiles. Reuters Textline, 20 June 1991. Chinese Foreign Ministry official, Sha Zukang, said China had not supplied Pakistan with M-11 missiles either before or after accepting MTCR guidelines. He claimed the United States had no evidence that China had supplied such missiles to Pakistan. Personal communication, 28 March 1994. Pakistan's Foreign Minister, Sardar Aseff Ahmed Ali, admitted that China had supplied Pakistan with Scud-type short range missiles but he strongly denied that Pakistan possessed any Chinese M-11 missiles. Islamabad, *The News*, 10 September 1994, p. 12.

62 Kristof, 'The Rise of China', p. 71.

63 Sha Zukang, Director, International Organisations, Ministry of Foreign Affairs, Beijing, personal interview.

64 *Xinhua*, Beijing, 5 October 1994.

65 ibid.

66 David Shambaugh, 'China's Security Policy in the post-Cold War Era', *Survival*, vol. 34, no. 2, Summer 1992, p. 94.

67 Statement by Winston Lord, Assistant Secretary of State for East Asia and the Pacific, before the Subcommittee on Trade, House Ways and Means Committee, Washington, 8 June 1993, US Department of State Dispatch, 14 June 1993, 4(24) p. 427; and Barber B. Conable and David M. Lampton, 'China: The Coming Power', *Foreign Affairs*, vol. 72, no. 5, Winter 1992, p. 139.

68 Guo Changlin, 'Sino-US Relations in Perspective', *Contemporary International Relations*, (Beijing), vol. 2, no. 7, July 1992, p. 6.

69 *Wen Wei Po*, (Hong Kong), 29 July 1994. US Secretary of Commerce, Ron Brown, Transcript of remarks, Beijing, 31 August 1994, USIS Wireless File, Canberra, 2 September 1994.

70 Yu Zemin,'The Strategic Thinking of Sun Tzu', in *Proceedings of China/United States Seminar on Methodologies in Defence Systems Analysis*, China Defence Science and Technology Information Center, Beijing, 1987, pp. 57–63.

71 Chow Ching-wen, *Ten Years of Storm*, Holt, Rinehart and Winston, New York, 1960 cited in Melvin Gurtov and Byung-Moo Hwang, *China Under Threat: The Politics of Strategy and Diplomacy*, Johns Hopkins University Press, Baltimore, 1980, p. 55.

72 A. Doak Barnett, *China and the Major Powers in East Asia*, Brookings Institution, Washington, 1977, pp. 154–56; and Chapter 1, 'A Century of American Policy, 1844–1943', *United States Relations with China: With Special Reference to the Period 1944–1949*, Department of State Publication 3573, Division of Publications, Office of Public Affairs, Washington, 1949.

73 Barnett, *China and the Major Powers in East Asia*, p. 155.

74 From Department of State, *Foreign Relations of the United States, 1945, volume 7, The Far East, China*, Government Printing Office, Washington, 1969, pp. 273–74, quoted in Barnett, *China and the Major Powers in East Asia*, p. 166.

75 Joseph W. Ballantine, *Formosa*, Brookings Institution, Washington, 1952, pp. 118–20; and Bruce Cumings, 'Telltale Taiwan', in Bruce Cumings (ed.), *The Origins of the Korean War: volume II. The Roaring of the Cataract*, Princeton University Press, Princeton, New Jersey, 1990, pp. 508, 533–36. See also US Department of State's Policy Memorandum on Formosa, 23 December 1949, in *Military Situation in the Far East*, Hearings before the Committee on Armed Services and the Committee on Foreign Relations, US Senate, 82nd Congress, 1st Session, Part III, US

Government Printing Office, Washington, 1951, p. 1668.

76 Ballantine, *Formosa*, p. 120.

77 See John Gittings, *The World and China 1922–1972*, Harper and Row, New York, 1974, p. 163ff; and Gurtov and Hwang, *China Under Threat*, p. 34ff.

78 US Senate, Committee on Foreign Relations, *Report on Mutual Defence Treaty with the Republic of China*, 8 February 1955, Senate, 84th Congress, 1st Session, Executive Report no. 2, US Government Printing Office, Washington, 1955, p. 8.

79 Michael Oksenberg, President of East-West Center, address to the Asia Society, Washington, 21 September 1993, USIS Wireless File, Canberra, 23 September 1993.

80 Strobe Talbott, 'The Strategic Dimension of the Sino-American Relationship', in Solomon (ed.), *The China Factor*, p. 83.

81 Xiao Bing and Qing Bo, *Zhongguo Jundui Nengfou Daying Xia Yi Chang Zhanzheng* (Can the Chinese Army Win the Next War), Chongqing, 1993, trans. FBIS-*China*, 5 May 1994, p. 3.

82 President Bill Clinton, statement on China, 26 May 1994, Washington, reported in the *Washington Post*, 27 May 1994.

83 Harry Harding, 'Asia Policy to the Brink', *Foreign Policy*, no. 96, Fall 1994, pp. 57–74.

84 Australian Foreign Minister, Gareth Evans, 'bluntly told US Secretary of State, Warren Christopher, that Australia did not accept the US position that China's trading status should be linked to human rights'. Reported in the *Australian Financial Review*, 10 March 1994. Singapore's Prime Minister, Goh Chok Tong, also warned that a break in Sino-US relations over China's human rights policies would have severe long-term consequences for the world. *Financial Times* (London), 21 April 1994. Japanese Prime Minister Morihiro Hosokawa told President Clinton in Seattle in November 1993 that the Western concept of human rights should not be blindly applied to all nations: *Washington Times*, 22 March 1994.

85 US Secretary of Commerce, Ron Brown, transcript of remarks in Hong Kong, 2 September 1994, in USIS Wireless File, Canberra, 6 September 1994.

86 ibid.

87 ibid.

88 Joan Spero, address to Korean Economic Institute of America, Washington, 19 October 1993, in USIS Wireless File, Canberra, 21 October 1993; and Conable and Lampton, 'China', p. 148.

89 George Black, 'Why the Debate? The Outcome was Clear: Business as Usual', *Los Angeles Times*, 27 May 1994.

90 Transcript of remarks by US Secretary of Commerce, Ron Brown, Beijing, 29 August 1994, in USIS Wireless File, Canberra, 31 August 1994.

91 Transcript of remarks by US Secretary of Commerce, Ron Brown, Beijing, 30 August 1994, in USIS Wireless File, Canberra, 2 September 1994.

92 *South China Morning Post*, 3 August 1993.

93 *Direction of Trade Statistics Yearbook 1989, Direction of Trade Statistics Yearbook 1993*, International Monetary Fund, Washington. Taiwan, by way of comparison, improved its position as a United States export market from fourteenth place in 1982 to sixth place in 1992.

94 Barber Conable and John C. Whitehead, 'United States and China Relations at a Crossroads', presentation to the National Press Club, Washington, 8 February 1994, in USIS Wireless File, Canberra, 9 February 1994.

95 Testimony to the US House Foreign Affairs Committee, 15 June 1994, USIS Wireless File, Canberra, 16 June 1994.

96 ibid.

97 *Wen Wei Po*, 18 August 1994, in *Foreign Broadcast Information Service — China*, 18 August 1994, p. 3. Both sides still operate joint missile monitoring facilities in Xinjiang.

98 Betts, 'Wealth, Power and Instability', p. 55.

99 Conable and Lampton, 'China', p. 149.

100 ibid., p. 143.

101 Manning, 'Clinton and China', pp. 193–205. The same point is made by a former United States ambassador to China, James Lilley, in 'Freedom Through Trade', *Foreign Policy*, no. 94, Spring 1994, p. 37.

102 Song Yimin, 'New Trends in the Post Cold War World', paper presented at a symposium at the Brookings Institution, Washington, DC, December 1992, China Institute of International Studies, Beijing.

103 Qian Qichen, address to the Asia Society, New York, 28 September 1993, Reuters Textline.

104 Gilpin, *War and Change in World Politics*, pp. 10-11.

105 ibid.

106 Admiral Richard C. Macke, speech, Royal United Services Institute, seminar on Regional Security in the Asia-Pacific: Towards 2001, Australian Defence Force Academy, Canberra, 23 September 1994.

6 Sino-Japanese Relations in the Post-Cold War World

Ian Wilson

No other foreign relationship maintained by China has as many facets or contradictions as that with Japan. Japan is variously admired, hated, feared, patronised and courted. It is seen as a cruel invader, an economic model, a military threat, and as an important source of aid, investment and technology — in ways to be preferred over the United States. It is not surprising, therefore, that there is little consistency in China's policy towards Japan, if only because of the different and often clashing bureaucratic interests involved. If China is to become less centrist and give more play to regional and sectional interests, we can expect these divergent and contradictory tendencies to increase and to be reflected in policies towards Japan even more than is the case at present. But whether China as a whole is heading towards a military confrontation with Japan stemming from economic rivalry and competition is a separate and more problematic issue. It requires a less complex model of China's decision-making process and a lot more evidence than is available to date. From what can be discerned thus far, quasi-alliance is at least as possible an outcome as open conflict.[1]

Japan's attitudes towards China are similarly difficult to characterise in simple terms, but again do not point to an inevitable clash of interests likely to result in major confrontation. Admiration as the source of much Japanese culture, attraction as a vast market for exports, profound war guilt, and fear as a potential aggressor all mingle in Japanese thinking. This takes place in a context in which an attitude of superiority prevails, Japan having succeeded while China is pitied as far less successful and still backward in many respects. Like China, Japan is also seeking to define for itself a new role in a vastly changed world order, but is doing so under a novice political leadership long excluded from foreign policy-making during the LDP era.

China's political leadership is operating under rather different constraints with the closing of the Deng Xiaoping era, but without resolving the succession problem, except to endorse a rather fragile and probably temporary Jiang Zemin–Li Peng coalition. Sino-Japanese relations are, therefore, at a point of transition and their future course remains problematic. A number of scenarios can be advanced, each dependent on the shape taken by the emerging world order: confrontation leading to conflict if China should seek regional hegemony; Sino-Japanese alliance if a triumphalist United States seeks to impose its will on others and embraces the economic protectionist option; and, should a genuine multipolar world develop in which Russia remains weak, and the United States, Japan and China face internal problems which prevent one-state dominance, then Sino-Japanese relations are likely to remain stable. This chapter suggests that relations will most likely follow the latter course.

The background

Sino-Japanese relations have always been very much a function of wider external power relations and balances. Superpower conflict in the region and the climate of the Cold War froze Japan's relations with China with the outbreak of the Korean War. Thereafter, the United States Security Treaty and its attendant links with Washington precluded any independent Japanese opening to China until the early 1970s. Although Japan, like other United States allies, was not informed beforehand of Dr Kissinger's secret flight to Beijing in mid-1971, and the prime minister was greatly embarrassed by the policy shift, Tokyo then moved more quickly than Washington to establish diplomatic and direct economic relations with the People's Republic. This was eagerly reciprocated because China's main preoccupation was the threat of further and more substantial attacks from the Soviet Union, a concern which had made Washington's overtures acceptable in the first place. Japan was recruited into this new triangular power relationship as an adjunct of the United States and thus allied with China against the Soviet Union. In China's eyes, this recruitment to the anti-Soviet camp was reinforced by including the standard 'anti-hegemony' clause in the document of recognition and the subsequent treaty — a term which had a much more vague meaning for Japan and remained for them no more than a statement of general principle.

Another axiom of China's foreign policy at the time was the strong insistence on a 'one China' formula for all those that sought diplomatic relations. Japan's recognition was employed to reinforce this requirement. Although ways were soon found around this formula, Japan was forced to sever all formal ties with Taiwan. Subsequent ambiguities were overlooked, but in general Japan's recognition fitted into a long list of diplomatic gains which flowed from Beijing's resumption of the China seat in the United Nations and

Nixon's opening towards China. Tokyo also provided a reluctant but significant boost to China's legitimation of its claim to Taiwan. For Japan, as with the United States, the prospects of great economic benefits in the long term outweighed the costs of temporarily less convenient trade with Taiwan.

China in the early 1970s was not altogether satisfied with the shape of the international system within which she was now a full participant, and Japan figured prominently in the several alternative patterns of power distribution debated in foreign policy circles and academic research institutes that were beginning to emerge after the long freeze initiated by the Cultural Revolution. China's rejection of the Stalinist 'two camp' thesis led to disillusionment with the Soviet alliance itself in the late 1950s and Japan was accorded a place in the second of the 'intermediate zones' that Mao Zedong developed in his new view of the world.

As such, Japan was no longer conceived of as irretrievably linked to the imperialist camp, but was seen as seeking greater independence of action, partially resistant to United States domination and also threatened by the Soviet superpower. One important policy implication of this formulation during the 1960s was for China to undermine the United States–Japan Security Treaty without provoking open retaliation by Washington. Again, trade was the mechanism employed and, although there were important economic benefits which flowed to China from the 'Memorandum trade' made possible by the Takasaki–Liao Zhengzhi meeting in 1962, their agreement had greater significance for the Chinese leadership by serving to separate Japan from the United States at the symbolic level because such trade was contrary to the spirit of Japan's treaty with the United States. Ironically, the deterioration of relations with the Soviet Union during the late 1960s, which culminated in armed border conflicts in 1969, led to a positive reassessment of the Security Treaty by the moderates in Beijing, a group which at the time included Mao and Zhou Enlai. They began to view the treaty as very useful in deterring perceived Soviet territorial ambitions in the region because it locked the United States into protecting Japan and the existing regional order.

Whether Japan was seen as resisting United States domination or as a convenient means whereby the United States guaranteed regional security, it acquired the status of a largely independent centre or point in the emerging multipolar configuration which China saw as gradually replacing the bipolar system that had prevailed since the end of the Second World War. Because of the diminished capacity of both superpowers to control their former satellites and satraps, a new pattern was identified by some observers which they depicted as a five-pointed star with Japan, Western Europe and the Third World challenging the power of the Soviet Union and the United States. That Japan's growing economic might would push it rapidly in this direction was seen as inevitable on neo-Marxist a priori grounds by Chinese observers. What had begun as a set of incidental political differences between Tokyo and Washington, stemming from the thwarting of Japanese economic and nationalist aspirations and drawing the two apart during the 1960s, had changed by the 1970s. It would in the future drive a greatly intensified epic rivalry.

Japan assumed a greater importance for China once the violent and assertive aspects of the Cultural Revolution began to give way to a more 'realist' world view, following diplomatic recognition and the announcement of the Four Modernisations campaign by Zhou Enlai in 1975. Japan was seen as an alternative source of aid, investment funds, technology, managerial skills and as a market for China's energy exports to finance the ambitious development plans launched at the Third Plenum in late 1978. Economic assistance from the United States was delayed by an inability to solve a range of issues, many centred on Taiwan. Some observers were also quick to note that the Chinese and Japanese economies were still complementary in a number of respects. Neither side particularly appreciated the references to the very similar relationship that had existed in the 1930s. This time, care was being taken to stress themes of equality, free choice and mutual benefit in economic exchanges. In fact, very little had changed apart from the rhetoric. Renewed fears of imminent Soviet attack were entertained by some of the dominant elements of the Chinese leadership, including Deng Xiaoping, and China was pushed towards a quasi-alliance with the United States in 1978–79. By extension, this also involved Japan because of the Security Treaty, but by mid-1982 China's fears began to recede following several strategic reassessments which downgraded Soviet capacities to project its power into the region because of costly commitments elsewhere. China's principal concern remained the 'great triangle', but there were now opportunities for manoeuvre within its confines by playing one superpower off against the other, particularly when President Reagan proved less compliant to Soviet pressure than President Carter. At the same time, a secondary regional quadrilateral which included Japan (but not yet Korea) began to figure in Chinese thinking about Northeast Asia. This conceptualisation emphasised some of the divisions between Japan and the United States because too close a relationship between the two economic giants was an unnerving prospect for China. An even more alarming prospect for China was that these two might join with the Soviet Union in the joint economic exploitation of the oil, gas, minerals and timber of Siberia and the Soviet Far East, possibly including South Korea as a minor partner and source of labour. Quadrilateralism along these lines would disadvantage and isolate China, so diplomatic pressure was applied to ensure such a consortium did not come to fruition. As it turned out, these fears came to nothing, largely because United States–Soviet relations deteriorated over a range of other issues, including intermediate-range ballistic missiles in Europe, human rights and the invasion of Afghanistan. Japan's unwillingness to invest large sums in the Soviet hinterland ensured the scheme's failure, although it is not clear to what extent political factors were involved in the decision. Tokyo was at least aware that an isolated and economically encircled China would not be conducive to a peaceful and stable regional environment.

Reform and opening up

In general terms, China's foreign policy underwent a change following the 1978 decision to pursue major economic reform and open the country up to outside trade, technology and investment. As Deng Xiaoping noted in 1987, 'When we decided on the policy of [domestic] construction, we adjusted our foreign policy ...' Economic development rested on trade and this required conditions of peace and stability to permit China's full participation in the international economic system. In specific terms, on the other hand, the course of very few bilateral relationships followed this pattern except in the longer term. Significantly closer relations with Japan took some time to mature and their uneven progress reflected the ambivalences and contradictions in Sino-Japanese relations mentioned at the beginning of this chapter. Some are worth examining for the light they shed on the direction they followed in a very different world order of the 1980s, and may take in the future.

For China, the world environment seemed to change very rapidly during the Deng reform era and these changes had an impact on the manner in which Beijing regarded Japan. Quite quickly, the possibility of a peaceful and stable environment conducive to expanded trade and reduced defence expenditure became a reality. Furthermore, the weakness and decline of the Soviet Union and the economic challenges to United States predominance indicated to the Chinese leaders that the old bipolar world was at last giving way to a multipolar configuration more favourable to China. New Year 1989 was, therefore, greeted with considerable optimism, although at home there were signs in the economy and the social order that all was not going well with the domestic reform agenda. Even so, there was little to prepare China for the twin shocks to come — the demonstrations and then the killings in Tiananmen Square in early June followed by the rapid decline of Marxist socialism in the Soviet Union and Eastern Europe, culminating in the loss of proletarian state power in most of these states and the collapse and dismemberment of the first socialist state itself following the failed August coup in 1991.[2]

The shifts in domestic political alignments also involved Japan, although only marginally. The political consensus carefully built up by Deng Xiaoping as the springboard for his reform program and the policy of 'opening up' began to break down in 1987. A relatively hard-line group of conservative reformers, grouped around Chen Yun, came into open conflict with the more radical reform group, initially led by Deng himself but moving at greater speed under Party General Secretary Hu Yaobang and Premier Zhao Ziyang and his advisers. This group wanted to accelerate the dismantling of central planning mechanisms by removing almost all price controls and leaving more and more economic decisions to the operations of the market. These policies met with resistance from vested interests and ideological beliefs. Hu Yaobang was also vulnerable on several grounds, one being his unwillingness to crack down hard on student and worker demonstrations in late 1985 and again at the end of 1986.

Anti-Japanese feeling had been a feature of both demonstrations, but was particularly so in 1985 when many Chinese were resentful of economic penetration, known as the 'second Japanese invasion'. Hu was criticised for failing to conduct relations with Japan on the basis of equality and reciprocity and for being over-polite to Prime Minister Nakasone. There were more important issues driving his attackers, but the Japanese question was certainly manipulated to his detriment. Memories of past atrocities, trade imbalances, allegations of bad faith over the Baoshan iron and steel complex and insensitive behaviour by certain Japanese politicians all struck sympathetic chords amongst many Chinese. Hu Yaobang found himself at odds with the conservatives but also with broader national opinion. Something of an admirer of Japan's modernisation, he allowed this to show when he welcomed Nakasone on a televised visit to his home. Several acquaintances thought him too obsequious, an impression not easily dispelled by his shortness of stature alongside the tallest postwar Japanese leader. Of greater significance was Hu's invitation to some 3000 Japanese youth for an expensive tour of China, a gesture the Japanese government did not reciprocate in kind, inviting only a very small group of young Chinese for a return visit. These seemingly petty matters were used against him, his opponents alleging dereliction of his duty to defend the national honour.

The eventual outcome was due to other factors, but finally Deng Xiaoping withdrew his support and Hu fell early in 1987. The patriarch seemed to align himself with the conservatives for much of 1987 and new premier Li Peng, enjoying the patronage of Chen Yun, prevailed over Zhao until the Party Congress in September. As Carol Lee Hamrin has shown, factional struggles within the Communist Party of China are fought out in terms of 'policy packages', aggregations of economic, ideological, political and foreign policy proposals.[3] The foreign policy debate cannot be separated from other issues but in general terms the conservative elders were less sanguine about the nature of the contemporary world than were Deng and his reformers. Japan figured prominently in these debates throughout the 1980s for a number of reasons.

Firstly, the conservative 'Old Guard' saw themselves as just that — namely, the protectors of the revolutionary tradition and the socialist state. For them, and for many others, Japan had invaded China, cruelly pillaged the homeland and contributed to decades of national humiliation. Any changes exhibited since then were seen as largely cosmetic. This nationalist rhetoric, so effectively captured by the conservatives, helps account for the solid support they enjoy within the People's Liberation Army. These links are reinforced by networks of *guanxi* relationships established by the old leaders with their successors within the High Command. Some of the conservatives, like Wang Zhen, were greatly respected within the PLA and exercised considerable influence. Wang Zhen's views on Japan had been forged in the 1930s and 1940s and, like many of his other positions, had undergone few changes since then.

Secondly, Japan represented many of the most hated facets of imperialism, Western capitalism and materialism to the older revolutionaries — particularly those recruited from the provinces of the north and the interior of China. Nowhere was this more clearly exemplified than in the fierce debate over the television series *He Shang*, screened in 1988. Its makers, for the most part younger reformers with liberal inclinations, attempted to show that China's salvation lay in looking outwards towards the 'blue' of the ocean. This embraced the West but also Japan and Southeast Asia. This view they contrasted with the 'yellow' mindset of the interior, characterised by traditionalism, xenophobia and general backwardness. The clear inference was that China must open up, reject aspects of the past which held back the development of the nation, and utilise appropriate foreign models. In many ways this debate simply repeated arguments that went back at least 150 years when the impact of the West was being felt and modernisation first became an issue. Zhao Ziyang praised the series and even showed episodes to visiting foreign leaders, including Lee Kuan Yew, but many senior figures did not share his opinions. The elderly and very conservative veteran, Wang Zhen, was quite incensed and dared the General Secretary to expel him from the Party for criticising a program which he saw as negating all that was of value in China's long history.

Japan's alleged manipulation of feasibility studies for the Baoshan project and the unwillingness of several ministers and the textbook industry to accept any responsibility for the invasion and massacres of the late 1930s were opposite sides of the same coin to many of that generation, who still use the term 'dwarf pirates', and will remain an obstacle to genuinely close Sino-Japanese relations for some time to come.

While the anti-Japanese issue may have been manipulated then by anti-reform factions, more spontaneous demonstrations are still frequent, particularly around the anniversaries of episodes in past relations, such as the Nanjing Massacre and the Marco Polo Bridge Incident. The official press sometimes provides the cue for agitation, but spontaneity cannot be ruled out altogether. The 1985 student demonstrations over economic penetration were tolerated by the authorities, probably to convey a message to Tokyo, but they attracted wider support. Regional state and co-operative enterprises, which were otherwise supportive of the reforms, joined in because their efforts to establish infant locality-based manufacturing industries could not meet the competition from cheaper Japanese products. Xian and Chengdu also experienced violence and Japanese showrooms, offices and cars were burnt.

Tiananmen and its consequences

A new and complex set of domestic factors, not directly linked to Japan, combined in mid-1989 to disturb social peace and with it the Chinese leadership's fairly sanguine view of the world. Rising urban prices, currency inflation, uneven distribution of the benefits of reform, sectoral unemployment and accounts of widespread corruption in the state and Party all fuelled the fires of discontent during early 1989. The impending visit of Mikhail Gorbachev and the sudden death of Hu Yaobang provided the circumstances for further demonstrations by young people in Beijing and then other major centres. However, it was the ineptitude of a divided leadership which led to the bloody massacre of 3–4 June and an immediate crisis in China's foreign relations.

Loans, credit facilities and projects were suspended across the country and Japan acted in concert with the Western nations to place China relations on 'hold'. It was to prove significant when the sanctions were lifted that Japan did not indulge in the same moralising but instead warned of the long-term danger of isolating China. Japan's obvious reluctance over sanctions was followed by some alacrity in having them lifted. During this period, Japan was the closest China had to a friendly state among the G-7 members.

Beijing's initial reaction to the somewhat unexpected ostracism by the West was to shore up support in Eastern Europe and the Third World, where criticism had been muted or nonexistent. Two top-level delegations were dispatched to Europe, with particular attention being given to the hard-line regimes in East Germany and Romania, but the returns were meagre. Regional trade was shifting to a hard currency basis and away from barter and non-negotiable currencies. Moreover, the bloc members were experiencing political crises of their own which were to topple even the tough Honecker and Ceausescu regimes by the end of 1989. But no grouping of Eastern bloc or Third World states could compensate for the loss of Western markets, capital and technology (although Taiwan helped cushion the impact of isolation by providing a source of new tourism and investment funds, and actually exceeded Japan's for the calendar year of 1989).

Some hopes were held out for a change in Moscow, as Gorbachev's conservative opponents seemed to be gaining ground, and China even offered a loan and credit facilities as evidence of good faith. While careful not to be seen as taking sides, the new Chinese leadership alliance clearly hoped the conservative forces would prevail, but the failure of the August 1991 coup put an end to such wishful thinking. Not only were the conservatives defeated and placed under arrest, but Gorbachev survived. Worse was to follow because he was soon replaced by the even less acceptable ex-Party member, Boris Yeltsin, who then presided over the dissolution of the Soviet Union itself. Political power had slipped from the hands of the proletariat, they complained, and China must develop a totally new approach in a key area of diplomacy. The reappraisal was agonising indeed because China's handy position in the strategic triangle between the United States and the Soviet Union was also lost.

The policy debate

A foreign policy debate ensued in which the optimistic view of a basically peaceful and congenial international environment was discredited and replaced by a world view which had China as the victim of a United States-led scheme to undermine socialism everywhere through a 'smokeless war', perpetrating the view that socialist states would evolve peacefully towards market economies and Western-style parliamentary political systems. In this way, the United States could achieve the world dominance which it had failed to win by force of arms. There was a paranoid element to this outlook and John Foster Dulles was disinterred to be the architect of the strategy of 'peaceful evolution', although one commentator managed to trace it back to the time of Lenin, who had conveniently warned against it. The Soviet Union and much of Eastern Europe were seen as having succumbed and China was painted as the *Jingkangshan* or bastion of world socialism.

On a more practical and operational level, some analysts advocated that China should forge direct linkages with Japan as an alternative to trying to repair relations with the United States. Thus it was hoped a new triangle could be constructed within which China could again enjoy freedom of manoeuvre as the swing weight, playing the Japan card when it suited. This strategic approach placed great store in the economic rivalry and conflict existing between Japan and the United States. An interesting articulation of this position came from a 'think tank' which included Chen Yuan, vice-governor of the People's Bank and the son of Chen Yun, the powerful conservative elder and consistent critic of radical market reform. Hong Kong sources dubbed this document the political platform of the so-called 'Princes' Party', a group made up of the sons and daughters of senior conservative figures. The document proposed that China should do what it could to exacerbate friction between Japan and the United States.[4] The subsequent failure of many of the 'party' to achieve high positions suggests that the views put forward in the document had little impact. They do, however, represent an interesting alternative standpoint on foreign policy.

An analyst from the Academy of the Social Sciences, He Xin, was the most forthright of those advocating a quasi-alliance with Japan. This line had some endorsement at high levels and was published in authoritative journals, including the *Beijing Review*, but came under stern attack and was later characterised as 'extreme left'.[5] The head of the Shanghai Institute for International Studies, and thus a person close to Party chief Jiang Zemin, had him in mind when he wrote, 'China has neither the intention nor the capability to persuade Japan or Russia to stand against the United States. Individual leftists in China may have advocated such a stupid idea, but it received little attention from Chinese specialists or the leaders in Beijing.' He Xin, a fairly young commentator, had as his mentor Deng Liqun, the senior ideologue and opponent of Deng Xiaoping.[6] As the paramount leader regained his room for manoeuvre after Tiananmen and could act once more in a balancing role, he was able to move away from the hard-line anti-United States faction. In Orwellian fashion, this line was given the 'extreme leftist' label and has now been generally discredited. Had it ever become the prescription for policy, China would have been locked into a relationship with Japan that would have allowed no leverage with the United States at all, and created a regional atmosphere of insecurity. Even the most superficial reading of China's post-1989 foreign policy shows that the maintenance of a link with Washington remains one cornerstone of Beijing's strategy.

An alternative view, which also has currency within the armed forces and the conservatives, confronts the data on Japan's military spending and draws pessimistic conclusions on likely regional and global intentions: that expenditure on what is a self-defence force now exceeds China's official defence budget and gives it third ranking in the world; that there are elements within Japan urging constitutional revision to allow greater spending and an unfettered role for those forces; and that a minority wants to reverse the position on nuclear arms. These points can all be used to revive old anxieties in China about Japan's longer-term ambitions.

The focus provided by the army professionals as well as the institutional resentment against a decade of budgetary restraint means that the main pressure for increasing China's defence spending accordingly comes from the Ministry of Defence and the PLA itself. The defence spending issue is canvassed more fully elsewhere in this volume, but it should be noted that the PLA advocates do not refer to extra-budgetary funding in China, or to the fact that Japan's spending provides it with a mere 240 000 or so military personnel, whereas China, with a smaller official amount, is able to afford some 3.2 million under arms.

Most Chinese statements of concern about Japanese rearmament have a very high rhetorical component and are taken less seriously at the leadership level. A symposium on the international environment conducted by the State Council's Institute of Contemporary International Relations in mid-1985 reported that Japan's assumption of more military responsibilities, '... does not indicate that it intends to become a major military power. We, however, must always sound the alarm about that. The "textbooks" incident was one alarm we sounded.' Mention was made of new anti-Japanese War Museums recently established in Nanjing and Lugouqiao and the commemoration of the 40th anniversary of the war against fascism. It concluded, 'All these activities are necessary. They warn the people not to forget history as well as not to repeat history.'[7] Interviews in 1985 at the Beijing Institute of International Relations, a research body under the Foreign Ministry, confirmed this interpretation. Analysts there saw no harm in Japan exceeding the 1 per cent of Gross Domestic Product (GDP) limit on defence or extending the operational range of Self-Defence Force naval vessels. Indeed, this was inevitable, the author was told: 'As the water rises, so does the boat.' That China would not insist on its publicly proclaimed stance was even conveyed to the Japanese government in 1980, admittedly at a time of very tense relations with the Soviet Union. In 1987 Japan did exceed its self-imposed spending limit when it went to 1.004 per cent of GDP and this did occasion loud protests, presumably because it threatened the fairly stable and peaceful regional environment which had allowed China to keep defence spending quite low.

Other commentators, including the missile expert and strategist Hua Di, played down the military aspects of the relationship. He argued that closer relations with Tokyo were far preferable to dealing alone with the one superpower.[8] These views were not always well received by the 'old guard' conservatives who remained concerned about a perceived growth in Japan's military capacity and remained fearful of a resurgence similar to the 1930s and 1940s. In her conversations with Chinese strategists, Bonnie Glaser also encountered the somewhat unusual opinion that Japan might seek to recruit China as an ally against the United States.[9] At the level of political diplomacy, Japan certainly used its voice to moderate United States positions on Most Favoured Nation conditions, human rights and China's re-entry to the General Agreement on Tariffs and Trade (GATT), and might sometimes hope Beijing could reciprocate when Tokyo and Washington are at odds.

There is, however, no strategic dimension to this relationship. There are periodic bilateral talks on regional security concerns but the idea of a military alliance directed against the United States is fanciful in the extreme. How much of this speculation was simply wishful thinking created by nostalgia for the old United States–Soviet triangle in which China carried real weight is difficult to assess.

China's Japan policy

Currently it would appear that different and not always clearly defined views on Japan have prevailed at the top level of Chinese decision-making in recent years. A revival of militarism has not been dismissed totally as a possible outcome and, in the current uncertain climate while the leadership succession in still unresolved, no leader can afford to be painted by their opponents as in any way 'soft on Japan'. It is a reflection of residual attitudes deeply embedded in some older Japanese that at almost regular intervals some recently appointed minister will commit a gaffe on the history of imperial aggression in the region, thus touching off a fresh burst of protests from China and other victims in Korea and the Association of Southeast Asian Nation (ASEAN) states. In 1985 and 1986 the Chinese government was able to make use of popular protests against Japan to strengthen its hand in negotiations over the unfavourable trade balance and meagre direct Japanese investment. This tactic has continued to prove useful but should not be taken as a sign of implacable opposition, let alone as the basis for inevitable conflict between the two states. The intention is rather to place Japan in an inferior bargaining position or at least provide some balance in a relationship within which Japan is otherwise the stronger. This is managed in many ways. Voluntary and truly independent associations in China are virtually unknown, but one organisation did spring up in 1992 to protest on behalf of the so-called 'comfort women' drafted for the use of Japanese soldiery during the war. Its continued existence and official toleration should not be taken as conclusive evidence of an emerging civil society because it clearly serves the purposes of the regime when it wishes to apply pressure to the Japanese government without seeming to do so at the state level.

Significantly, its leader was kept out of the capital at the time of the visit by the Crown Prince of Japan. That visit in itself showed that the attitude which prevails most of the time is generally friendly towards Japan without being effusive. The leadership concedes that, like it or not, China needs Japan.

Japan's China policy

Japanese attitudes towards China are no less complex and ambivalent. At the strategic level of analysis, there is a concern that China might one day flex its military muscles in the region and considerable effort is directed towards averting such a possibility. To develop a credible counter-force is out of the question, although Japan's technically sophisticated Self Defence Force has some deterrent capability against China's larger but now very dated arsenal. The preferred strategy is to bring China into a set of bilateral and multilateral economic and political relationships which will create a degree of interdependence and make of the Middle Kingdom a responsible and co-operative neighbour and great power. Conflict would be a marked failure of this strategy, as it would be for Deng Xiaoping's policy of reform and opening up to the world.

The Japanese decision-making is no more monolithic than is the Chinese system and different interests and factions have their impacts on the final policy outcome. Among older Japanese, the sense of cultural debt coupled with feelings of war debt have produced a benign tolerance towards China's sometimes errant behaviour. Younger Japanese are less constrained and may well look towards the time when Chinese economic growth rates, if sustained, will give that country a leading edge in the region and globally. Surveys conducted by Fukuyama and Oh found that Japan desires neither a weaker China, rent by political or economic collapse, nor a militarily stronger China.[10]

To avoid the first possibility, Japan has become the major source of aid, loans and credit to China and has, belatedly in the eyes of the Chinese, become a major direct foreign investor. Gerald Chan notes that direct investment stood at US$439 million in 1990 and US$580 million in 1991 but had burgeoned to US$1800 million by 1992.[11] In November 1990, Japan concluded a loan agreement for Y36.5 billion as the first stage of Japan's third loan package of a massive Y810 billion for the 1990–95 period.[12] Further long-term trade agreements were concluded soon after, including one for US$8 billion in technology and machinery to be paid for in oil coal supplies to Japan's energy industry. Between 1990 and 1992, Sino-Japanese trade swelled from US$17 billion to about US$29 billion. As the *Japan Times* reported on an earlier agreement, signed on China's National Day in 1988 but still appropriate, 'In expressing their gratitude for economic cooperation from Japan, Chinese leaders noted that such assistance would also be profitable to Japan in the long run. We in Japan certainly have no objection to this view,' wrote Sakutaro Tanino.[13] This highly profitable aid and trade has not compromised Japan's independence, whereas China is exposed. The PRC accounts for less than 5 per cent of Japan's total trade, whereas Japan accounts for some 25 per cent of China's total trade.[14]

To avert significant military strengthening in China, Japan has fewer means at her disposal and thus far no agreement has been reached on how to react should Beijing act with aggression in the region. Whereas Japan's policy towards Russia has remained fairly firmly in the grasp of the Ministry for Foreign Affairs, China policy is arrived at only after some struggle between the professional diplomats, the Ministry of International Trade and Industry (MITI), the Defence Agency and various corporate and private operators involved with aid and trade.[15] Even within the Gaimusho, there can be differences between the China desk officials and those dealing with security policy.[16] In the post-Tiananmen months, for instance, Japan's bankers feared their exposure in China should internal crisis and foreign isolation bring about even partial economic collapse. Their lobbying efforts no doubt speeded the lifting of sanctions and the resumption of aid, although the Foreign Ministry was able to make it appear that Japan was not seriously out of step with the other G-7 members by waiting until the eve of the first United Nations resolutions on the Gulf War before acting.[17] Interests providing plant and equipment to China under Overseas Development Aid (ODA) have had some success in persuading the government to provide further infrastructural assistance and thus create a more favourable environment for direct private investment. In general, Japanese business is heavily reliant on government assistance. To do what it can to promote stability, these and other interests have generally favoured fairly free transfers of technology to China, whereas the Foreign Ministry and the Defence Agency have been more cautious where that technology might have military uses. This has not always been at the behest of the United States or Co-ordinating Committee for Export to Communist Areas guidelines. It is therefore not clear what punitive steps Japan could or would take against China.

Conclusion

While there are complex uncertainties on both sides which defy confident prediction of outcomes, there is nevertheless considerable agreement on broad issues between China and Japan. Both want to expand the present levels of trade and investment and will act together to promote this, as can be seen from Japan's support for China's re-entry to the GATT. Both share an optimism about the prospects for Pacific Basin growth and prosperity and generally support the development of structures that might enhance these prospects, whether or not it is Asia-Pacific Economic Cooperation (APEC) or some other arrangement and as long as it does not exclude them. Both fear protectionism in international trade, although both pursue protectionist policies themselves, and the North America Free Trade Agreement (NAFTA) is therefore viewed with suspicion and alarm. In security matters, there is also some congruence of positions. Despite its fading relevance since 1991, the Security Treaty retains support in that it provides a mechanism for a continued United States regional presence, although for China it is seen as a possible curb on Japan whereas Tokyo hopes it can be invoked against other threats to the peace.

The Washington–Tokyo–Beijing axis that operated in a general sense during the years when Northeast Asia could be described in terms of a quadrangular balance still exists because it has utility for Japan and China. Both are alarmed at the prospect of a nuclear North Korea, more because it would trigger moves for a nuclear capacity in South Korea and Japan. On the other hand, neither shows the enthusiasm of the United States to break the DPRK through economic sanctions, let alone return it to the topography of a parking lot. Both are interested in talks on security and regional arms control. Both continue to support the United Nations, and China softened its opposition to Japanese minesweepers being deployed in the Gulf by agreeing to a Japanese peacekeeping presence in Cambodia, where both countries suffered casualties. China does not support permanent Security Council membership for Japan (or Germany and India) but appreciates its peacekeeping role. Both remain sceptical about Russia's role in the region but the trend is more towards co-operative ventures as China can envisage a future when Siberian and Far Eastern minerals and energy reserves will be needed to sustain domestic development, a conclusion Japan had faced much earlier.

The argument thus far appears dismissive of the possibility of confrontation between China and Japan, but that is not the intention. There are too many uncertainties in the equation and one or more may operate to produce confrontation, although not in the short term. Japan's domestic politics remain uncertain and the search for an acceptable leadership may produce mood swings and a resort to narrow nationalism, much as happened when China's leadership was weak and seeking legitimacy in 1989. Since China must re-enter such a phase with the passing of Deng Xiaoping, the combination could be explosive. The pretexts for confrontation exist over the Senkaku Islands or Diaoyutai. If John Garver is correct in identifying a strong PLA Navy faction, led by Politburo Standing Committee member Liu Huaqing, behind policy in the South China Sea and able to outgun the Ministry of Foreign Affairs, then there is cause for pessimism. The seabed around the Senkaku rocks may also contain mineral and energy reserves which the navy can argue are vital to China's future development and must be secured, presumably by a better funded maritime arm.[18] Allen Whiting, while pointing out that Sino-Japanese relations have not been better since 1972, warns that 'Nationalism is not likely to fade on either side; on the contrary, it is likely to grow in order to bolster the dubious legitimacy of Chinese Communist rule and as a prideful consequence of an expanded Japanese role abroad.'[19]

A final imponderable which makes prediction difficult is the likely course China may take and the extent to which it will remain an integrated, unitary state. It is now clear that the People's Republic is not about to break up in the manner of the Soviet Union. Nor will the Party relinquish political power, despite the succession issue and the immobilism it has created. On the other hand, the centre has lost some of its power over the periphery and parts of the heartland as well. Regions and provinces now enjoy a level of economic power and independence unknown in the past and now seek some control over foreign policy decisions which may affect their interests. Shandong, Liaoning and Heilongjiang had trading offices with South Korea before Beijing deserted the DPRK and recognised Seoul. Shanghai and the coastal provinces have particular interests in opening up to the region and Guangdong does not share Beijing's sense of national honour over Hong Kong if it interferes with existing co-lingual and collinear trading arrangements across the southeast. The province has already defied the centre over new taxation measures and in 1992 bought the oil it was denied by Beijing by chartering tankers and going to the spot market.

Some form of institutional recognition of these realities must come. Provided always that China's ecological decline remains slow and there is no sudden crisis, some form of federalism must emerge eventually. A federal China will be less egalitarian and will not solve the many social problems but it will be easier for Japan to deal with. The general trend will continue to be competitive and often co-operative but the chances of a confrontational or conflictual relationship will be reduced. The current weakness of Russia diminishes the Japanese and United States need for a strong and united China as a counterweight, although complete disintegration would present disastrous consequences. Much depends therefore on the capacity of the post-Deng leadership to reshape the Chinese state and create a new source of political legitimacy. The prospects do not look promising at this stage but may improve once the post-Deng leadership is installed and has time to look beyond the next medical report. Any premature attempts by either Japan or the United States to exploit the situation would open the way for the hardline conservative forces so influential in the PLA to advance a set of narrowly nationalistic policies that would make of China a much more awkward neighbour for the region and a very prickly great power on the world stage.

Notes

1 Gerald Segal, 'The Coming Confrontation between China and Japan?', *World Policy Journal*, vol. 10, no. 2, Summer 1993, pp. 27–32.

2 Much of the foregoing argument draws upon my chapter, 'China and the New World Order', in Richard Leaver and J.L. Richardson (eds), *The Post-Cold War Order: Diagnoses and Prognoses*, Allen & Unwin, Sydney, 1993.

3 Carol Lee Hamrin, *China and the Challenge of the Future*, Westview, Boulder, Col., 1990.

4 *Zhongguo Zingnian Bao* [China Youth Daily], Ideology and Theory Department, 'Realistic Responses and Strategic Choices for China after

the Soviet Upheaval'. I am indebted to Dr David Kelly of the Contemporary China Centre, Australian National University, for his translation.

5 Qimao Chen, 'New Approaches in China's Foreign Policy', *Asian Survey*, vol. 33, no. 3, March 1993, p. 248.

6 Lu Chinyang, 'A Secret History of He Xin, a Newly Elected CPPCC Member ... ', *Ching Pao* (Hong Kong), 10 April 1991; translated in FBIS - *China Daily Report*, 91-073, pp. 26–29.

7 Shen Yun, 'The International Political Environment and Our Modernisation in the Latter Half of the 1980s', *Issues and Studies*, vol. 22, no. 10, October 1986, pp. 132–33.

8 Hua Di, 'China in the 1990s: A Friendly Member of the East Asian Community Confronting the US Superpower', paper presented to the Asia-Pacific Defence Conference 1992, held under the auspices of the Institute of South East Asian Studies (ISEAS), Singapore, 26–28 February 1992.

9 Bonnie Glaser, 'China's Security Perceptions: Interests and Ambitions', *Asian Survey*, vol. 33, no. 3, March 1993, p. 254.

10 Francis Fukuyama and Kongdan Oh, *The US–Japan Security Relationship After the Cold War*, Rand, Santa Monica, 1993, p. 12.

11 Gerald Chan, 'Foreign Policy', *China Report, 1993*, Chinese University of Hong Kong, Hong Kong, 1994.

12 John Garver, 'China and the New World Order', in William A. Joseph (ed.), *The China Briefing 1992*, Westview for the Asia Society, Boulder, Col., 1993, p. 73.

13 Quoted in Christopher Howe, 'China, Japan and Economic Inter-dependence in the Asia Pacific Region', *China Quarterly*, no. 124, December 1990, p. 662.

14 Robert A. Manning, 'Burdens of the Past, Dilemmas of the Future: Sino-Japanese Relations in the Emerging International System', *Washington Quarterly*, vol. 17, no. 1, 1993, p. 53.

15 Motohide Saito, 'Japan's "Northward" Foreign Policy', in G.L. Curtis (ed.), *Japan's Foreign Policy After the Cold War*, M.E. Sharpe for Columbia University, Armonk, NY, 1993, p. 290.

16 Peter Polomka made this useful contribution in discussion.

17 Uldis Kruze, 'Sino-Japanese Relations', *Current History*, vol. 90, no. 555, April 1991, pp. 156–59, 179.

18 John W. Garver, 'China's Push through the South China Sea: The Interaction of Bureaucractic and National Interests', *China Quarterly*, no. 132, December 1992, pp. 999–1028. Garver quotes naval sources arguing in terms of *'lebensraum'* for the Chinese people.

19 Allen S. Whiting, 'China and Japan: Politics Versus Economics', *Annals of the American Academy of Political and Social Science*, no. 519, January 1992, p. 50.

7 Russian Influences and Mutual Insecurity

Greg Austin

Fin de siècle, the mood of decline and loss of optimism which characterised the arts in Europe in the late nineteenth century, is now being replayed in this century in politics — and nowhere with more savage irony than in Russia and the PRC.[1] But this mood might, given its intensity and significance, more appropriately be labelled *fin de millennium*. This last decade of the second millennium is witnessing the final unravelling of the most powerful millenarian movement ever visited upon humanity, in the two countries which for so long were its most devoted advocates and adherents.

Future relations between the two formerly communist giants will be profoundly influenced by this irreversible trend: the collapse of domestic ideology and the remaking of national identity. As of mid-1994, the new national identity both governments were trying to create included notions of global interdependence, economic reform inspired by market forces, need for foreign investment and political liberalisation. The presence of those elements in the new national ideology leads both countries to strive for friendly relations with all major powers, including each other. The persistence of these elements in the emerging national identities will be the main determinant of continuity in relations between the PRC and Russia, and between each of them and the rest of the world. A marked trend away from these liberal-inspired values by either the PRC or Russia would provoke a downturn in relations between it and major Western powers. If the same trend toward draconian rule and a chauvinist, isolationist posture emerged in both countries simultaneously, then the prospects of some sort of entente between the PRC and Russia against Western pressure on human rights must be considered likely.

This chapter looks at three broad outcomes for Russian influence on the PRC's status as a great power in the next decade: normal, correct and co-operative relations; close allies;[2] and bitter enemies. The new starting point for such an analysis as of 1994 has become the close relationship unequalled in its intensity since the 1950s, but one which both sides refuse to characterise as an alliance. Moves toward an alliance or renewed hostility would therefore require a fundamental change of circumstances from that existing in mid-1994.

Approaches to Sino-Russian relations

The political transformations underway in the PRC and Russia have important similarities relevant to any analysis of their future international relations. The collapse of an entrenched totalitarian regime in each is, in several important respects, the same political phenomenon, even though the loss of confidence so prevalent in many parts of Russian society is confined largely to several groups in the PRC — the conservative wing of the Chinese Communist Party (CCP), minority groups, dissident intellectuals and poor peasants and factory workers. Many other people in the PRC are filled with optimism about the imminent end of the communist era, and prosperous economic circumstances in which they find themselves.

The collapse in Russia was accompanied by dramatic events, such as the fall of the Berlin Wall in 1989, the independence of the Baltic Republics in 1991, the August 1991 coup against Gorbachev and the Soviet parliament, and the final breakup of the Soviet Union into independent states based on the constituent republics in December 1991. *But the process of collapse in Russia did not start and end with these dramatic events.* The collapse was gradual, as the Soviet regime itself, through Gorbachev, unleashed a process of political liberalisation that eventually swept it away. And the process of political liberalisation was forced on the regime by the stagnation of the national command economy in the years before Gorbachev came to power.

In the same way as the collapse was a process over many years, the remaking of national identity will be a process over many years, in which a new social contract between the rulers and the ruled will have to be established. As this social contract is negotiated, rulers may come and go, and the terms of the negotiation will be profoundly affected by the economic circumstances of the rulers and the ruled over this formative period. Political stability in Russia is a long way off. The struggle for power in Russia between the democrats and the conservatives has not been resolved, and this domestic power struggle continues to constrain and shape Russian government decisions, particularly in respect of foreign policy.[3]

Similarly, in the PRC, 'the collapse' has been gradual and has been accompanied by dramatic events, such as the forced resignation of CCP Secretary-General Hu Yaobang, the Tiananmen Square demonstrations in 1989, the violent termination of those demonstrations, a possible attempted 'coup',[4] and serious civil disturbances throughout the country. The obsolescence of communist authority in the PRC has been accelerated by the economic and political reforms unleashed by Deng Xiaoping, by the prospects for greater political freedom offered briefly by Hu Yaobang and, to a lesser extent, Zhao Ziyang, and by serious disaffection with rampant corruption. When Deng Xiaoping and Chen Yun have gone, and important restraints are removed from the already naked competition for political power in the CCP leadership, there is a very high likelihood that the struggle to establish a stable social contract in the PRC could be as lengthy a process and as tortuous a route as it has been in Russia.

The scale of the current social unrest in the PRC and the diversity of its causes are so great that it is difficult to accept the line coming out of Beijing that 'the national mood is for a smooth generational transition', that the 'popular feeling is for order and against big change', and that 'any attempt to rock the boat ... will only court strong national indignation'.[5] Even the author of this particular iteration of the CCP line admits that, unless the Party is able to reform itself, and clean politics replace money politics, then the 'boat' will overturn.[6]

The political rivalry in both the PRC and Russia is not just about which side of politics will govern, with particular variants of policy. The political contest is a struggle about what sort of country each should be, about a new national identity. In both countries, the choice is the same: between a fairly rigid authoritarian model, where state interests are paramount and where these are best protected and advanced through a chauvinist ideology of the nation; and, on the other hand, a more liberal model, trying to find greater room for personal freedoms, including freedom of speech, freedom of enterprise and freedom of assembly, in an enlightened and just legal system. The domestic political poles have their counterpart on the international plane: the primacy of state sovereignty, naked, unadorned and unlimited, where power is the primary medium of exchange; contrasted with a more internationalist approach, where peaceful settlement of disputes, recognition of mutual security and some surrender of sovereignty in the interests of international stability are the guiding principles, if not the consistent practice.

The crisis in ideology and identity for the PRC and Russia has removed long-standing points of reference for scholars of international relations and politics, as well as foreign governments keen to anticipate the foreign policies and military strategies of the once great communist powers. And the loss of a reference point does not only apply in isolation to the analytical work of scholars and government officials.

The broader social environment in the industrialised countries which opposed communism with greatest ferocity, at home and internationally, is characterised by the same mood of uncertainty defined in large part by this *fin de millennium*. The final rejection of the legitimacy of communism in the PRC and Russia, and the resultant changes in international affairs, have redefined the spectrum of policy choice and method of justification of it, both in foreign as well as domestic affairs, and in the balance between the priority to be accorded international or domestic issues.

The policy choice in the developed world in respect of international security policy revolves in large part around the two theoretical poles of 'realism' and 'interdependence or new world order': whether a country should expect the great powers to act as they did in the nineteenth century and up to 1945; or whether a country can expect the great powers to act with a sense of enlightened benevolence inspired by notions of common good and sovereign equality. Thus scholars and governments alike are now asking whether we are indeed at the 'end of history' (the optimistic view) or whether we should prepare for a new version of the 'great game' in which balance of power considerations are paramount (the pessimistic view).[7]

Historiography of PRC–Soviet relations has been influenced by perspectives of a romanticised China and a demonised Soviet Union. In particular, the suggestion that the PRC–Soviet military disputes between 1963 and 1969 were caused in the first instance by Soviet pressure on the PRC, and not by the trend towards radicalism in PRC foreign and domestic policy at that time, has left a nearly permanent mark on interpretations of subsequent PRC foreign policy motivations, even though most scholars accept now that the PRC's actions toward the Soviet Union at the time were provocative and were caused in part by domestic political struggles.[8]

Moreover, current realist interpretations remain influenced by the 'all-or-nothing', 'us against them' syndrome so prevalent in Soviet and United States policy preferences during the Cold War, and in the PRC's propaganda about its own independence from the superpowers. In practice, international relationships are more subtle, often highly variable across a broad range of policy choice. Even if countries move toward some sort of alliance, this can have many shades and nuances. The Cold War tendency to relate alliance loyalty to moral choice has blurred the understanding of its essential character, which is mere expediency. Alliances can be comprehensive, embracing all security relationships, or can be more particular, addressing only one mutual security relationship. Moreover, by slight moves in relations with other great powers, one can threaten or feint a change in the global balance of power.

Another new issue of perspective is the importance to be assigned the newly independent countries of Central Asia, where countries such as the United States, Japan and Germany have almost no direct strategic interest, but where Russia and the PRC have fundamental strategic interests, including the most fundamental of all: the security of borders and the national loyalty of the citizens within those borders.

There are competing views in the scholarship on the current direction of the PRC's security thinking. One view is that Beijing is evolving a strategy built on assumptions of interdependence;[9] the other is that the PRC is not posturing for interdependence, but 'seems locked in pre-cold war, almost turn-of-the-century modes of quasi-imperial competition for regional hegemony'.[10] Opinion appears divided by a fairly stark divide: a PRC with internationalist tendencies versus a PRC with chauvinistic tendencies.

This may not so much be the result of one side or the other being wrong, but the relatively subdued attention given to detailed analysis of the likely political fortunes of the two competing tendencies. Closer attention to this question might expose the specific institutional origins within the PRC of statements about international perceptions attributed to the PRC government as a whole. Subsequent assessment of the relative foreign policy influence (current and prospective) of the originators of the statements might throw a different light on the more generalised observations about likely PRC intentions.

Interpretations of the outside world lie close to the heart of Chinese communist ideology, and have therefore figured prominently in the many battles that have left serious scars on the PRC's body politic over the past decades. For example, real or imagined attitudes to the United States ('capitalist road') or the Soviet Union ('revisionism') among CCP leaders have been a cause for political victimisation or a basis for political alignment on a fairly consistent basis since 1959.

In the face of continuing competition in both the PRC and Russia for political ascendancy by groups espousing opposing interpretations of the outside world and the position the country should take on issues such as relations with the United States, and economic liberalisation, the analyst is denied the opportunity of firm precedent in assessing how relations between the PRC and Russia will unfold. This chapter therefore considers alternative outcomes, making plain the important assumptions on which these outcomes would be based, and comments on the sorts of consequences that might flow from the alternative outcomes. The ultimate variables for PRC–Russian relations will be the fate of the domestic political order in both countries. Other important variables include the domestic political circumstances in Mongolia, Kazakhstan and Xinjiang; and regional strategic stability in Northeast Asia. This chapter assumes continuity in the international trading and fiscal system, and broad continuity in the international policies of the United States and the European Community.

Close relations: The new starting point

Few people would describe the current relationship between Russia and the PRC as an alliance: neither government chooses to characterise it thus as of mid-1994.[11] The Russian Ambassador to Beijing, Rogachev, has supported the public PRC position that relations between the two countries should not harm the interests of any third country.[12] This was emphatically reiterated during talks between Boris Yeltsin and the Secretary-General of the Chinese Communist Party, Jiang Zemin, in September 1994. Foreign Minister Qian Qichen told journalists that 'the two sides will not counteract each other, but they will not make a bilateral alliance either'.[13]

The official PRC view is that bilateral relations entered a new phase after President Yeltsin's visit to the PRC in late 1992, when healthy and stable development of mutual co-operation became the guiding principle.[14] The visit to Russia by Jiang Zemin in 1994 was further testimony to this.

Russia and the PRC signed a 'Joint Declaration on the Basis of Relations' during Yeltsin's visit in December 1992. The agreement provides that neither party should join any military or political alliance against the other, nor harm the sovereignty or security interests of the other.[15] While the PRC may not want to regard this document as a treaty, it has the same effect. The Russian newspaper *Izvestia* described it as such,[16] and it has the same language as a treaty between the PRC and Mongolia signed in April 1994.[17]

Apart from the normalisation of trade opportunities and issues that once set the two countries at loggerheads — especially the border demarcation — prospects for a thriving but non-alliance relationship are based on Russia's desire for Chinese investment and labour in return for transfer of high technology, most notably in energy development and military equipment.[18]

The joint communiqué issued at the end of the visit to the PRC by Russia's Prime Minister, Chernomyrdin, in May 1994, demonstrated the quickening pace of a very productive and fruitful relationship, including co-operation in sensitive areas such as border delimitation, military and public security affairs.[19] During Jiang Zemin's visit in September 1994, several more agreements were signed, including a comprehensive document on principles for deepening bilateral relations.[20] The PRC and Russia held their first consultations on consular affairs (since the collapse of the Soviet Union) in May 1994.[21] Li Peng was scheduled to visit in 1995.

In June 1994, the two countries agreed on the alignment of the western section of the border, after the fifth round of talks established specifically for this purpose.[22] By that time, the PRC and a group of the four former Soviet republics which border on the PRC, including Russia, had completed twelve rounds of talks on border delimitation and confidence-building measures.[23] The two countries have exchanged 'basic data' on border deployments.[24]

Trade between the two countries enjoyed spectacular growth between 1991 and 1993, with the PRC becoming Russia's second biggest trading partner (after Germany) in 1993.[25] Russia ranked seventh on the PRC's list of international trading partners in 1993.

Military trade and co-operation are of considerable importance. Whether the report of Russian approval of PRC manufacture of SU-27 aircraft[26] proves to be accurate, the PRC was determined, as of mid-1994, to purchase large amounts of Russian military technology and equipment. Other aspects of bilateral military cooperation were also improving. For example, in May 1994, the PRC Navy sent three ships to Vladivostok for a goodwill visit, reciprocating a similar visit in August 1993 by three ships from Russia's Pacific Fleet to Qingdao.[27]

Investment was also growing rapidly by 1994. For example, in the Khabarovsk region, by January 1994, 199 PRC-funded enterprises (144 joint ventures and 55 wholly PRC owned) had been established on the Russian side of the border area, accounting for 45 per cent of the total number of foreign-funded enterprises, although total capital of US$11 million represented only 10 per cent of the region's registered total assets.[28] In March 1994, the State Council developed a three-year plan on aid to Russia in the light industry, food and textiles sectors.[29]

Both sides looked to an intensification of the relationship, particularly in trade and economic co-operation,[30] exploiting as fully as possible the advantages of contiguity.[31] The PRC asserted the need for good PRC–Russian relations as arising not only from the fundamental interests of the two countries but important for global strategic reasons.[32]

By the time Jiang and Yeltsin signed the joint statement on deepening relations in September 1994, the two countries were ready to commit themselves to joint action on a number of fronts. These included co-operation in the reform processes in the two countries; solving residual border demarcation disputes; no first use of nuclear weapons; a commitment not to target strategic nuclear weapons against each other; a quicker pace in border disarmament and mutual confidence-building measures; carving out a new role for the United Nations; and mutual support in opposing 'expansionism' — that is, the United States policy of exerting pressure on foreign governments to advance what it sees as appropriately democratic and liberal values, particularly in the field of human rights.

The two governments committed themselves to work together as great powers in addressing security problems, both at the global level as well as in the Asia-Pacific region. Specific issues identified included proliferation of 'weapons of mass destruction and relevant delivery vehicles'.

Yet the increasingly productive relationship between the PRC and Russia is not all sweetness and light. The first quarter of 1994 showed a sharp turnaround in trade between the two countries, with a drop of 43.5 per cent over the same period in 1993.[33] By mid-year, the scale of the drop for the first half of the year was still of much the same order: 39 per cent.[34] There has been a decline in Russian visitors to the PRC since May 1993, with figures for the first six months of 1994 showing a decline of 39.5 per cent from the same 1993 period.[35]

There are differences over the number of PRC citizens in Russia, with Russian legislators keen to restrict the number of Chinese in Russia. Some 2.5 million people reportedly crossed the border in 1993,[36] and illegal immigration (Chinese citizens in Russia) is now a serious problem. The management of the relationship by the two governments was criticised by the Chairman of the Foreign Affairs Committee of the Russian Duma for lacking a co-ordinated long-term strategy.[37]

Suspicions clearly remain on both sides, as evidenced by the PRC's failing to take up Soviet and Russian proposals since 1990 to cut forces on their common border, particularly forces assigned to the military regions (beyond 100 kilometres from the border where the main disparity in forces — in the PRC's favour — lies).[38] There are also technical difficulties such as distinguishing regular units from other kinds of armed forces. (Most of China's 50 000 troops within 100 kilometres of the border are People's Armed Police or militia units, compared with 150 000 regular Russian troops or heavily armed border guards within 100 kilometres on the other side.) Nevertheless, these suspicions are probably more in the nature of doubts about the possibility of an eventual return to the acrimony and confrontation of the past than about any fear that this is either imminent or likely.[39]

Alliance and internationalism in PRC security thinking

In mid-1994, the PRC government's declared line on foreign policy was to pursue independence in international affairs and opposition to membership of alliances.[40] This foreign policy line, echoed consistently in official PRC statements, was laid down by Deng Xiaoping, according to a probably reliable report. Deng reportedly told the Standing Committee of the Politbureau of the Chinese Communist Party in April 1994 that it was 'not advisable to be impatient to establish partnership or treaty relations' with Russia. He is reported to have said, 'I think for quite a long time to come there will not be major conflicts between China and Russia.' This was consistent with the general line he reportedly outlined in December 1990 to high-level figures of the CCP: 'We fear nobody, but we offend nobody. We handle affairs in accordance with the five principles of peaceful coexistence ...' He described the essence of this strategy in September 1989: 'First, observing coolly; second, securing our position; third, dealing with things calmly ... attending to our own affairs ...'[41]

An example of the new non-threatening line in official PRC foreign policy can be seen in the 1992 Joint Declaration of Non-aggression with Russia. It is also visible in the replacement of the 1960 Treaty of Co-operation and Mutual Assistance with Mongolia by a Treaty of Co-operation which was signed in Ulaanbataar on 29 April 1994.[42] The PRC still has serious concerns about the political loyalties of inhabitants in its inner Mongolia area, and some concerns about Russia's long-term position, but was prepared to surrender what it had regarded in 1960 as an important tool to guarantee its interests in Mongolia in the face of Soviet pressure. The new treaty (Article Four) committed both parties to the policy line of no military or political alliances. A similar border treaty between the PRC and Kazakhstan was signed by Li Peng and President Nazarbaev in Almaty on 26 April 1994.

The consistent trend by China towards settlement of border disputes with most of its neighbours — a trend in place since the mid-1980s — is also testimony to China's 'good neighbourly' policy, not just in words but in deed.[43] The PRC has moved to settle or defuse all border conflicts and territorial disputes, the only possible exception being the dispute over the Spratly Islands in the South China Sea. Yet, even there, the PRC's motivation can be attributed mostly to its judgment that it needs to use limited force to give credibility to its claim. The PRC has not taken any action since 1988 which might be construed as attempting to dislodge the military forces

exotic

of any rival claimants. The PRC and Vietnam have jointly reaffirmed their stand to resolve territorial disputes peacefully, and widen economic and cultural relations.[44]

But evidence for the even handed and 'non-offensive' line in PRC foreign policy can be found in the relatively good relationships with the rest of the world, including the United States after the September 1994 visit of United States Commerce Secretary Ron Brown to the PRC.[45]

The basis for the PRC's current line of following an independent strategy could flow from assessments of the new international order after the end of the Cold War, where greater fluidity, inconsistency and uncertainty exists in inter-state relations. For example, one *People's Daily* commentator observed:

> Gone are the days when a clear line between friend and foes could be drawn and confrontation between groups could be seen. A new picture, more complicated and characterised by a condition in which one is neither friend or foe or both friend and foe has emerged. Proceeding from their own basic interests, Russia, the United States, and other major western powers attack, defend, charge, and retreat in the big chess board of international politics.[46]

The Foreign Minister, Qian Qichen, reported to a Party meeting that the current world is proceeding in the direction of multipolarisation, with various political forces disintegrating and realigning, producing 'drastic and complicated changes'.[47] A number of commentators in the PRC talk as if the end of the Cold War brought little joy for the world. For example, the view is commonly expressed that 'the United States and Russia are on guard against each other and suspicious about each other'.[48] There are warnings of the re-emergence of European fascism and Russian chauvinism, and assertions that United States strategic interests are still very much tied to Europe. In particular, there is a view that the 'geopolitical interests of Russia and the United States ... remain unchanged'.[49]

The need for the PRC to remain independent is not a sudden innovation in PRC foreign policy flowing from the end of the Cold War.[50] As a rhetorical element, it has been present since the end of the Sino-Soviet alliance, and has meant different things at different times. But in its current meaning, of 'no political alliances', and normalised relations with all great powers, this line has been followed in word and deed since the early 1980s — when it began to be fairly clear that the old order in Russia was undergoing substantial change. It was in this period that PRC military pressure on Vietnam's border took a noticeable downturn.

A robust or strident approach to respect for sovereignty remains an important element of PRC foreign policy. This was visible in its approach to United States pressure for sanctions over North Korea's refusal to apply internationally acceptable safeguards to its nuclear facilities. Yet, even here, the PRC's position in key votes was to abstain, rather than vote against sanctions.[51] The PRC's action on the United Nations Security Council resolution approving Chapter VII sanctions against Iraq for its refusal to withdraw from Kuwait in 1991 was to abstain, not use its veto power.

This highlights the essential new element in the PRC's official foreign policy since the end of the Cold War: desire to avoid confrontation ('offend nobody'). Qian Qichen has advocated to a closed Party meeting a calm approach ('it is important to take advantage of all favorable factors and get rid of unfavourable ones to create a peaceful environment'), one that would not unnecessarily put China into a position of open strategic enmity with any country.[52]

The PRC government has not only pursued Deng's line of 'offend nobody', but has gone somewhat further. Another aspect of the current declared foreign policy line is to rely on the United Nations' system and to exploit the end of great power hostility to craft a stable international environment, to 'make efforts together with all UN member states to establish a new international political and economic order'.[53] People with fairly strong internationalist tendencies, such as the Foreign Ministers of the two countries, Kozyrev and Qian Qichen, currently dominate the foreign policy apparatus. Qian Qichen talks of a 'virtuous cycle of mutual promotion' between economic stability and political development in the Asia-Pacific region.[54] The political leaders of both countries look to maximise their country's international authority in a world in which they do not yet see a serious international threat to their security and where close co-operation with other great powers is seen as the best way of maintaining that position.[55]

Both Russia and the PRC are comfortable with the international security structure established after the Second World War by the victorious allies — the United Nations system which accorded the great powers (Russia and China included) superior standing in global management through permanent membership of the Security Council and the attendant veto power. Both Russia and the PRC are comfortable with the principles of common security which relegate unqualified views of national interest (and realist theory) to second place.[56]

With the collapse of messianic communism,[57] all of the great powers have fairly happily returned — for the moment, at least — to this system set up by the Allies, who styled themselves as the 'united nations'. Once again, therefore, Russia and China (this time, the PRC) are allies in this very important sense, as part of a re-emerging system of common security.[58] Thus, notwithstanding the claims by the two countries that their relations will not be to the detriment of third parties, they are linked by a shared commitment to great power (Security Council) intervention in the affairs of lesser powers. Of course, the level of intervention which the PRC would tolerate in the internal affairs of other countries is much lower than that favoured by the United States, but PRC claims to be pursuing a foreign policy which places the sovereignty of other countries as the supreme value are not borne out by its actions.

It would not be uncontroversial to characterise the operating principles of the new alliance[59] of which Russia and the PRC find themselves active partners.[60] One thing is clear, however. The principle of unlimited state sovereignty, which for so many years underpinned and constrained the operations of the United Nations Security Council, and which was a fundamental tenet of Soviet and Chinese approaches to international law, has now been sufficiently diluted in recent practice to allow a more vigorous and arguably more effective role for the Council in enforcing a collective security regime.[61]

The move by the PRC and Russia to a more accommodating position — in fact, a well integrated position — in respect of a common body of international law is a far cry from the days when both states rejected 'bourgeois international law' as something not applying to them. This move has not been a recent one. In the case of the Soviet Union, the trend became noticeable in the immediate aftermath of the Second World War, with more hopeful signs of consolidation through the 1970s, and a high point in Gorbachev's declarations in the second half of the 1980s concerning a common humanity with common interests. In the PRC's case, the move only really began in the early 1980s after the economic and political reforms launched by Deng Xiaoping in 1978 began to take hold, and the effects of 'open door' policy began to be felt.

The new internationalist position of the PRC since 1981 has been well sketched by Samuel Kim, who describes it as a 'mixture of the Westphalian sovereignty-centered and UN Charter-based world order systems'.[62] PRC foreign policy has relaxed its concept of absolute state sovereignty (except where its suits it for domestic purposes, especially in respect of human rights), and moved to a position of active support for United Nations peacekeeping operations.[63]

The political will among other permanent members of the Security Council, and other important governments, such as Japan and Germany, to reinforce this trend of integration of the Soviet Union (later Russia) and the PRC into global governance faltered badly in the late 1980s. By 1994, that reluctance seems to have faded substantially, with the PRC firmly in APEC, and Russia a 'partner for peace' with NATO, an 'associate' member of the G-7 plus one, and a member in waiting for APEC.

A most remarkable aspect of the move by the PRC and Russia into the system of co-operative global governance is that it has been at a time when the United States, the former great nemesis of both and now sole superpower, was in charge — standing and crowing as victor in the Cold War, and prepared to lead the United Nations Security Council on uncharted paths. The preparedness of both the PRC and Russia to co-operate in an international security directorate led by the United States has considerable weight as evidence of the strength of the new quasi-alliance tying Russia and the PRC together. The domestic political risks to which the governments of both countries have exposed themselves by pursuing this course stand as testimony to the importance of the trend (and also to the reality that the trend remains hostage in part to domestic politics and will take some time to consolidate).

Thus, the first question about the future course of PRC–Russian relations is not whether the two countries will form some exclusive alliance directed against other great powers, but whether the existing great alliance — however loose, fragile or newborn — will fracture, remain intact or gain in strength.

Failure to appreciate the significance of this trend has marked scholarly analyses of PRC foreign policy for the most part, and this failure stems from the persistent, but incomplete Cold War images of PRC politics and the scope of an alliance.[64] Of course, both the PRC and Russia have signalled the limits to their tolerance of the United States vision of intervention in their own domestic affairs, and this fact will remain an important counterweight to any new internationalist tendencies in either country.

Oppose the United States — the chauvinist element?

In fact, there is a view in the PRC that its foreign policy is too passive, that it does not give enough backbone to the PRC's position internationally, and that the government may be too positively disposed to the United States. This view has gained ground since the United States' shift to confrontation with the PRC over issues that the United States was prepared to leave under the table during the Cold War.

The People's Liberation Army (PLA) General Staff and the Policy Research Office of the Central Military Commission have called for Chinese leadership of a global united front against hegemony, interference, subversion and aggression[65] — all code-words for activities currently being undertaken or mooted by the United States.[66] This line is apparently in direct contradiction of the policy of the Standing Committee of the Politbureau, which has determined that while such a front already exists, and while its work is complementary to the PRC's foreign policy aims, the PRC should definitely not be the leader of such an organisation. Qian Qichen was reportedly excluded from a meeting of party secretaries and propaganda chiefs at which Hu Jintao and the Chief of the General Staff, Zhang Wannian, made strident speeches against United States policies of interference. Zhang is reported to have said: 'We shall not challenge other nations, but we must keep our strength in order to defeat the challenge from hegemonism and colonialism.'[67]

It is not just that these party and military officials were concerned merely about United States pressure on the PRC, such as linkage between renewal of most favoured nation (MFN) status for the PRC and its domestic human rights policies, but the Clinton doctrine of 'expansion', the United States policy which seeks to go beyond containment and force an expansion of the liberal democratic regime to non-democratic countries. The groups were calling for a new policy, openly advocating what Deng Xiaoping had himself explicitly opposed: Chinese leadership of a political alliance of 'antihegemonic' countries. Deng reportedly opposed this because of the risks associated with tying China's international prestige and standing to such a group. In 1993, 100 military officials had petitioned Deng for a revision of the PRC's policy towards the United States.

The new, hostile sentiment toward the United States does not equate to support for an alliance with Russia, but it does provide some basis for it in the future. Advocates of an anti-United States posture in foreign policy are obviously positioned closer to this outcome since Russia has not — in recent years at least — interfered in PRC domestic policy in the same way as the United States. The fact that the actions by the United States between 1989 and 1994 have squandered a good deal of positive sentiment among the younger, reform-minded officers of the PLA will probably affect relations between the two countries in the next decade more than the period of bitter Sino-Soviet relations (1965–69) because that bitter period, now 25 years distant, may well be understood, at least implicitly, by most officers in the PLA, to have been caused by the radical policies of the Cultural Revolution period. Moreover, bitter historical memories — as often as not irrelevant to whether states form alliances — can be reshaped.[68] As Chi Haotian put it:

> The Russian people and Armed Forces have accomplished great achievements in the war against fascism. Both China and Russia should make their own contributions to enhancing the traditional friendship between the Chinese and Russian peoples …[69]

It is almost certainly the case that some influential people in the PRC see a closer relationship with Russia as some form of protection against United States pressure. An account of leadership views published in a Hong Kong newspaper in mid-1994 has 'some party, government and military elders' supporting the development of 'good neighbourly relations' with Russia, in contrast to what the article describes as Deng's 'unique view'.[70] Two of six reasons given by informed sources for the PRC's interest in a new closer relationship with Russia related to containing hegemony and power politics or curbing United States hegemonic strategy toward the PRC. The final reason given was that Russia's advanced science and technology and advanced military equipment are precisely what China needs in its economy and national defence.

The strong interest of elements of the General Staff and the Ministry of National Defence in a stronger military element in the relationship with Russia is evidenced by a proposal submitted in March this year to the Central Committee of the CCP, the Central Military Commission and the State Council. The proposal called for exchanges in intelligence, technology, high-level visits and military academy cadets.[71]

It is difficult to see any difference in the rhetoric used by Deng Xiaoping and Jiang Zemin in respect of the importance of good relations between the PRC and Russia, and in respect of good relations between the PRC and the United States. For example, Jiang spoke to Henry Kissinger in May 1994 in the following terms:

> China and the United States bear an important responsibility for the future of the world and the destiny of mankind … Although there are some disputes … efforts should be made to improve relations between

them ... In the past, Sino-US relations developed more smoothly when-ever both sides were able to overcome their differences in social systems and value concepts ... and treated each other on an equal footing.[72]

While several PRC leaders have called for the handling of the bilateral relationship with Russia 'strategically with an eye on the 21st century',[73] the same language has been used of the PRC's relationship with Japan.

Yet the prospect of a serious breach in relations between the United States and the PRC has clearly been signalled. Jiang was telling Kissinger that unless the relationship was managed with the 'foresight of a strategist' and the 'courage of a statesman', the 'very profound' historical lessons about setbacks and regressions in United States–PRC relations would repeat them-selves with important consequences for 'world peace and stability'. There was clearly a propaganda element on this line, in terms of the MFN threats being made by the United States at the time. But Jiang's reported remarks reflect the tone of private Central Committee documents and work in schol-arly institutes about the long-term trends in United States policy towards China: that it is becoming the new 'hegemon'. Even Qian Qichen charac-terised United States policy as a factor of instability in the Asia-Pacific.[74] Some PRC leaders recall the great impact on the international situation of the close relations ('the alliance'?) with the Soviet Union in the 1950s.[75]

A move by the PRC and Russia to form a close alliance would be a sign of recognition by at least one of them that without the alliance it is unable to defend its interests against encroachments by other powers; and that the threat of such encroachments provides an important opportunity for the other to enter into an alliance.

It would not be unreasonable to suggest that the PRC and Russia have a very strong interest in an alliance to enable each to 'secure the periphery'. This is a motivation attributed by some diplomats in Beijing to China's inter-ests in close relations with Russia.[76] As Professor Harry Rigby put it, 'West Turkestan (Kazakhstan) is now liberated, East Turkestan (Xinjiang province) is not.'[77] Both the PRC and Russia face a decade of social upheaval in which the identity of each nation-state faces significant threats. This process was unleashed in Russia in 1991 with the collapse of the Soviet Union and the demise of the communist political system. The process is threatened in the PRC as the economic liberalisation breeds radical calls for political liberal-isation and direct physical threats to the internal security regime of the gov-ernment. To the extent that other great powers demonstrate any serious interest in exploiting these pressures, as recent United States administra-tions have done, and as subsequent administrations are likely to do, then con-siderable potential exists for an alliance between Moscow and Beijing.

But such an alliance, founded solely on a defensive reaction to internal security pressures, is likely only in the event of direct foreign involvement in the domestic political processes or the coming to power in both coun-tries of politicians who falsely claim such intervention. While prominent Russian and Chinese politicians have railed against United States interference in the domestic affairs of their countries, both governments have consistently demonstrated a surprising and increasing level of tolerance for such interference. This new tolerance stems from the dependence of both the PRC and Russia on the goodwill of other major powers for economic and technological assistance. And in both countries, certain political forces favour such intervention, since they see it as advancing their own political purposes.

As of mid-1994, the PRC probably felt it had the measure of the United States government, and that the United States would have to abandon its policy of pressure. Some PRC government sources were claiming that the country's growing economic strength and successful diplomacy had overcome the isolation forced on it by the United States and others in 1989.[78] Yet it was not entirely convinced that this would come about, assessing that if the United States persisted with its policy of 'global democratisation' on its own terms, then the prospects for continuing international co-operation would be gloomy.[79]

In any event, while the views of the PLA generals remain of considerable importance, the broader PRC interests in access to United States assistance, technology and markets will probably continue to have a more effective constituency in PRC power politics. This outcome has already been foreshadowed in the formulation in current PRC policy that the PRC will continue to oppose 'hegemonism', but only on specific issues, thereby avoiding the unnecessary consequences that flow from targeting a particular country.[80]

Thus, as of 1994, the main import of the prospect of alliance between Russia and the PRC remained its value to both countries as an implied threat, a remote but not impossible condition to which either could threaten to move, if the other great powers (the United States, Japan, the European Community) do not give either of them what it wants. It may be no coincidence that the closer ties between Russia and the PRC, and the agreements on technology and arms transfers, occurred at a time when the United States was denying the PRC access to military technology, and after a period of severe chill in the PRC's relations with the other great powers.

Fundamental changes: The variables and a ten-year prognosis

The circumstances in which the Russian and PRC governments now find themselves, in terms of their ability to influence both international and domestic order, are likely to worsen, and each government will be in similar positions of contested domestic legitimacy, notwithstanding the great disparity between their economic productivity.

In the case of the PRC, the contest of legitimacy comes from two sources: one within the Communist Party (the conservatives) and the other in the

society at large, from those groups seriously disaffected by the social contract (liberals, minorities and poor workers). Political stability would therefore depend on both the defeat of the conservatives and the creation of a
new social contract. The prospects for either outcome are not good in the
short term. Sustained efforts by Deng Xiaoping since 1980 to give the PRC
a new political system and new operating principles succeeded in producing a vigorous progressive momentum, but were met at almost every stage
with strong opposition. Once Deng passes from the scene, the absence of
such a powerful figure will compound the deep divisions existing within the
Party. Since the reformist tendency in the Party at present has no visible
claim on the PLA, the internal security apparatus or the propaganda organs,
there must be little hope for their early victory. Internationalist tendencies
in PRC foreign policy are likely to be subdued in such circumstances.

If there was a strong move away from the internationalist tendency, the
PRC is more likely to return to its traditional doctrine of robust independence and uninhibited sovereignty rather than look for a great power ally,
such as Russia.

Russia, for its part, is likely to want to keep its border with the PRC as stable as possible for a number of years, in the face of mounting secessionist
threats from within Russia, and intractable problems of political instability
in some of the southern Muslim republics. Some prospect of a break with the
PRC must, however, exist if the chauvinistic line in Russian politics becomes
dominant. In such circumstances, the question of border delimitation and
illegal immigration may be exploited to create difficulties with the PRC.

If, within five to ten years, a new social contract is established in the PRC
— perhaps a federal political system and more equitable distribution of
power and income — then the importance of the secure northern and northwestern borders will have less domestic significance and relations with
Russia would probably receive less priority, but in all likelihood would
remain normal.

If both the PRC and Russia respond to their political crises with force
and suppression, then the two countries will find common ground in opposing efforts by other great powers to interfere in their domestic politics on
human rights grounds. Yet even the likelihood of such suppression on the
part of the PRC will be reduced after Deng Xiaoping dies. It was Deng after
all who steeled the Party to dare to use force against the demonstrators in
Tiananmen Square: 'do not fear bloodshed,' he told them.

A serious political crisis in Mongolia, Kazakhstan or Xinjiang, if it involved
any threat to domestic political stability in the PRC or Russia, or to the survival of one of the two governments, would almost certainly provoke a re-
evaluation of PRC–Russian ties. A chauvinistic government in the PRC or
Russia (by definition, seeking to isolate itself from the world) could attempt
to exploit such a crisis to put pressure on the other, but it is more likely that,
for both countries, stability in these border countries will remain a common
security interest. The prospect of co-ordination of policy between the PRC
and Russia in such circumstances will be strong.

A major change to regional strategic stability in Northeast Asia, such as the withdrawal of United States forces accompanied by an increase in Japan's military spending, or the reunification of Korea, might provoke new interest in an alliance between the PRC and Russia. Yet even those sorts of changes are unlikely to adversely affect the relative power of the PRC to the point that it feels itself forced to abandon its traditional doctrine of an independent foreign policy.

Very close relations with Russia, verging on a quasi-alliance, might be considered by some in the PRC to give it a freer hand to take military action against Taiwan, but there is little evidence for this.

Conclusion

Prospects for a continuation of close, co-operative relations between the PRC and Russia are very good for the next few years. The only circumstance likely to dim those prospects is the early coming to power in Russia of a chauvinist government which seeks to revive border disputes or provoke further unrest in the already unstable PRC provinces. Yet even a chauvinist Russian government would have interests in common with the PRC government in the immediate future, and both governments would look to a continuation of close relations as part of a strategy to 'secure the periphery'. Mutual concern over the threat of any pan-Turkic or pan-Islamic political movement affecting border security or territorial integrity will be a powerful force keeping relations between the PRC and Russia at a very good working level.

The scope of PRC–Russia relations in the next few years will be comprehensive. They will include military co-operation, some disarmament measures and military sales. But it is more than likely that both governments will avoid any appearance of a formal alliance in order to keep open their access to the capital, technology and markets of the United States, Japan and the European Community. Some difficulties, such as illegal immigration, will arise from time to time but will probably only serve as temporary obstacles to good relations.

If the United States returns to an aggressively interventionist foreign policy (Clinton's 'expansion' doctrine) to the disadvantage of the PRC, there is every likelihood that the PRC will move toward a policy of 'opposing the United States'. An unambiguous move by the PRC to align itself against United States interests would signal acceptance (probably quite reluctant) that the diplomatic, economic and technological gains to be had from close relations with the United States were outweighed by corresponding gains to be had from aligning with anti-United States countries.

The implications of such a move would probably be a strengthening of relations between the PRC and Russia , based on the PRC's need to get access to relatively modern technology. But Russia will have little else to offer the PRC, except a commitment to a peaceful border and military technology. In fact, the PRC will continue for some time to be a source of assistance for Russia.

It is indisputable that talk of alliance between Russia and China has a different substantive content in an era where interdependence has become more than a theory, where interdependence is in fact a goal that both the PRC and Russian governments have actively pursued and continue to pursue. The PRC might seek an alliance with Russia to protect itself from United States blandishments and pressure, but the scope of that alliance would be confined to narrow economic co-operation as long as the Russian government continued its current policies of active co-operation with the United States.

In the longer term, if the political circumstances in the PRC turn in favour of the liberal outcome, and those in Russia continue on a downward trend of economic and political instability, the closeness of relations between the two countries will fade, probably quite dramatically.

The period of close relations will represent an enhancement of the power of the PRC, but there are now few signs that over the next decade the PRC will seek to utilise its enhanced power to the disadvantage of regional stability. Domestic political and economic stabilisation will remain profoundly consuming preoccupations and provide a solid basis for a consolidation of Deng's line of 'offend nobody'. This line, while not typical of PRC foreign policy in the past, is equivalent to normal participation in the civilised community of states. It is in this respect that we can now evaluate the PRC's relations with Russia.

Notes

1 In this chapter, the term 'PRC' is used instead of China to refer to the country ruled by the national government in Beijing.
2 The essence of an alliance is the fact of 'alignment', not the mechanism by which the 'alignment' is recorded. See George Liska, *Nations in Alliance — The Limits of Interdependence*, Johns Hopkins Press, Baltimore, 1962, p. 12.
3 See Mette Skak, 'Post-Soviet Foreign Policy: The Emerging Relationship Between Russia and Northeast Asia', *Journal of East Asian Affairs*, vol. 7, no. 1, Winter 1993, pp. 137–85.
4 Wen Shi 'Newsletter from Beijing', *Ming pao* (Hong Kong), 4 December 1992, p. 9, translated in JPRS-CAR-093 (Joint Publications Research Service), 11 December 1992, p. 40 quotes a CCP document to the effect that Yang Baibing, a PLA general who was formerly General Secretary of the CCP's Central Military Commission and former Director of the PLA's General Political Department, held a military meeting without authorisation in an attempt to 'usurp Army leadership' and tried to change the leadership with Jiang Zemin at the core into a Party central committee under the command of military forces. The incident reportedly happened at the time of the 14th Party Congress, and was engineered by the political commissar of the Beijing Military Region, Zhang Gong.
5 Ma Zhongshi, 'China Dream in the Global 1990s and Beyond', *Strategic Digest*, January 1994 , p. 71. The article is reprinted from the PRC journal

Contemporary International Relations, vol. 3, no. 7, July 1992. This line is common amongst the privileged members of PRC society and Party members.

6 ibid., p. 77.

7 An excellent overview of the competing analyses as they apply to Northeast Asia can be found in Skak, 'Post-Soviet Foreign Policy'. A recent alarmist commentary on the strategic policies of the PRC can be found in Larry M. Wortzel, 'China Pursues Traditional Great Power Status', *Orbis*, vol. 38, no. 2, Spring 1994, pp. 157–75.

8 Most studies of Sino-Soviet relations seem to give some weight to the view that the PRC's foreign policy after 1978 was heavily influenced by fear of the Soviet Union. See, for example, David Shambaugh, 'China's Security Policy in the Post-Cold War Era', *Survival*, vol. 34, no. 2, Summer 1992, p. 90; and Michael Yahuda, 'Deng Xiaoping: The Statesman', *China Quarterly*, no. 135, September 1993, p. 561. A contrary view, suggesting that PRC concern with a Soviet threat at the time of greatest PRC tilt toward the United States was disingenuous, is given by Sheng Lijun, 'China's View of the War Threat and its Foreign Policy', *Journal of Northeast Asian Studies*, vol. 11, no. 3, Fall, 1992, pp. 47–69.

9 Bonnie S. Glaser, 'China's Security Perceptions: Interests and Ambitions', *Asian Survey*, vol. 33, no. 3, March 1993, p. 268.

10 Larry M. Wortzel, 'China Pursues Traditional Great-Power Status', *Orbis*, vol. 38, no. 2, Spring 1994, p. 157.

11 The Secretary General of the Chinese Communist Party, Jiang Zemin, described relations during the visit of the Russian Prime Minister, V.S. Chernomyrdin, in May 1994 as 'mutually beneficial cooperation in various fields': 'Jiang Zemin Meets Russian Prime Minister', *Xinhua*, 27 May 1994, FBIS-CHI-94-104, 31 May 1994, p. 10. Russia's President Boris Yeltsin proposed to Jiang in early 1994 that the two countries develop a 'constructive partnership', which is presented by Russian officials as 'a normal relationship of good neighbourliness': '*Xinhua* Interviews Russia's Chernomyrdin on Upcoming Visit', *Xinhua*, 25 May 1994, FBIS-CHI-94-102, 26 May 1994, p. 7.

12 '*Renmin Ribao* Interviews Russian Ambassador', FBIS-CHI-94-111, 9 June 1994, p. 4.

13 ITAR-TASS news agency (World Service), Moscow, 4 September 1994.

14 'Jiang Zemin Meets Russian Prime Minister'.

15 Ya-chun Chang, 'Peking–Moscow Relations in the Post-Soviet Era', *Issues and Studies*, vol. 30, no. 1, January 1994, p. 90.

16 ibid.

17 'Text of Amity, Cooperation Treaty', *Xinhua*, 29 April 1994, in FBIS-CHI-94-084, 2 May 1994, p. 16.

18 '*Renmin Ribao* Interviews Russian Ambassador', p. 4.

19 '*Xinhua* Publishes Sino-Russian Communiqué', FBIS-CHI-94-104, 31 May 1994, pp. 11–12. One section reads:

> The two sides positively appraised the ongoing negotiations on borders and cutting the military presence in the border areas and enhanc-

ing mutual trust in the military field; and agreed to stick to the provisions in the agreement on the eastern section of the Sino-Russian border, be willing to continue talks on the left-over border issues, and speed up preparation for the agreement on the western section of the Sino-Russian border. The two sides believe that it is of great significance to reach an agreement as soon as possible on cutting the military presence by both sides in border areas and enhancing trust in the military field. (p. 11).

The agreement on the eastern section of the border was reached in May 1991, with a settlement still to be made for two small areas (one near Khabarovsk, the other near the Ergun River).'

20 The text was carried by *Xinhua* Domestic Service in Chinese on 3 September 1994. See BBC *Summary of World Broadcasts.*

21 'Beijing, Moscow Consult on Consular Affairs', *Xinhua*, 13 May 1994, in FBIS-CHI-94-094, 16 May 1994, p. 7.

22 'China, Four CIS States End Fifth Round of Border Talks', FBIS-CHI-94-115, 14 June 1994, p. 8.

23 'Border Disarmament Talks Held with Four CIS States', FBIS-CHI-94-114, 15 June 1994, p. 14. A thirteenth round has since been held.

24 'Border Troop Information Exchanged with Russia', *Lien Ho Pao* (Hong Kong), 5 May 1994, p. 9, in FBIS-CHI-94-088, 6 May 1994, p. 8.

25 Bilateral trade in 1992 was US$5.862 billion, an increase of 50 per cent over the 1991 figures for PRC–Soviet trade. In 1993, the figure reached US$7.679 billion, an increase of 30.9 per cent over 1992. 'Russian Minister Davydov Views Sino-Russian Trade', FBIS-CHI-94-102, 26 May 1994, p. 9, broadcast of *Xinhua* Domestic Service, 25 May 1994.

26 'Russia to Grant License to Manufacture SU-27 Fighters', FBIS-CHI-94-102, 26 May 1994, p. 10 citing Hong Kong newspaper article, Kuo Hung-chih, 'Russia to Authorise China to Manufacture Sukhoi-27 SU-27 Fighters', *Lien Ho Pao*, 26 May 1994, p. 9.

27 'Naval Task Force Reportedly Enroute to Vladivostok', broadcast of an article by Lin Kang, 'Chinese Naval Task Force to Visit Russia for First Time', *Lien Ho Pao*, 12 May 1994, p. 1, in FBIS-CHI-94-092, 12 May 1994, p. 12.

28 '"Newsletter" Depicts Economic Cooperation with Khabarovsk', FBIS-CHI-94-101, 25 May 1994, p. 10, Broadcast of *Xinhua* Domestic Service, 23 May 1994.

29 Jen Hui-wen, 'China's Strategic Considerations in Developing Sino-Russian Relations', *Hsin pao* (Hong Kong), 27 May 1994, p. 34, in FBIS-CAI-94-105, 1 June 1994, p. 11.

30 See, for example, the account of Li Peng's views in 'Premiers Hold Talks', *Xinhua*, 27 May 1994, in FBIS-CHI-94-103, 27 May 1994, p. 10; 'Jiang Zemin Holds Talks with Delegation', *Xinhua*, 16 May 1994, in FBIS-CHI-94-094, p. 6; and 'Qiao Shi Meets Russian State Duma Delegation', *Xinhua*, 14 May 1994, in FBIS-CHI-94-094, 16 May 1994, p. 7.

31 *'Renmin ribao* Interviews Russian Prime Minister', p. 4. The Russian Prime Minister observed that the two countries had yet to exploit the advantages of contiguity.

32 See, for example, the account of Li Peng's views in 'Premiers Hold Talks', *Xinhua*, 27 May 1994, in FBIS-CHI-94-103, 27 May 1994, p. 10.

33 'Russian Minister Davydov Views Sino-Russian Trade', FBIS-CHI-94-102, 26 May 1994, p. 9, broadcast of *Xinhua* Domestic Service, 25 May 1994. Both countries were inclined to regard this drop in trade as a temporary phenomenon which could be overcome. However, questions about trade diversion for hard currency by both countries and availability of better quality goods from other markets suggest that the drop may not be as short-lived as the two countries might like.

34 Reuters, 16 August 1994, citing PRC customs figures.

35 ibid.

36 'Legislator Says China "Foreign Policy Priority" for Moscow', *Xinhua*, 13 May 1994, in FBIS-CHI-94-095, 17 May 1994, p. 11.

37 'Russian Parliament Hearing Views Ties with China', *Xinhua*, 7 May 1994, in FBIS-CHI-94-092, 12 May 1994, p. 13.

38 'Border Troop Information Exchanged with Russia', from the Hong Kong newspaper *Lien Ho Pao*, 5 May 1994, p. 9, in FBIS-CHI-94-088, 6 May 1994, p. 8.

39 For an account of these sorts of concerns, see Glaser 'China's Security Perceptions', pp. 254–56; and Shulong Wu, 'The PRC Girds for Limited, High-Tech War', *Orbis*, vol. 38, no. 2, Spring 1994, pp. 182–83.

40 The PRC Permanent Representative to the United Nations, Li Zhaoxing, affirmed this line in an address to a forum in Washington on 5 May 1994, saying that China will never participate in any political or military blocs, is opposed to power politics (that is temporary alliances), and follows a path of independence in foreign policy by 'opening up in all directions' — an allusion used often by PRC leaders from Charles de Gaulle's policy '*a tous azimuths*'. 'Envoy to UN Addresses Forum, Notes Beijing's Foreign Policy', Beijing Central People's Radio in Mandarin', 6 May 1994, FBIS-CHI-94-089, 9 May 1994, p. 2.

41 'Article Views China's Policy on Ties with Russia', a broadcast of an article from a Hong Kong newspaper, *Xin Bao*, 'Beijing's Strategic Considerations in Developing Sino-Russian Relations' written by Jen Huiwen in Beijing on 25 May 1994, FBIS-CHI-94-105, 1 June 1994, p. 11.

42 'Text of Amity, Cooperation Treaty', *Xinhua*, 29 April 1994, in FBIS-CHI-94-084, 2 May 1994, p. 16.

43 For example, in April 1994, the PRC signed a new agreement with Laos and Burma demarcating the triborder point. See 'Tripartite Border Agreement with Laos, Burma', *Xinhua*, 8 April 1994, in FBIS-CHI-94-069, 11 April 1994, p. 9.

44 Qimao Chen, 'New Approaches in China's Foreign Policy — The Post-Cold War Era', *Asian Survey*, vol. 33, no. 3, March 1993, p. 247.

45 The visit was marked by subdued United States interest in PRC human rights issues, and talks of a possible visit by President Clinton.

46 'Article Views American-Russian Relations', *Renmin ribao*, 4 June 1994, p. 6, 'International Forum' column by Gu Ping, FBIS-CHI-94-110, 8 June 1994, p. 3.

47 'Qian Qichen Views International Situation', *Xinhua*, 10 June 1994, FBIS-CHI-94-112, 10 June 1994, p. 1.

48 '*Liaowang* Views US Strategic Focus', FBIS-CHI-94-087, 5 May 1994, p. 15, text of broadcast of article by Wang Shu, 'Is the US Strategic Focus Shifting Eastward', *Liaowang*, no. 17, 25 April 1994, p. 61. See also Liu Yongping, 'Has US–Russian "Partnership" Matured?' *Shijie Zhishi*, no. 5, 1 March 1994, pp. 2–4, in FBIS-CHI-94-102, 26 May, 1994, p. 6.

49 'Article Views American–Russian Relations', p. 3.

50 See, for example, Thomas Fingar (ed.), *China's Quest for Independence: Policy Evolution in the 1970s*, Westview Press, Boulder Col., 1980.

51 For example, on 10 June 1994, the PRC abstained on a vote in a meeting of the Board of Governors of the International Atomic Energy Agency to suspend non-medical forms of technical assistance to North Korea. See FBIS-CHI-94-113, 13 June 1994, p. 5.

52 'Qian Qichen Views International Situation'.

53 See Li Zhaoxing's remarks, 'Envoy to UN Addresses Forum, Notes Beijing's Foreign Policy', p. 2.

54 'Qian Qichen Speaks at Asia-Pacific Security Symposium', *Xinhua*, 11 May 1994, FBIS-CHI-095-091, 11 May 1994, p. 4.

55 The great alliance between the Soviet Union and the PRC in the 1950s was based at least in part on a shared messianic, universalist ideology that tended to confound, if not counteract, narrow preoccupation with individual national interest. The grounding of current PRC and Russian officials in the internationalist or utopian ideology may have left an idealistic stamp on their current foreign policy practices not quite matched in the case of United States officials raised in the 'realist' tradition.

56 That the Cold War, and the messianic ideology of communism, came between the former allies does not alter this fact. The surprise is that the architecture of the international security system devised in the 1940s in the form of the United Nations Security Council survived into the 1990s.

57 The PRC is struggling to keep some modified version of communism alive and has abandoned all thought of exporting it.

58 Some commentators have preferred the term 'collective security', which they see as more limited in scope than the more utopian 'common security'.

59 The new alliance has substantially differing foundations than the United Nations system established in 1945. The prospect then of a concert of great powers (only the victorious ones) organising the affairs of a post-war world of vast and largely self-contained colonial empires has almost

no commonality with the international system in prospect for the third millennium. This system is marked not so exclusively by a small number of great powers in contact (or conflict), but over 200 individual national societies connected through vast networks of trade, investment, financial dealing, information exchange, and social ties arising from migrations on a scale previously unknown and unimagined. Ernst-Otto Cziempiel, 'Internationalizing Politics: Some Answers to the Question of Who Does What to Whom', in Ernst-Otto Cziempiel and James N. Rosenau (eds), *Global Changes and Theoretical Challenges — Approaches to World Politics for the 1990s*, Lexington Books, Lexington, 1989, p. 32, makes the point that we should give up the concept of the state and the terminology that has traditionally accompanied it in international relations theory because reality knows only political systems interacting with their societal environments and providing one medium for 'demand conversion' for their societies on the international stage.

60 Perhaps they include the following: armed aggression by one community or state against another should be reversed by the international community if possible; great powers should not exploit domestic politics of others for strategic gain; and civil revolution arising from the exercise of democratic principles, recognition of human rights, and the rule of law is in fact a good thing notwithstanding the pain and threats that go with it, and notwithstanding differing interpretations of how human rights should be protected by a society.

61 The radical departure from the operating principles of the United Nations in the current world order is that the firm rule against intervention in the internal affairs of other states has been abandoned. The United Nations has intervened in civil wars, such as in Bosnia, and in the internal military policies of states, such as North Korea's nuclear intentions, in ways that were not acceptable to most United Nations members in 1945 or for most of the time since then.

62 Samuel S. Kim, 'Mainland China and a New World Order', *Issues and Studies*, vol. 27, no. 11, November 1991, p. 1.

63 As Kim points out, in 1981 the PRC voted for the first time in support of a peacekeeping force, and in 1988, with Soviet prodding and support, sought membership of the United Nations' Special Committee on Peacekeeping Operations: ibid., pp. 11–12.

64 This assertion will no doubt be controversial. But for two accounts which illuminate this view, see Qimao Chen, 'New Approaches in China's Foreign Policy', and Sheng Lijun, 'China's View of the War Threat and its Foreign Policy'.

65 The supporters of the global united front claimed the support of more than 20 countries for the specific proposal.

66 In June 1994, 80 PLA generals, including some of the highest rank, wrote a joint letter to the Politbureau complaining that the United States had never stopped its attempts to subvert, penetrate, interfere in and under-

mine China. See Jen Hui-wen, 'China Insists Foreign Countries Should Accord Li Peng Equally Courteous Reception', *Hsin pao* (Hong Kong), 8 July 1994, p. 23, FBIS-CHI-94-134, 13 July 1994, p. 2.

67 'Military Said Behind "Hard-Line" Policy on US', FBIS-CHI-94-087, 5 May 1994, p. 13, text of a broadcast of an article from the Hong Kong paper *Cheng Ming*, no. 199, 1 May 1994, pp. 10–12. Much of the information in the article is sourced to the General Office of the Central Military Commission.

68 As Coral Bell has pointed out, the United States and Japan formed an alliance only six years after their bitter war; and the French and British governments signed an alliance treaty with West Germany a decade after their bitter war. Comments to a seminar at the Australian National University, 25 August 1994.

69 'Discuss Ties in Moscow', *Xinhua* Broadcast, FBIS-CHI-094-94-135, 14 July 1994, p. 5.

70 'China's Strategic Considerations in Developing Sino-Russian Relations', pp. 10, 11.

71 ibid.

72 'Jiang Zemin, Kissinger Discuss Sino-US Relations', Beijing Central Radio, 12 May 1994, FBIS-CHI-094-093, 13 May 1994, pp. 10–11.

73 'Jiang Zemin Meets Russian Prime Minister'.

74 'Qian Qichen Speaks at Asia-Pacific Security Symposium', *Xinhua*, 11 May 1994, FBIS-CHI-095-091, 11 May 1994, p. 4.

75 ibid. See also 'China's Strategic Considerations in Developing Sino-Russian Relations', p. 10.

76 'China's Strategic Considerations in Developing Sino-Russian Relations', p. 11.

77 Comments to a seminar at the Australian National University, 25 August 1994. Rigby was not expressing sympathy with this view, but rather illustrating the important threat the PRC now faces in its province of Xinjiang.

78 See Jen Hui-wen, 'China Insists Foreign Countries Should Accord Li Peng Equally Courteous Reception'; and Sa Benwang, 'The Expansionist Strategy Practised by the United States is Impeded', *Liaowang*, no. 26, 27 June 1994, pp. 58–59, FBIS-CHI-94-136, 15 July 1994, pp. 3–5.

79 See Sa Benwang, 'The Expansionist Strategy Practised by the United States is Impeded', p. 5.

80 See Qimao Chen, 'New Approaches in China's Foreign Policy', p. 243.

8 India's Relations with China Post-Soviet Union: Less Co-operation, More Competition

J. Mohan Malik

Introduction

In early September 1993, India and China signed an agreement 'to maintain peace and tranquillity' along their disputed Himalayan border. This agreement requires both sides to respect the Line of Actual Control (LAC) — that is, maintain the status quo, pending a peaceful, final boundary settlement and reduce military forces along the border in accordance with the principle of 'mutual and equal security'. The agreement was described as 'a significant step forward' in Sino-Indian relations.[1] It was a logical culmination of developments since the late 1980s, including the visit of India's premier to Beijing in 1988 and the reciprocal visit of China's premier to New Delhi in 1991; the dramatic changes in the post-Cold War global strategic environment; and the overall improvement in relations between China and India.

However, the fact that Sino-Indian relations today seem to be better than at any time during the last four decades should not lead one to assume that all the hurdles in the relationship have been overcome. This chapter examines the factors underlying the current *detente* and argues that Asia's two regional heavyweights are poised to become rivals for regional dominance and influence in the multipolar world of the twenty-first century.

Sino-Indian dialogue: An exercise in conflict management

Sino-Indian relations have been soured by several issues, notably the rejection by the Chinese of the British-drawn McMahon Line of 1914 separating Tibet and India, the flight of the Dalai Lama to India in 1959, and the dispute remaining from the 1962 Sino-Indian border war — in which China occupied 14 500 square miles of territory in the Ladakh region of the Jammu and Kashmir state. Since the 1962 war, relations between the two Asian giants have been characterised by mutual antagonism, rivalry, distrust and hostilities. The Sino-Pakistani alliance further exacerbated rivalry between the two most populous countries of the world. Border skirmishes took place in 1965 during the India–Pakistan War and in 1967 on the Sikkim–Tibet border. Relations were revived in 1976 with an exchange of ambassadors, but there was no meeting of minds. Throughout the 1970s and 1980s, China aligned itself with Pakistan and the small neighbouring states of Sri Lanka, Nepal and Bangladesh to undermine India's attempts to establish its regional predominance in South Asia. India responded by establishing closer ties with China's rival in Indochina and Vietnam, and expressing support for the Hanoi-backed Hun Sen government in Cambodia.

Following exchanges at Foreign Minister level in 1979 and 1981, both sides agreed to negotiate a solution to the boundary dispute. Eight rounds of talks were held between 1981 and 1987, without success. The period from June 1986 to May 1987 saw a marked deterioration in Sino-Indian relations over alleged Chinese intrusions in Sumdorong Chu Valley, renewed tension and armed clashes on the border, and a fresh spate of accusations and warnings from Beijing. Tensions were defused, however, through high-level dialogue. At the eighth round, held in November 1987, a decision was reached to upgrade the level of talks from the bureaucratic to the political level. During Indian Prime Minister Rajiv Gandhi's official visit to China in December 1988, both sides agreed to a joint working group to create conditions for 'a fair and reasonable settlement' and 'to maintain peace and tranquillity in the border region'.[2] The two countries also agreed to improve bilateral relations. Agreements were signed to establish direct commercial flights and to increase scientific, technological and cultural exchanges.

Many observers have long argued that since neither India nor China would ever give up the areas they occupy at present, the most feasible settlement would be the acceptance by both sides of the existing Line of Actual Control, with some minor adjustments in the eastern and western sectors. After all, the possession of Aksai Chin in the western sector is as vital for China as possession of Arunachal Pradesh is for India in the eastern sector. Since a negotiated border settlement has proven to be too difficult to achieve, the two sides have now decided to put it on the back burner. The 'peace and tranquillity' agreement signed by Prime Minister Narasimha Rao and Premier Li Peng in September 1993 should be seen as an acceptance of 'ground realities' by Beijing as well as New Delhi.

A Sino-Indian rapprochement?

In the post-Cold War world, India and China find themselves at the receiving end of changes in the global strategic environment. Deprived of the benefits of the bipolar world, where New Delhi and Beijing could maximise their leverage and independence, they see themselves as victims of geopolitical movements that have realigned the political landscape. Beijing has been resentful of Washington's pronouncements on the issues of human rights, weapons sales, nuclear technology transfers and trade issues. India, long allied with the Soviet Union, has been thrown off balance by the disintegration of its former ally. It has come under pressure from Washington on a range of issues — from nuclear weapons and missile proliferation to intellectual property rights and economic liberalisation. Both are concerned that the industrialised North is setting the international economic and political agenda 'in total disregard of the developing world's interests and views' on issues such as environment, human rights, non-discriminatory access to technology and a new world order.[3] China and India suspect that the basic premise of American strategy in the post-Cold War world is 'to prevent the emergence of any great power that can challenge American dominance in Europe or in Asia'.[4] Both are keen to emerge as independent power centres in a multipolar world, which means a world where America's relative power declines and regional powers dominate in their respective spheres of influence.

While in the long term China sees its strategic military prowess and growing economic power as offsetting American hegemony, in the short term Beijing sees its role as the leader of a bloc of nations challenging American supremacy.[5] It is against this background that China sees some benefit in making common cause with India so as to resist 'arm-twisting' by the United States. Chinese leaders reportedly told the visiting Indian president that 'if Third World countries like China and India did not unite and co-operate they would be "left behind", and "bullied" by others'.[6] While pointing out the differences in the Indian and Chinese political systems, the Indian side agreed that 'as great and ancient civilisations', India and China 'cannot be told what to do' by the United States on subjects such as human rights.[7] Apparently, with the disappearance of a countervailing power in the former Soviet Union, the two Asian giants do see some mutual gain in co-operating to match the United States in Asia.

However, India's desire to mend fences with China extends beyond the need to counter the United States-dominated world order. Bereft of Soviet military and diplomatic support, India is working on new alignments and security arrangements to assert itself in Asia. Given its deteriorating relationship with Pakistan in recent years, a crucial step for India is to improve relations with China.[8] From New Delhi's perspective, a durable peace with China will help India concentrate on the more vexatious internal security problems in Kashmir, Assam and elsewhere and on its poor relations with Pakistan. Detente with China affords the opportunity to free up at least two-thirds of the Indian mountain divisions on the Chinese borders. The redeployment of five of these divisions and a half dozen fighter squadrons on the India–Pakistan border is supposed to give India a decisive military edge over Pakistan and help in counter-insurgency (COIN) operations in Kashmir.[9] Besides, the acquisition of electronic and photo-intelligence capabilities of surveillance on the Chinese border has imparted a sense of security and confidence in the Indian defence establishment which now feels that 'the short-term Chinese threat is all but over'.[10]

Like India, China has its own separatist problems in Tibet and Xinjiang and is aware that the biggest threat to its security comes from within and not from without.

This is not to say that the post-Cold War world has turned the two 'natural rivals' — India and China — into 'natural allies'. Post-Cold War realism demands peaceful coexistence with old enemies finding new areas of common interest. What it has shown them is that their common interests are likely to outweigh their differences, at least over the next decade.[11] A number of developments indicate a warming of relations between the two Asian giants: for the first time, Beijing has promised not to use 'the Pakistani card' against India, and offered 'flexibility' on Sikkim. More importantly, the Chinese have adopted a neutral stance on the Kashmir dispute, favouring a bilateral India–Pakistan negotiated solution. In return, India has reassured China on the Tibetan question.[12] Chinese naval vessels called at Indian ports for the first time in December 1993 and talks have been held to promote defence co-operation between the two countries.[13]

These developments have led some observers to speculate whether Beijing has finally come round to accepting the idea of some sort of cross-recognition of spheres of influence: China's acceptance of Indian pre-eminence in South Asia in exchange for Indian acceptance of Chinese pre-eminence in Southeast Asia.[14] One analyst wonders whether the next logical step would be to reach a similar tacit understanding to delineate naval spheres of influence between the northern Indian Ocean and the South China Sea.[15]

Indian perspectives on Sino-Indian relations

Following the end of the Cold War and the bipolar system, New Delhi is trying to come to terms with what it sees as a shifting, but complex and potentially troublesome, security environment. India's military planners visualise a multipolar world in the twenty-first century, with the likely emergence of several new powers in the Asia-Pacific, such as China, Japan and India. New Delhi is keen to carve out a large sphere of Indian influence stretching from the Persian Gulf to the Straits of Malacca. India's actions in Sri Lanka (1987–90) and the Maldives (1988) are a manifestation of its desire and capability to emerge as an independent power centre in the emerging multipolar global power structure by the early twenty-first century. However, it is clear to the policy-makers in New Delhi that the realisation of this objective is dependent, to a great extent, upon three variables: the management of India's relations with other great powers (especially the United States and China); the resolution of India's internal security problems; and the success of its ongoing economic reforms.

Conversations with India's China-watchers, the Ministry of External Affairs (MEA), Defence Ministry officials and opinion makers reveal that given the new strategic realities, there is a general support for the Indian government's efforts to improve relations with China. However, when it comes to the future direction of Sino-Indian relations, differences exist within the Indian defence and foreign policy establishments. Whereas the foreign policy makers are quite upbeat about India's relationship with China, defence planners remain very cautious.[16] An overwhelming majority of Indian policy-makers and analysts fear China's expansionist ambitions and want to keep a close eye on developments across the Himalayas. Of particular concern to New Delhi is the challenge China's growing economic and military power might pose for India's own aspirations for regional leadership.[17] While Indian academics like Giri Deshingkar believe that increasing cultural and economic links will enhance mutual understanding, defence planners voice concern over a Chinese superpower.

Some Indian commentators fear that Chinese nationalism could be more threatening to its Asian neighbours than was Chinese communism, and that a wealthy, powerful China will assert itself in world affairs as every other powerful nation has done. Amidst all the euphoria about the twenty-first century being the 'Asian-Pacific Century', some Indians wonder what that would mean for their country. They point out that the Chinese do not talk about the next century as being an 'Asian Century'; they talk about the next century as the 'Chinese Century'. Unless Japan and India respond to the growing power of China, China will dominate the whole of the Asia-Pacific region and become increasingly influential beyond it. This, it is argued, 'must not be allowed to happen'. Indian analysts believe that there are only two alternatives before the Asian countries: either accept Chinese hegemony or take steps to contain and balance Chinese power. New Delhi hopes and believes that the latter alternative would be more acceptable to China's neighbours. Sooner rather than later, the region will have to evolve counterweights to China. India, which has the size, might and numbers of China, seeks to manoeuvre itself into a dominant position in order to offer itself and, more importantly, be seen as a counterweight to the Chinese power in Asia.

Indians are also optimistic that a shared interest in containing China's growing economic and military influence in Asia would cement India's relations with the United States, Japan and ASEAN countries. The improvement in Indo-United States relations since the end of the Cold War has led some observers to conclude that changing strategic realities would encourage the United States to look for an alternative Asian power to contain Chinese and Japanese influence. Washington's growing economic and military ties with New Delhi indicate that United States strategic planners also feel that a co-operative relationship with a regional power like India could be mutually beneficial in the long term.[18] In short, New Delhi wants United States economic and military help in gaining and maintaining pre-eminence in the region as a counterweight to China. India now supports the American presence in Southeast Asia to contain Chinese influence.[19] While New Delhi may express outrage over American concern for the human rights situation in Kashmir or over nuclear and missile proliferation in South Asia, there is no enthusiasm for a joint platform with the Chinese against the United States — India's largest trading partner and the source of much-needed capital, investment and advanced technology.

In the long term, Indians maintain that a powerful China will force the Japanese to play a greater military role, while China's actions in the Spratlys or elsewhere will require them to seek co-operation with ASEAN and India to counter China. They see in the geostrategic location of the two countries — India southwest of China and Japan northeast of China — a facilitating factor in bringing the two together to contain the rising power of greater China.[20] Unlike the East Asians, Indian strategists welcome a greater Japanese military profile in the Asian region to counter the Chinese. Furthermore, Indian policy-makers would like New Delhi, Tokyo, Hanoi and Jakarta to co-operate on policy towards the world's fastest-rising power which is 'a challenge as much in military terms as in economic terms'.[21] To this end, India is also keen to establish closer ties with fast-growing East Asian countries. New Delhi has repeatedly expressed its desire to become a formal dialogue partner of the Association of Southeast Asian Nations (ASEAN) and to join Asia-Pacific Economic Co-operation (APEC).

Strategically, Indian defence planners are very wary of China's growing military strength. Indian strategists feel that the military equipment that a 'cashed-up' China is acquiring from Russia and other countries would upset the balance of power in Asia by the end of the decade.[22] Of particular concern is China's air and naval buildup. In a recent interview with *Jane's Defence Weekly*, Indian Air Force Chief S.K. Kaul said: 'It is a militarist China' that 'India has to watch over the next decade.'[23] Following the withdrawal of the Soviet and American fleets, India's powerful navy was hoping to fill the vacuum in the Indian Ocean which it has long viewed as 'India's Ocean'. However, China's recent forays into the Indian Ocean have challenged that assumption as well.

Pakistan's China connection, coupled with the growing insurgency in Kashmir, worries Indian policy-makers. Despite Chinese assurances not to play 'the Pakistani card' against India, Indian strategists believe that China will continue to prop up Pakistan so as to tie down Indian military assets on the India–Pakistani border.[24] Nor is New Delhi optimistic about curbs on Chinese arms sales to India's other smaller South Asian neighbours which are seen as nothing less than 'pitching an armed dragnet around India'.[25] After all, it is through these arms sales that China has come to have 'a finger in every geopolitical pie from North Korea to Burma'.[26] Furthermore, while India's economic problems have slowed down, and its military expansion and internal security preoccupations have constrained the country's ability to play a wider role in the broader Asian region, China has raced ahead.

A majority of India's China-watchers and opinion-makers challenge the prevalent view that an economically strong China will enhance peace and stability in the region.[27] One article in *Indian Defence Review* cautioned that though China has been very careful to adopt a non-threatening posture, 'there is no cause for lowering armed guard at a time when China is determined to achieve superpower status' and the focus of its defence strategy is shifting from its northwestern border to its southeastern borders.[28] India's military has also kept a close eye on China's aggressive posturing on the Spratlys since 1988 which shows Beijing's willingness to use force to settle territorial disputes. As Denny Roy has observed:

China's current 'open door' orientation should not be misinterpreted: Beijing tolerates interdependence with its potential enemies because this is at present the best way of hastening economic development, which will increase China's security in the long term. But the cooperative posture which China favors at this stage of its development in no way rules out a resort to force in the future.[29]

Many maintain that India cannot pin too much hope on the current phase of the Sino-Indian detente because China is known to befriend enemies in times of adversity. As one Asian diplomat pointed out, the dramatic improvement in Sino-Indian relations occurred in the immediate aftermath of the Tiananmen Square massacre when the communist regime in Beijing was feeling isolated and vulnerable. But in future, the chances of an economically and militarily powerful China taking more interest in India's neighbourhood are assured, particularly if its designs are frustrated in Southeast Asia by Japan and/or ASEAN.

As regards the Sino-Indian dialogue, many observers believe that China has gained at India's expense during recent high-level talks.[30] For example, Beijing's attempts to create the impression of a common Sino-Indian front on human rights during Premier Li Peng's visit to New Delhi in December 1991 drew sharp criticism from the Indian media and opinion-makers.[31] That is why, at the September 1993 Rao–Li Peng meeting, the Indian External Affairs Ministry spokesman was at pains to stress that human rights issues were not a problem for India because '[w]e're a democracy and they're not'.[32]

India's China-watchers also draw attention to the anti-India tirade in the official Chinese press which continues to highlight India's troubles with its South Asian neighbours while downplaying India's socio-economic achievements since independence.[33] The press in China has also remained conspicuously indifferent to the recent visits of Indian prime ministers and president. Besides, New Delhi maintains that the Chinese fail to sufficiently appreciate 'the complex nature of India's problems with its South Asian neighbours'. Chinese academics, who generally reiterate the official line, continue to criticise India's 'hegemonic behaviour' in South Asian academic forums. Furthermore, China is perceived as willing to co-operate with India only on specific issues considered important to Beijing, such as human rights, environment and American hegemony, while doing little to assuage India's security concerns by curbing arms sales to Pakistan or making its intentions clear in Burma. Nor is Beijing willing to endorse India's bid for permanent membership of the United Nations Security Council.[34]

And finally, like other Asians, Indians are concerned that their northern neighbour would undergo a major political transition which could produce instability at home and more aggressive policies abroad. However, unlike East and Southeast Asians who worry more about the destabilising consequences (for example, refugee flows) of a weak, unstable post-Deng China, Indians believe that a strong China would constitute a greater threat than a weak, unstable China.

But though the faultlines of suspicion and mistrust still run deep between New Delhi and Beijing, India's elite understands that New Delhi would gain little from direct confrontation with Beijing. As a prominent China-watcher and politician, Subramaniam Swamy, remarked at the time of heightened tensions in 1987: 'China is our competitor, not Pakistan. We have to find common ground with China to regulate this underlying competition. Otherwise, there will be "cut throat" competition. We must know where to punch China, and when to roll with it.'[35] India's determination to develop a degree of regional dominance comparable with China means that, some time early next century, New Delhi might slip into the role of the main counterweight to its giant neighbour.

Chinese perspectives on Sino-Indian relations

Chinese leaders and strategists have time and again pointed out that China would not be satisfied with merely being a second-rate power or a regional power but would like to become a world economic and military power.[36] Many Chinese analysts see the recent changes in the global and regional strategic environments as providing a window of opportunity for the Chinese leadership to claim the Middle Kingdom's 'rightful' place in the regional and global power structure. At the same time, the Chinese also want to thwart attempts by other countries to form a formal or informal alliance against the 'China threat'. Beijing's 'peace and friendship' diplomacy reflects this concern.

Chinese policy-makers and foreign policy analysts, given their deftness in playing balance of power games, have always been strong champions of a multipolar world. A multipolar world system is supposed to give the Chinese more opportunities to enhance their country's leverage and international role by exploiting contradictions and differences among their friends and enemies. Since regional rivalries and jealousies between China and its major neighbours are unlikely to diminish in the post-Cold War world, China's strategists want to form 'balanced relationships' in which major powers in the region — the United States, Russia, China, Japan and India — may keep each other in check.[37] These relationships, the Chinese argue, will 'no longer [be] based upon confrontations aiming at weakening any side. Rather ... [these relationships would allow] both competition and cooperation'.[38] Richard K. Betts has called this strategy 'containment without confrontation — polite containment which need not preclude decent relations'.[39] China's decision to mend its fences with India (and other Asian countries) is undoubtedly motivated by this foreign policy framework.

During their summit meetings with Indian leaders, the Chinese have proposed a united front for opposing Western interference in the internal affairs of developing countries; for upholding the principle of inviolable state sovereignty; for working towards the establishment of a multipolar world; and for opposing the Western stance on human rights and environment protection. With India's support, China has obtained observer status in the Non-Aligned Movement.[40] China's fears of increased instability and turbulence, both internal and external, following the Soviet fragmentation, probably added further incentive to its search for a tranquil environment with India. At a time when Chinese foreign policy is driven by its economic interests and is focused on the United States and East Asia, it is clearly in China's interests to keep its western and southern frontiers quiet.[41]

Despite a significant thaw in Sino-Indian relations, China remains apprehensive about India's backing for the Dalai Lama and Tibetan resistance. Chinese strategic literature continues to list India as one of China's most likely opponents in regional conflicts on China's southern borders in the 1990s and beyond (the others being Vietnam and Taiwan).[42] A Chinese strategist told the *Far Eastern Economic Review*: 'We still regard India as a threat because they still occupy Chinese territory, though not as ominously as a few years ago'.[43] One Chinese South Asian analyst, Ye Zhengjia, cautions that a key objective of India's revamped China policy is a desire 'to isolate Pakistan in the new international environment'.[44] Chinese analysts believe, perhaps rightly so, that China serves as a convenient tool for the Indian military to justify its high defence expenditure and regional hegemonic policies. Chinese strategists are also increasingly questioning India's view of its status in the Indian Ocean. A high-ranking People's Liberation Army (PLA) officer and Director of the Chinese Academy of Military Sciences, General Zhao Nanqi, was quoted in 1993 as saying that China would extend its naval operations farther than the South and East China Sea to check attempts by India to 'dominate' the Indian Ocean and other regional waters. Accusing India of seeking to develop a navy to rival that of 'large global powers', General Zhao said that 'this is something which we cannot accept ... we are not prepared to let the Indian Ocean become India's Ocean'.[45]

Another 'problem', from Beijing's perspective, is that, while China looms large in Indian policy considerations, India does not occupy such an important role in China's foreign policy agenda. China has always seen itself as a superpower and Chinese policy-makers, who always compare their country with the United States, France, Britain, Russia and Japan, regard comparisons with India as demeaning to their country's status. They continue to 'think of India as weak and divided and economically such a catastrophe'.[46] From Beijing's perspective, a great power must have multidimensional capabilities — economic, military, technological, political and diplomatic — or what they call the 'comprehensive national strength' (*zhonghe guoli youshe*). By these standards, China's India-watchers believe that, despite India's ambition to become a great power like China, it falls short because of its poor economic performance, weak political system, chronic social instability and failure to convince other Asian nations of its paramountcy.[47]

Beijing's rhetoric regarding a new democratic and egalitarian international political order notwithstanding, the status-conscious Chinese also view with concern Indian (and Japanese) demand for permanent membership of the United Nations Security Council. This is understandable because such demand has the potential to seriously undermine China's status as the sole representative of Asian interests in the world organisation and undercut China's regional and global influence. Chinese attitudes towards India have been succinctly summed up by Gary Klintworth: 'China perceives India to be an ambitious, overconfident yet militarily powerful neighbour with whom it may eventually have to have a day of reckoning.'[48]

Sino-Indian rivalry

The foregoing analysis shows that multiple objectives underlie Beijing's courtship of New Delhi and vice versa. The recent momentous changes in the global and regional strategic environment have undoubtedly facilitated improvement in Sino-Indian relations in recent years. But there is certainly no reason to expect a revival of Nehru's heady dreams of Indian–Chinese brotherhood. Other factors, apart from the territorial dispute, contribute to the fractious Sino-Indian relationship. These include the anti-Indian overtones of China's ties with South Asian neighbours, arms sales (especially the supply of nuclear and missile technology to Pakistan, Saudi Arabia and Iran), asymmetry in international status, unrest in Tibet, China's refusal until recently to recognise Sikkim as part of India, nuclear and naval competition, great power ambitions and a rivalry for the leadership of the Third World. Even if the territorial dispute were resolved, India and China would retain a competitive relationship in the Asia-Pacific region.

Indeed, no possible boundary agreement would reduce the need for deployment of Indian armed forces along the Chinese frontier. The underlying power rivalry between the two Asian giants, and their self-images as natural great powers and centres of civilisation and culture, will continue to drive them to support different countries and causes. India will strive to emerge, not only as an independent power centre in the multipolar world, but as a counterweight to Chinese power and influence. For this reason, Indian strategists have always held that India's military strength and strategy should be seen 'in relation to the People's Republic of China'.[49]

Conversely, China's ambitions as a global and regional power and as a Third World standard-bearer bring it into competition with India's similar ambitions. For their part, the Chinese are equally anxious to assert their power and expand their influence — in other words, fill the 'power vacuum' in the Asian region — to counteract similar moves by other regional powers at a time when the superpowers are in a 'state of withdrawal'. Inevitably, these factors introduce a more competitive aspect into the Sino-Indian relationship.

Therefore, the current phase of detente in Sino-Indian relations should be seen as a short-term tactical move on the part of both countries at a time of their vulnerability in a United States-dominated unipolar world. Sino-Indian rhetoric notwithstanding, their declared goal to establish 'a new structure of international relations involving a new set of alliances' is likely to remain what it is — a goal. Both need the West — and its capital and technology — more than they need each other. Both are scrambling to step into the power vacuum that would be created if Washington should withdraw from the region — or at least be in a position to block the other from doing so. Both remain suspicious of each other's long-term agenda and intentions, and both see themselves as newly rising great Asian powers whose time has finally come. The game of encirclement and counter-encirclement has by no means come to an end with the end of the Cold War. On the contrary, the old balance of power game between India and China seems to have acquired a fresh lease of life in post-Cold War Asia (witness Burma and Mongolia). China's and India's preference for a balance of power approach in interstate relations inevitably leads them to provide military/political support to those countries which can serve as a counterweight to the perceived enemies and rivals of each other.[50] Their rivalry for hegemony in South Asia, Southeast Asia, Indochina and Central and Inner Asia is coming into sharper focus with the lifting of the United States–Soviet shadow from Asia. Over the next decade, a serious contest is shaping up between Asia's two giants — both in the military and economic spheres. However, this contest for influence will be accompanied by sincere efforts to maintain peace on their disputed border and increase bilateral cooperation.

Nuclear and missile competition

Contrary to common perception of the India–Pakistan nuclear contest, India's nuclear and missile capabilities owe much to the dynamics of Sino-Indian rivalry. It is the adversarial nature of the Sino-Indian relationship which has driven India's and, in turn, Pakistan's nuclear weapons program.

China tested its first atomic bomb in 1964, two years after India's humiliating defeat in the 1962 border war. India followed suit in 1974. Beijing responded by providing nuclear weapons designs and technology to India's arch-rival Pakistan so as to prop up a counterweight to tie down India's nuclear assets. Similarly, India's development of long-range ballistic missiles in the 1980s led Beijing to provide substantial missile assistance to Pakistan. China and India are also competing with each other to supply civilian nuclear technology. In a move which might be seen as tit for tat, when China and Pakistan signed a nuclear co-operation deal in 1989, India responded by agreeing to help China's arch-rival in Southeast Asia, Vietnam, with its 'atomic energy program for peaceful purposes'.[51] After the United States forced India to withdraw from a deal to sell a nuclear reactor to Iran, China exported a mini-reactor to Teheran. In 1988, New Delhi leased a Charlie-class nuclear attack submarine from Moscow as part of its plans to offset China's small fleet of SSBNs. Beijing, in turn, responded by offering to sell Islamabad a nuclear-powered Han-class submarine.[52] Again, it was no coincidence that India's intermediate-range Agni missile test took place only a few days after China detonated its largest ever nuclear explosion in May 1992 during the Indian president's official visit to China. Clearly, Chinese nuclear forces are central to the Sino-Indian-Pakistani nuclear triangle and arms control process.

India's objection to a South Asian Nuclear Freeze Zone (the time for a South Asian Nuclear Free Zone has already passed), and to Indian ratification of the Nuclear Non-Proliferation Treaty (NPT), is principally that they exclude China. Though India and China have made some progress in instituting conventional confidence-building measures (CBMs) on their disputed border, the nuclear dimension of the problem has not yet been addressed.[53] A number of proposals have been put forward to curb the subcontinental nuclear arms race. These include: a freeze on the production of nuclear weapon materials; freezing ballistic missile technology; a regional test ban treaty; and five-power talks. However, none of the proposals has succeeded nor is likely to succeed because of India's insistence on placing restraints on Chinese nuclear forces. In view of sharp differences on the nuclear question, the joint communiqué issued at the end of Premier Li Peng's December 1991 visit to India did not mention the idea of a South Asian nuclear-free zone or the five-power talks.[54]

The proposal to hold five-power talks (United States, Russia, China, India and Pakistan) on nuclear arms control in South Asia failed because Beijing let it be known that 'in any such summit, China will participate as an outside power and not as a regional player whose own arsenal could be on the negotiating table'.[55] This stance is consistent with the Chinese arms control strategy of keeping Chinese nuclear arms out of all bilateral or multilateral nuclear arms reduction talks.[56] This is unacceptable to India. An ex-Indian ambassador to China, K.S. Bajpai, told the *Far Eastern Economic Review* (15 April 1993) that 'the whole world cannot get India and Pakistan to give up the nuclear option without China giving up the option'.

In the meantime, India is committed to pursuing its nuclear and missile programs despite strong Western opposition. According to the *Indian Defence Review*, India's major strategic goal is to 'build a small but credible nuclear deterrent against its northern neighbour China'.[57] Apparently, there has long been what Gary Klintworth calls 'a competitive duality' in the Sino-

Indian nuclear relationship.[58] However, the worrisome aspect of this competition is that it might be carried over into an open nuclear arms rivalry in the region. And this will have 'adverse consequences for regional security and stability' if 'pressure develops for neighbouring countries to follow suit or choose sides'.[59]

Force doctrine and force structure

With the withdrawal of the former Soviet Union and reduction in the United States military presence, defence strategists in New Delhi are pointing to China's defence capabilities and military expenditure as the rationale for India's ongoing military modernisation and force acquisition program.

Strong economic growth has enabled Beijing to nearly double its defence budget to finance weapons procurement, from a 1990 level of US$6.06 billion to a 1993 level of US$12 billion. Much to India's chagrin, China's arms buildup has been assisted by cheap arms sales from its former ally, Moscow, with the emphasis being on rapid reaction and force projection forces.

These developments have been noted with concern by the Indian defence community, coming as they did at a time when India's military brass was struggling to come to terms with a near-crippling resource crunch. A commonly expressed fear is that China will not take India seriously if it is not seen as a militarily powerful nation. However, it should be noted that India's force acquisition and modernisation plans have not been abandoned. Despite the fiscal crunch, New Delhi continues to give its military research and development program high priority on the principle of 'keeping one step ahead of Pakistan and at par with China'.

India's nuclear weapons and ballistic missile programs are already at an advanced stage. While Agni provides India the capability to place all of Pakistan, much of the Indian Ocean and many cities in southern China within the range of its missiles, Trishul and Akash — if deployed as anti-tactical ballistic missiles (ATBM) — could provide India with the capability of protecting itself from incoming missiles. Work on nuclear-powered submarines is continuing. As *Jane's Defence Weekly* (3 June 1989) put it, New Delhi is moving toward a strategy of 'limited deterrence' *vis-à-vis* Beijing as well as Islamabad. Despite some drawdown in force levels on the Sino-Indian border following the September 1993 agreement, the Indian military wants to keep at least six out of eleven mountain divisions deployed there. As a result of India's perception of China's growing profile in Rangoon, there is also a greater need to police the long-neglected Indian border with Burma.

Economic competition

For nearly a decade, Indian economists have watched China's economic boom with envy and awe while Indian strategists have debated its implications for China's military capability and Indian security. Now India has taken a leaf out of China's book and embarked upon a similar path of export-oriented and investment-driven economic prosperity. With India joining China in the worldwide rush for scarce capital, investment, resources and markets, an interesting race has just begun. This economic competition is pitching India and China headlong into the global marketplace, 'with their fast opening economies and liberal investment laws replacing missiles and missives with money-making opportunities, hoping that while they make profits for others, they also profit from the development of their largely poor countries'.[60]

However, India has a lot of catching up to do. It was only in 1991 that India snapped the straps on its Soviet-style socialist straitjacket and acknowledged that free market and free trade were the right way to go.[61] China, having initiated the economic liberalisation reforms in 1979, has a fifteen-year advantage over India, and is reaping the benefits at a much higher level. Whereas China received pledges for $80 billion in direct foreign investment (DFI) and around US$15 billion in actual monies in 1993 alone, India attracted just US$3 billion.[62] China's economic growth rate is perhaps three or four times that of India. China's exports are about to cross the $US100 billion-mark — four times that of India. China is the world's thirteenth largest exporter, India, by contrast, ranks a mere 33rd. What's more, China's exports are cutting into traditional areas of India's strength: China has overtaken India in fields such as garments, leather, spices and aquaculture. Unlike the military battlefield, where India has achieved a certain parity with China, in the new economic battlefield, China is way ahead of India in every sphere.[63] And that is a cause of worry for New Delhi. Many thoughtful Indians voice concern that if India does not take immediate steps to narrow the gap, it will fall further behind China and will come under increasing pressure from China over a whole range of issues in the future. As a former Indian ambassador to the United States, Abid Hussain, put it: 'Like China, India should have a "grand strategy" of striving to become a major economic power by the turn of the century which would consequently give it leverage to become an equally powerful military power.'[64]

Indian policy-makers remain optimistic that India is set to emerge as one of the top five or six powerful economic players alongside China.[65] Most multinationals are already looking at India as the next major centre of manufacturing, service and consumption.[66] It has been pointed out that India's economic strengths are China's weaknesses: an educated, urban middle class of 300 million,[67] the widespread use of English; the third largest skilled workforce in the world; a thriving private enterprise base; reliable statistics; an awesome industrial base; growing managerial and technological prowess; a better patent protection environment than China; functioning capital markets and a long stockmarket tradition; a commercial code (that China still lacks); and an impeccable record of repatriation of foreign capital.[68]

More importantly, unlike China, India has no fundamental conflict between its political and economic systems. Politically, India is the world's largest democracy with a parliamentary system of government, rule of law, a free press and independent judiciary. While China is still struggling with the means to ensure a peaceful, smooth political succession, India settled the question of political succession way back in 1947. Furthermore, the Indian diaspora is expected to play a role similar to that of the overseas Chinese. Many India–China watchers and businesspeople believe there is no reason why these advantages should not enable India to outdo China. Already there are signs that the Indian economy has taken a turn for the better.

In contrast, bilateral trade between India and China has grown to just $330 million in 1993. Since India and China are on 'parallel tracks of development', there is a general perception that the two giants have little potential for trade expansion. Besides, the lack of direct banking relations, air links or good transportation facilities has also hampered any increase in bilateral trade.[69]

The point is that the Indian government is taking the 'China challenge' very seriously indeed. Finance Minister Manmohan Singh is using China as a benchmark for domestic reforms both to silence his domestic left-wing critics and to integrate the country with the fast-developing Pacific economies.[70] The security implications of a higher economic growth are not lost on Indian policy-makers. With a sustained economic growth rate of 6 to 8 per cent, it is hoped that India will be able to play the role of checking and balancing the influences of other major powers in a world where 'economic competition might replace the old politico-military contests for supremacy'. The emergence of China and India as economic giants will undoubtedly throw a huge new weight on to the world's geopolitical balance. This in itself should not be a cause for worry. As Sandy Gordon points out, a competitive relationship between the two 'would only become threatening if other aspects of relationship, and particularly those relating to security, continue to be troubling'.[71]

Competing for dominance and influence in Asia

In addition to competition in military and economic spheres, there is also an interesting mutual game of containment being played out between New Delhi and Beijing in South Asia, Southeast Asia, and Central and Inner Asia.

South Asia

Tibet

The origins of the Sino-Indian rivalry can be traced back to the Chinese occupation of Tibet in 1951, which eliminated a buffer between the two Asian giants and transformed the Indo-Tibetan boundary into a Sino-Indian boundary. Tibet still remains a bone of contention between India and China, though neither side would publicly admit as much. Frequent disturbances and protests in and outside Tibet make the issue of Tibet acute for Sino-Indian relations.

Chinese leaders are concerned about the resurgent nationalist movements based on ethnicity and religion in the border provinces of Tibet, Inner Mongolia and Xinjiang at a time when the whole of Central and Inner Asia is in flux. The cause of Tibet's independence has received a boost from recent international events, especially the collapse of the Soviet Union, and the gaining of independence by the Baltic states, the Ukraine and Central Asian republics which share similar historical experiences. The Western countries, particularly the United States, are also more receptive to Tibet's cause than they were during the Cold War, when relations with China were viewed as a useful counterbalance to Soviet power. At a time when the Chinese are under heavy criticism from the West for human rights violations in Tibet and are facing a rising tide of Tibetan nationalism, they apparently need Indian help to legitimise their rule. And this presents difficulties for India. As one observer has pointed out, Sino-Indian relations:

> will continue to be haunted by 'the inescapable dilemma of Tibet ... for India to be indifferent to the reality of Tibetan suffering ... in pursuit of ... *realpolitik* would be to sacrifice some of the most cherished constitutive principles of modern Indian society and polity: human rights, personal dignity, religious freedom, cultural autonomy, political liberties. And, it would cede control over the Indo-Tibetan border to China.[72]

A number of articles in Indian defence journals and print media in recent years have called upon the government to keep its options open on Tibet in the fast-changing international situation. Some of India's China-watchers argue that India's repeated protestations that Tibet is 'an autonomous region of China' are unnecessary. Asks Sujit Dutta of the government-run Institute for Defence Studies and Analyses (IDSA): 'Even if our statement on Tibet is the existing position, why should we keep repeating it when the Chinese have actually made no effort to fulfil their promise of autonomy to Tibet?'[73] Another China expert, Surjit Mansingh, advises that in view of the 'unpredictable dynamics of change in Central Asia ... [and] the still growing prestige of the Dalai Lama, it would be well for the Indian government to formulate a long-range policy on Tibet taking into account contingent factors'.[74] Policy-makers in New Delhi are also aware that any boundary agreement under present conditions may not be in their interests because the issue of the future status of Tibet *vis-à-vis* China is yet to be resolved. Besides, an India–China boundary agreement at this stage will undoubtedly inflame Tibetan opinion against India. Not only that, there is a general consensus that the long-term security of India's northern frontiers lies in the restoration of Tibet's independence. From New Delhi's perspective, the expulsion of hostile influences from Tibet and the establishment of a friendly or neutral government in Lhasa would go a long way to ushering in a peaceful and stable environment in South Asia. The removal of a threat from China through

Tibet on India's northeast could make New Delhi more conciliatory in its disputes with Pakistan and other South Asian neighbours.

Having said that, it should be noted that there has been no change in India's official stance on 'Tibet as an autonomous region of China'. Nor is there likely to be. In fact, successive Indian governments have bent over backwards to reassure the Chinese on Tibet. But the Chinese still worry. 'Being eminent realists they know that India has contiguity and historical relations with Tibet, and more important, the Dalai Lama and 100,000 refugees who have to go back one day.'[75] In short, since the Sino-Indian boundary is essentially an Indo-Tibetan border, any change in Tibet's status will have important implications for the future of Sino-Indian relations and for the Asian balance of power as a whole, just as it did 50 years ago when Tibet fell to Chinese communists.

Pakistan

Since the mid-1980s, Indo-Pakistan relations have deteriorated sharply. Military buildups, mutual hostility and support to secessionist elements have led to a perpetual game of brinkmanship, sabre-rattling and war hysteria. The Indo-Pakistani border remains heavily militarised.

Despite the thaw in Sino-Indian relations, Sino-Pakistani military links remain as strong as ever. Though China's changed policy on Kashmir now undoubtedly favours the Indian position over the Pakistani stance, there has been no change in China's strategy of shoring up Pakistan's defences in order to contain India, nor is there likely to be.[76] Soon after the signing of the so-called 'landmark agreement' between India and China in September 1993, the Chinese reassured the worried Pakistanis that 'moves [to improve ties with India] will not be made at your cost'. Chinese Premier Li Peng has promised to continue arms sales to Pakistan and the supply of a 300 megawatt nuclear power plant.[77] While Beijing has tried to keep its relationships with Pakistan and India apart, stressing the bilateral nature of ties, India continues to perceive a Sino-Pakistani military nexus, which goes back to the 1960s, as 'hostile' and 'threatening' in both intent and character.[78] What irks India most is the Chinese transfer of nuclear and missile technology to Pakistan.[79]

Obviously, China is not going to become less friendly to Pakistan following normalisation with India because the combined strategic and political advantages that China receives from its relationship with Pakistan (and through Pakistan, other Islamic countries) easily outweigh any advantages China might accrue from a closer relationship with India. Above all, Pakistan is the only country that stands up to India and thereby prevents Indian hegemony over the region. This fulfils a key strategic objective of China's South Asia policy.

Like Pakistan, India's other smaller South Asian neighbours resent India's hegemonic ambitions in the region and have tried to resist the imposition of the Indian version of the 'Monroe Doctrine' by seeking security links with extra-regional powers, primarily China. This has led to an ongoing conflict between South Asia's largest state and its smaller neighbours.

Soon after independence from the British, in 1949–50, India signed treaties with the Himalayan kingdoms of Bhutan, Nepal and the small princely protectorate of Sikkim, thereby sending a clear signal to China that the security of their northern borders was India's responsibility. Since the 1962 war, India has kept a watchful eye on China's relations with Nepal and Bhutan. Whenever Nepalese rulers have tried to play 'the China card' in their relations with India, problems have arisen (for example, the 1989–90 blockade) and tremendous pressure has been brought on Nepal to toe the line. Sikkim was annexed by the Indira Gandhi government in 1975 to bolster India's defences *vis-à-vis* China. India's involvement in the conflict in Sri Lanka is another example of New Delhi's attempts to enhance its strategic position *vis-à-vis* China, while at the same time containing the domestic political fallout from Tamil ethnic separatism.

Although the Chinese have tried to dissuade South Asian countries from assuming Beijing's partisan involvement in their disputes with India (for example, in 1990 the Chinese kept New Delhi informed of the Sri Lankan and Nepalese requests for arms transfers and of the scale and delivery details),[80] India remains apprehensive of China's 'high profile in South Asia' as evidenced by Beijing's continuing arms transfers to Bangladesh, Nepal and Sri Lanka.[81]

Southeast Asia

In Southeast Asia, India has always maintained close political and security ties with China's prime adversary, Vietnam. In post-Cold War Asia, New Delhi is also exploring the possibilities of establishing closer ties with ASEAN countries, especially Indonesia, for it sees both Indonesia and Vietnam sharing India's geopolitical interest in checking the spread of Chinese influence and reach in Southeast Asia. For its part, China maintained military pressure on Vietnam and has built close ties with Thailand, the Khmer Rouge in Cambodia and the SLORC government in Burma.[82]

Burma

More than anywhere else, it is in Burma (or Myanmar) that Beijing and New Delhi are waging an open and determined struggle for influence and domination. Faced with increasing international isolation and pressure following the suppression in 1988 of the democratic movement in the country, the military junta in Rangoon has developed close military and diplomatic ties with Beijing. China is reported to have supplied more than US$1.4 billion worth of arms to Burma, including fighter aircraft, naval patrol boats, heavy artillery, tanks, and anti-aircraft missiles and guns. Most of the Chinese weaponry is now reportedly deployed on the Indo-Burmese border, with the number of battalions on Burma's borders with India and Bangladesh going up from five in 1988 to 32 in 1992.[83] Indian military planners are also closely monitoring the tense situation on the Bangladeshi–Burmese border.

The growing military relationship between Beijing and Rangoon has not only marked the end of Burma's traditional non-aligned orientation, it has also aroused Indian apprehensions.[84] It has forced New Delhi, for the first time, to pay increasing attention to events across its eastern frontier with Burma. As one observer of Burmese affairs noted: 'Just as China's support for Pakistan puts pressure on India to the west, so closer Chinese ties with Burma adds to India's strategic concerns in the east.'[85]

This *de facto* military alliance between Burma and China in the early 1990s coincided with a serious deterioration in relations between India and Burma. While China strengthened its political and security ties with the Burmese military regime, the Indian government publicly aligned itself with the democratic movement led by Aung San Suu Kyi and condemned the Burmese military regime for violations of human rights. With several key Burmese opposition figures seeking refuge in India, and Rangoon accusing New Delhi of interfering in its internal affairs, the two countries have become increasingly suspicious of each other.

Reports of Beijing's involvement in the development of a Burmese naval base at Hainggyi Island and a radar station at Coco Island, southwest of the Burmese coast (both of which are close to the Indian territory of Andaman and Nicobar Islands in the Bay of Bengal) and their possible military use by Beijing, have introduced a whole new dimension to India's threat perceptions from a powerful neighbour.[86] Articles in *Jane's Defence Weekly*, the *Far Eastern Economic Review*, Indian defence journals and by the media have mentioned a number of possibilities ranging from the establishment of SIGINT facilities by China to monitor Indian missile launches conducted between Orissa and the Andamans, maritime reconnaissance or communication and naval facilities for Chinese naval vessels, and a listening post, to a deep water port for Chinese nuclear submarines.[87]

China's inroads into Burma, when juxtaposed with China's ties with Bangladesh are, from New Delhi's perspective, serious encroachments into India's sphere of influence. For Indian strategists, China is now seen as constituting a threat in the north as well as in the east. As one analyst at IDSA put it: 'In dealing with China we have to consider what it is doing in the east rather than see it only as a northern threat'.[88] China's forays into Burma have been variously described by India's China-watchers as a direct challenge to New Delhi's strategic interests.[89]

Despite growing regional concern about Chinese intentions, Beijing's reluctance to clarify the matters has further complicated the situation.[90] However, observers of Chinese and Burmese affairs have attributed several motives to China's desire to expand its economic and strategic influence down to the Bay of Bengal. A major one, of course, is Chinese economic planners' desire to open the Old Burma Road to link up the poorer inland provinces such as Yunnan, which have lagged behind the booming coastal provinces, with the fast growing economies of Southeast and South Asia.[91] From the strategic viewpoint, arms sales and/or military co-operation have always been an important means of funding the PLA's modernisation drive and of expanding China's influence abroad. For example, through its military assistance, Beijing has come to acquire considerable political influence over Rangoon, thereby affording China the opportunity to mediate the conflict between Burma and Bangladesh over the Rohingya Muslim refugees.

To counterbalance China's influence, New Delhi has now decided to follow a policy of 'constructive engagement' with Rangoon, thus abandoning its earlier stance of isolating the Burmese military regime. Indian Foreign Secretary J.N. Dixit paid a surprise, low-key visit to the Burmese capital in March 1993 to hold talks on issues of mutual concern. This first high-level official contact since the Burmese army's crackdown on pro-democracy demonstrations in 1988 confirmed New Delhi's policy shift. In return for the Burmese army's co-operation in curtailing the drug and arms traffic in India's volatile northeast and maintaining peace along Burma's 1600 kilometre border with India, Dixit reiterated India's stand of non-interference in Burma's internal affairs.[92]

The second prong of India's strategy is to find a complementarity of interests with those Southeast Asian countries which share New Delhi's perception of 'the China threat'. To assuage Southeast Asian countries' fears about India's own military buildup, New Delhi has proposed defence ties and joint naval exercises with Malaysia, Indonesia, Singapore and the Philippines.[93] Jakarta, always wary of Beijing's extra-territorial ambitions, accepted India's invitation to conduct joint naval exercises in early 1994 not far from Coco Island. Similarly, Thailand, a close ally of China during the Cambodian conflict, is equally uncomfortable with Beijing's support for Burma. Indian Prime Minister Narasimha Rao is said to have raised the issue of 'India as a possible strategic counterbalance to China in Asia' during talks with his Thai counterpart, Chuan Leekpai, in Bangkok in April 1993.[94] There is some evidence to suggest that the region's smaller nations, Singapore and Brunei, also see India's powerful military as a useful counterweight to China.

Clearly, China's forays in Burma have brought about some strategic consensus between India and Southeast Asian countries on the need to counter Chinese expansion into the Indian Ocean. In one sense, Burma's China connection has proved to be a blessing in disguise for New Delhi. India has been able to endear itself to the countries of Southeast Asia by convincing them of India's security relevance to the region; at the same time, it has diverted the attention of Southeast Asian countries from New Delhi's strategic ambitions to those of Beijing's expansionist moves.[95] Critics also point out that, by exaggerating the potential Chinese threat to the region, New Delhi could be hoping to put regional pressure on the State Law and Order Restoration Council to modify its hardline political stance, distance itself from China, and 'not to go ahead with the Hainggyi Island project'.[96] Since some of the exaggerated accounts of Sino-Burmese relations have originated from India's defence establishment, it is also possible that an attempt was being made by the Indian military to 'assert [its] relevance ... during a period of tight finances and defence cuts'.[97]

Despite all the hype about Chinese incursions into the Indian Ocean, objective observers concede that the 'major interest of the Chinese Navy lies in dominating the South China Sea'.[98]

Whatever the case, the fact remains that, in recent years, Burma has moved too close to China for India's comfort. It does not matter whether China's expansion is dictated by economic interests or by strategic interests. What matters is that Beijing's Burma policy is seen in New Delhi as a manifestation of a Chinese desire to dominate both the Pacific and Indian Oceans. It is also a demonstration of the potential for a Chinese naval presence in the Indian Ocean, should it ever wish it in the future. The net result is that Burma, occupying as it does a critical strategic position between the two Asian giants, has become a source of friction in the Sino-Indian equation. What's more, Burma has added a maritime dimension to traditional Sino-Indian rivalry. Even if some accounts of China's military nexus with Burma are untrue, the fact that they are so easily believed in New Delhi (and in Southeast Asian capitals), shows the degree of residual distrust and suspicion in Sino-Indian relations.

Central and Inner Asia

Central Asian Republics

Finally, the emergence of five independent Central Asian states has the potential to extend traditional Sino-Indian rivalry to a new volatile geopolitical region of Central and Inner Asia.

China and India lost no time in establishing diplomatic relations with all Central Asian states. Both Chinese and Indian prime ministers have visited the Central Asian republics and signed a number of bilateral agreements since 1991. Both China and India are home to large Muslim populations but, despite a commonality of interest in containing Muslim separatism at home, it seems there will be more competition between Beijing and New Delhi in Central and Inner Asia.

India's key diplomatic objective in Central Asia is to prevent the formation of a pro-Pakistani, pro-Iranian pan-Islamic confederation based on common strategic and economic interests. Geostrategically, India seeks to checkmate its traditional rivals, China and Pakistan, from gaining advantage and influence.[99] New Delhi seeks to curb the growth of Islamic fundamentalism because of its destabilising impact on Kashmir and India's 120 million-strong Muslim minority. To counter strategic moves by China and Pakistan and to promote secular democratic forces, New Delhi seems to be according special importance to its relations with Kazakhstan, Kyrghyzstan and Uzbekistan. Some Indian strategists envisage Kazakhstan, India and Mongolia moving closer to counterbalance the might of China and Pakistan. Policy-makers in New Delhi are concerned that China is working hard to promote economic ties with the Central Asian states so as to pre-empt competition from other Asian states.

In the heady days of the Soviet empire and Indo-Soviet friendship, India used to enjoy privileged trade access to Central Asian markets. Now it has to compete not only with China, but also with the oil-rich Persian Gulf states as well as the Asian newly industrialising economies (NIEs). Already, Chinese food products, light machinery, consumer goods, agricultural and industrial technology, equipment and raw materials have found a good market in Central Asia.

Beijing looks towards the region as a vast market for Chinese exports and has proposed joint venture projects and offered liberal economic aid and investment. China's and Pakistan's geographic proximity coupled with ethnic and Islamic ties with Central Asian states could mean that, over the longer term, Beijing and Islamabad might come to play a more important role in the region, both strategically and economically.

But, unlike India, China shares a common, disputed border with Central Asia, and therefore has a lot more at stake. Strategically, the challenge before China's defence planners is to secure their country's northwestern and southwestern frontiers which are no longer as secure as they were during the Cold War or in the days of the Soviet Union. Iran-backed Islamic fundamentalism and Turkey-supported Pan-Turkism are both seen as long-term threats to China's security. China's strategy is to exploit the inter-regional rivalries and contradictions to establish a strategic environment favourable to Chinese interests. Fearful of Turkish domination of the region, especially in view of Xinjiang's historical links with Turkey, Beijing has moved closer to Iran and Pakistan to counter Turkey's moves.[100] Religious unrest in Xinjiang could damage China's ties with Islamic countries. China's main interest is to stop instability spilling over into the strategically important Muslim-majority province of Xinjiang (also called Chinese Turkestan) which borders three Central Asian states — Kazakhstan, Kyrghyzstan and Tajikistan. The Uighurs, Kazakhs and Kirghiz people of rebellious Xinjiang province remain far from reconciled to Chinese rule and seek independence or unification with their brethren across the border. Not only that, with the disintegration of the former Soviet Union, the Sino-Soviet territorial dispute in the western sector has now been transformed into Sino-Kazakh, Sino-Tajik and Sino-Kyrghiz border disputes. Though Chinese territorial claims on Central Asian territory are in abeyance, their possible revival cannot be ruled out in the event of strained relations between China and its Central Asian neighbours.[101]

In short, the political map of Central Asia is now up for grabs, with China, India, Pakistan, Turkey and Iran all actively wooing the newly freed Central Asian republics.

Mongolia

In Inner Asia, India is strengthening its ties with Mongolia following the end of the special relationship between Ulaanbataar and Moscow. Deprived of the Soviet counterweight to China, Mongolia is keen to establish new relationships with Asian countries so as to expand its horizons beyond the narrow geopolitical confines of Russia and China. During his recent visit to India, the Mongolian President, P. Ochirbat, declared that 'Kashmir is an integral part of India, and what happens there is an internal affair of India'.[102] In return, New Delhi has offered to assist in the developmental programs as well as in the restoration of Buddhist monasteries.

A large land-locked Buddhist state sandwiched between China and Russia, Mongolia has assumed 'immense strategic importance' to India in the post-Cold War, post-Soviet balance of power games being played out between the two Asian giants. Given the existence of large Buddhist populations in Inner Mongolia and Tibet in China, and Tuva and Buryat in Russia, the political implications of a nexus between Mongolia and India could not have gone unnoticed in Beijing and Moscow. What is of special significance is that 'secular' India — with its large Buddhist population and as the birthplace of Buddhism — is now seeking to exploit religion by playing the pan-Buddhist card to counter the growing strength of Islamic fundamentalism in Central Asia and to strengthen its relations with Southeast and East Asian countries. Mongolia is described as the first country where 'Buddhism is laying the foundations of a new diplomatic relationship' and as 'the linchpin of India's new policy' in Central and Inner Asia.[103] In one sense, India's growing relationship with Mongolia can also be interpreted as India's response to Chinese diplomacy in Burma.[104]

Conclusion

Despite a thaw in Sino-Indian relations, the basic insecurities of the two nations will continue to bedevil their relationship. Historic rivalries and common sense suggest that a fair amount of tension between these continent-sized neighbours, which also happen to be the world's two most populous nations, is inevitable.

India and China share similar aspirations towards status and influence, with China further advanced than India. This inevitably introduces a more competitive aspect into the Sino-Indian relationship. Apparently the notion of 'the China threat' also serves a number of Indian foreign policy objectives: one, it elevates India's international status; two, it takes the heat off criticism over India's NPT stance; three, it justifies high defence spending; four, it legitimises India's nuclear and missile programs and its demand for a permanent seat in the United Nations Security Council; five, it undermines Pakistan's attempts to gain strategic parity with India; and last but not least, it diverts regional attention from India's regional supremacy ambitions to China's expansionist designs and thereby brings India closer to Southeast and East Asian countries.

Both India and China are on 'parallel tracks of development'. On present trends, China and India will emerge as the engines of Asia's economic growth and will dominate world industrial production within a generation or so. It is possible that new economic prosperity, first in China and then in India, would reawaken nationalist pride and self-assertiveness with unknown consequences for the region's peace and stability. Their weight on geopolitical balance will depend on the manner in which ongoing internal economic reforms are managed to maximise gain and minimise pain in both countries. Provided China and India are successful in maintaining their unity and territorial integrity against all odds, the two Asian giants will emerge as major power centres in the long term, and the future of the Asia-Pacific region will be shaped increasingly by the kind of relations that will exist between them and Japan.

In the short to medium term, neither New Delhi nor Beijing will do anything which destabilises their bilateral relationship or arouses the suspicions of their smaller Asian neighbours. Their efforts will be aimed at consolidating their power and position while striving to resolve more pressing domestic problems. Instability in Tibet coupled with China's military links with Pakistan would pose a continuing complication in Sino-Indian relations. At the same time, both will continue to monitor closely each other's activities to expand influence and gain advantage in the wider Asian region, and will attempt to fill any perceived power vacuum or block the other from doing so. In other words, bilateral co-operation and peaceful competition will be the hallmarks of the Sino-Indian relationship in the foreseeable future.

In the long term, however, neither Indian nor Chinese defence planners can rule out the possibility of a renewed confrontation.

Notes

1 Shekhar Gupta and S. Chakravarti, 'Sino-Indian Relations: Vital Breakthrough', *India Today*, 30 September 1993, p. 22; Lincoln Kaye, 'Bordering on Peace', *Far Eastern Economic Review* [hereafter *FEER*], 16 September 1993, p. 13; and 'Hands across the Himalayas', *Economist*, 11 September 1993, p. 21.

2 For details, see J. Mohan Malik, 'Hands across the Himalayas', *Pacific Defence Reporter*, March 1989, pp. 43–45.

3 Kaye, 'Bordering on Peace'; J. Mohan Malik, 'India Copes with the Kremlin's Fall', *Orbis*, vol. 37, no. 1, Winter 1993, pp. 69–87.

4 *FEER*, 15 April 1993, pp. 10–11. According to the Pentagon's 'Defense Planning Draft, 1994–1999', Washington proposes to 'discourage Indian hegemonic aspirations over the other states in South Asia and on the India Ocean'. See *New York Times*, 8 March 1992.

5 B.S. Glaser, 'China's Security Perceptions: Interests and Ambitions', *Asian Survey*, vol. 33, no. 3, March 1993; Chang Ya-chun, 'Peking's Asia-Pacific Strategy in the 1990s', *Issues & Studies*, vol. 29, no. 1, January 1993, p. 85.

6 Zheng Ruixiang, 'Shifting Obstacles in Sino-Indian Relations', *Pacific Review*, vol. 6, no. 1, 1993, p. 65.

7 Kaye, 'Bordering on Peace'.

8 Nirmal Mitra, 'Coming Closer', *Sunday* [Calcutta], 23–29 August 1992, p. 59.

9 Gupta and Chakravarti, 'Sino-Indian Relations', pp. 24–25; *Indian Defence Review*, April 1992.

10 Manoj Joshi, 'Shy Hands Across the Himalayas', *Asia-Pacific Defence Reporter*, April–May 1993, p. 15.
11 *Economist*, 11 September 1993, p. 21.
12 British Broadcasting Corporation, *Summary of World Broadcasts*, FE/1789/G/2, 9 September 1993; Gupta and Chakravarti, 'Sino-Indian Relations', p. 23.
13 After a gap of 30 years, the deputy chief of the general staff of the Chinese PLA, General Xu Huizi, visited New Delhi in December 1993. See Ranjan Gupta, 'India, China to Withdraw Troops', *Australian*, 1–2 January 1994, p. 9.
14 John W. Garver, 'Chinese–Indian Rivalry in Indochina', *Asian Survey*, vol. 27, no. 11, November 1987, pp. 1216–17.
15 Ramesh Thakur, 'Normalizing Sino-Indian Relations', *Pacific Review*, vol. 4, no. 1, 1991, p. 15.
16 China's forays into Burma since 1990 seem to have bridged the gap in thinking lately.
17 C. Uday Bhaskar, 'Role of China in the Emerging World Order', *Strategic Analysis* (New Delhi), vol. 16, no. 1, April 1993, pp. 3–19.
18 See Ranjan Gupta, 'US Sees India and Pakistan in a New Light', *Australian*, 15 April 1994, p. 16.
19 Pravin Sawhney, 'Hastening Slowly: Developing Indo-US Relations', *Indian Defence Review*, April 1993, pp. 57–63; *Indian Defence Review*, April 1992.
20 Lt Gen K.S. Khajuria (Retd), 'Security in South West Asia Region — Post Cold War and India's Defence Concerns', *Indian Defence Review*, July 1993, p. 44. Conversations with India's Japan experts, 1992.
21 Bhaskar, 'Role of China in the Emerging World Order', p. 8.
22 Sandy Gordon, 'Sino-Indian Relations After the Cold War', *SDSC Newsletter*, March 1993, pp. 1, 4.
23 *Jane's Defence Weekly* [hereafter *JDW*], 6 November 1993, p. 56. Minister of State for External Affairs, R.L. Bhatia, told the Parliament on 6 August 1992 that the government was fully aware of the apprehensions of defence analysts and editorial writers about the potential threat to India's security arising from Chinese military expansion plans. Cited in B.M. Chengappa, 'India–China Relations: Issues and Implications', *Strategic Analysis*, vol. 16, no. 1, April 1993, p. 39.
24 Brahma Chellaney, 'The Challenge of Nuclear Arms Control in South Asia', *Survival*, vol. 35, no. 3, Autumn 1993, pp. 121–36.
25 Chengappa, 'India–China Relations', p. 41.
26 Bhaskar, 'Role of China in the Emerging World Order', p. 9.
27 'Like most Asians, Indians fret about the security implications of a rich and powerful China in the next century': *Economist*, 11 September 1993, p. 21.
28 *Indian Defence Review*, April 1992, p. 14.
29 Denny Roy, 'Consequences of China's Economic Growth for Asia-Pacific Security', *Security Dialogue*, vol. 24, no. 2, June 1993, p. 184.

30 A section of China-watchers feels that 'India has stooped too low to please the Chinese' in recent years. A former ambassador to China and ex-foreign secretary, A.P. Venkateswaran complains: 'The Chinese haven't resiled on anything, while we keep talking of achievements'. See Mitra, 'Coming Closer'.

31 Rita Manchanda, 'Unequal exchange', *FEER*, 26 December 1991, pp. 10–11. Critics argue there is no need to support China's position on human rights. Sujit Dutta asks: 'How can we declare commonality on human rights with China, a socialist state that does not believe in democracy?', see *Sunday*, 23–29 August 1992, p. 59.

32 Kaye, 'Bordering on Peace'.

33 *Hindustan Times*, 13 January 1993, p. 14; Conversation with Sujit Dutta, Institute for Defence Studies and Analyses, January 1993.

34 Surjit Mansingh, 'An Overview of India–China Relations: From When to Where?' *Indian Defence Review*, April 1993, p. 76; Ranjan Gupta, 'India Walks a Tightrope in Pursuit of Security Council Role', *Australian*, 8 October 1993.

35 Subramaniam Swamy, 'Are we Heading for a War with China?' *Sunday*, 1–7 February 1987, p. 33.

36 Gerald Segal, 'As China Grows Strong', *International Affairs*, vol. 64, no. 2, Spring 1988, pp. 217–31.

37 Xu Xin, 'Changing Chinese Security Perceptions', North Pacific Co-operative Security Dialogue Working Paper no. 27, April 1993, York University, Ontario, Canada, p. 12.

38 ibid.

39 Richard K. Betts, 'Wealth, Power, and Instability', *International Security*, vol. 18, no. 3, Winter 1993/94, p. 54.

40 Mansingh, 'An Overview of India–China Relations', p. 76; Ruixiang, 'Shifting Obstacles in Sino-Indian Relations', p. 67.

41 *India Today*, 30 September 1993, pp. 22–37.

42 Ye Zhengjia, 'India's Foreign Policy in the Restructuring International Relations', *International Studies* [*Guoji Wenti*], vol. 3, 1992. A banned Chinese book authored by a serving PLA official sees the United States, India, Vietnam and Taiwan as potential military enemies. *Weekend Australian*, 20–21 November 1993, p. 16.

43 Tai Ming Cheung, 'Smoke Signals', *FEER*, 12 November 1992, pp. 29–30.

44 Ye Zhengjia, 'India's Foreign Policy', p. 13.

45 'China's Plan to Build up Navy', *Hindustan Times*, 13 January 1993, p. 14. See also *Time*, 10 May 1993, p. 39.

46 *India Today*, 30 September 1993, p. 26.

47 Conversations with Chinese analysts Li and Hua Di, May 1991.

48 Gary Klintworth, 'Chinese Perspectives on India as a Great Power', in Ross Babbage and Sandy Gordon (eds), *India's Strategic Future: Regional State or Global Power?*, Macmillan, London, 1992, p. 96.

49 Jasjit Singh, 'Indian Security: A Framework for National Strategy', *Strategic Analysis*, November 1987, p. 898.

50 For example, China's nuclear and missile assistance to Pakistan has the double advantage for China of gaining a military counterweight on India's left flank while keeping in close contact with the Islamic world.
51 *Xinhua*, 16 August 1988.
52 *FEER*, 18 January and 6 September 1990; also cited in Klintworth, 'Chinese Perspectives on India', p. 101.
53 Chellaney, 'The Challenge of Nuclear Arms Control in South Asia'.
54 *Arms Control Today*, June 1993, pp. 7, 17–22; Ruixiang, 'Shifting Obstacles in Sino-Indian Relations', p. 69.
55 Shekhar Gupta and W.P.S. Sidhu, 'Indo-US Relations: Cautious Manoeuvres,' *India Today*, 30 June 1992, p. 35.
56 For details, see J. Mohan Malik, 'China's Policy Towards Nuclear Arms Control', paper presented at the conference on Nuclear Proliferation and Nuclear Arms Control After the Cold War, La Trobe University, Melbourne, 25 March 1994.
57 *Indian Defence Review*, April 1993, pp. 59–60.
58 Klintworth, 'Chinese Perspectives on India', p. 101.
59 ibid., p. 105; Sandy Gordon, 'The New Nuclear Arms Race', *Current Affairs Bulletin*, vol. 69, no. 6, November 1992, pp. 28–89.
60 *India Today*, 30 September 1993, p. 29.
61 'Asia Survey: Measuring up the Giants', *Economist*, 30 October 1993, pp. 14–15.
62 *Australian Financial Review*, 8 July 1993, p. 67. Foreign investors have committed US$4.38 billion to projects in India since 1991. United States companies were the top investors last year with pledges worth US$1.15 billion. Eric Ellis, 'India's Economic Revolution', *Australian Financial Review*, 7 February 1994, p. 14.
63 *India Today*, 30 September 1993, p. 29.
64 *Indian Voice* [Melbourne], November 1993, p. 4.
65 *FEER*, 17 March 1994, p. 49.
66 As a result of the recent economic reforms, the global investment community now regards India as the most exciting market in the world. 'China may have had its day', *Australian*, 15 November 1993, p. 19; Cameron Forbes, 'Indian Summer', *Weekend Australian*, 5–6 March 1994, p. 24.
67 According to India's National Council of Applied Economic Research, about a third of India's 900 million people earn at least US$1000 a year. 'Credit card giant VISA estimates at least 40 million Indians, a number twice Australia's population, have annual incomes up to US$30 000'. See Eric Ellis, 'India's Economic Revolution', *Australian Financial Review*, 7 February 1994, p. 14.
68 Richard Sproull, 'India Challenges China Investment', *Australian*, 27 July 1993, p. 38. Many Indians believe that Western investment would switch from China to India as Beijing struggled to reconcile its fledgling market economy with communist political rule. Also see *FEER*, 17 March 1994, p. 49; 'Asia Survey: Measuring up the Giants', *Economist*, 30 October 1993, pp. 14–15; 'India in a Hurry', *Economist*, 5 March 1994, p. 13.

69 According to one report, Indian commodities such as iron ore, drugs and engineering goods have a ready market across the Himalayas, while Chinese goods such as raw silk, precious stones and petroleum products are welcomed by Indian businesspeople. See *India Today*, 30 September 1993, p. 36.

70 *India Today*, 15 October 1993, p. 87.

71 Gordon, *The Search for Substance*, p. 75.

72 Thakur, 'Normalizing Sino-Indian Relations', p. 14.

73 Mitra, 'Coming Closer'.

74 Mansingh, 'An Overview of India–China Relations: From When to Where?', p. 76.

75 Joshi, 'Shy Hands Across the Himalayas', p. 16.

76 On Sino-Pakistan military ties, see Mushahid Hussain, 'Pakistan–China defense co-operation', *International Defense Review*, February 1993, pp. 108–11; 'No Change in Complexion of Sino-Pak Relations', *Asian Defence Journal*, February 1994, p. 122.

77 ibid. Also see Gupta and Chakravarti, 'Sino-Indian Relations', p. 26. The figure on arms sales to Pakistan is from the *Asian Wall Street Journal*, 28–29 January 1994, p. 6.

78 Joshi, 'Shy Hands Across the Himalayas'; Mansingh, 'An Overview of India–China Relations'.

79 British Broadcasting Corporation, *Summary of World Broadcasts*, FE/1789/G/2, 9 Sep 1993; *FEER*, 16 September 1993, p. 13; 'India Complains Over Pakistan–China Links', *Australian*, 16 December 1991, p. 7.

80 'India Tipped Off', *FEER*, 9 August 1990, p. 5; Editorial, 'China's Non-interference', *Hindustan Times*, 18 November 1989.

81 Mansingh, 'An Overview of India–China Relations', p. 75; conversations with India's China-watchers.

82 Garver, 'Chinese–Indian Rivalry in Indochina'; Klintworth, 'Chinese Perspectives on India'.

83 P. Stobdan, 'China's Forays into Burma: Implications for India', *Strategic Analysis*, vol. 16, no. 1, April 1993, p. 35; Bertil Lintner, 'Burma: Arms for Eyes', *FEER*, 16 December 1993, p. 26.

84 *FEER*, 28 November 1991.

85 Andrew Selth, 'Burma: "Hidden Paradise" or Paradise Lost', *Current Affairs Bulletin*, November 1991, p. 7.

86 *Jane's Defence Weekly* reported recently that 'about 70 Chinese personnel have been attached to the Burmese Navy as instructors and technicians. China is helping to build a new naval base at Hainggyi Island and to upgrade facilities at Sittwe (Akyab), Mergui and Great Coco Island'. See *JDW*, 27 November 1993, p. 11.

87 Tai Ming Cheung, 'Smoke Signals'; William Ashton, 'Chinese Naval Base: Many Rumors, Few Facts', *Asia-Pacific Defence Reporter*, June–July 1993, p. 25.

88 Mitra, 'Coming Closer'.

89 Stobdan, 'China's Forays into Burma'.
90 As is their wont, the Chinese vehemently denied that they were 'up to anything' when Indian Defence Minister S. Pawar and Prime Minister N. Rao raised the topic of Chinese arms flows into Burma and the buildup of naval facilities there during their visits to China in 1992 and 1993. See *Sunday*, 23–29 August 1992, pp. 58–59 and *FEER*, 16 September 1993, p. 13.
91 Stobdan, 'China's Forays into Burma', p. 34; Ashton, 'Chinese Naval Base: Many Rumors, Few Facts', p. 25. 'China has already undertaken the large-scale development of towns and infrastructure near the Myanmar border to cater to its burgeoning cross-border trade, now valued at over $1.5 billion.'
92 *FEER*, 3 February 1994, p. 14; 'Indo-Myanmar Relations: Coming Slowly Closer', *India Today*, 31 January 1994, p. 40.
93 *Indian Defence Review*, April 1993, pp. 8–9; Bertil Lintner, 'Burma: Arms for Eyes'.
94 *FEER*, 22 April 1993, p. 9.
95 There still remain several outstanding problems between India and Southeast Asia. India's military buildup, Kashmir and Hindu–Muslim conflicts create misgivings in ASEAN's Islamic-majority countries. Hamish McDonald, 'The Wooing Game', *FEER*, 27 January 1994, p. 28.
96 Ashton, 'Chinese Naval Base: Many Rumors, Few Facts'; Gordon, 'Sino-Indian Relations After the Cold War'.
97 Gordon, 'Sino-Indian Relations After the Cold War', p. 1.
98 R. Roy-Chaudhury, 'The Indian Navy in the 1990s', *Indian Defence Review*, October 1992, p. 64.
99 One commentary in the *Indian Defence Review* called upon the Indian government to 'follow an activist policy in this region in order to negate external hostile [read, Sino-Pakistani] influences'. See *Indian Defence Review*, April 1993, pp. 8–9. For example, the Pakistanis are dreaming of a strategic Islamic bloc, consisting of Pakistan, Iran, Turkey, Afghanistan and some of these new Central Asian states, that could stand up to United States pressure, act as a counterweight to India, support the Kashmiri Muslims' struggle for self-determination and provide Islamabad long-sought 'strategic depth' in the event of a war with India.
100 Lillian Craig Harris, 'Xinjiang, Central Asia and the Implications for China's Policy in the Islamic World', *China Quarterly*, no. 133, March 1993, pp. 111–29. Chinese media reports suggest that Beijing is watching with concern the growing pro-independence activities of Uighur and Kazakh separatists living in Kazakhstan and Kyrghyzstan.
101 Anthony Hyman, 'Moving Out of Moscow's Orbit: The Outlook for Central Asia', *International Affairs*, vol. 69, no. 2, April 1993, p. 301.
102 Ranjan Gupta, 'Buddhism Goes Full Circle in Enlightened India', *Weekend Australian*, 26–27 February 1994, p. 13.

103 ibid. Interestingly, the head Lama of Ladakh has been appointed as the Indian ambassador to Mongolia. According to one observer: 'A new awareness of Buddhism is fostering ties between Buddhist societies in Central Asia, particularly those of Mongolia, Bhutan, Tibet, Burma and the Buddhist rim of northern India. There is a chance of spreading the initiative to Southeast Asia'.

104 One wonders if New Delhi is signalling Beijing: 'if you continue to support our neighbours against us or open new fronts against us, we will do the same to you'. Rivalry in Central and Inner Asia is thus just one component of a larger pattern of Sino-Indian rivalry.

9 China and the ASEAN Region
Leszek Buszynski

China's relationship with the Association of Southeast Asian Nations (ASEAN) has been markedly transformed since the Maoist era when the People's Republic was regarded with deep suspicion. That relationship has been shaped by geopolitical and historical factors which prevented any significant improvement until the termination of the Cold War. One way or another, the often cruel reality of geopolitics would be sufficient for the ASEAN countries to feel concern about China.

In any part of the globe, small and fragmented states direct their attention towards larger neighbours who would by their presence alone become a source of apprehension. The ASEAN states are only too well aware of the disparity that exists between themselves and a populous and relatively homogeneous state with a long tradition of centralised rule. Size, organisation and resources distinguish China from its southern neighbours, who remain ethnically and politically divided and, in some cases, beset by the kind of mutual suspicions that prevent co-operation between them. Moreover, the states of the ASEAN region are by and large the products of decolonisation, Thailand excepted, and their legitimacy is questionable in the absence of the long tradition which characterises China. On the basis of proximity alone, ASEAN leaders would be concerned about the actions of their giant northern neighbour which could have disproportionate consequences for their own security.

The impact of history

Added to the above are three other factors which have shaped China's relationship with the region, the impact of which continues to be felt today. The first factor was China's former assumption of suzerainty over Southeast

Asia. The kingdoms of Southeast Asia, whether Angkor, Majapahit or Burma, developed trade relations with China which the Chinese then defined in the context of their tributary system. The Chinese world view spawned the myth of suzerainty which sustained the tribute system.[1] China conferred titles and recognition upon its 'vassals' in Southeast Asia and protected them against the predatory actions of neighbours. Champa, for example, appealed to the Emperor against Vietnam and Malacca against Siam in confirmation of the Emperor's role as the enforcer of order. The historian D.G.E. Hall referred to China's 'overlordship' of Southeast Asia which complicated Britain's position in Burma in the late Ch'ing Dynasty and wrote that such attitudes influenced the Guomindang in its view of the region.[2] Indeed, according to Wang Gungwu, similar attitudes can be found today amongst Taiwanese scholars and, in this author's experience, they form the basis of a populist Chinese interpretation of Southeast Asian history that is not easily eroded.[3] On occasion, the idea of 'overlordship' finds a place in foreign policy as in the case of China's response to Vietnam's alliance with the Soviet Union in 1978.

Secondly, there was the issue of the Chinese in Southeast Asia, which for Malaysia and Indonesia formed a prism through which China was viewed. The historian C.P. Fitzgerald wrote about the Southern Expansion of the Chinese People in 1972 in terms of waves of pioneering ventures and as population overspill from China.[4] The Imperial Government in 1909 passed a nationality law which claimed that Chinese parents made one a Chinese subject and this was reaffirmed by the Guomindang in 1929. The Guomindang regarded the Chinese of the region as Chinese subjects according to the doctrine of *jus sanguinis* (citizenship by parentage).[5] The People's Republic moved to affirm the doctrine of *jus solis* (citizenship by birth) when it signed the dual nationality treaty with Indonesia in April 1955. That treaty eliminated dual nationality for the regional Chinese and made them either local citizens or citizens of the PRC, depending on their choice. According to Wang Gungwu, the PRC also dropped the term Huaqiao, 'Chinese sojourner', which was previously applied to all Chinese in the region and retained it to describe only those Chinese who refused to opt for local citizenship.[6] Under the dual nationality treaty, these Chinese remained citizens of the PRC. Nonetheless, China's attempt to protect the Chinese in Indonesia when the retail trade ban was imposed in 1959 — its alleged involvement in the events leading to the abortive coup of 30 September 1965 — unfortunately undermined the position of the local Chinese in that country, as they came to be regarded as a fifth column for Beijing.[7] The Chinese in Indonesia still suffer from this stigma, and under the 1967 Internal Security Act, dragon dances, firecrackers and the public display of Chinese characters were banned; many Chinese subsequently thought it appropriate to adopt Indonesian names. Since 1990 the ban has been partially lifted to permit the establishment of Chinese schools for Taiwanese businesspeople and the importing of textbooks in Chinese characters for those schools. Taiwan was by then Indonesia's sixth largest investor. The Chinese in Indonesia, however, still have their identity cards marked in a way that reveals their ethnic origin.

The third factor was Maoist China's support for revolutionary movements in the region, which varied according to the state of China's relationship with the government in question.[8] Support for the Communist Party of Thailand (CPT) escalated after Thailand accepted an American military presence during the Vietnam War.[9] China offered the Burmese Communist Party (BCP) sufficient armed support throughout the 1970s to ensure Burma's neutrality and to remind its military leadership of the need to avoid alliance with the West.[10] Support for the CPT and the BCP began to decline when Vietnam invaded Cambodia in 1978 and as China in response sought ASEAN support. Nonetheless, China continued to offer moral support to the revolutionary groups of the region and allowed them to broadcast their propaganda from Chinese territory. The Voice of the People of Burma and The Voice of the Thai People were programs broadcast from transmitters located in southern China, while The Voice of the Malayan Revolution, which acted as a major irritant in Malaysian relations with China, was located in southern Thailand/northern Malaya. From the ASEAN point of view, Maoist China's effort to improve relations with the region on the basis that ties with the revolutionary movements could be ignored was hypocritical.

China's policy towards the ASEAN region in the Deng Xiaoping era

Immediately after the death of Mao Zedong in September 1976, China embarked upon an effort to improve relations with Indonesia. Diplomatic relations with Indonesia were suspended during the Cultural Revolution when Chinese Embassy staff in Jakarta openly proclaimed their revolutionary credentials. On 5 August 1967, the Chinese Embassy was sacked by Indonesian crowds and on 24 October 1967, diplomatic staff were withdrawn. China moved to repair the damage with Indonesia once policy had been freed of the radicalism of domestic politics after the defeat of the 'gang of four'. In November 1977, Vice-Premier Li Xiannian's call for the establishment of diplomatic relations with Indonesia was repeated by Party Chairman Hua Guofeng in his speech to the 5th National Peoples' Congress in March 1978. The party chairman announced that China would establish relations with the countries of Southeast Asia and would also support the Zone of Peace, Freedom and Neutrality (ZOPFAN).[11] This was China's first step towards a post-Maoist policy towards Southeast Asia that was motivated largely by a concern to rectify the tragic errors perpetrated in relation to Indonesia. Chinese leaders understood that their efforts to wield influence in peripheral or contiguous areas as a product of Sino-Soviet rivalry required the repair of the relationship with Indonesia. President Suharto responded on 11 March 1978 when he endorsed the establishment of diplomatic relations with China as a long-term aim.[12] Thereafter, the Indonesian leader emphasised the condition that China should assure the region that it would no longer support revolutionary movements in the region.

Vietnam's alliance with the Soviet Union, which was announced on 3 November 1978, and its consequent invasion of Cambodia in the following December, intensified China's efforts to improve relations with the region. China's aim was the establishment of a regional coalition directed against Vietnam, which would prevent it from consolidating its position in Cambodia. In this context *Xinhua* graphically characterised Vietnam as 'a knife placed by the Soviet Union at the back of China'.[13] At the global level, China's policy towards the region was shaped by the need to contain Soviet influence and to prevent the Soviet Union from gaining additional allies. Declaratory policy was framed in terms of the three worlds theory outlined by Deng Xiaoping in the United Nations General Assembly in February 1974, in which closer third world unity was demanded against 'superpower hegemonism'. Deng Xiaoping's only visit to Southeast Asia took place in October–November 1978 when he attempted to alert the region to the danger posed by Vietnam. As the region assumed a prominent role in China's anti-Vietnam strategy, specific efforts were made to reduce support for insurgent groups. China formed a *de facto* alliance with Thailand against Vietnam when the then Thai Premier, Kriangsak Chamanand, agreed in February 1979 to allow Chinese arms to be shipped through Thai territory to the Khmer Rouge in Cambodia. The CPT ceased being a domestic threat to Thailand as Chinese support attenuated and as Prem Tinsulanonda's amnesty programs took effect. The mass surrenders of CPT personnel over 1981–82 depleted the party's ranks and reduced it to being merely a nuisance.

The Cambodian conflict marked a critical stage in China's relations with ASEAN as the idea of China as a stabilising force coexisted with the intensified perception of threat. China's leaders desired stability along their southern borders and attempted to ensure that peripheral areas would not be dominated by hostile coalitions linked with the Soviet Union. To that extent, Chinese interests merged with those of Thailand and Singapore in particular, these being particularly sensitive to territorial aggrandisement on the Asian mainland by force of arms. China became a guarantor of Thai security and a source of reassurance for Thailand, Malaysia and Singapore, who initially interpreted Vietnamese aims in terms of expansion and regional conquest. Lee Kuan Yew expressed gratitude for China's limited invasion of northern Vietnam in February–March 1979. He claimed that if China had not taken this step, the situation would have been 'disastrous' for Thailand and the rest of the region, as Soviet influence would have been paramount.[14] Indeed, ASEAN leaders recognised China's role in underpinning their diplomatic position over the Cambodian issue and in their demands for a withdrawal of forces from Cambodia.

Nonetheless, within Malaysia and Indonesia, the spectre of China as a threat to the region was raised by her involvement in the Cambodian conflict. First, China's effort to forge a united front against the Vietnamese and Soviet 'hegemonists' aroused a negative response in these two countries according to the view that China's actions drew Vietnam into Cambodia and the Soviet Union into the region. Chinese pressure upon Vietnam during 1977–78, when the Khmer Rouge unleashed their murderous forays against Vietnamese villages, placed it in the position of a victim according to Malaysian and Indonesian opinion. A widespread view in these countries was that the problem of Soviet intrusion in the region was one related to Chinese inability to accept an independent Vietnam that had only recently completed its reunification.[15] Secondly, China's armed support for the Khmer Rouge after they had been toppled from power by Vietnam stimulated regional fears about China's links with other insurgent groups within the region. In this vein, Malaysian Home Affairs Minister Ghazali Shafie claimed that the Cambodian conflict gave China an excuse to arm the Khmer Rouge and to support regional communist parties.[16]

Fear of China was expressed in various ways and came to influence Malaysian and Indonesian views of the Cambodian issue. Indonesia, as a consequence of these events, formed the view that Vietnam was a buffer against China whereas previously its military held a negative view of all communist powers as potential threats. Malaysia's Tun Hussein Onn and President Suharto affirmed the Kuantan principle when they met in the Malaysian city of the same name in March 1980. According to this principle, ASEAN would compromise with Vietnam over the Cambodian issue to allow it to break with the Soviet Union. Vietnam could then join a wider Southeast Asian community that would resist Chinese pressure. This was an underlying vision frequently expressed within Indonesia.

The Kuantan principle was never translated into practical policy, as ASEAN unity demanded support for Thailand's position. Nonetheless, Malaysian Prime Minister Mohamed Mahathir vociferously drew attention to China as a potential threat to the region which could, as he put it, be tempted to venture into the region.[17] Malaysia's Deputy Foreign Minister Sheikh Kadir Fadzir pointed to the dangers inherent in an American effort to utilise China as a counterweight to the Soviet Union. He specifically objected to any American attempt to devolve responsibility for the security of the region on to China in the context of the United States' containment of the Soviet Union.[18]

China had become a divisive issue for ASEAN which periodically threatened the diplomatic unity of the organisation. Premier Zhao Ziyang visited Malaysia and the Philippines in August 1981, the first occasion when a Chinese premier had travelled to both countries. In Kuala Lumpur, Zhao Ziyang met newly elected Malaysian Prime Minister Mahathir and attempted to downplay China's links with the regional communist parties which for Malaysia were an obstacle to relations with that country. The Chinese premier explained that insurgency was a product of local conditions and could not be directed by external actors. The Voice of the Malayan Revolution was closed down in July in preparation for Zhao's visit and began broadcasting with the less objectionable name of the Voice of the Malayan Democracy. The Malaysian leadership anticipated something more from the Chinese Premier than he was prepared to offer and Mahathir declared that the maintenance of links with insurgent groups was unacceptable to Malaysia.[19] The distinction between state-to-state and party-to-party relations which the Chinese retained was rejected by Malaysia on the basis that they were contradictory. China made a gesture of releasing former Communist Party of Malaya (CPM) Central Committee member Musa Ahmed in early 1981 but questions were raised about the CPM leader Chin Peng who was still resident in Beijing.

Chinese attempts to downplay links with the insurgent movements were never convincing in Malaysia or Indonesia. The Chinese insisted that their ties were a matter of principle, similar to those retained by the labour or socialist parties of the developed world with each other and could not constitute a threat. From the Malaysian or Indonesian point of view, China's credibility as a responsible power hinged upon a repudiation of those ties. The Chinese claimed that they had done everything possible to remove party-to-party ties as an obstacle to state-to-state relations. This was not strictly correct. China prompted the CPT into mass surrenders in the early 1980s as a strategic alliance was established between Thailand and China. According to the Malaysians and the Indonesians, China should have done the same with the CPM. As it was, the CPM ceased to be an issue for Malaysian relations with China only in December 1989, when Chin Peng (then 67 years old) emerged from Beijing to sign surrender agreements with Malaysia and with Thailand's internal security command in Haadyai (southern Thailand). Under these agreements, some 1188 CPM guerillas surrendered and the CPM was disbanded. The Malaysians claim that the surrender of the CPM could have been arranged earlier to coincide with CPT capitulations. The Chinese argued that rivalry with the Soviet Union prevented China from repudiating its ties with the regional communist parties or from arranging a surrender of the CPM before 1989. In reality, however, China had no incentive to sacrifice the CPM before 1989 while Malaysia maintained what was regarded as a 'hostile' attitude, thereby demonstrating yet again how ties with insurgent groups were closely linked with state-to-state relations.

Chinese relations with ASEAN after the Cambodian issue

The Paris Peace Conference of 1989–91 marked the end of the Cambodian issue as an international conflict and signalled the removal of a major obstacle in Chinese–ASEAN relations. Firstly, the strategic conflict between China and the Soviet Union ceased to be an issue for ASEAN when Gorbachev elevated relations with China to front-rank position in his Asia-Pacific agenda. All the ASEAN countries were concerned about the Soviet facility in Cam Ranh Bay in varying degrees. Singapore and Thailand regarded the Soviet position as a menace to their own security either because of the protection it afforded to Vietnam or because it represented a staging post towards a greater design. Within Malaysia and Indonesia, the view was expressed that Cam Ranh Bay served a useful function in deterring or balancing China, in which case the Soviet presence in the region was not unwelcome. As long as Cam Ranh Bay was balanced by the United States military presence in the Philippines, it could be tolerated. Once Gorbachev began to improve relations with China, however, the issue of Sino-Soviet rivalry, and the consequent linkage established with global superpower conflict, was removed from ASEAN discussions.

Secondly, China had played a crucial role in the Paris Conference which eventually resulted in the United Nations-sponsored peace settlement for Cambodia in 1990. China's support for the Khmer Rouge had been criticised by Malaysia and Indonesia, in particular as preventing the Vietnamese from coming to the negotiating table over the issue. China's preference for the Khmer Rouge in the diplomatic moves leading up to the ASEAN co-ordinated Khmer coalition agreement of June 1982 was an irritant because it was surmised that China's aim was to guide them back into power in Cambodia.

Subsequently, however, China reduced its support for the Khmer Rouge in response to regional and international concerns about their brutal record. The Chinese delivered weapons to the other factions in the anti-Vietnamese Khmer coalition headed by Sihanouk and Son Sann, and endorsed the quadripartite declaration of March 1986 in which the Khmer Rouge was given a place equal to that of the other factions. China pushed the Khmer Rouge to accept the United Nations peace plan over 1989–90 when they were inclined to resist all diplomatic pressure. Chinese armed support for the Khmer Rouge ceased in August 1990 when Li Peng declared in Jakarta that China would not accept them in a dominant role in Cambodia and would not push them into power.[20] China's efforts in contributing to a comprehensive settlement of the Cambodian issue endeared it to ASEAN and removed much of the suspicion and resentment that had accumulated within the region.

Thirdly, the ASEAN countries became more conscious of China as a potential trading partner, especially after the short-lived recession of 1985. Within Indonesia, the Chamber of Commerce and Industry (KADIN), headed by Sukamdani Gitsardjono, advocated the establishment of direct trade links with China which would eliminate intermediaries in Singapore and Hong Kong. On the Indonesian side, the decline of oil prices in 1982 was a reminder of the danger of relying on petroleum or gas exports and a stimulant to a diversification of exports — plywood, textiles and other manufactured products. According to official figures, exports to China increased from $8.3 million in 1981 to $84.5 million in 1985, not including indirect trade funnelled through Hong Kong and Singapore. These were outweighed by imports ($249 million in 1985). A direct trade agreement was signed by

KADIN and the China Council for the Promotion of International Trade (CCPIT) in Singapore on 5 July 1985. China despatched three trade delegations to Indonesia in 1985, and in May and August of that year, the first direct exports of Indonesian products under the new order were arranged; they included 875 tonnes of coffee from Bali and 2500 tonnes of palm oil.[21] In April 1986, Indonesia shipped its first consignment of oil (1.5 million barrels) to China's southern provinces, which found it more convenient to purchase oil from Indonesia than from northern China.[22] Indonesia's trade relations with China, however, were distinguished from political relations which would take more time for their restoration. Chinese Foreign Minister Wu Xueqian visited Jakarta for the 30th anniversary of the Bandung conference in April 1985, but failed to extend his visit to meet President Suharto.

A similar interest in trade relations with China was observable in Malaysia, which had been affected by the decline of world commodity prices in 1985. As part of the effort to diversify economic relations, a special cabinet meeting on China was held on 6 June 1985 which was chaired by Deputy Foreign Minister Sheikh Kadir Fadzir. The meeting produced a 200-page document on Malaysia's relations with China entitled 'Managing a Controlled Relationship with the People's Republic of China', and decided that it was time to develop trade with that country.[23] In November in the same year, Mahathir visited Beijing for the first time to boost economic relations despite the Malaysian concern about China's links with the CPM. In Beijing, Mahathir drew attention to the trade balance which was in China's favour and called upon China to import more from Malaysia. Official statistics revealed that Malaysia's exports to China almost doubled from $88 million in 1981 to $161 million in 1985 but were outweighed by imports from China which in 1985 amounted to $251 million. Mahathir, like the Indonesians, wanted to remove the intermediaries in Singapore and Hong Kong who had profited from Malaysia's trade with China. In talks with Zhao Ziyang on 21 November, he reached agreement on joint trade ventures with China and the formation of a Sino-Malaysian trade council to replace the intermediaries. Mahathir also moved to head off the advantages that the Malaysian Chinese would naturally assume in any trading relationship with China and called for special consideration for 'indigenous' Malaysian businesses.[24]

By the end of the Cambodian conflict, the ASEAN countries had become receptive to the idea of expanded relations with China. But ASEAN's relations with China were dependent upon the China–Indonesia relationship and could improve only according to the pace of change in that relationship. Thailand's relationship with China had introduced significant strains into ASEAN, with Indonesian suspicions of China compelling Thai leaders to direct more attention to the maintenance of ASEAN unity. Thailand had established diplomatic relations with China in July 1975, but Singapore could not follow suit because of its concern to avoid establishing diplomatic relations with China until Indonesia had done so first. Brunei also had reservations about developing relations with communist powers and awaited Indonesia's move.

President Suharto played a major role in the effort to prepare Indonesia for normalised relations with China. Indonesian society had developed an antipathy towards China as a consequence of the factors mentioned previously, and this feeling pervaded the military in particular. When the first trial balloons were floated in true Javanese fashion in 1989, key figures in the military establishment either expressed their opposition or insisted on the condition that the president had previously emphasised. They demanded that China renounce its ties with the PKI or that it apologise for 'interference' in Indonesia's internal affairs through its support of the PKI and the coup of October 1965. In his speech to parliament on 1 March 1988, Suharto insisted that China give Indonesia an assurance of non-intervention in its internal affairs. Yoga Sugama, who was Head of the National Intelligence Co-ordinating Board (BAKIN) until 1989, and Admiral Sudomo, Co-ordinating Minister for Security and Political Affairs, both demanded that before diplomatic relations could be restored, China should pledge not to intervene in Indonesia's internal affairs. The then Governor of the National Defence College, Major-General Soebiyakto Prawirasubrata, similarly called for caution, claiming that China would continue to protect its interests in the region through subversion or military means. Soebiyakto also stated that Indonesia had been lulled by the West into complacency about China and expressed the resentment in that country over America's support for China.[25]

Political pressure, however, was mounting for the normalisation of diplomatic relations with China. Chief of the Indonesian Armed Forces, and subsequently Defence Minister, Benny Murdani, as early as 1988, publicly discounted China as a threat to Indonesia and argued that Indonesia was ideologically prepared for diplomatic relations with China.[26] From the security perspective, it was understood that Indonesia could no longer remain isolated from global trends and eventually would have to come to terms with China. Foreign Minister Ali Alatas stressed that Indonesia could only assume a role in shaping regional security if it had established a working relationship with China. More specifically, Indonesia could not act as Co-chair of the Paris Conference on Cambodia when it was first convened in July without such a relationship with China, which was one of the key actors in the conflict. In February 1989, however, Ali Alatas declared that the time was not ripe for the normalisation of relations with China and at that stage it seemed that this position was official policy.[27]

However, after Suharto met Qian Qichen in Tokyo later the same month, Ali Alatas became an open proponent of the restoration of relations with China as it became clear that the president was behind the move. On 23 February 1989, Suharto and Qian Qichen agreed in principle to normalise relations. Thereafter, Ali Alatas claimed that Suharto's condition for a pledge of non-interference in Indonesia's internal affairs had been met, although in reality it had been dropped.[28]

Besides the security rationale for the move, there was pressure to expand trade relations with China which was the most compelling argument in favour of the restoration of diplomatic relations.[29] Indonesia's businesses had become interested in exporting to China as KADIN became an active lob-byist for China. Moreover, the president's family, with its far-flung and extensive business interests, was reportedly behind KADIN over this issue.[30] The Direct Trade Agreement, which was signed in 1985, had not operated effectively as trade continued to be diverted through third parties. Indonesia's non-oil exports had increased as a percentage of total exports from 27 per cent in 1983 to 60 per cent in 1988.[31] Eighty per cent of those exports in 1988 derived from manufacturing and as the profile of the Indonesian economy changed, the pressure for alternative markets was strengthened. State Secretary Murdiono, who was chairman of an interde-partmental committee which co-ordinated relations with China, similarly became a proponent of expanding trade with China and predicted that exports to China would surge in future years. Murdiono's prognosis was based on the observation that exports to China had increased sharply from $393 million in 1985 to $887 million in 1988.[32]

Once Indonesia restored diplomatic relations with China on 8 August 1990, a chapter in the region's history had closed. Singapore followed suit on 3 October 1990 and Brunei on 1 October 1991. China had established formal rela-tions with all of the ASEAN countries and had ceased being regarded as the public threat in a way that was characteristic during the Cambodian conflict.

The challenge that ASEAN faced was the integration of China into the wider Asia-Pacific community without, however, subordinating the inter-ests of the regional organisation or those of its constituent members. Lee Kuan Yew in Shanghai warned that the world would have to change its ways when China became an economic superpower and declared that how a country the size of China would react after it had been marginalised for the past 200 years would depend upon how it was treated by the world.[33] Singapore's Defence Minister Yeo Ning Hong similarly warned that China should not be isolated by the West and claimed that whether China would be a 'responsible player or not' would depend upon its integration into the international economy.[34]

Singapore has emerged as a vocal proponent of China's integration into the Asia-Pacific region and has criticised the West's concern with China's human rights record after the Tiananmen Square incident of June 1989. Singapore's Foreign Minister Wong Kan Seng has emphasised that China should be given a stake in the region and that ASEAN should allow it to assume a constructive role.[35] Over this issue, Singapore has the support of the other ASEAN countries — though in varying degrees, as the conse-quences of China's economic transformation are assessed. The ASEAN coun-tries cannot associate with punitive or corrective Western policies directed towards China which would introduce unnecessary tensions in their own relationships with that country. Such tensions, indeed, may have deleteri-ous repercussions in the future when China's position *vis-à-vis* the region is strengthened. At this point, Western and ASEAN views of China diverge.

Within the context of a constructive relationship, outstanding issues such as the South China Sea or the Vietnamese–Chinese territorial dispute hopefully may be resolved. Indeed, the idea of a constructive relationship with China is itself intended to make China's leaders more sensitive to regional security and political concerns through dialogue and public discussion. China's position over the Khmer Rouge was altered as ASEAN interests were accommodated and there is no reason why a similar dialogue may not affect China's position over other outstanding issues. This, at least, is the ASEAN expectation.

The ASEAN effort to engage China in multilateral security dialogue can be understood in the above context. The actual process of engagement may act as a corrective mechanism which will make China more aware of the needs of the regional states and supportive of the idea of underlying security equilibrium on the basis of which economic integration could be encouraged. China was a special guest of the 25th ASEAN Annual Ministerial Meeting (AMM) held in Manila in July 1992 which was attended by Foreign Minister Qian Qichen. At the 26th AMM in Singapore in July 1993, ASEAN Foreign Ministers decided to establish an Asia-Pacific political and security forum which will be attached to the AMM and which will include eighteen states as well as China and Russia. China has proposed that it conduct a 'special relationship' with ASEAN entailing dialogue partner status similar to that assumed by the United States, Japan, Australia, New Zealand, Canada, South Korea and the European Community. China also proposed a separate security dialogue with ASEAN which would raise such issues as the South China Sea. The first China–ASEAN forum, at deputy foreign minister level, was held in Hangzhou in April 1995. ASEAN also strives to involve China in other multilateral discussions. Singapore has called for China's adherence to the Treaty of Amity and Co-operation (TAC) which was signed by ASEAN members during the first Bali summit of February 1976. The treaty pledges members to renounce the use of force, to avoid interference in each other's internal affairs and to respect the independence and territorial integrity of members. Ali Alatas, however, has opposed the proposal to broaden the membership of the TAC to include external powers as it raises fears of external domination of ASEAN. As a response to Indonesian concerns, Qian Qichen declined to pursue Singapore's suggestion. Nonetheless, aside from the obvious security and political motive in ensuring China's integration with the region, two factors bring ASEAN and China closer — economics and human rights.

ASEAN countries have responded with alacrity to China's open door economic policy and their business communities are at present in the grip of what has been described as 'China fever'. For China, the ASEAN region is not a major source of trade or investment and cannot be compared to the United States, Japan or Taiwan and Hong Kong (see Tables 9.1 and 9.2). China can tap the wealth and business experience of the regional Chinese in a supplementary role, but the major contribution in this respect will be from Taiwan and Hong Kong. The development of economic relationships with the ASEAN region serves the political purpose of easing China's integration with the Asia-Pacific region and overcoming lingering suspicions of

China's intentions in the region. From the Chinese perspective, ASEAN hardly rates a mention in terms of the scale of its economic contribution to China's modernisation, though specific industries and projects may benefit from ASEAN involvement.

Table 9.1 ASEAN trade with China (US$ millions)

		1988	1989	1990	1991	1992
Indonesia*						
	Total	917	805	1250	1883	2024
	Exports	681	582	849	1402	1553
	Imports	236	223	401	481	471
Malaysia						
	Total	879	1044	1222	1330	1474
	Exports	570	692	852	803	829
	Imports	309	352	370	527	645
Philippines						
	Total	403	322	295	383	364
	Exports	135	83	90	130	155
	Imports	268	239	205	253	209
Singapore						
	Total	2512	3191	2865	3075	3265
	Exports	1018	1499	849	1062	1236
	Imports	1494	1692	2016	2013	2029
Thailand						
	Total	1145	1256	1240	1268	1317
	Exports	633	756	386	421	424
	Imports	512	500	854	847	893

* Figures do not include indirect trade
Source: International Monetary Fund, Direction of Trade Statistics, IMF, Washington, DC, various years.

China, however, is the new economic frontier for ASEAN and its booming economy has been regarded by President Ramos of the Philippines as an 'economic model' for the region.[36] In a similar view, Mahathir declared that China could act as a 'vehicle of growth' for ASEAN in recognition that the region's economic future could be increasingly intertwined with that of China.[37] At a time when ASEAN exporters fear that markets in the Western world will close, through protectionism, increased competition or saturation, China offers new opportunities for continuous growth. China's share of ASEAN trade is still limited but is expanding rapidly. Figures for 1992 indicate that 3.6 per cent of Indonesia's trade was directed to China, an increase over 2.6 per cent in 1990. For Malaysia, Thailand and Singapore, the 1992 figures were 1.8 per cent, 1.8 per cent and 2.4 per cent respectively, indicating little change over the 1990 figures. Up until 1992, China was still a second-rank trading partner for the ASEAN countries, with Japan and the United States in the first rank. Australia remained a larger market for Thai and Singaporean exports and South Korea a more important market for Indonesia; for Malaysia, China was a trading partner comparable to Australia and a smaller market for its exports than South Korea. Despite Mahathir's expectations, China in 1992 was Malaysia's ninth trading partner, the same rank it occupied in 1988, and took a modest 2.2 per cent of Malaysia's exports, a slight increase over the 2.0 per cent in 1988; the first four months of 1993, however, reported a 20 per cent increase in trade with China which is expected to join the front rank of Malaysia's trading partners within the next five years.[38]

Singapore is becoming a financial and service centre for China and is able to utilise its ethnic connections with that country to good effect. Figures from the *China Statistical Yearbook* show that Singapore has been consistently the largest ASEAN investor in China, far outstripping the other ASEAN countries. According to this source, over 1985–89, Singapore's cumulative direct investment in China amounted to $73.2 million, well ahead of Thailand in second place with $3.5 million; Singapore's figure was dwarfed by Hong Kong/Macau with $8 billion and by Japan's $1 billion.[39] Trends continued throughout 1990 and 1991, as Table 9.2 shows; Singapore's direct investment in China for those years was $76 million and $68 million respectively; reports indicate that the figure escalated in 1992 to reach $1 billion as businesses took advantage of China's economic boom.[40]

If Chinese figures are in any way indicative of trends, they demonstrate a dramatic change in 1992 as China became the largest recipient of direct investment in the developing world — increasing by 100 per cent over the 1991 figure to reach $11 billion.[41]

The role of Singapore proportionately expanded to the point where it became a financier and source of funds for China. In 1993, for the first time, Chinese banks approached Singapore and raised some $517 million in loans, indicating an interest in going beyond Hong Kong* for regional capital.[42] China is also engaging Singapore's skills and experience in developing industrial processing zones of the kind completed in Jurong or under development at Batam Island. In May 1993 Singapore negotiated an agreement to develop an industrial township at Suzhou on the Shandong peninsula. Suzhou will require joint investment of up to $20 billion and will be given the status of an open coastal city along with fourteen others which enjoy the concessional corporate tax rate of 15 per cent as opposed to the usual 30 per cent.[43]

Table 9.2 Direct foreign investment in China (US$ millions)

	1990	1991
Hong Kong/Macau	2432.00	2925.00
Taiwan	222.30	472.00
Japan	3021.00	1894.00
Indonesia	1.00	2.18
Philippines	1.67	5.85
Thailand	7.52	19.73
Malaysia	0.64	1.96
Singapore	75.85	68.21

Source: China, *Statistical Yearbook 1992*, State Statistical Bureau of the People's Republic of China, Beijing.

Singapore's involvement in China's modernisation brings with it dilem-mas of another kind relating to the status of Singapore's Chinese popula-tion in the region. Singapore's leaders have consistently emphasised that its ethnic Chinese population belongs to the region and have judiciously avoided open identification with China in a way which would stimulate the suspicions of its Malay neighbours. Prime Minister Goh Chok Tong empha-sised that relations with China were 'strictly business' and would never result in the marginalisation of the Malay or Indian population of Singapore.[44] In his National Day rally speech, the Prime Minister warned that if Singapore concentrated upon China its neighbours may misunder-stand its intentions, in a poignant reminder of its vulnerability.[45] The issue may be aggravated by the role of the regional Chinese in funnelling capi-tal to China, depriving their host countries of much-needed investment. Already the ASEAN countries regard China as a competitor for direct for-eign investment and international bankers have warned that China may 'crowd out' other Asian countries because of its huge capital demands.[46] The outflow of capital from Indonesia has been a source of concern as ven-tures in Indonesia are starved of funds. In 1992 a reported $800 million of Indonesian capital was invested in China, mainly in property, which cor-respondingly reduced the funds available for national development pro-jects.[47]

Malaysia's interest in developing economic relations with China was affirmed when Mahathir visited that country for the second time in June 1993. The prime minister led a 290-member delegation to Beijing, which was the largest Malaysian mission ever to visit China. The issues discussed included human rights, China's support for Mahathir's proposal for an East Asian Economic Caucus (EAEC) and trade. The Malaysians called upon the Chinese to reduce the 28 per cent import duty on palm oil, one of their major exports to China.[48] Reports circulated that the Malaysians were interested in purchasing weapons from China or in establishing joint ventures in avi-ation and ammunition production.[49] Though such reports were denied by Defence Minister Najib, Mahathir subsequently agreed in principle to the production of Chinese armoured personnel vehicles in Malaysia.[50] Some 36 Memorandums of Understanding and contracts totalling $586 million were signed with Chinese corporations during the Mahathir trip.

Thailand's business community has similarly been captivated by the image of boundless opportunities in China. Previous governments pro-claimed that Thailand was the 'gateway to Indochina', a phrase used by Anand Panyarachun when he was prime minister (February 1991–March 1992, May 1992–September 1992) or that Indochina was a natural economic hinterland for Thailand. The Thai business community, however, has shown a decided preference for China over Vietnam, for which there are several rea-sons. The obvious size of China's market is one reason but the lure of quick profits in China's booming economy may be even more significant as an explanation, given that Vietnam is a place for the longer-term investor. Deputy Prime Minister Amnuay Viravan claimed that proximity was an important consideration: Yunnan was only 250 kilometres from northern Thailand, China had abundant cheap labour, energy and raw materials and its economy showed a similar pattern of development to that of Thailand.[51] Several major Thai companies have moved into China, taking advantage of China's cheap labour and its relatively undervalued property market. Siam Cement has negotiated agreements to construct plants in Hainan and Guangzhou; Bangkok Land and MK Real Estate have invested in residential property in cities such as Shanghai; the paint manufacturers TOA, with their Japanese partners, relocated a joint venture from Vietnam to China where the market was larger.[52]

Thailand has visions of including southern China in a northern growth triangle linking Yunnan, Myanmar and Laos with northern Thailand. Thai companies have already taken the first steps in the construction of a road 225 kilometres in length linking Yunnan with northern Thailand and Myanmar. A feasibility study was undertaken in February 1993 and the project was submitted to Yangon for approval. Thai Prime Minister Chuan Leekpai joined the queue of ASEAN leaders travelling to China when he visited Beijing in August 1993. Chuan, accompanied by 120 Thai businessmen, called upon China to reduce the trade deficit with Thailand and to invest more in Thailand.[53] China was Thailand's second largest market for rubber but the Thai prime minister hoped to promote exports of manufactured goods.

Despite the commercial relationship that has rapidly developed between Thailand and China, the Thais have not subordinated their interests to China in a way initially feared within ASEAN. The relationship that Thailand established with China was a product of the Cambodian conflict when Thailand felt threatened by Vietnam. That deferential relationship did not carry over into the post-Cambodian era, particularly after the events of May 1992 when democracy was restored under a civilian leadership. The Chuan Leekpai government invited the Dalai Lama to Thailand in February along with eight Nobel Peace Prize laureates. Sensitivity to China prevented Thailand from inviting the Dalai Lama on at least three other occasions, in 1984, 1987 and 1990. Army Chief Vimol Wongwanich complained that the visit would send the wrong signals to China and Myanmar and that the visitors would use Thailand as a platform to criticise neighbours; the army, as a consequence, prevented the Dalai Lama from being interviewed on its own television channel.[54] The military, however, no longer ruled Thai politics and it was compelled to back down over this issue. Foreign Minister Prasong Sunsiri, who is known for his links with the national security establishment, claimed that the decision to invite the Dalai Lama was in line with the 'pro-democracy' stance of the present government.[55]

Deputy Foreign Minister Surin Pitsuwan declared that the visit would 'show the world that Thailand would uphold human rights'.[56] After the Cambodian conflict, Thailand's relationship with China was liberated from the limitations imposed by strategic need and came to be based on the perception of business opportunities.

Human rights in ASEAN–China relations

The issue of human rights is another factor which draws together ASEAN and China. United States relations with China have been strained since the Clinton administration gave notice that human rights and democratisation held a prominent place in its Asia-Pacific policy. China complains of a United States-led anti-China coalition as revealed by a leaked Ministry of Foreign Affairs document according to which the United States was intensifying its anti-China campaign over human rights issues. In this document, America's support for Russia and Vietnam's effort to normalise relations with the United States were specifically noted.[57] The Clinton administration's crusade for human rights may push China to assume the role of champion of Asia and defender of what are considered to be Asian as opposed to Western values. ASEAN countries feel keenly that Western human rights activists do not understand or appreciate the cultural differences between Western and Southeast Asian societies or that political democracy requires a conducive cultural context for its success. Only in Thailand, of all the ASEAN countries, is there a press that shares the West's values over this issue and criticises China and Indonesia for human rights abuses.[58]

This emerging consensus between ASEAN and China in relation to human rights was seen at the Vienna Conference on Human Rights which was held in June 1993. For a start, China won ASEAN gratitude by insisting that non-government organisation (NGO) representatives be excluded. Deputy Foreign Minister Liu Huaqiu expressed China's opposition to the Western definition of human rights at the conference more forcefully and cogently than the ASEAN representatives could do by themselves. ASEAN representatives were constrained by their ties to the West and gained some satisfaction from China's advocacy of an Asian position over this issue. Liu insisted that human rights constituted a country's internal affairs and accused the West of interference.

This view has been expressed by ASEAN leaders on different occasions and with different degrees of emphasis. Lee Kuan Yew claimed that the 1945 Universal Declaration of Human Rights was a Western document written by the victorious allied powers at the conclusion of the Second World War. As such, it needed revision through the inclusion of an Asian view of human rights.[59] As to what an Asian interpretation of human rights would entail, two points have been regularly emphasised by ASEAN leaders. The first is the idea that the most basic human right is economic development, without which there can be no real democracy. From the ASEAN perspective, this right constitutes the foundation upon which are constructed all the other rights that the West seeks to protect.[60] Secondly, the universal element inherent in the concept of human rights should be distinguished from the particular which relates only to specific cultures. ASEAN foreign ministers have attempted to formulate their own concept of human rights, taking account of the specific features of their societies. Singapore's Foreign

Minister Wong Kan Sen claimed that press freedom, pornography and trial by jury were all relative to the societies concerned and could not therefore be imposed on Asian societies.[61]

The tendency to seek China's support is strengthened as ASEAN countries are subject to United States criticism for human rights abuses. Mahathir, who has been a strident critic of the West over this issue, has found a staunch ally in China. During his visit to Beijing in June 1993 Mahathir agreed with Li Peng that, as they put it, the West was attempting to subvert Asian governments by utilising human rights.[62] Mahathir declared that Malaysia and China had identical views of this issue in a platform that may attract other Asian governments that find themselves under attack.

Indonesia has been targeted by the United States for its human rights record but pride prevents its leadership from turning to China for support. The United States eliminated education and training funding for the Indonesian military, prevented Jordan from selling F-5s to Indonesia because of the East Timor issue and threatened to withdraw GSP privileges if the Indonesian government did not improve its attitude towards labour. On 8 September 1993, the United States Senate Foreign Relations Committee passed the Feingold Amendment which was attached to the Foreign Assistance Authorisation Bill of 1993–94. The amendment proposed to ban all arms sales to Indonesia unless it complied with all United Nations resolutions over East Timor and improved its human rights record. The Senate subsequently voted against the amendment, but the impression of increasing pressure from the United States over this issue remains. Indonesian leaders have not publicly reacted by condemning the West in the way characteristic of Mahathir. The Foreign Ministry's Director-General for Political Affairs, Wiryono Sastrohandojo, claimed, however, that if Indonesia became a victim of United States pressure, relations could reach breaking point.[63] Indonesia's Ambassador to China, Abdurahman Gunadirdja, declared that Indonesia and China share similar principles and foreign policies based on peaceful coexistence and mutual non-interference.[64] Such statements would not have been heard publicly several years ago and are indicative of future trends.

ASEAN relations with China are far too complicated to claim that Western human rights policies will compel threatened Asian countries to form a counter-group. Mahathir has promoted the idea of the EAEC as an economic grouping of Asian states which could assume a political dimension in relation to the issue of human rights. For Mahathir, the EAEC as an exclusive Asian grouping is a weapon in his campaign against the West and its irritating assumption of moral superiority. For the other ASEAN countries, the idea of the EAEC is either divisive, threatening to aggravate relations with major trading partners in the West, or it raises the fear of domination by larger Asian powers — Japan or China. Nonetheless, Western human rights campaigns could certainly accelerate trends towards an ASEAN–China alignment over this specific issue.

ASEAN security concerns

Despite the effort to engage China diplomatically and economically with-in the region, concerns continue to be expressed about China's intentions over several key issues. Malaysian leaders have made a deliberate attempt to deny that China is a threat or a security problem to facilitate China's integration into the Asia-Pacific region. During the Cambodian conflict, Mahathir had publicly identified China as a regional threat and now his diplomacy of accommodation demands the repudiation of the past. In Bangkok in August 1993, Mahathir declared that China was no 'potential enemy' and saw no purpose in discussing regional security arrangements 'as though China was the enemy'.[65] At the 7th ISIS Roundtable Conference in June 1993, Defence Minister Najib claimed that China was a 'benign power' and criticised the Western media for the portrayal of China as a regional threat.[66] In a previous decade, at a time when the West regarded China as an ally against the Soviet Union, it was Malaysia which warned the West about China and stigmatised it as a threat. Despite public pronouncements, there are three security issues which concern ASEAN — China's defence modernisation program, the South China Sea and China's support for Myanmar.

In a general sense, the ASEAN countries recognise China's sovereign right to develop a modern defence capability since they are doing the same themselves. China's defence spending increased by 12.5 per cent in 1993 and by up to 60 per cent in real terms over the past five years, which represents an expansion of some magnitude in comparison with ASEAN. China's representatives claim that their economy can sustain such increases anyway, that defence spending as a percentage of GDP declined from 7.2 per cent in 1985 to an estimated 1.5 per cent in 1993, and that much of the budget increase would be used to maintain the living standards of the 3.2 million men in the People's Liberation Army (PLA) in the face of inflationary pressure.[67] Total defence spending ($7.3 billion) may be low in comparison with the United States ($274 billion) or Japan ($37.7 billion), but it is only slightly smaller than the combined defence budgets of all the ASEAN countries in 1992 ($9.44 billion). In any case, China's actual defence spending is greater than official figures suggest and may be around the $10–15 billion mark, much larger than ASEAN's combined defence budget. Ali Alatas declared that China had a legitimate need to ensure its security, but recognised that a Chinese military buildup would impact upon the South China Sea and would be of concern to ASEAN.[68] Najib attempted to distinguish between what ASEAN could and could not accept in China's defence modernisation and drew the line at offensive weapons systems — a long-range air strike capability and aircraft carriers.[69]

More disturbing for the ASEAN countries are confusing reports about China's desire to purchase or manufacture an aircraft carrier. Chinese Foreign Ministry representatives deny the intention and are contradicted by reports attributed to PLA officers. Naval Air Force Commander Wang

Xudong declared that a carrier would symbolise a nation's strength and claimed China has decided to construct one.[70] General Zhao Nanqi, Inspector-General of the Logistics Department of the PLA, reportedly stated that a carrier would be deployed in 1997.[71] It is unclear exactly what the Chinese have in mind, but after rejecting purchase of the Varyag from the Ukrainians, some reports claim that China has decided to construct a small carrier of around 30 000 tonnes. An aircraft carrier would give China the means to deploy SU-27s or MiG-29s, configured for carriers, in the South China Sea. China may not have an escort capability to protect a carrier against Western navies, but against Vietnam or ASEAN extensive carrier protection will not be required.

A similar ambiguity surrounds Chinese policy towards the South China Sea. Foreign Ministry officials may call for joint development of the area's resources and the suspension of territorial claims, but there has been no progress in this direction. At ASEAN's 25th AMM in July 1992, Foreign Minister Qian Qichen declared that, when conditions are ripe, China will be ready to promote a settlement of the dispute. The same intention was repeated by Chinese Foreign Ministry representatives at the 26th AMM. Yet the question is why conditions are not ripe now. Indonesia has sponsored several informal workshops, bringing together the claimants to the South China Sea. Ali Alatas' aim is a solution based on the Australian–Indonesian Timor Gap Treaty of October 1989 which specified an area over which both sides shared sovereignty. When Alatas proposed to move from informal discussions to a formal government-to-government dialogue over the issue, the Chinese refused.[72] China also opposed a Philippine proposal for an international conference over the South China Sea, stating that the discussions should be kept to the claimants. While China opposes or avoids practical proposals for a resolution of the issue, the situation may become complicated and difficult to resolve. At the Surabaya workshop in 1993, Ali Alatas thought the situation in the South China Sea 'potentially explosive' and voiced his fear that diplomatic positions could harden if significant deposits of oil were discovered in the area.[73] China's occupation of Mischief Reef in February 1995 highlights these concerns.

The issue of the South China Sea has become a touchstone of China's relationship with the region and various interpretations of China's behaviour have circulated, based on views as to who represents official policy in Beijing. The first, or benign, view has it that the Foreign Ministry and its representatives express official policy and that the ultimate priority is a settlement on the basis of joint development on terms favourable to China. According to this view, China has too much at stake in terms of expanding trade relations with the Asia-Pacific to risk escalation and conflict over this issue. The second view is that the Foreign Ministry is covering up for the PLA and is adopting delaying tactics over the issue according to a hidden agenda which includes eventual possession of the islands. Proponents of this view point to China's naval buildup as evidence, as well as the territorial law which was passed in February 1992 which turned the South China Sea into China's inland waters and which gave the Chinese Navy the right to eject foreign intruders. As a third view, it is more likely that China has no defined policy over the South China Sea and that the proponents of joint development jostle for influence against the nationalist advocates in the PLA who oppose compromise over the issue.[74] While the situation remains unclear, the Foreign Ministry can only stall, generating suspicions within ASEAN security circles that China harbours malignant intentions.

The third issue that concerns ASEAN is China's links with the military regime in Myanmar which presents the region with a dilemma. On the basis of the narrow calculation of security alone, a strengthening of the Myanmar military prevents that country's internal collapse at the cost of continuing human rights abuses. On the other hand, however, a stronger Myanmar military will be less likely to compromise with the domestic opposition over the constitution which has been under discussion since January 1993. The postponement of internal political change brings with it the danger of a sudden eruption at some later date with consequences which cannot be assessed. Moreover, the military would be more likely to engage in border clashes with Thailand if it were confident of China's support. In 1992 Thai and Myanmar forces clashed over an obscure part of the border (Hill 491), during which the Thai military threatened escalation. In 1992 China provided the Myanmar military with an estimated $1 billion in military equipment and agreed to support an expansion of its size from 300 000 to 400 000.[75] More significant for ASEAN as a grouping was the report of China's interest in naval facilities at Bassein, an island in the Irrawaddy delta. If reports of China's desire to develop a naval presence in the Indian Ocean to counter India are correct, the danger arises of Sino-Indian naval rivalry which would be a detrimental development for ASEAN's security.

The balance of power in ASEAN strategy

Uncertainty still surrounds China's integration into the region. There is the hope that regional and global economic trends would create cross-cutting networks within the Asia-Pacific region and would remove the above issues as obstacles or areas of tension. Nonetheless, the integration of China into the Asia-Pacific region has been accompanied by a corresponding search for a security framework that would provide ASEAN with a counterbalance. China's smaller Asian neighbours cannot expect economic trends to resolve all of their dilemmas of national security as economic competition can be a source of new tensions in a way illustrated by fishing disputes or Exclusive Economic Zone conflicts in the South China Sea. Moreover, those responsible for the national security of their countries look beyond the current phase of economic expansion and wonder how China would behave in the case of an economic downturn. Economic growth and integration may not necessarily be a permanent constraint upon the ambitions of states: they may reflect a current phase that may not last.

The ASEAN interest in a multilateral security framework that would involve the United States and Japan is a product, in part, of the need to ensure the successful regional integration of China. Indeed, China's sheer presence, along with that of Japan, has redirected policy in Malaysia and Indonesia away from the Zone of Peace, Freedom and Neutrality (ZOPFAN) towards a variant of the balance of power approach to security. Both Malaysia and Indonesia were proponents of the idea of regional security autonomy, that ASEAN could define its own security without the presence of external powers and in particular the United States. ZOPFAN symbolised these aspirations during the decades of the Cold War when the United States maintained its military presence in the Philippines. Since the Cold War era, however, both Malaysia and Indonesia have expressed the need to retain a continuing American presence in the region. Ali Alatas, in his speech to the NUS society in Singapore in October 1992, outlined Indonesian thinking in the post-Cold War era in terms of 'strategic equilibrium'. The Indonesian Foreign Minister used the terms 'fluidity' and 'instability' to characterise the new global security environment in which case the move towards a balance of power approach towards regional security was not surprising.[76]

Conclusion

As China and ASEAN forge their relationship in the post-Cold War era, the question is will it be based primarily on mutual economic advantage or defined in hierarchical terms? ASEAN involvement of other external powers, the United States and Japan, in a multilateral Asia-Pacific security framework, is intended to influence Chinese policy away from the idea of a predominant regional role which would entail ASEAN's subordination. Without external support, ASEAN would face China alone and the pressure to surrender to China over the South China Sea would be overwhelming over the long term. Economics alone will not necessarily eliminate the concerns that have been expressed in regard to China's intentions as long as outstanding territorial disputes remain and while China builds up her naval strength.

Much will depend upon domestic Chinese politics and the nature of the regime that will emerge in the post-Deng Xiaoping era. A smooth succession and a successful transfer of power to the reformists could strengthen integrative trends within the region and could remove the ambiguity around China's policy towards the South China Sea. Joint development in that area may become a reality if a reformist leadership in China felt sufficiently secure to deflect pressure from the nationalists and the advocates of great power politics. There are fears, however, that the PLA will strengthen its position in a post-Deng Xiaoping crisis and that it may step in directly to maintain order as it did during the Cultural Revolution and the arrest of the radical 'gang of four' in 1976–77. Party Secretary Jiang Zemin referred to the PLA as the chief guarantor of social stability in China in an article in the *People's Daily* on 23 March 1993.[77] With the decline of central authority, conditions for military intrusion into politics are more conducive than they ever have been.[78] A PLA that has assumed the role of guardian of the state will have its own demands in terms of long-range offensive capabilities and in relation to the South China Sea. One way or another, ASEAN security is indeed dependent upon political events in China.

Notes

1 Leonard Y. Andaya in Nicholas Tarling (ed.), *The Cambridge History of Southeast Asia*, vol. 1, Cambridge University Press, Cambridge, 1992, p. 340.

2 D.G.E. Hall, *A History of Southeast Asia*, Macmillan, London, 1970, p. 866.

3 Wang Gungwu, *China and the Chinese Overseas*, Times Academic Press, Singapore, 1991, p. 75.

4 C.P. Fitzgerald, *The Southern Expansion of the Chinese People*, ANU Press, Canberra, 1972.

5 Tao-Tai Hsia and Kathryn A. Haun, *Peking's Policy toward the Dual Nationality of the Overseas Chinese: A Study of its Development*, Law Library, Library of Congress, Washington DC, April 1976, pp. 12–14.

6 Wang Gungwu, *China and the Chinese Overseas*, p. 224.

7 On the Chinese in Indonesia see Mary F. Somers Heidhues, *Southeast Asia's Chinese Minorities*, Longman, Melbourne, 1974, pp. 80–83; Leo Suryadinata, *'Overseas Chinese' in Southeast Asia and China's Foreign Policy: An Interpretative Essay*, Research Notes and Discussion Paper, no. II, Institute of Southeast Asian Studies, Singapore, 1978.

8 Melvin Gurtov, *China and Southeast Asia — The Politics of Survival*, Heath Lexington, Lexington, Mass., 1971, p. 164.

9 Peter Van Ness, *Revolution and Chinese Foreign Policy: Peking's Support for Wars of National Liberation*, University of California Press, Berkeley, 1970, p. 137.

10 Jay Taylor, *China and Southeast Asia: Peking's Relations with Revolutionary Movements*, Praeger, New York, 1974.

11 *Straits Times*, 7 March 1978.

12 ibid., 12 March 1978.

13 *Xinhua*, 2 November 1983.

14 *Straits Times*, 7 February 1982.

15 Leszek Buszynski, *The Soviet Union and Southeast Asia*, Croom Helm, London, 1986, p. 222.

16 *New Straits Times*, 3 June 1981.

17 *Sunday Monitor*, Malaysia, 12 August 1984.

18 Kuala Lumpur Service, 31 July 1984, British Broadcasting Corporation, *Summary of World Broadcasts*, FE/7711/A3/5, 2 August 1984.

19 Reuters, 11 August 1981.

20 *Straits Times*, 9 August 1990.

21 ibid., 25 September 1985.

22 ibid., 21 May 1986.
23 James Clad, 'An Affair of the Head', *Far Eastern Economic Review*, 4 July 1985.
24 Kuala Lumpur Radio, 21 November 1985, British Broadcasting Corporation, *Summary of World Broadcasts*, FE/8116/A3/3, 23 November 1985.
25 *Jakarta Post*, 3 July 1989.
26 ibid., 2 May 1988.
27 *Sunday Times*, Singapore, 5 February 1989.
28 *Straits Times*, 24 February 1989.
29 Hadi Soesastro, *After the Resumption of Diplomatic Relations: Aspects of Sino-Indonesian Economic Relations*, Centre for Strategic and International Studies, Jakarta, June 1991, p. 3.
30 Hamish McDonald, 'Breaking the Ice', *Far Eastern Economic Review*, 9 March 1989, p. 10.
31 *Jakarta Post*, 18 August 1989.
32 ibid., 16 March 1990; KADIN figures on Sino-Indonesian trade from Soeasastro, *After the Resumption of Diplomatic Relations*, p. 7.
33 *Straits Times*, 15 May 1993.
34 ibid., 1 July 1993.
35 ibid., 27 July 1993.
36 Reuters Textline, 27 April 1993.
37 *Straits Times*, 21 August 1993.
38 *Business Times*, Singapore, 26 July 1993, Reuters Textline.
39 Zafar Shah Khan, *Patterns of Direct Foreign Investment in China*, World Bank Discussion Papers, The World Bank, Washington, DC, September 1991.
40 *Economist*, 21 August 1993, p. 52.
41 'China's Economy in 1992 and 1993: Grappling with the Risks of Economic Growth', paper written by the Central Intelligence Agency for submission to the Subcommittee on Technology and National Security of the Joint Economic Committee: Congress of the United States, 30 July 1993, p. 2.
42 *Business Times*, Singapore, 21 July 1993, Reuters Textline.
43 *Straits Times*, 12 May 1993; 8 July 1993.
44 Reuters, 15 August 1993.
45 ibid., 16 August 1993.
46 *Australian Financial Review*, 22 June 1993.
47 *Nikkei*, 19 April 1993, Reuters Textline.
48 *Straits Times*, 9 June 1993.
49 ibid., 25 May 1993.
50 Michael Vatikiotis, 'Political Weapons', *Far Eastern Economic Review*, 26 August 1993, p. 12.
51 *Bangkok Post*, 1 September 1993.
52 *South China Morning Post*, 19 May 1993, Reuters Textline.
53 *Straits Times*, 27, 28 August 1993.

54 *Bangkok Post*, 16 February 1993.

55 ibid., 20 February 1993.

56 ibid.; also editorial 'Military Thinking out of Tune with the Times', 20 February 1993.

57 Lu Yu-shan, 'The CCP is Worried about US-led Anti-China Alliance', *Tangtai*, 15 June 1993, British Broadcasting Corporation, *Summary of World Broadcasts*, 24 June 1993, Reuters Textline.

58 See editorial, 'Human Rights does not Stop at Vietnam Conference', *Nation*, 2 July 1993.

59 *Straits Times*, 17 June 1993.

60 See views of Datuk Musa, Malaysia's Permanent Representative to the United Nations, *Straits Times*, 28 June 1993.

61 ibid., 17 June 1993.

62 *Xinhua*, British Broadcasting Corporation, *Summary of World Broadcasts*, 15 June 1993, Reuters Textline.

63 *Straits Times*, 14 September 1993.

64 Antara 241/A, 19 August 1993.

65 *Straits Times*, 21 August 1993.

66 ibid., 10 June 1993.

67 *South China Morning Post*, 10 March 1993, Reuters Textline.

68 *Straits Times*, 4 September 1993.

69 *Bangkok Post*, 13 July 1993.

70 *Kyodo*, 27 June 1993, Reuters Textline.

71 *Observer*, 11 April 1993, Reuters Textline.

72 Reuters, 23 August 1993.

73 ibid.

74 On bureaucratic conflict and its impact on China's position, see John W. Garver, 'China's Push through the South China Sea: The Interaction of Bureaucractic and National Interests', *China Quarterly*, no. 132, December 1992, pp. 999–1028.

75 Reuters, 8 February 1993.

76 'The Emerging Security Environment in East Asia and the Pacific: An ASEAN Perspective', address by Ali Alatas before the NUS Society, Singapore, 28 October 1992.

77 *Bangkok Post*, 24 March 1993.

78 See Harlan W. Jencks, 'Party Authority and Military Power: Communist China's Continuing Crisis' in Bih-Jan Lin, et al. (eds), *The Aftermath of the 1989 Tiananmen Crisis in Mainland China*, Westview Press, Boulder, Col., 1992; on the other hand, Michael Swaine argues that the 14th Party Congress of October 1992 reduced the likelihood of PLA intervention when Deng Xiaoping had Yang Shangkun and Yang Baibing removed. Nonetheless, Swaine also concludes that 'the key to China's political future will continue to rest in large part with the PLA': Michael D. Swaine, *The Military and Political Succession in China: Leadership, Institutions, Beliefs*, Rand Corporation Monograph R-4254 AF Rand Corporation, Santa Monica, California, 1992.

10 Vietnam's Strategic Readjustment

Carlyle A. Thayer

Introduction

Vietnam suffers from 'the tyranny of its geography'. It is located on China's southern border and cannot escape the geopolitical fact that China is large, populous and more powerful. Prior to the technological developments brought by the twentieth century, Vietnam managed its relations with the Middle Kingdom through its participation in the tributary system.[1] Only in the twentieth century did it become possible to counterbalance Chinese influence and pressures by the maintenance of an 'over-the-horizon' alliance with the Soviet Union. As long as the socialist camp existed, Vietnam could comfortably frame its foreign policy within familiar ideological structures.[2] Prior to the Gorbachev era, Vietnam espoused the model of 'three revolutionary currents'.[3] During the Gorbachev years, Vietnam adjusted its foreign policy frame of reference to suit the 'new political thinking' emanating from Moscow.[4] This enabled Vietnam to open its doors to foreign capitalist investment and to seek the normalisation of relations with China.

In the post-Cold War era, Vietnam finds itself in a rather unique position. It is no longer dependent on or subservient to any single power. It owes no homage to any particular ideological model of foreign relations.[5] It is now free to design its own foreign policy framework. However, given geopolitical realities, Vietnam must always take its northern neighbour into account. After all, in population terms, Vietnam is roughly equivalent to a single Chinese province. Foreign China specialists visiting Vietnam for the first time liken Hanoi, Vietnam's capital, to a provincial Chinese city.

It has been argued elsewhere that from May 1989 to the end of 1991 — that is, from the Beijing summit which normalised Sino-Soviet relations until after the abortive anti-Gorbachev coup and the collapse of the Soviet

Union — China flirted with the idea of creating an 'Asian socialist community' embracing the Soviet Union, North Korea, Mongolia and Vietnam.[6] During this period, elements within the Vietnam Communist Party (VCP), particularly the military, sought to normalise relations with China on the basis of shared ideology. They were not adverse to joining a grouping of Asian socialist states and were even prepared to offer a 'red solution' to the Cambodian problem as the price of admission.[7]

During 1990–91, Vietnam experienced an intense inter-party debate on the question of relations with China. In September 1990, key party leaders secretly journeyed to Chengdu in southern China to discuss normalisation issues with their Chinese counterparts. But it was only in June 1991 that Vietnam's 'pro-China lobby' gained ascendancy at the VCP's Seventh National Congress. After the congress, this group not only pushed for the normalisation of relations with China, but the restoration of some form of 'alliance' relationship. Party-to-party relations were formally normalised at a summit meeting of party leaders held in Beijing in November 1991 and were codified in an eleven-point joint communiqué.[8]

During the two-year period from normalisation until late 1993, Vietnam has sought to develop its relations with China within the larger foreign policy context of relations with the world in general. This framework contains few of the ideological tenets of the past. Increasingly Vietnam is attempting to formulate a foreign policy framework based on national interests set within the context of what it perceives to be acceptable norms of international state behaviour. Vietnam explicitly seeks to 'multilateralise' its relations with all countries in the Asia Pacific region.

In pursuing its national interests, Vietnam has undertaken actions which appear highly provocative from China's point of view. For example, during Vietnam's long struggle for independence, it made no public protests over Chinese claims to territory in the South China Sea and indeed supported them. Yet, after unification, Vietnam reversed its stance. In 1975 Vietnam occupied a number of islands in the Spratly archipelago and subsequently pressed territorial claims to the entire South China Sea. As Foreign Minister Nguyen Manh Cam has admitted:

> Our leaders' previous declaration on the Hoang Sa (Paracel) and Truong Sa (Spratly) archipelagoes was made in the following context: At that time, under the 1954 Geneva agreement on Indochina, the territories from the 17th parallel southward including the two archipelagoes were under the control of the South Vietnam administration. Moreover, Vietnam then had to concentrate all its force on the highest goal of resisting the US aggressive war to defend national independence. It had to gain support of friends all over the world. Meanwhile, Sino-Vietnamese relations were very close and the two countries trusted each other. China was according to Vietnam a very great support and valuable assistance. In that context and stemming from the above-said urgent requirement, our leaders' declaration [sup-

porting China's claims to sovereignty over the Paracel and Spratly Islands] was necessary because it directly served the fight for the defence of national independence and the freedom of the motherland. More specifically, it aimed at meeting the then immediate need to prevent the US imperialists from using these islands to attack us. It has nothing to do with the historical and legal foundations of Vietnam's sovereignty over the Truong Sa and Hoang Sa archipelagoes.[9]

Since then, Vietnam has expanded its presence to include twenty-one islands, while China now occupies nine. Some of these have been garrisoned and fortified. After China's 1992 promulgation of a law on territorial waters, Vietnam moved to reinforce its sovereignty claims by encouraging economic activity. It built a lighthouse, a port and offered tax breaks to Vietnamese firms willing to relocate. According to a Vietnamese political source:

We have a lot of islands, but up to now they haven't been occupied. We had sovereignty in principle but no people. That left open the opportunity for them to be occupied by others. Now our policy is to have a presence on all of them. Not a military presence — we don't want to shock the Chinese. Economic means are more subtle.[10]

Vietnam's national interests dictate that it not capitulate fully in the face of Chinese power. Indeed, Vietnamese expansion into the South China Sea may be viewed as a testing of the limits of its relationship with its northern neighbour. Vietnam has tried to smooth the rough edges in bilateral relations by emphasising the two countries' common ideological heritage. For example, Vietnam argues that the two share a commitment to building socialism (whatever their different paths) and that both are faced by the common threat of 'the strategy of peaceful evolution' and demands to 'democratise' society by permitting political pluralism and internationally acceptable standards of human rights. Vietnam has even gone to the extent of plagiarising Chinese phraseology to stress this commonality.[11] Vietnam, therefore, argues that ideology provides a common ground for developing party-to-party relations as both countries face similar problems in the transition to a market economy.[12]

At the same time, Vietnam has had to cope with what it regards as 'traditional' Chinese behaviour in dealing with matters which are in contention.[13] On 25 February 1992, for example, within months of Sino-Vietnamese normalisation, China promulgated a law on territorial waters which reiterated its claim to the South China Sea and which reserved the right to use force in this area to prevent any violation of its sovereignty. That same month, Chinese troops physically took possession of Da Bau Dau (Three Headed Rock), an unoccupied islet in the Spratly Islands. In May, China granted a concession for oil exploration to the American firm Crestone Energy Corporation in the Tu Chinh bank, a disputed area located on Vietnam's continental shelf. In June, Chinese troops planted a territorial marker on Dac Lac reef, also in the Spratly archipelago. In August, two Chinese ships erected a drilling platform in a disputed area of the Gulf of Tonkin which the two sides had earlier agreed to leave vacant. China also began impounding Vietnamese ships sailing from Hong Kong which it claimed were bringing goods to Vietnam which would be smuggled into southern China. Finally, in May 1993, Chinese ships again intruded into Vietnamese territorial waters off its central coast.

Vietnamese sensitivities to Chinese 'traditional' behaviour may be illustrated with reference to the Crestone affair. In May 1992, Nguyen Van Linh, a senior adviser to the party Central Committee and former VCP Secretary General, visited Beijing and held discussions with Chinese Communist Party (CCP) General Secretary Jiang Zemin and Premier Li Peng in the Great Hall of the People. Hours before Linh's reception, Chinese officials and representatives of the Crestone Energy Corporation signed an oil exploration agreement in the same hall (and in the presence of a United States embassy official). Vietnamese officials interviewed in Hanoi in July 1992 said this was a calculated act designed to complicate the normalisation of United States–Vietnamese relations.

Chinese actions in the Spratly archipelago provoked heated argument at the third plenum of the party's Central Committee which met from 18–29 June 1992. The plenum debated whether or not China was a long-term threat to Vietnam's security. Some party officials argued that China 'has continued on the road to socialism, so we should make allies with the Chinese and ignore small conflicts'. Other party officials argued that China was two-faced and was using 'socialism as a rope to tie Vietnam's hands'.[14] Do Muoi, the party Secretary General, reportedly called China 'expansionist', the first time this expression was used in inner party circles since the early 1980s. The plenum remained divided and unable to reach a firm conclusion on whether China had 'expansionist' designs on the region. Nonetheless, the Foreign Ministry was given the green light to be more vocal in making Vietnamese misgivings public.

By the time of the Crestone affair, Vietnam had overcome its diplomatic isolation in the region and had normalised its relations with all states in Southeast Asia. In the past, such as March 1988 when Chinese and Vietnamese naval forces clashed briefly in the Spratlys after Chinese forces had landed on an unoccupied island, Vietnam was perceived by regional states as a Soviet surrogate. Chinese actions, however much they may have aroused private regional misgivings at that time, were seen essentially as an appropriate form of pressure on Vietnam to force its withdrawal from Cambodia. In the post-Cold War circumstances of 1992, however, regional misgivings were now directed at China. More importantly, they were made in public and in concert. In July 1992 the Association of Southeast Asian Nations (ASEAN) foreign ministers, meeting in Manila, issued a statement of concern which called on unnamed parties to the conflict to exercise restraint. The ASEAN statement was clearly aimed at China. It was issued just after Vietnam had acceded to the ASEAN Treaty of Amity and Co-operation.

ASEAN's statement on the Spratlys, coupled with more vocal reactions, including a warning from the United States, put China on the backfoot diplomatically speaking. In late November–early December, Chinese Premier Li Peng, while on an official visit to Vietnam, declared, 'China will never seek hegemony nor practice expansionism and power politics of all descriptions'.[15] In August 1993, discussions on border issues, which had been stalled since they began in September the previous year, finally produced a result. These were ratified in October, when an agreement on basic principles to resolve territorial and border disputes was signed by deputy foreign minsters Vu Khoan and Tang Jiaxuan. This agreement concerned only the land boundary and delineation of the Gulf of Tonkin but not the Spratly Islands. A joint communiqué stated that both agreed to speed up negotiations to reach a border settlement, to avoid actions that could create complications and to shun the use of force over border disputes.

With this as background, this chapter will now explore Sino-Vietnamese relations within the context of Vietnam's new foreign policy framework.

China and Vietnam's world view

According to an unpublished confidential report by the Vietnamese Foreign Minister to the National Assembly in September 1992,[16] the combination of the revolution in science and technology and the impact of the collapse of the socialist camp had resulted in 'a complex pattern of development and revealed new international relationships'. In Cam's view:

The world political revolution is at an ebb while the developed capitalist countries still maintain their rate of development and stability, completely reversing the situation of relatively balanced forces between East and West to an unfavourable disparity for socialism and the world's revolutionary forces. The world order established by the Soviet Union and the United States after the Second World War has ended; the new world order is taking shape with diversified prospects based on national interests. International relationships have thus become more complicated due to the different interests of independent countries.

In this new world situation, every country has to adapt its foreign policy to the changed situation. Larger countries, in particular, are rapidly adjusting their strategies in order to gain a favourable position in the new world order.

The United States, he said, had emerged in a 'temporarily superior political position' and sought 'to set up the new world order under its control'. The United States, however, was constrained by 'fierce rivalry' with Japan and Western Europe and had been forced to reduce its military commitments in Southeast Asia to a secondary priority. The United States now conducted a policy of 'balancing its own forces with those of its competitors', he argued.

In these changed circumstances, how then did Vietnam perceive China's role? According to Cam:

China has confirmed that the new world order is not unipolar but multipolar. China desires to become one of the pivotal countries in the future. China is adopting a flexible foreign policy in order to become a superpower in the Asian-Pacific region by taking advantage of economic, military, scientific and technical weaknesses in the region, thus creating an image of China which can be judged by international standards — a China which is ready to establish cordial relationships with other countries, a China worthy of its position as a member of the UN Security Council. China has liberalised its foreign policies targeting in particular the United States and Western Europe. It will avoid confrontation with the US except in the direct interests of China.

The above remarks were taken from the general section of the report which gave an overview of the world situation. Later, in the section dealing with bilateral relations, the Foreign Minister stated:

Since early 1992, normal relations have been restored with China after thirteen years of confrontation. However, we have to deal with complications in this relationship because of Chinese incursions into our territory and the agreements signed between our two countries in November 1991. In these circumstances, we have continued to advocate a solution to the problems through peaceful negotiation in order to gradually improve our relations with China. We have endeavoured to maintain our relations with China but at the same time to defend our sovereignty and integrity. However, this has been a long and complicated process.

At the conclusion of his report, Foreign Minister Cam listed fourteen priority tasks. First among them was 'to find solutions through peaceful negotiation to the problems in Sino-Vietnamese relations, but at the same time to promote co-operation between the two countries on the basis of equality and mutual benefit'. In late 1992, according to a former party official, the VCP Central Committee 'redefined ... (Vietnam's) foreign policy in a secret resolution which categorises Vietnam's relations with various countries according to a list of priorities. In the first category are China, Cuba and North Korea ... since they are all considered to be Marxist-Leninist states'.[17]

Vietnam's strategic readjustment

The communist regime in Vietnam, which first came to power in August 1945, has been almost continually at war for four decades.[18] In the changed international environment of the post-Cold War period, Vietnam appears secure from a sudden major attack by an external power. But at the same time, Vietnam's military is perhaps at its most vulnerable stage, having been cut off from all foreign military assistance in 1991. Vietnam's military arsenal is rapidly deteriorating and it has no hard currency to purchase major items, let alone keep up with the force modernisation programs of its neighbours.

Throughout the Cold War period in the 1970s and 1980s, Vietnam declared that Indochina was a 'single theatre of operations' and that its 'special relations' with Laos and Cambodia were 'a law of development'. Further, Vietnam maintained that its alliance relationships with Laos and Cambodia were part of a structure which stretched back to the Warsaw Pact.[19] China was clearly Vietnam's main threat. In mid-1978, on the eve of the Third Indochina War, Vietnam's Central Committee (fourth plenum) secretly concluded that China was the 'main and immediate enemy' of the Vietnamese people.[20] At the 5th National Party Congress held in March 1982, the Central Committee's *Political Report* reiterated (with reference to the 1979 border war) that 'the Chinese ruling circles unmasked themselves as a direct and dangerous enemy of our people'.[21] Elsewhere the report stated:

> The Chinese leaders have all along been pursuing expansionist and hegemonic ambitions. They have not yet given up their scheme to put Vietnam, Laos and Kampuchea under China's tutelage, regarding the three Indochinese countries as primary targets for aggression and annexation on their path of expansion into Southeast Asia.[22]

At the 6th Party Congress in December 1986, after Gorbachev had signalled Moscow's intention to normalise relations with China, Vietnam adopted a far-reaching reform program (known as *doi moi*, or renovation, in Vietnamese). *Doi moi* signalled a complete turn-about in declaratory policy towards China. The Party's *Political Report* now stated:

> The Vietnamese Government and people consistently treasure the friendship between the peoples of the two countries and are resolved to do their best to restore it and have put forward many proposals aimed at an early normalisation of relations between our country and the People's Republic of China. Our stance is to set great store by the fundamental and long-term interests of the two countries. We hold that the time has come for the two sides to enter into negotiations to solve both immediate and long-term problems in the relations between the two countries. Once again we officially declare that Vietnam is ready to negotiate with China at any time, at any level and in any place to normalise the relations between the two countries, in the interests of the two peoples, and of peace in Southeast Asia and the rest of the world.[23]

The following year, Vietnam quietly adopted a new defence doctrine which it termed 'people's war and all-people's national defence' and which led to a strategic readjustment of Vietnam's military posture. In brief, Vietnam made the decision to withdraw its forces from Cambodia and Laos and to cut the size of its main forces in half.

Vietnam's 'all-people's national defence' was a defensive strategy designed to cope with the perceived main threats to Vietnam's security. These were identified as the two 'hot spots' — Vietnam's border with China and the Spratly Islands. It was felt that tensions in either area could erupt at any time and escalate into local armed conflict or even full-scale war. After the collapse of socialist regimes in Eastern Europe, Vietnam also listed the 'strategy of peaceful evolution' as a major threat to national security.

In response to these identifiable threats, Vietnam adopted a policy of 'ending and preventing armed conflicts from bursting into wars' by 'applying measures of maximum self-restraint so as to avoid intensifying and spreading hostile activities'.[24] According to the 'National Defence Tasks and Guidelines, 1991–95':

> Since 1987, we have advocated the policy of self-restraint, intensified the propaganda campaign to motivate the Chinese people and troops to cease hostilities and restore normal relations, gradually reduced the scale of conflicts by not resorting to gun battles all the time, and made the Chinese people and troops clearly understand our good will and practical deeds, thus creating conditions for ending the war. This is, of course, a dangerous and difficult ideological struggle. Our troops have had to endure and even though they have at time questioned the situation, they have always scrupulously implemented the policies of the higher echelons.[25]

By late 1989, according to the then Minister for National Defence, Le Duc Anh, the security situation in the two 'hot spots' had become 'stable for the time being'. In light of events in Eastern Europe, Vietnam now began to stress 'the strategy of peaceful evolution' as the main threat to its national security. As party Secretary General, Nguyen Van Linh, put the matter:

> There are still simmering hotbeds that can easily explode into localised armed conflicts or full-scale wars. This is because [our] enemies have still not given up their sinister schemes to be implemented against the Vietnamese revolution and the revolutions of the three Indochinese countries as a whole through the application of mainly economic, political, and psychological measures and by means of localised armed aggression, localised nibbling attacks, and wars of aggression on various scales, including large-scale ones which, though unlikely to occur in the near future, cannot be completely ruled out …
>
> This strategy uses mainly peaceful evolution … while always remaining ready to use military force in various forms whenever the need arises, such as partial armed conflict, low intensity conflict, proxy war, and limited war.[26]

The 7th National Congress (June 1991) reconfirmed that Vietnam's national defence strategy must 'meet the objective requirements of defeating several forms of sabotage activities and modern war of aggression, including the "fourth generation war", of reactionary imperialist forces'.[27] According to Major-General Nguyen Van Phiet (1992):

> Today, the factors threatening our socialist regime's existence and our fatherland's independence stem not only from certain counter-revolutionary armed violence in the country, or from the deterrent, aggressive military strength of imperialism from the outside; they are also shaped and influenced by our country's weaknesses and deficiencies in the economic, social, political, ideological, cultural, educational, and artistic fields as well as in our life-style. These are weaknesses and deficiencies caused by the socio-economic crisis. Pursuing their scheme of abolishing socialism, hostile forces inside the country and imperialism are deepening our weaknesses and carrying out many policies and tricks of sabotage, confrontation, and aggression against our people in all domains of social life. In conjunction with applying military deterrence, they are implementing the 'peaceful evolution' strategy, launching attacks and sabotage activities in the economic, political, ideological, educational, and cultural fields and in daily life, while colluding with reactionary forces inside the country for the purpose of overthrowing the present political regime. They are concentrating on undermining the unity among the party, state, people, and armed forces, and on inciting enmity among nationalities [sic] ... These are the factors threatening the security of our regime and endangering the independence and sovereignty of the Vietnamese fatherland. This could even be called an undeclared, non-shooting 'war of aggression'.[28]

In summary, in the current period Vietnam identifies low-level or limited conflict as the most likely threat to Vietnam's security.[29] Such conflicts could arise from disputes along its land and sea borders, offshore territories in the Eastern Sea (South China Sea), or as a result of deliberate instigation by 'imperialist and reactionary' forces employing the 'strategy of peaceful evolution'. Vietnam's repeated references to 'the strategy of peaceful evolution' indicate that it — and not aggression from China — is perceived as the main threat to Vietnam's national security. Witness this assertion by General Doan Khue that Vietnam is the deliberate target of such a strategy:

> Following the failure of socialism in Eastern Europe and the Soviet Union, the adversary forces, on the one hand, have been expanding the results of their victory in those countries, and, on the other, stepping up their offensive against the remaining socialist countries, which include Vietnam.
>
> Their plot and action are aimed at accelerating the combined use of unarmed and armed measures against us to undermine in a total

manner our politics, ideology, psychology, way of living, and so on, and encircling, isolating, and destroying us in the economic field, with the hope that they could achieve so-called 'peaceful evolution' and make the revolution in our country deviate from its course. They have been trying to seek, build, and develop reactionary forces of all kinds within our country; at the same time to nurture and bring back groups of armed reactionaries within our country; and to combine armed activities with political activities, hoping to transform the socio-economic crisis in our country into a political crisis and to incite rioting and overthrowing when opportunities arise. They may also look for excuses to effect an intervention, to carry out partial armed aggression, or to wage aggressive wars on various scales.

Our people thus have the task of dealing with and being ready to deal with any circumstances caused by the adversary forces; peaceful evolution, riot and overthrow, encirclement, blockade, surprise attacks by armed forces, aggressive wars on various scales. The politico-ideological front is a hot one to fight back the 'peaceful development' and to defend the fatherland.[30]

In order to prepare for such contingencies, Vietnam has assigned its best trained and equipped regular forces and reserves to defend its most vital areas,[31] such as offshore islands, oil and gas exploration zones and border regions. In addition, each military region, province and district must also designate its own strategic areas and turn them into special defence zones.

In Military Region 4, for example, three separate defence areas have been identified: the sea (designated a national defence 'hot spot'), cities along national highway one, and the forested mountain region.[32] Military Region 5 has designated the Paracel and Spratly Island archipelagoes and the tri-border region where Vietnam joins Laos and Cambodia as sensitive defence zones.[33] Military Region 9 in the Mekong Delta has identified territorial waters in the Gulf of Thailand and the southwest border with Cambodia as special defence zones.[34] These special defence zones have been fortified and efforts made to link economic production and military defence. In the initial stages of limited conflict, the responsibility of meeting and countering an external attack would rest with local forces, militia and self-defence forces. At a later stage, the main forces, supplemented with ready reserves, would be employed.

Finally, Vietnam had to be prepared to meet 'all eventualities', including subversion, rebellion, blockade, biological warfare, 'localised armed aggressions and war of aggression ... [and] round-the-clock surprise massive, lightning air, sea and ground assault conducted by enemies with high-tech weapons'.[35] Vietnam's 'people's war and all-people's national defence' strategy is a doctrine which attempts to integrate all aspects of Vietnamese society — economic, social, cultural, political, military, internal security and foreign relations — in defence of the homeland and socialist regime.

Vietnam and China: 'Comrades but not allies'

The process of disintegration among the socialist states in Eastern Europe and the Soviet Union provoked debate in Vietnam about future national security policy. The party leadership was divided about whether or not to lean towards China. One group, centred in the Vietnamese People's Army (VPA), advocated that priority be assigned to the normalisation of relations with China and the re-establishment of formal military–security ties.[36] The majority view within the VCP was that the best guarantee of Vietnam's security was to pursue a multi-directional foreign policy within the Asia Pacific region, attempt to normalise relations with China and the United States simultaneously, and develop good relations with as many countries as possible.

In July 1991, immediately after the 7th Party Congress, Vietnam received a confidential invitation from the Chinese Communist Party to send a senior official to Beijing to brief Chinese leaders on the outcome of the congress. Vietnam dispatched General Le Duc Anh, second-ranking Politburo member and then Minister for National Defence. As a result of his visit, the path was cleared for normalisation. The signing of the Cambodian peace accords in Paris in October then set the stage for the final act in the normalisation process. The following month a summit of high-level party leaders was held in Beijing. Reportedly, it was at this summit, or immediately after it, that Vietnam pressed China to expand the relationship to include security guarantees or a form of military alliance. China rebuffed these approaches, stating that China and Vietnam could be 'comrades but not allies'.[37] Nevertheless, Vietnam continued to press for a military component to the normalisation package on subsequent occasions.

Following the normalisation of party and state relations, the Vietnam People's Army and the People's Liberation Army (PLA) took determined steps to restore relations. In February–March 1992, for example, Major-General Vu Xuan Vinh, head of the VPA's External Relations Department, went to China to discuss 'the restoration and development of friendship between the armed forces of the two countries'. General Vinh held discussions with Senior Lieutenant-General Chi Haotian, the PLA's Chief of the General Staff. A return visit by Major-General Fu Jiaping, head of the PLA's Foreign Affairs Bureau, took place in May. The question of Chinese arms sales to Vietnam may have been discussed at this time.[38]

This was followed by the exchange visits of Defence Ministers. General Doan Khue visited Beijing in December where he met not only his counterpart, but CCP Secretary General Jiang Zemin. During this visit, General Khue was careful to thank his hosts for their past 'precious assistance and support', a formulation which led some observers to conclude that Vietnam was seeking to acquire Chinese arms and equipment.[39] General Khue also stated he hoped that existing problems (territorial disputes) would not prevent the strengthening of bilateral relations and that such differences should be solved through negotiations.[40]

China's Defence Minister, Senior Lieutenant-General Chi Haotian, reciprocated with a nine-day trip to Vietnam in May 1993.[41] He called in at the command staffs in Military Regions 5 (in the centre) and 7 (south). A joint statement issued at the end of his visit stated, 'friendly relations between the two countries are historic and should be developed'. This suggested 'that China may be about to fill the arms and equipment gap left by the ending of Soviet military assistance to Vietnam'.[42]

In December Vietnam hosted a visit by General Yu Yongbo, director of the PLA's General Political Department. General Yu and his counterpart, General Le Kha Phieu discussed co-operation in army political work. He was also received by Defence Minister Doan Khue and party chief Do Muoi. The latter declared, 'at present, the armies and the people of Vietnam and China are uniting in national defence and construction', an expression which seemed to indicate that military relations were slowly evolving.[43]

Towards the future

In interviews conducted with a wide spectrum of government officials in Hanoi in May 1993, it was repeatedly stressed that China had a 'South Sea strategy' aimed at filling the power vacuum left by the collapse of the Soviet Union and the withdrawal of the United States from the Philippines. This posed the problem for Vietnamese foreign policy-makers of how to reach accommodation with its northern neighbour without exchanging one dependent relationship for another. One Foreign Ministry official argued that Vietnam had three options:

> There are three possible ways of organizing our relations with China: (1) confrontation (2) satellite status similar to North Korea or (3) a median position between the two. Satellite status provides no guarantees. North Korea was sacrificed by China when it turned to South Korea. Also, even if Vietnam were to be a good satellite, China would not leave us alone. They will always pressure us and try to dominate Southeast Asia. We tried for a full year to forge new relations with China but we failed. Take its occupation of Bay Tu Chinh (an island in the Spratly archipelago) and the Crestone affair. Okay, we distrusted China but it was only with Bay Tu Chinh that we understood that China follows its national interest. That game is in the nature of international politics.

Since these remarks were made, Vietnam and China negotiated and signed, on 19 October 1993, an 'agreement on the basic principles for the settlement of border territory issues' (for example, the land border, the border in the Tonkin Gulf and the South China Sea). Before a final accord is reached, both sides have agreed they should not take any action which complicates the disputes, nor should they resort to use of force or threaten the use of force. Vietnam and China also agreed to set up joint working groups for the land border and for demarcating the Gulf of Tonkin. Both agree that the land border is a technical issue. And, according to Vietnam's chief negotiator, China has agreed that it would return land if it is found to be on Vietnamese territory.[44]

According to Vietnamese officials, there are three separate 'issue areas' to be dealt with in the South China Sea: bilateral conflicting claims to the Paracel Islands, multilateral overlapping claims to the Spratly Islands and demarcation of Vietnam's continental shelf. The South China Sea remains the most contentious issue as it involves not only conflicting claims between China and Vietnam but conflicting claims with Taiwan, Malaysia, the Philippines and Brunei as well. China occupied the Paracels in January 1974 and will not discuss their status.

On the second anniversary of Sino-Vietnamese normalisation, Vietnam's former defence minister and now president, Le Duc Anh, paid an official state visit to China. This was the first such visit since 1955 when President Ho Chi Minh travelled to Beijing. One of the main purposes of his visit was to review progress in implementing the fourteen separate agreements that had been signed since November 1991. After review, both sides agreed that progress had been slow and that steps must be taken to speed up implementation. Anh's visit was proceeded by an unprecedented visit to Singapore and Thailand by Do Muoi, the Secretary General of the Vietnam Communist Party. These events clearly indicate that Vietnam and China have managed to overcome existing irritants and to codify their bilateral relations in a series of mutually beneficial accords. Vietnam has also managed to place its relations with China in the broader context of its relations with Southeast Asia. In other words, Vietnam has been successful in its pursuit of 'option three' — the median approach.

Vietnam and China both need a stable and peaceful external environment in order to carry out their domestic reform programs while integrating their economies with the world economy. In this context, both have a common interest in controlling and regulating border trade between them. As Brantly Womack has demonstrated, while the value of China's border trade with Vietnam is a small portion of total trade, it is especially significant for Guangxi province where Vietnam ranks as its second largest trading partner after Hong Kong.[45] The border trade is significant for Vietnam where the importation of lower-priced Chinese goods threatens to overwhelm domestic industries. The border trade thus serves as both a bridge to better relations and an irritant. Womack assesses the balance and concludes, 'as both countries develop and institutionalise their general policies of international economic openness, it should become more difficult for each to intervene in the continued development of the bilateral economic relationship'.[46] In brief, 'the border trade is likely to play a stabilising role. It is the major expression of a shared material interest in cooperation.'[47]

Vietnam began its 'long march' to re-evaluate relations with China in the mid-1980s. In 1987, Vietnam undertook a strategic readjustment of its military forces, withdrew from Laos and Cambodia, and then concentrated on developing a doctrine of defence self-reliance. Despite Chinese assertiveness in the South China Sea, as reflected in the Crestone affair and island-grabbing in 1992 and 1995, Vietnam has not been deflected from this course. It has continued to push for the full normalisation of relations, especially economic and commercial relations. It has tried to develop special influence in Beijing by restoring military and party-to-party linkages. At the same time, Vietnam has counterbalanced its ties with China by multilateralising its relations with the Asia-Pacific region and pushing for the complete normalisation of relations with the United States.

If there is any country in Southeast Asia which should be fearful of China's military modernisation program it is Vietnam. In December 1992, for example, Vietnam reacted to Russian arms sales to China by cancelling discussions with Moscow on the future of Cam Ranh Bay.[48] But Vietnam has also been circumspect in its public reaction to China's resumption of nuclear testing. In October 1993, after China exploded a device, a foreign ministry spokesperson merely declared, 'This issue should be settled through negotiations, on the basis of guaranteeing the security of all nations, especially those without nuclear weapons.'[49]

These two cases illustrate an ambivalence within Vietnamese policy-making circles about how to manage relations with China. Given the disparities of power and the 'tyranny of geography', Vietnam is unlikely to pursue the path of alarmism or confrontation. Instead, Vietnam will be sensitive to the nuances of China's regional and global status. Priority will continue to be given to developing breadth and depth in the bilateral relationship, with special attention to economic relations. The rationale behind this strategy was explained by a foreign ministry official in this way:

Sino-Vietnamese relations will be meshed within the much larger regional network of interlocking economic and political interests. It is an arrangement whereby anybody wanting to violate Vietnam's sovereignty would be violating the interests of other countries as well. This is the ideal strategic option for Vietnam. It is also the most practical.[50]

Notes

1 Anne Gilks, 'The Breakdown of the Sino-Vietnamese Alliance, 1970–79', *China Research Monograph*, no. 39, Center for Chinese Studies, Institute of East Asian Studies, University of California, Berkeley, 1992.
2 Gareth Porter, 'Vietnam and the Socialist Camp: Center or Periphery?', in William S. Turley (ed.), *Vietnamese Communism in Comparative Perspective*, Westview Special Studies on South and Southeast Asia, Westview Press, Boulder, Col., 1980.
3 Carlyle A. Thayer, 'Vietnamese Perspectives on International Security: Three Revolutionary Currents', in Donald H. McMillen (ed.), *Asian Perspectives on International Security*, Macmillan Press, London, 1984.

4 Carlyle A. Thayer, 'The Soviet Union and Indochina', in Roger E. Kanet, Deborah Nutter Miner and Tamara J. Resler (eds), *Soviet Foreign Policy in Transition*, Cambridge University Press, Cambridge, 1992.

5 William S. Turley, 'Political Renovation in Vietnam: Renewal and Adaptation', in Borje Ljunggren (ed.), *The Challenge of Reform in Indochina*, Harvard Institute for International Development, Cambridge, Mass, 1993.

6 Carlyle A. Thayer, 'Sino-Vietnamese Relations: The Interplay Between Ideology and National Interest', *Asian Survey*, vol. 34, no. 6, June 1994, pp. 513–55; and Thayer, 'Comrade Plus Brother: The New Sino-Vietnamese Relations', *Pacific Review*, vol. 5, no. 4, September, 1992, pp. 402–6.

7 During Sino-Vietnamese discussions on Cambodia in September 1990, Vietnam reportedly suggested a settlement based on a coalition between its protégés in Phnom Penh with the Khmer Rouge. This is the so-called 'red solution'.

8 The communiqué set out principles to govern party-to-party and state-to-state relations. It also set out the terms governing Vietnam's relations with the Republic of China on Taiwan.

9 Remarks to a press conference in Hanoi on 2 December 1992 carried by Vietnam News Agency, 3 December 1992.

10 Quoted by Andrew Sherry, AFP, Hanoi, 27 October 1993.

11 This point was made by Richard Rigby (director of the Indochina Section, Department of Foreign Affairs and Trade, Australia) in his comments as discussant on my original paper. Dr Rigby served in China prior to his current post.

12 Author's interview with Pham Van Chuong, Deputy Director, Department of Foreign Affairs, Central Committee of the Vietnam Communist Party, Hanoi, 13 May 1993.

13 Interview with Nguyen Ngoc Truong, general editor of *Quan He Quoc Te*, a periodical published by Vietnam's foreign ministry, Hanoi, 7 May 1993.

14 Murray Hiebert, 'Unhealed Wounds', *Far Eastern Economic Review*, 16 July 1992, pp. 20–21.

15 AFP, *Business Times* (Singapore), 2 December 1992.

16 Nguyen Manh Cam, 'Bao Cao ve Tinh Hinh The Gioi, Cong Tac Doi Ngoai 9 Thang Nam 1992 va Phuong Huong Cong Tac Thoi Gian Toi' [Report on the World Situation, External Affairs in the First Nine Months of 1992 and the Outlook for the Future]. Typescript marked confidential, Hanoi, 17 September 1992.

17 Bui Tin, Breaking the Ice: The Memoires of a North Vietnamese Colonel, draft manuscript to be published by The University of Hawaii Press and C. Hurst Publishers, London, p. 153.

18 This includes the anti-French war (1945–54), the war for national liberation and anti-American war (1959–75) and the wars with Cambodia and China (1977–89).

19 Thayer, 'Vietnamese Perspectives on International Security', pp. 72–73.
20 Gareth Porter, *Vietnam: The Politics of Bureaucratic Socialism*, Cornell University Press, Ithaca, 1993, p. 202.
21 'Bao Cao Chinh Tri cua Ban Chap Hanh Trung uong Dang Tai Dai Hoi Dai Bieu Toan Quoc Lan Thu Nam', *Nhan Dan*, 28 March 1982, p. 2.
22 ibid., 29 March 1982, p. 5.
23 *6th National Congress of the Communist Party of Vietnam Documents*, Foreign Languages Publishing House, Hanoi, 1987, p. 128.
24 Le Duc Anh, interview with Tap Chi Quoc Phong Toan Dan, Hanoi Domestic Service, 4 December 1989. In US Foreign Broadcast Information Service, *Daily Report* EAS-89-234, 7 December 1989, pp. 70–71.
25 'Report of the Party Central Committee's Military Commission on the Implementation of the 1986–90 National Defence Tasks and Guidelines and the Tasks for the 1991–95 Five-Year Period' *Tap Chi Quoc Phong Toan Dan*, June 1991, pp. 40–51. In US Foreign Broadcast Information Service, *Daily Report* EAS-91-143, 25 July 1991, pp. 62–69.
26 Nguyen Van Linh, 'Consolidate Peace, Uphold Vigilance, and Develop the Integrated Strength for National Defence', *Tap Chi Quoc Phong Toan Dan*, December 1989. In British Broadcasting Corporation, *Summary of World Broadcasts* FE/0643, 19 December 1989, B/4-5.
27 'Fourth generation war' refers to psychological warfare directed at the population, and the destruction and sabotage of the industrial, political and social infrastructure of the targeted country.
28 Nguyen Van Phiet, 'Applying Results of Study on Democracy–Discipline Measures in Air Defence Service', *Quan Doi Nhan Dan*, 17 March 1992, p. 2. In US Joint Publications Research Service, *Report* SEA-92-010, 15 May 1992, pp. 38–39.
29 Le Bang, 'Build the People's Armed Forces and the Vietnam People's Army in the Direction of Renovation', *Tap Chi Quoc Phong Toan Dan*, June 1991. In British Broadcasting Corporation, *Summary of World Broadcasts* FE/1099, 15 June 1991, B/5-6; Nguyen Hai Bang, untitled article, *Tap Chi Quoc Phong Toan Dan*, March 1992, pp. 3–8. In US Joint Publications Research Service, *Report* SEA-92-012, 10 June 1992, pp. 19–22.
30 Doan Khue, 'Consolidating and Building Mobilization Reserve Forces and Militia and Self-Defence Forces of Good Quality Everywhere to Contribute to Building Strong Defence Areas', Hanoi Domestic Service, 28 June 1989. In US Foreign Broadcast Information Service, *Daily Report* EAS-89-138, 20 July 1989, pp. 75–76.
31 ibid. Mobilisation reserve forces are located in all provinces, cities and special zones. Reserve forces can be assigned to the regular force as necessary to conduct mobile combat operations throughout the country (militia and self-defence forces always remain in their localities).
32 Nguyen Quoc Thuoc, 'The Experience of the 4th Military Region — Changes in the Building of the All-People National Defence in the 4th

Military Region', *Tap Chi Quoc Phong Toan Dan*, May 1992, pp. 49–53. In US Joint Publications Research Service, *Report* SEA-92-017, 12 August 1992, pp. 10–13.

33 Phan Hoan, 'Firmly Maintaining Security and Consolidating National Defence in the 5th Military Region', *Tap Chi Quoc Phong Toan Dan*, October 1992, pp. 46–50. In US Joint Publications Research Service, *Report* SEA-93-004, 25 March 1993, pp. 18–20.

34 Tran Minh Phu, 'The 9th Military Region Develops and Defends its Sea Area', *Tap Chi Quoc Phong Toan Dan*, September 1992, pp. 60–66. In US Joint Publications Research Service, *Report* SEA-92-002, 16 February 1993, pp. 55–60.

35 Q.S., 'On the Socialist, Modern All-People National Defence of Vietnam', *Tap Chi Quoc Phong Toan Dan*, May 1992, pp. 39–42, 90. In US Joint Publications Research Service, *Report* SEA-92-016, 6 August 1992, pp. 47–49.

36 Thayer, 'Sino-Vietnamese Relations'.

37 Author's discussion with a Vietnamese Foreign Ministry official, Singapore, 5 October 1992.

38 Jacques Bekaert, transcript of interview on BBC 'Dateline East Asia', 31 July 1992. In Republic of Singapore, *Foreign Broadcast Monitor* 176/92, 1 August 1992, pp. 8–9.

39 A Russian diplomat, identified as having long experience in both countries, later confirmed that 'China gave Vietnam some spare parts for the army'. Jacques Bekaert, 'Vietnam and China: Towards Peaceful Coexistence', *Bangkok Post*, 21 January 1993, p. 5.

40 Xinhua News Agency, 8 December 1992.

41 General's Chi's predecessor, Qin Jiwei, was scheduled to visit Hanoi in February 1993 but the visit was cancelled due to illness.

42 Economist Intelligence Unit, *Indochina: Vietnam, Laos, Cambodia Country Report*, no. 2, 1993.

43 *Nhan Dan*, 6 December 1993, p. 4.

44 Author's interview with Vu Khoan, Deputy Minister for Foreign Affairs, Canberra, 17 November 1992.

45 Brantly Womack, 'Sino-Vietnamese Border Trade: The Edge of Normalization', unpublished paper presented to a seminar at Cornell University, Ithaca, October 1993, p. 7.

46 ibid., p. 14.

47 ibid., p. 15.

48 Robert Karniol, 'Trade Dispute Halts Cam Ranh Talks', *Jane's Defence Weekly*, 20 March 1993, p. 12.

49 Reuters, Hanoi, 7 October 1993.

50 Nguyen Hong Thach, 'Vietnam–China Ties: A New But Not Easy Era', *Business Times* (Singapore), 31 December 1992. In *Vietnam Newswatch* (Singapore), no. 117, 16–31 December 1992, pp. 105–6.

11 The Conflicting Contexts of the China–Korea Relationships

James Cotton

In this chapter on Korea, a review of China's transformation is the starting point of the analysis. It then turns to a consideration of the host of geographic, economic and historical factors and trends — notably the existence of two Korean states — which complicates relations between China and the Korean peninsula. It is argued that the complexity in question is at least as great as that which commentators have detected in the Beijing–Washington nexus. Specifically, China and South Korea are major trading partners and are also being drawn into a dynamic regional economic and social complex; at the same time, Beijing and Pyongyang are still bound by a mutual defence arrangement entered into in 1961 as well as by the residue of ideological ties. Korea may not be a superpower, but it is arguable that next to relations with the United States and with Japan, China's interests now require that the closest attention be paid to the Beijing–Seoul–Pyongyang triangle.

The function of 'China' in an analysis of China's relations

Before reviewing the dimensions of the China–Korea relationships, it is necessary to interrogate the key term in this discourse. Following the Sino-Soviet split and prior to 1979, the meaning of 'China', at least from the point of view of international relations, was relatively clear. The government in Beijing had the pretensions of a strong state, and for the purposes of external relationships was largely able to match those pretensions with policy.

China was not enmeshed in significant transnational connections of an economic, cultural or communications kind — all of which tend to derogate from national sovereignty, or expose governments to the needs of contradictory policy objectives. And China was not party to the host of international mechanisms and requirements — human rights instruments, nuclear and other weapons non-proliferation agreements, trading and finance regimes — which have now become the norm in world politics. This is not to suggest that the regime's actual and realisable policy options were not heavily constrained, but rather that policy remained integrated and more or less articulated by the authorities in the capital.

Between 1979 (the beginning of the reform era) and 1994, this integrated notion of 'China' has definitely begun to unravel, though this development has not always been sufficiently noticed by analysts of China's foreign relations. Accordingly, it is now necessary to treat the term 'China' with caution, in particular paying attention to instances where the regime's strong state posture runs up against economic priorities or assumed international obligations.[1]

Without considering this topic in detail, the following points are made by way of illustration. The regime in Beijing still possesses strong state pretensions. These derive from the residues of the Marxist state project, from the attempt to shift the grounds of legitimation of the regime towards economic performance — which is still presented as chiefly a state accomplishment — and from the challenges which the regime faces from inside the country. The pressures and forces which are eroding these pretensions are both transnational or regional, and international. Since 1979, the integration of the Chinese economy into the Northeast Asian regional economy has been a striking phenomenon. Significant investment from the Chinese of Southeast Asia has also been important, leading to the use of the expression 'greater China' to encompass not merely China, Hong Kong, Macau and Taiwan, but the network of Chinese entrepreneurs and traders beyond. The use here of the term 'the Chinese economy' can, however, be misleading, since both of these developments have been decidedly uneven. One can now speak of a 'Pearl River economy' (incorporating Hong Kong) and otherwise differentiate the Fujian, Zhejiang and Shanghai coastal zones, with their strong Taiwan links, from inner and interior China.[2] Local systems have also emerged in the cultural and communications spheres, with Hong Kong fashions and Taiwan music exerting a strong influence. Beijing's recognition of and adjustment to these phenomena has been slow, though Beijing's participation in Asia-Pacific Economic Co-operation (APEC) does provide some institutional expression.

The enmeshment of China is a phenomenon larger than the East Asian region. China has also become part of several world regimes which, though still weak in effect, are now constraining government policy and forcing China to adopt some elements of an internationalist stance. Even less than ten years ago, the government in Beijing did not regard discussion of China's record on human rights as legitimate, nor was it at all receptive to suggestions that the country should practise transparency in arms doctrine, or attend to such global issues as the environmental crisis. China's low level of trade with the market economies made self-sufficiency a still realisable option, and Beijing often inveighed against the nuclear monopoly which lay behind the Nuclear Non-Proliferation Treaty (NPT). In each of these areas, China has had to adjust policy to meet the demands of internationalist pressures.[3] China is now a member of the NPT regime. In receipt of loans from the World Bank, and seeking membership of the General Agreement on Tariffs and Trade (GATT), much of China's present booming growth is sustained by a large trade surplus with the United States.

The points to be concluded from this analysis are plain. China's policy is now constrained. In different areas, policies are made by a variety of actors whose actions are often not co-ordinated or whose goals may be in conflict. In the case of Korea, the ten dimensions of the China–Korea relationships chosen for analysis illustrate this more general conclusion. Different actors or interests make up different elements of China's 'policy' towards the Koreas, and often these policies, wittingly or unwittingly, are not entirely consistent.

Dimensions of the China–Korea relationships

China's long-standing cultural links with Korea

The indebtedness of Korea to Chinese culture is substantial. Indeed, in premodern times Korea was known to the Chinese as the nation of scholars — that is to say, the only foreign country to have properly understood the profundities of Chinese culture. Insofar as such cultural factors play any part in the making of foreign policy — as is maintained by at least one school of foreign policy analysts — the China–Korea relationship should possess special significance.

There can be little doubt that China's long-standing and patient solicitude for North Korea is connected with the Chinese perception that the country is a younger cultural sibling. Similarly, with the shift to 'economics in command' after 1978, China has been particularly chagrined that a former cultural protegé, South Korea, has been so much the more successful in achieving rapid economic transformation. The vogue for the study of Korea in the mid-1980s, though it had a political bearing (which is discussed below), had more than a little connection with the view that cultural affinity meant that China could more easily learn from the Korean experience.

China's former role of suzerain and the geopolitics of the Korean peninsula

Korea was for a long period a state dependent upon China for the ultimate legitimacy of its institutions, though independent in a practical sense for most of its history.[4] China's cultural role in Korea was the foundation for this relationship, though in time it took on an economic and also a strategic dimension.

From the Chinese perspective, Korea has acted as an historical bridgehead to and from Japan, and Japanese interest in Korea has generally been accompanied by challenges to China's predominance on the peninsula. In 1592 and again in 1597, Japan under Hideyoshi invaded Korea with the ultimate intention of subjugating the country and turning it into a base from which to invade China. Ming forces helped repel the Japanese, the effort required contributing to the demise of the dynasty shortly afterwards. As early as the 1870s, advocates of Japan's territorial expansion looked first to Korea, and between 1884 and 1895 China and Japan were locked in a struggle for influence on the peninsula, with the modernising school in Beijing committed to transmuting a vague suzerainty into something more akin to a European-style protectorate arrangement. This project was frustrated, however, by China's inability to match Japan's power. Japan fought a major war with Russia on Chinese territory for control of the peninsula and dominance in the region, and from the 1920s Korea became a base first for the annexation of Manchuria, and then for the war with China.

Korea's geographic position raises acute conventional strategic problems for China. Korea is the closest foreign country to the capital, to the key heavy industries of the northeast, and to the burgeoning lower-Yangzi economic region. Korea is also a few minutes flying time to the routes followed by much of China's trade through the ports of Tianjin, Dalian and Shanghai. Both of the Korean states are in possession of advanced armaments including submarines, surface craft, jet interceptors and bombers, all of which could pose considerable dangers to the territory and forces of China. To the factor of geographical proximity needs to be added that of political instability (discussed below).

To the conventional security perspective, further observations need to be added. Though Beijing is still obsessed with statist pretensions, the reality of China's growing economic interdependence with the regional and world economies has eroded the capacity of the central authorities to control developments in many of the provinces. Japan, Taiwan and Hong Kong, through investment, trade and proximity, have all exerted a powerful social, economic and now political attraction. In the case of Korea, and longer term, it is not impossible to imagine the peninsula as a very much larger member of the species now identified with Hong Kong, acting as a bridgehead to the Pacific economy, providing advanced technology and capital, and drawing in immigrant labour. Even without direct land transportation between the two systems, some of these developments can already be detected. Korea's role as an investor in Shandong and in the northeastern provinces has proved crucial for the economic advancement of those regions. In addition, the presence of the ethnic Korean minority in Jilin gives Korea a special interest in that (peripheral) part of China, while providing Korean enterprises with the ideal intermediaries for commercial exchanges.

The Tumen River and Northeast Asian economic integration

China's participation in the Tumen River co-operation scheme illustrates Korea's centrality in any scheme of regional integration.[5] In 1990 and again the following year, the United Nations Development Program (UNDP) sponsored a series of conferences devoted to the possibility of integrating the development of the riparian countries of the Tumen region — China, Russia and Korea, plus Mongolia. In October 1991 the participating countries agreed to inaugurate a Program Management Committee, with the UNDP funding a $3.5 million feasibility study for the Tumen River Area Development Program.

The economic and geographic rationale for such a scheme has been fairly clear to the countries of the region for a century, if not longer. While Korea was a Japanese colony, Rajin became an important infiltration point for the training and dispatch of agents to Manchuria, and likewise Koreans fighting in Manchuria played an important role in China's resistance to Japanese encroachments on the continent. As a result of Tsarist Russian annexation in 1860, China lost its coastline on the Sea of Japan (East Sea), though Chinese merchants continued to trade from the port of Hunchun (on a tributary of the Tumen, and a Treaty Port from 1906) in Jilin province. The river mouth was blocked in 1938 after the Soviet–Japanese clash at Changkufeng, and Sino-Soviet differences from 1960 prevented any resumption of Chinese navigation on the lower Tumen.

China now seeks a port outlet in this area (at Hunchun, or perhaps Fangchuan), to be associated with an export processing zone. Russia seeks to relieve the overcrowding of its Pacific ports, and also to take advantage of the fact that the ice-free port of Rajin is connected without break of gauge to the railway land-bridge to Europe. Mongolia wishes to secure guaranteed access to an international port, and South Korean corporate interests have been drawn to the prospect of investing in an area where Korean labour is available at a very low comparative cost. By opening the Tumen region, North Korea hopes to take advantage of its geographical position to host at least some of these activities, and particularly to derive benefit from the fact that the country borders the booming provinces of northeast China.

Since 1984, North Korea has been experimenting, albeit in a limited fashion, with plans to attract foreign capital and technology. Following the announcement, in December 1991, of the formation of the Tumen River Free Economic and Trade Zone, these plans have received much greater emphasis. In 1992–93, a series of regulations were introduced, governing prospective foreign business activity in North Korea, which appeared to indicate that some elements in North Korean policy-making circles were prepared to take a leaf from the Chinese reform text. On the one hand, China is offered the opportunity to take part in a potentially profitable exercise which will have a significant impact, especially in the northeast. On the other hand, participating in the Tumen River scheme (along with South Korea) may be the best means to keep the North Korean economy afloat (thus avoiding the refugee, social disorder and other problems inherent if the Pyongyang regime implodes) while introducing some market elements into the North Korean system.

China's former role in Korea and the Korean War

With regard to this factor, the China–Korea relationship is quite without parallel. China was the cradle of the Korean revolution, and the origin of much that is still distinctive in the North Korean political style. Kim Il-sung, while a member of the Chinese Communist Party fighting the Japanese on Chinese soil, learned his guerilla craft from his Chinese superiors, Yang Jingyu and others. He also learned — the struggle in Manchuria being overseen not from Yan'an but by the Far Eastern Commission of the Comintern in Vladivostok — of the baleful effects of direct external intervention in a national revolution.[6] Kim's desire, clearly articulated in the 1950s, to describe his ideology as an adaptation of Marxism-Leninism to Korean practice, was directly borrowed from Mao Zedong's Yan'an program of the 1940s. With some irony, Kim more recently rewrote history to support the claim that he anticipated Mao by several years. The watchword of the Korean revolution over the past two decades, *juche* (self-reliance), is to be understood in large part as an extrapolation of this position.

In late 1950, Beijing's decision to intervene in the Korean War rescued the Kim regime from oblivion. The Chinese did not, however, choose to interfere in internal Korean party affairs, which gave Kim a free hand to elevate to exclusive leadership his personal clique, again by a historical irony purging those Korean communists who had been Mao's comrades in Yan'an. Specific policies and general organisational attitudes — from the Great Leap Forward to the mass line — have had their Korean echoes, and Kim's personality cult owed something to the example of Mao, though here — perhaps with much less talent — Kim's performance exceeded that of his teacher.

Pyongyang's 'socialist' regime

It is also still of some consequence that North Korea is avowedly a 'socialist' country. Post-Tiananmen and after the dissolution of the Soviet Union, the regime of the People's Republic of China confronts a unique challenge. It is no longer credible to maintain that socialism is a world movement or in any respect the wave of the future, yet it is upon such foundations that the communist party regime subsisted for the first three decades of its rule. Since 1978 there have been a number of attempts to seek a new foundation, but all have run up against the ineluctable fact that if a new standard of legitimacy is to be propounded, how can those first three decades be accounted for except as a usurpation.[7]

Some notion of socialism must, accordingly, be retained. This exigency is reflected in Deng Xiaoping's 'Four Cardinal Principles', which amount, apart from the proposition that there should be no disagreement with the communist party, to a blanket prohibition on all attempts to tamper with the party's definition of socialism. This forces Beijing to hang on to whatever 'socialist' elements their foreign policy might be described to contain, especially as this policy pertains to the survival of other socialist regimes. There is some precedent for this, of course, in the Beijing–Tirana axis of the late 1960s. Succour of and support for North Korea — the regime in the name of which Communist China sustained more battle casualties than in all its other wars combined — fits this category. Thus the Chinese regime has been remarkably patient with North Korea when a conventional 'security' or 'economic' calculus would suggest other approaches. Similarly, the Chinese leadership is endeavouring to come to terms with Vietnam despite recent history. Indeed, according to the Hong Kong press, criticism of China within and internal to the leadership of the Korean Workers Party has been almost completely ignored, although recently Deng Xiaoping is supposed to have advised the regime to reform if it does not want to perish, and has also refused repeated requests from Pyongyang to cancel North Korea's debts.[8] The death of Kim Il-sung may provide the impetus necessary for a further re-evaluation of Beijing–Pyongyang ties, although much will depend upon the policies chosen by the new leadership.

The division of the peninsula

Although there have been 40 years of peace on the Korean peninsula, and both Korean states have for the last three years been members of the United Nations, the longstanding and intense competition between the two Korean states for legitimacy has yet to abate. North Korea still describes the foreign relations of the government in Seoul as the activities of a less than sovereign entity, and tensions between the two remain high as a consequence of Pyongyang's inability to negotiate with the South as an equal interlocutor. China, as a signatory with the North of the 1953 armistice agreement, has also had a vested interest in protecting North Korea's state pretensions. As late as 1975, Beijing had signalled that it supported North Korea's long-term aspiration of communising the South.

For their part, while they had to deal with the unhappy legacy of China's role in the Korean War, policy-makers in Seoul sought in the 1980s to improve relations as part of the 'Northern policy' which was aimed at detaching North Korea from its patrons. Seoul was careful in handling the return of a hijacked Chinese aircraft to Beijing in 1983, and generous inducements were offered to encourage China's participation in the 1986 Asian Games and the 1988 Olympics. But the pace of improvement in relations with the Soviet Union under Gorbachev was much more rapid. For a period, there was a possibility of Beijing exercising a veto to prevent South Korea from seeking entry to the United Nations. It was not until 1991 that South Korea exchanged trade offices with China, and full diplomatic relations were not agreed until August 1992.

Whereas the Soviet Union and the successor Russian Republic were able to dispense with the security treaty which bound them to North Korea, those other considerations already identified in Chinese policy-making left no such option. Beijing was aware — especially having confronted the question of the existence of Taiwan as a state — that policy towards the Koreas was almost zero-sum in composition. It is therefore the case that the communiqué which announced the initiation of diplomatic ties between the two countries was a great affront to Pyongyang, although North Korean reaction was muted by comparison with the response to Gorbachev's agreement to recognise Seoul. It should not be supposed, however, that Beijing has abandoned Pyongyang completely. There has been no cessation of military co-operation, nor severance of trade relations between China and North Korea. Even while International Atomic Energy Agency (IAEA) teams were investigating North Korean nuclear facilities, military delegations from China were visiting Pyongyang. China has replaced the Soviet Union/Russia as North Korea's chief trading partner, and it appears that China is still extending credit to finance a surplus trading balance.

The Washington–Seoul alliance

In this respect, Beijing's policy must again accommodate conflicting objectives and perspectives.[9] The Washington–Seoul alliance is a direct consequence of the Korean War, and for many years was the most tangible evidence of Beijing's charge that the United States sought to exercise hegemony over East Asia. With the demise of the Cold War, and given the immense resurgence in the power and potential of Japan, United States involvement in Korea and thus the Northeast Asia region may now well be preferable to a re-armed Japan exercising, after the Macarthur engineered years of denial, the full sovereignty of an independent foreign policy.

The nuclear issue

The development of nuclear weapons by North Korea, especially in the light of the withdrawal of United States nuclear weapons from South Korea in 1992, presents particular problems. In the past, China assisted in the development of North Korea's nuclear capacity, a fact which reflected their close co-operation in such activities as arms transfers.[10] China has also been vocal in support of the principle of a nuclear weapons-free Korean peninsula, a position which has been (and remains) North Korea's stated policy. At every available opportunity, China has lauded progress on the negotiation of better relations on the peninsula. The December 1991 agreement between the two Korean states to abandon all nuclear weapons was praised, as was the progress in 1993 in setting up a North–South committee to deal with nuclear issues. More recently, the two series of official talks between Pyongyang and Washington which produced a *pro tem* agreement — subject to further

North–South Korean talks and to North Korea accepting full IAEA scrutiny of its nuclear facilities — were welcomed.

Beijing's interest in defusing this issue is clear. Once North Korea's possession of a nuclear weapon is confirmed, tensions in the region will rise sharply. The United States may reinstate its nuclear weapons in Korea, or South Korea may attempt to replicate the North Korean arsenal. It is noteworthy that South Korea did endeavour to develop its own nuclear capacity in 1974–75, a strategy which was checked by United States intervention. It is doubtful whether pressure from Washington could achieve such a result today, even if it were desired. Conventional military conflict could break out as a result of a pre-emptive strike on North Korea's nuclear facilities — a move publicly mooted by some figures in South Korea in 1991, and again threatened by some American spokespersons in 1994 — or nuclear weapons could actually be used in a theatre or other context.

As much of a concern, however, is the effect that these developments might have on Japan. At present, Japan's official position on nuclear weapons conforms to the longstanding 'three no's' policy, though it is also the case that Japan acts as host to an extensive United States nuclear arsenal. Japan is also committed to the plutonium fuel cycle for the development of power generation capacity, and thus holds an already extensive reserve of potentially fissile material. It is not impossible that a nuclear armed North Korea might induce a future government in Tokyo to develop similar weapons, thus undermining China's claim to be the power of greatest consequence in the region. Already North Korea's missile program — Pyongyang testing an enhanced 1000 kilometre range version of the Soviet SCUD, the *Nodong*-1 in mid-1993 — has alarmed Japanese policy-makers sufficiently to induce them to investigate the introduction of anti-missile defence technology.

China's regional concerns need to be seen also in terms of other international objectives. Although a signatory of the Nuclear Non-Proliferation Treaty in 1992, China has remained a critic of the advantages that the established powers derive from the NPT. Thus Beijing chose to resume nuclear testing in 1993 despite an American moratorium and international appeals not to do so. During the events which preceded North Korea's announcement of its decision to withdraw from the NPT, at which time the North Korean nuclear issue was debated before the IAEA and then in the United Nations Security Council, China's approach was always to urge a conciliatory line, though never to the extent of exercising the veto in the latter body. Thus China (along with Vietnam and Iraq) abstained from the November 1993 vote in the United Nations General Assembly which called on North Korea to comply fully and expeditiously with the nuclear safeguards regime of the International Atomic Energy Agency. This attitude presents a facet of a wider approach to international obligations. China no longer contests the application of such concepts as human rights to international behaviour, but seeks to constrain their operation. If international pressure upon North Korea, orchestrated by the United States, succeeds in its objectives, quite apart from humbling an erstwhile 'socialist' ally, this may well open the way to greater international scrutiny of the Chinese legal system, of the situation in Tibet, of China's approach to intellectual property, and of a host of other issues where China's behaviour has been found wanting. In the early days of the Clinton administration, a rash of opinion pieces appeared affirming the need for America, now the only superpower, to pursue the goal of democratisation around the world. While this objective has taken a battering in Somalia, Haiti, Georgia, Bosnia and elsewhere, it has not been abandoned.[11]

South Korea's economic strength

South Korea's remarkable economic performance over almost the last three decades has raised a complex of issues for China. After 1978 South Korea became something of an economic model, and more recently it has been seen as a source of capital, technology and intermediate goods, as well as a market for Chinese raw materials and light industrial manufactures. The potential for South Korea–China economic relations can be judged by the fact that two-way trade is now running at over US$8 billion, comparable to the volume of trade between China and Taiwan via Hong Kong. Korea's economic strength, and especially the immense size of its largest business conglomerates, does, however, pose challenges for deepened economic relations. Commercial dealings with the Korean *chaebôl* might be very much determined by their priorities rather than by China's, a difficulty already experienced in Sino-Japanese economic relations.

A similar picture emerges if the overall dimensions of the economic relationship are considered. South Korea has become within a few years China's fifth largest trading partner. In earlier years, China ran a considerable surplus with South Korea, as Korean conglomerates explored the China market for alternative sources of commodity supply and in the context of government encouragement that such economic exchange also paid political dividends. But by 1993 this surplus had changed to a deficit, with the prospect that this would be the pattern for some time to come. When it is recalled that for the last three decades South Korea has run a trade deficit with Japan, which continues as Japan supplies important added value components for items which have become traditional Korean exports, there is some possibility that this structure may be reversed in the China–South Korea commercial relationship.

South Korea as a political model of managed authoritarianism

The question of the legitimisation of the communist regime in China is one which has already been noted. Between 1978 and 1989, an attempt was made to supplement — if not substitute for the traditional socialist goals — China's economic performance. Both *practically* and *ideologically*, South Korea provided a powerful and appealing example to the Chinese regime. *Practically*, South Korea demonstrated that it was possible for an authoritarian leadership to remain firmly in charge while overseeing rapid economic development and a greater integration into the world economy. *Ideologically*, the example of Korea (and other of the newly industrialised economies (NIEs), especially Singapore) provided a counter to the related arguments that democratisation was the inevitable consequence of market opening, and that the market democracies would dominate the post-Cold War era.[12]

Even despite events in South Korea since the democratic upsurge of 1987, the appeal in China of the NIE model has not disappeared. South Korea is still dominated by a political party with hegemonic potential, the institutions of civil society are weak, and the country still practises an etiolated version of managed trade. From the perspective of the Chinese leadership, it must surely seem remarkable that many of the same political elites have remained in power even while Korea has experienced such rapid social and economic transformation.

In Korea, in the communications field, there are some notable checks on free access to information — it is still illegal to view Japanese films in Korea, and the government is acting to restrict the spread of satellite dishes which can easily receive Japanese and other television channels. Here China's policy mirrors that of Korea, with Beijing moving in similar fashion to limit popular access to world media.

Conclusion

This chapter has sketched some of the complexities of Sino-Korean relations, in the context of an analysis of the transformation of 'China' and the country's policy-making mechanisms since 1979. Economic and political priorities would seem to impel conflicting policies on Beijing's part. Further complications are caused by the existence of the two Korean states. Economic priorities (including notions of regional integration) would suggest an abandoning of Pyongyang and closer ties with Seoul. Political priorities, on the other hand, do not recommend a clear policy. Even if some support of 'socialist' Pyongyang is thought appropriate, with the legitimation of the Chinese Communist Party in transition, the authoritarian party-hegemonic system of South Korea holds up at least one model for possible emulation. When refracted through historical, cultural, and geostrategic perspectives, it can be appreciated that Korea policy presents awkward but vital choices for Beijing.

Notes

1 Lucian W. Pye, 'China: Erratic State, Frustrated Society', *Foreign Affairs*, vol. 69, no. 4, 1990, pp. 56–74; Shih Chih-yu, *China's Just World. The Morality of Chinese Foreign Policy*, Lynne Rienner, Boulder, Col., 1993.

2 Sung Yun-wing, *The China–Hong Kong Connection. The Key to China's Open-Door Policy*, Cambridge University Press, Cambridge, 1991; Lynn White and Li Cheng, 'China's Coast Identities: Regional, National, and

Global', in Lowell Dittmer and Samuel S. Kim (eds), *China's Quest for National Identity*, Cornell University Press, Ithaca, 1993; Huang Yasheng, 'China's Economic Development: Implications for its Political and Security Roles', *Adelphi Paper* 275, 1993, pp. 49–57.

3 Ann Kent, *Between Freedom and Subsistence. China and Human Rights*, Oxford University Press, Hong Kong, 1993; Si Chu, 'Confidence Building in Asia-Pacific', *Beijing Review*, vol. 34, no. 9, 4–10 March 1991, pp. 10–12.

4 Chun Hae-jong, 'Sino-Korean Tributary Relations in the Ch'ing Period', in John K. Fairbank (ed.), *The Chinese World Order. Traditional China's Foreign Relations*, Harvard University Press, Cambridge, Mass., 1968.

5 James Cotton, 'Signs of Change in North Korea?', *Pacific Review*, vol. 7, no. 2, 1994, pp. 223–27.

6 Lee Chong-Sik, *Revolutionary Struggle in Manchuria: Chinese Communism and Soviet Interest, 1922–1945*, University of California Press, Berkeley, 1983.

7 John W. Garver, 'The Chinese Communist Party and the Collapse of Soviet Communism', *China Quarterly*, no. 133, 1993, pp. 1–26; Michael B. Yahuda, 'Chinese Foreign Policy and the Collapse of Communism', *SAIS Review*, vol. 12, no. 1, 1992, pp. 125–37; David Kelly, 'Chinese Marxism Since Tiananmen: Between Evaporation and Dismemberment', in David S.G. Goodman and Gerald Segal (eds), *China in the Nineties: Crisis Management and Beyond*, Clarendon Press, Oxford, 1991.

8 '"Ching Pao" on China–North Korea Rift', *Summary of World Broadcasts*, Far East/1631, A2/3-4, 8 March 1993; 'Hong Kong Magazine on Sino-North Korean Tension', *Summary of World Broadcasts*, Far East/1709, A1/12-13, 8 June 1993; 'Deng Xiaoping's Personal Intervention over North Korean Nuclear Issue Reported', *Summary of World Broadcasts*, Far East/1733, A2/1-2, 6 July 1993.

9 Jia Hao and Zhuang Qubing, 'China's Policy Toward the Korean Peninsula', *Asian Survey*, vol. 32, no. 12, December 1992, pp. 1137–56; Samuel S. Kim, 'China as a Regional Power', *Current History*, vol. 91, no. 566, September 1992, pp. 247–52.

10 Leonard S. Spector with Jacqueline R. Smith, *Nuclear Ambitions. The Spread of Nuclear Weapons 1989–1990*, Westview, Boulder, Col., 1990, pp. 118–37.

11 Morton H. Halperin, 'Guaranteeing Democracy', *Foreign Policy*, no. 91, 1993, pp. 105–22.

12 Barry Sautman, 'Sirens of the Strongman: Neo-Authoritarianism in Recent Chinese Political Theory', *China Quarterly*, no. 129, 1992, pp. 72–102.

12 China's Relationship with Taiwan

J. Bruce Jacobs and Lijian Hong[1]

In late 1949 the Chinese Communist Party (CCP) established the People's Republic of China (PRC). At the same time, the defeated Chinese Nationalist Party (Guomindang) fled to Taiwan, where it established a temporary capital for the Republic of China (ROC). From 1949 to the end of 1978, the PRC and ROC regimes tried to destroy each other. However, beginning with the Third Plenum of the Eleventh Central Committee, which set China on its post-Mao reform road and confirmed the 'normalisation' of Sino-American relations, the CCP radically altered its policies toward Taiwan to allow peaceful coexistence. This has led to a vast growth in mainland–Taiwan economic relations and to increased 'non-governmental' political contacts, metamorphoses which were inconceivable prior to the mid-1970s when both Mao Zedong and Chiang Kai-shek were still alive.

While the economic relations between the mainland and Taiwan continue to expand rapidly and some improvement continues in the 'non-governmental' political sphere (e.g. the April 1993 Wang–Koo talks in Singapore), we believe two simultaneous developments — one on the mainland and one on Taiwan — have increased the tension in the military relationship between Taiwan and the mainland since 1989. Firstly, the CCP leadership's perceived need to use the military to suppress the (northern) Spring 1989 student and popular demonstrations has strengthened the position of the military in China. The budgets of the Chinese military have increased substantially and the Chinese military has obtained many modern weapons from the Soviet Union. The Taiwanese response of purchasing F-16 and Mirage 2000 aircraft and other arms has escalated tension over the Taiwan Straits.

Secondly, while China has endured a period of political repression, Taiwan has undergone a remarkable period of political democratisation.[2] Under the authoritarian rule of Presidents Chiang Kai-shek and Chiang Ching-kuo, the mainlander minority dominated the Taiwanese majority. The Guomindang justified this minority rule by arguing that the minority Guomindang regime, as the only 'legitimate' Chinese government, represented the whole of China and not simply Taiwan. Taiwan's recent democratisation process has undercut this argument and compelled political forces in Taiwan to seek support from the majority Taiwanese. This has given the opposition Democratic Progressive Party (DPP) the opportunity to express publicly its support for 'Taiwan Independence', a position the CCP regards as anathema. It has also forced the ruling Guomindang to 'Taiwanise' and emphasise its Taiwan base rather than its former mainland links. This, too, has induced the KMT-led ROC government on Taiwan to advocate *de facto* 'two China' or 'one China, one Taiwan' positions, which the CCP also decries as unacceptable. Ironically, as Taiwan ceases to become a military threat to the mainland and no longer claims to be the legitimate government of the mainland, Taiwan's democratisation now poses a major ideological threat to the CCP because Taiwan's democratic existence decisively disproves the dogma that Chinese culture and democracy are incompatible.[3]

A hostile relationship: 1949–1978

Despite the claim in the recent Chinese White Paper on Taiwan that 'Early, in the 1950s, the Chinese government had already tentatively planned (*shexiang*) using peaceful means (*fangshi*) to solve the Taiwan question',[4] the Chinese emphasised the use of military force to 'liberate' Taiwan before the end of 1978. According to a senior Chinese government adviser, the 'peaceful liberation of Taiwan' during the 1950s 'demanded the realisation of a single social, economic and governmental system for [both] Taiwan and the Motherland's mainland, thereby incorporating Taiwan within the "one nation, one system" implemented for the whole of China'.[5] The CCP leadership correctly perceived the Guomindang regime on Taiwan as a competitor attempting to replace it as the government of China.

Despite the Communist failure to take the Nationalist-held offshore island of Jinmen (Quemoy) in October 1949, CCP military successes on the Chinese mainland and on Hainan Island led most of the world to believe the CCP would 'liberate' Taiwan in 1950. At the Third Plenum of the Seventh Central Committee in June 1950, General Su Yu, Deputy-Commander of the East China Military Region, reported on the preparatory work of the People's Liberation Army (PLA) to 'liberate' Taiwan.[6]

The North Korean invasion of 25 June 1950 into South Korea gave the KMT in Taiwan a reprieve. President Truman, uncertain whether the North Korean action was local or a prelude for further Communist military action in Asia and/or Europe, placed the Seventh Fleet in the Taiwan Straits to prevent both the Chinese Communists from attacking Taiwan and the Chinese Nationalists from attacking the mainland. Chinese intervention in the Korean War compelled the PLA to move substantial forces to Korea and the northeast (Manchuria), leaving only limited numbers of troops in Fujian and Zhejiang opposite Taiwan.

At the conclusion of the Korean War, the PLA renewed its attacks on Guomindang-held offshore islands along the Zhejiang and Fujian coasts. The Korean War had seriously affected the mainland's economy and delayed reconstruction, but militarily the war had strengthened the PLA. Still the world's largest army, the PLA had engaged in modern warfare with the United States. The PLA airforce had expanded from virtually no useable aircraft in 1949 to the world's third largest air force, with more than 3000 planes.[7] Just prior to and during the Korean War, the PLA navy also expanded.[8] By the end of 1955, the PLA navy had a total of 519 warships (including 132 landing ships), 341 support ships and 515 aircraft.[9]

In mid-1954, the Chinese launched a major campaign to 'liberate Taiwan'.[10] On 3 September 1954, the Communists, to use their own description, 'violently bombarded' Jinmen and little Jinmen, which they 'enveloped in flames and smoke'.[11] This bombardment, according to Stolper,[12] hit the islands 'with an unprecedented number of shells'. In January 1955 the PLA launched a series of military actions and captured several Guomindang-held offshore islands along Zhejiang coast including the Dachen (Tachen) Islands.[13] Strategically, these actions improved the mainland's lines of marine transportation and eliminated Guomindang military threats to China's most developed economic area, Shanghai, and the East China region. Moreover, since most military actions involved joint operations of army, navy and airforce, the occupation of these small islands demonstrated the PLA's improved ability to conduct modern warfare and its potential to fight across the sea.

From late March 1955[14] to 1957, tensions in the Taiwan Straits declined after Premier Zhou Enlai expressed the Chinese wish to discuss the situation with the United States (resulting in the Warsaw talks of July 1955) and, as he reported to the National People's Congress in 1956, the willingness of the Chinese to negotiate a peaceful solution.[15] But, according to both Chinese and Taiwanese sources, China continued to strengthen its military preparations in Fujian opposite Taiwan.

By 1958, the Chinese completed a railway between Xiamen, Fujian (just opposite the key Guomindang-held island of Jinmen) and Yingtan, Jiangxi, which dramatically increased Chinese capabilities to supply the Fujian military front. At the same time, the PLA also built nine airports in Fujian and Jiangxi for jet fighters and eight naval bases along the Fujian coast.[16] In July 1958, the 28th and 31st armies, with a total of nine infantry divisions, three artillery divisions and two anti-aircraft artillery divisions, moved into Fujian opposite Jinmen and Mazu (Matsu). The PLA Navy transferred three destroyers, two frigates and several other ships from naval bases in Shanghai and Zhejiang to Fujian.[17] The PLA Airforce deployed 520 MiG-17 aircraft to six Fujian airbases.[18] Significantly, the PLA's newly formed marine corps first appeared in Fuzhou and Xiamen.[19] Many senior PLA leaders believed the time to 'liberate' Jinmen and Mazu had arrived.[20]

On 23 August 1958, the PLA artillery launched a sudden bombardment on Jinmen. Within the 85 minutes, more than 30 000 shells fell on the tiny island. A Taiwan source estimates 475 000 shells were fired during the two-month bombardment.[21] According to a Chinese source, the bombardment, the largest in the history of Guomindang–CCP military conflict, destroyed Jinmen's communications system, several artillery emplacements and warships. Hundreds of soldiers, including several senior officers, and civilians on Jinmen were killed.[22]

The prompt United States response to the 1958 bombardment of Jinmen quickly ended the crisis.[23] Four factors reduced Chinese military pressure on Taiwan during the next two decades. Firstly, the economic disaster following the Great Leap Forward forced the Chinese to reduce defence expenditures during the early 1960s, thus preventing further pressure on Taiwan. Secondly, during the Cultural Revolution of the late 1960s, the Chinese turned inward and fought pitched battles among themselves, again leaving little energy and few resources for the 'liberation' of Taiwan. The policy towards Taiwan remained hostile, however, as many native Taiwanese who had gone over to the Communists and lived in China, as well as many Chinese with relatives in Taiwan, suffered grievously for these connections during the Cultural Revolution. Thirdly, as the Sino-Soviet dispute worsened in the late 1960s, Chinese strategy shifted from emphasising the defence of east and south China against possible attack from the United States and Taiwan to the defence of north China against possible Soviet attack. Following the Sino-Soviet border clash of 1969, the General Staff Department convened its 'Three Norths Meeting' (sanbei huiyi), referring to northeast, north and northwest China, and decided that China's greatest threat came from the Soviet Union. The consequent movement northward of Chinese military forces also reduced pressure on Taiwan. Finally, the importance to the Chinese of the Sino-American rapprochement (which followed the Kissinger and Nixon visits to Beijing in 1971 and 1972) for the Chinese efforts to ensure their security against the Soviet threat also forced the Chinese to put the Taiwan issue on the back burner as threats to Taiwan would have upset the Americans.

Yet, less than ten months before the monumental policy shift which occurred at the end of 1978, the Chinese still vowed to 'liberate (jiefang) Taiwan', a phrase which clearly connoted the use of military force to incorporate Taiwan within the PRC and the establishment of CCP rule in Taiwan. An article, which summarised speeches commemorating the 31st anniversary of the 28 February (1947) Uprising, repeatedly proclaimed 'liberation of Taiwan' would be the means to 'reunify the Motherland' (tongyi Zuguo).[24] On 5 March 1978, the Fifth National People's Congress enshrined this policy in the Preamble of the new state Constitution: 'Taiwan is China's sacred territory. We definitely will liberate Taiwan and complete the great undertaking of reunifying the Motherland.'[25]

Peaceful reunification: 1979–1989

The Third Plenum of the Eleventh Central Committee, which met during 18–22 December 1978, must be seen as a key event in China's post-Mao development. Firstly, it set China on its course of reform. Secondly, it validated the 'normalisation' of Sino-American relations, which was announced two days before the plenum actually began.

Taiwan clearly loomed large in the Chinese decision to establish diplomatic relations with the United States. The *People's Daily* prominently printed both the text of Chairman Hua Guofeng's press conference, in which four of six questions concerned Taiwan, as well as a story highlighting Hua's responses on Taiwan.[26] The Communiqué of the Third Plenum, which devoted only two sentences to reunification, explicitly tied the establishment of diplomatic relations with the United States to reunification: 'The Plenum believes, with the normalisation of Sino-American relations, the return of our sacred territory Taiwan to the bosom of the Motherland and the prospect of achieving the great undertaking of reunification has already come one step closer.'[27]

A week later, on New Year's Day, the Standing Committee of the National People's Congress issued a 'Letter to Taiwan Compatriots', which enunciated the new policy:

> Our national leaders have already shown their determination definitely to consider present circumstances in completing the great undertaking of reunifying the Motherland. When solving the problem of reunification, they will respect Taiwan's present situation and the opinions of various groups of people in Taiwan, and use fair and reasonable policies and methods to assure the people of Taiwan do not suffer losses.[28]

The 'Letter' also announced the Chinese would cease shelling the Nationalist-held offshore islands.[29] One month later, on 30 January 1979, Deng Xiaoping told both houses of the United States Congress, 'We will no longer use [the formulation] of liberating Taiwan.'[30]

From February 1979 to September 1981, as China's leadership unfurled the banners of reform, Taiwan policy clearly had low priority. Reunification of Taiwan with the Motherland received brief mention only in the final paragraphs of several major policy documents.[31] The Fifth Plenum of the Eleventh CCP Central Committee, concerned with the elevation of Hu Yaobang and Zhao Ziyang to the Political Bureau Standing Committee, the purge of the 'whatever faction', the re-establishment of the Party Secretariat, and the rehabilitation of Liu Shaoqi did not even mention Taiwan in its Communiqué.[32]

Two slogans epitomise the post-1979 Chinese policy towards Taiwan: 'peaceful reunification' (*heping tongyi*) and 'one nation, two systems' (*yiguo liangzhi*). The roots of these policies go back to the Third Plenum, though the actual policies took some time to evolve. The slogan 'peaceful reunification' became Chinese policy only on 30 September 1981 when, according to the New China News Agency, the Chairman of the Standing Committee of the

National People's Congress, Ye Jianying, 'went a step further toward clar-
ifying about the return of Taiwan to the Motherland and the policies of
achieving peaceful reunification'.[33] In prefacing his famous Nine Points, Ye
Jianying used the term 'peaceful reunification' twice.[34]

The slogan 'one nation, two systems' had roots in an internal briefing
Deng Xiaoping gave on 15 December 1979, the day before the announcement of 'normalisation' between Beijing and Washington. In order to achieve
the reunification of China, Deng wanted to have a third period of
Nationalist–Communist co-operation (the first two periods being 1923–27
and 1937–46). After unification, Taiwan's 'social and economic system,
lifestyles, and foreign investment will not change. The military will become
local militia.'[35]

Ye Jianying's Nine Points of September 1981 also clearly contained the
concept of 'one nation, two systems'. The Nine Points included proposals for
talks between the Chinese Communist and Chinese Nationalist parties on
the basis of equality, Taiwan enjoying a high degree of autonomy and retain-
ing military forces following reunification, and the maintenance of Taiwan's
current social and economic systems including private ownership.[36]

The use of the term 'one nation, two systems' became more explicit on
11 January 1982 when Deng Xiaoping used the expression for the first time to
epitomise the solution of the Taiwan question.[37] Following this, many Chinese
leaders, including Hu Yaobang, Zhao Ziyang, Li Xiannian, Deng Yingchao,
Peng Zhen, Ji Pengfei, Wu Xueqian and Deng himself, used the term repeatedly.[38] Article 13 of the new State Constitution, approved on 4 December 1982,
stated: 'When required, the state may establish special administrative districts. The *systems* implemented in the special administrative districts will be
established by laws passed by the National People's Congress in accord with
concrete conditions.'[39] In his Government Work Report of 15 May 1984,
Premier Zhao Ziyang said, 'we propose, after reunification of the Motherland,
that we can implement the plan of "one nation, two systems"'.[40]

As well as these high-level precedents, the Sino-British negotiations over
the future of Hong Kong provided an important impetus for developing
the policy of 'one nation, two systems'. Only in October 1984, when Deng
Xiaoping spoke to 'a group of foreign guests and compatriots from Hong
Kong and Macao', did the concept receive 'such a comprehensive, systematic and penetrating analysis'.[41] In fact, Hong Kong provided the first realistic opportunity for China to implement 'one nation, two systems' and in
this talk Deng emphasised Hong Kong, though he stated that 'China's plan
for Taiwan is the same'.[42]

To implement its reunification as well as its modernisation policies, the
post-Mao Chinese leadership has used a United Front (*tongyi zhanxian*) strategy. Such a strategy attempts to develop a broad political alliance in support of a policy. Seeking wide support, United Front stresses unity, rather
than struggle against enemies. The broad United Front coalition typically
includes groups which normally would not support the Communists, such
as intellectuals, minority nationalities, religious groups, former industrial-

ists and businesspeople, overseas Chinese and residents of Taiwan and Hong Kong. Not coincidentally, the Chinese language uses one word (*tongyi*) both for the 'United' of United Front and for 'reunification'.

Profound ignorance about Taiwan, a result of China's self-imposed policy of sealing itself off from the outside world before 1979 has hindered the development of China's Taiwan policies. A leading Taiwanese Communist, Li Chunqing, writing in the *People's Daily* a year after the opening to Taiwan, indicated this lack of knowledge:

> Owing to the long isolation between Taiwan and the Mainland ... Mainland compatriots also do not have much understanding of Taiwan and Taiwanese. Many people mistakenly believe Taiwan is a minority nationality area; they do not know that ninety-seven per cent of Taiwan's residents are Han.[43]

Well into the early 1980s, according to numerous Taiwanese living on the mainland, many mainland residents believed Taiwan was primarily an island of aborigines led by the Han Chinese Nationalist government.

To increase their understanding of Taiwan, the Chinese have established a large number of Taiwan offices in the Party and government as well as Taiwan Research Institutes in government think tanks and universities. Increasing contacts with Taiwanese and overseas Taiwan scholars have improved Chinese understanding of Taiwan, but many Chinese officials appear to wear ideological blinkers which inhibit their understanding of the major social, economic and political changes which have occurred on the island, and the insights of the more perspicacious research institutes rarely seem to percolate to high decision-makers in Beijing.

The Chinese leadership has also been slow to realise that the process of democratisation in Taiwan has changed negotiating parameters. Based on historical circumstances, the CCP has called for party-to-party talks with the Guomindang. Naturally, the DPP has objected and the Guomindang too has now rejected party-to-party talks. The CCP government assumes even officially 'unofficial' talks have an official nature. They do not realise the importance of public opinion in restricting the Taiwanese authorities' scope of operation. This is an important asymmetry. While the CCP sees 'national reunification' in relatively simple terms, no democratically elected Taiwan government — be it Guomindang or DPP — can make an agreement which does not consider the aspirations of Taiwan's population.

The Nationalist leadership on Taiwan has viewed the Communist United Front policies towards Taiwan with suspicion. The long course of Communist–Nationalist interaction, which began shortly after the founding of the Communist Party in 1921 and ended with the Nationalist defeat of 1949, has led Nationalist leaders to view the Communist United Front policies as designed to defeat the Nationalist government in Taiwan by obtaining Communist support in Taiwan and overseas Chinese communities.

The Nationalists have also been concerned that Taiwan might become economically dependent upon the mainland. According to the Nationalists, the strong Communist control over the Chinese economy would enable them to use Taiwan's dependence to extract political concessions.

The Nationalists responded to the dramatic Communist policy changes with their 'three no's' policy: 'no contact, no negotiations, no compromise'. In fact, in the last years of President Chiang Ching-kuo's reign and since the accession of President Lee Teng-hui in 1988, the Nationalists have become considerably more pragmatic, allowing large numbers of Taiwanese to visit the mainland, sending government ministers to international meetings on the mainland, establishing the Straits Exchange Foundation to conduct 'non-governmental' talks with the mainland authorities as well as permitting Taiwanese foreign investment on the mainland and indirect Taiwan–mainland trade. Nevertheless, most Nationalist leaders still fundamentally distrust the Communist regime.

Perhaps the most critical change in Taiwan's policy towards China occurred in October 1987 when President Chiang Ching-kuo allowed Taiwanese to visit the mainland. This decision followed considerable lobbying and demonstrations on the part of retired mainlander servicemen desiring to visit their native places before they died. Although only persons with relatives on the mainland who did not hold government positions in Taiwan were originally allowed to visit the mainland, in fact these restrictions have loosened dramatically and millions of Taiwanese have visited the mainland as tourists.

More than any other factors, the Taiwanese visits to the mainland (which the PRC welcomed) and the Beijing massacre have damaged the prospects for implementing Beijing's 'one nation, two systems' policy. For almost 40 years, Taiwanese were not allowed news of the mainland, and many felt the mainland could not be as bad as Nationalist anti-Communist propaganda had portrayed. The Taiwanese visits to the mainland, in perhaps their most important, though unintentional, consequence, punctured the myths about the mainland which existed on Taiwan.

Expanding economic ties (1987–present)

Since 1987, mainland–Taiwan trade has expanded rapidly. No one (including the Chinese and Taiwan governments) knows the full extent of this trade. As direct trade is illegal and much of the trade goes through Hong Kong, Hong Kong statistics provide the most reliable source for at least a portion of the trade. The trade is heavily in Taiwan's favour. The Beijing massacre appears to account for the greatly reduced rate of increase during 1989–90.

Taiwan also appears to be the second largest source of foreign investment on the mainland after Hong Kong. Investment statistics are even less reliable than trade statistics because many Taiwan investors do not report their investments to Taiwan's government. Mainland Chinese specialists also admit their government does not know how much Taiwan investment exists on the mainland. Furthermore, much Taiwan investment is disguised as coming from Hong Kong or even from the United States and Japan.

Table 12.1   Mainland–Taiwan trade through Hong Kong (1987–93, US$ millions)

Year	Total trade	% increase	Taiwan exports to mainland	% increase	Mainland exports to Taiwan	% increase
1987	1515.47	58.60	1226.53	51.18	288.94	100.35
1988	2720.91	79.54	2242.22	82.81	478.69	65.67
1989	3483.39	28.02	2896.49	29.18	586.90	22.61
1990	4043.62	16.08	3278.26	13.18	765.36	30.41
1991	5793.12	43.26	4667.16	42.36	1125.96	47.11
1992*	7400.00	27.90				
1993**	9000.00					

Sources: Zhang Xuping, 'Haixia liang'an jingmao guanxi yu zhanwang' (Trade and Economic Relations and Forecast between Both Sides of the Taiwan Straits), *Zhonggong yanjiu* (Chinese Communist Research), vol. 26, no. 7, July 1992, p. 29, from Hong Kong Government statistics.
* Florence Chong, 'Talks Signal Start of Better Relations', *Australian*, 10 September 1993, p. 12.
** Tony Walker, 'Taiwan Contemplates a Future Closer to China', *Age*, 21 August 1993, p. 22.

A few recent journalistic examples indicate the range of estimates. A Taiwan source told an Australian journalist that direct utilised Taiwan investment on the mainland exceeds US$2000 million with many times that figure committed. This source estimates that 12 000 Taiwan companies have investments on the mainland.[44] Another Australian journalist says official investment is about US$5000 million, but as many as 10 000 Taiwan companies may have invested as much as US$20 000 million. Using Chinese statistics, a recent Chinese-language source reported the PRC approved Taiwan investments for 2073 projects worth US$2131 million during the first quarter of 1993. These figures are 2.93 and 5.74 times the respective 1992 figures.[45] The same source also reported that the Taiwanese government had approved US$510 million of indirect investment on the mainland for the first five months of 1993, an amount seven times the same period in 1992 and more than the US$480 million invested in all other countries and regions.[46]

According to a Hong Kong economist, Taiwan ranked first among foreign investors in China during 1992. Official Taiwan estimates of Taiwan capital on the mainland totalled US$19 400 million as of November 1992, of which US$4500 million was invested. This amount greatly exceeds the US$1500 million which the Taiwan government had approved as of 20 May 1993, 'but estimates among unofficial Taiwan circles are much greater than this figure'.[47] In the first four months of 1993, Taiwan enterprises indirectly invested US$280 million, a figure almost five times the equivalent period in 1992.[48]

A military threat?

China's plans to reunify Taiwan with the mainland have incorporated an internal contradiction. While they emphasise that 'peaceful reunification is an established policy (*jiding fangzhen*) of the Chinese government',[49] the Chinese refuse to forgo the possibility of using military power to reunify Taiwan with the mainland. The Chinese argue that they have sovereignty over Taiwan and thus, as a sovereign power, can do what they like with Taiwan. The White Paper puts the argument thus: 'Every sovereign state has the right to use any measures which it considers necessary, including military measures, to protect its sovereignty and territorial integrity.'[50]

Clearly, people in Taiwan view this contradictory policy with suspicion. 'If China desires peaceful reunification,' they ask, 'why can't it forgo the possibility of using military power to force reunification?' A senior Chinese specialist on Taiwan affairs argues that China's statement assumes two types of military threat: a declaration of Taiwan independence; and foreign intervention.[51] The assumption in each case is that Taiwan cannot defend itself. But Taiwan does have military power to defend itself, and thus China's threat to use military power is dysfunctional for its attempts to convince Taiwan's population that it desires peaceful reunification.

In recent years, Taiwan has greatly changed its military posture from preparing to 'recover the mainland' to focusing on the defence of Taiwan. Thus the army, which needed to be large to invade and occupy the mainland, has been reduced in favour of increased expenditure on the navy and airforce, which have missions centred on Taiwan's defence.[52] The Nationalist army does not possess the capacity to recapture the mainland, 'nor do its forces organise, train or deploy to attempt such an adventure'.[53]

At the same time, China has substantially increased its military spending as the military has increased its political power in the aftermath of the Beijing massacre of June 1989. Since 1989, the Chinese military budget has increased from RMB25 100 million in 1989, to RMB29 000 million in 1990, RMB33 300 million in 1991, RMB37 300 million in 1992 and RMB49 000 million in 1993.[54]

Since 1990, China has reportedly purchased a variety of advanced weapons and military technologies from the United States, Britain, France, Italy, Russia and Israel to upgrade its obsolete equipment and improve the combat capacity of its army, navy and airforce. These include the purchase of an early warning system for the PLA airforce (from Britain), an anti-air-craft system for the Chinese navy (from France), co-operation in research and production of an American tank and purchase of a super-computer system (from America), SU-27 jet fighters (from Russia) and co-operation in mod-ification of the Chinese Q-5 fighter (with Italy).[55] According to the Taiwan Ministry of Defence, the Commander of the PLA General Logistics Department announced at the end of 1990 that China would spend US$1300 million in 1991 to purchase high-tech weapons from abroad.[56] In October 1993, the CIA alleged that Israel sold military technology to China which 'could be worth "several billion dollars"'.[57]

In recent years, Taiwan has also modernised its weapons. In 1988–89, Taiwan's defence budget was US$6700 million, one-third of the government budget and a 16 per cent increase over the previous fiscal year. The budget was also US$1000 million greater than the PLA budget.[58] In 1992, Taiwan obtained approval from the United States and France to purchase 150 F-16 and 60 Mirage 2000-5 fighters planes. In May 1993, the first Taiwan-made missile frigate offi-cially went into service, with seven others of the same class to follow.[59]

The apparent arms race on both sides of the Taiwan Straits, together with China's unwillingness to renounce the use of force with respect to Taiwan, has created apprehension in the international community concerning the possible destabilisation of the Taiwan Straits. Table 12.2 compares the armed forces of China and Taiwan.

Table 12.2 Comparison of armed forces

	China	Taiwan
Total armed forces	3 030 000	442 000
Army		
Strength	2 300 000	312 000
Group armies	24	3
Infantry divisions	74	15
Armoured divisions	10	6
Main battle tanks	7 500–8 000	509
Navy		
Strength	260 000	60 000
Submarines	47	4
Destroyers	18	22
Frigates	38	10
Missile craft	215	52
Torpedo craft	160	none
Mine warfare vessels	126	13
Landing ships	61	*29
Amphibious vessels	51	26
Support ships	150	28
Marines	6 000	30 000
Naval airforce		
Bombers	160	none
Fighters	600	none
Ground attack fighters	100	none
Armed helicopters	65	none
Airforce		
Strength	470 000	70 000
Bombers	470	
Ground attack fighters	500	
Fighters	4 000	398
Transport aircraft	600	81
Armed helicopters	400	23
Strategic missile forces		
Intercontinental ballistic missiles	8	none
Intermediate-range ballistic missiles	60	none
Medium-range ballistic missiles	*50	none

Sources: International Institute for Strategic Studies, *The Military Balance 1993–1994*, Brassey's for IISS, London, 1993, pp. 152–55, 168–69.

* Martin L. Lasater, *The Taiwan Issue in Sino-American State Relations*, Westview Press, Boulder, Col., 1984., p. 124.

Table 12.2 suggests that China has far superior military capabilities compared to Taiwan.[60] Theoretically speaking, in a full-scale conflict involving China, Taiwan would be defeated.

We believe, however, that the likelihood of full-scale conflict between China and Taiwan remains small. Firstly, the reduction of the tension between China and Taiwan since 1979 has created an atmosphere which makes it highly unlikely that the Chinese people or the Chinese military would accept a military solution. Of course, the Chinese leadership might be able to motivate the PLA to fight 'Taiwan Independence' in a manner similar to that used to suppress popular opinion in China in 1989.

Secondly, as the earlier discussion demonstrated, Taiwan has become important in China's current economic development. In terms of economic development, peaceful coexistence across the Taiwan Straits is more important for China than for Taiwan. The events of 1989 caused a drastic (though temporary) decline in foreign investment. In the post-Cold War world, a war against Taiwan would lose China considerable international support, and would create international sympathy for Taiwan and give Taiwan an excuse to claim independence.

Thirdly, the rapid economic growth in Taiwan has enabled Taiwan to buy expensive modern weapons systems and military technology. According to a reliable source, Taiwan's 1992 defence budget of US$10 290 million exceeded the Chinese defence budget of US$6710 million. Taiwan's 1993 defence budget of US$10 450 million also greatly exceeds the PLA's budget of US$7310 million.[61] Of course, Chinese wages and other costs are less than Taiwan's, but Taiwan can buy more on the international market. China would find it difficult to engage in an arms race with Taiwan (provided Taiwan could find suppliers willing to sell it advanced weapons).

Fourth, the PLA cannot focus most of its military forces on Taiwan. In a large country like China, the leaders must concentrate troops to defend other regions and to control internal unrest in such minority nationality areas as Tibet and Xinjiang. Even though China's diplomatic relations with Russia, South Korea and India have greatly improved in recent years, considerable foreign military forces are located near China's borders. For example, 60 per cent of former Soviet land forces, 70 per cent of fighter aircraft (including 80 per cent of sophisticated fourth-generation fighters) and 80 per cent of bombers are presently deployed in the Far East near China's northern border. It is believed that the quality of forces in the area has actually increased as tanks, armoured fighting vehicles, artillery, tactical aircraft, attack helicopters and other military equipment removed from the European part of Russia have been placed in the Russian Far East.[62] On China's southwest border, India's military buildup has achieved impressive results since the Sino-Indian border war.[63]

Only five of China's 24 Group Armies are stationed in areas relevant to Taiwan. The Nanjing Military Region, which has responsibility for Taiwan, has only three group armies (about nine infantry divisions) facing Taiwan's 442 000 troops with thirteen infantry divisions, two mechanised infantry divisions, two airborne brigades, six armoured brigades and two tank groups. The Guangzhou Military Region, with two group armies, could be used to support the Nanjing Military Region in any confrontation with

Taiwan, but the Guangzhou Military Region also has responsibility for Vietnam, Hong Kong and the disputed islands in the South China Sea over which China has evinced increasing concern.

Most of China's group armies are located elsewhere in the Shenyang Military Region (five group armies), Beijing Military Region (six), Lanzhou Military Region (two), Chengdu Military Region and Jinan Military Region (four each). Except for the last-mentioned, which act as strategic support troops, these group armies are located near the northern and southwestern borders. In other words, most of China's troops are still deployed along China's extended land border. This suggests that China has not significantly altered its defence posture since the end of the Cold War.

Fifth, in any Taiwan Straits conflict, the side which controls the air and sea will win. Although China has an impressive number of jet fighters, warships and main battle tanks, most are obsolete. Most of its jet fighters date from the 1960s and 1970s. The PLA also lacks modern communication, electronic tracking and guidance technologies. It is doubtful that the PLA's navy and air force could provide sufficient protection to enable an amphibious assault across the Taiwan Strait without very heavy casualties and, indeed, the risk of embarrassing defeat. Moreover, the existing transportation capability of the PLA navy seems inadequate to deliver sufficient troops and equipment to land on Taiwan and fight 442 000 Nationalist troops who would be waiting in well-prepared defensive positions. It will be many years before the PLA has enough air and naval forces to overpower the quantitatively small, but qualitatively better equipped Nationalist navy and airforce.The Taiwan Straits will, moreover, continue to be an excellent natural defence for Taiwan as they constitute a major obstacle for any PLA invasion.

Sixth, China has developed a strategic nuclear force, but it seems almost impossible for the Chinese leaders to use this in a 'civil war' against Taiwan. And a destroyed Taiwan would have little to contribute to China. Furthermore, the use of nuclear weapons against Taiwan would make China a pariah and might cause other great powers to intervene. Thus, to some extent, nuclear weapons are, as Mao said, 'paper tigers'. On the other hand, Taiwan has also developed a nuclear industry and could possibly produce nuclear weapons within a short time of any outbreak of war.[64] (In fact, Taiwan may already have nuclear weapons.)

Finally, the quality of an army depends on the calibre of its military personnel as well as its weapon systems. This is especially true in modern warfare, which uses large numbers of high-tech weapons. Although the PLA has purchased many modern weapon systems in recent years, it will take time for the PLA to absorb and master them. The Nationalist army appears much more highly trained and familiar with Western weapon systems.

For these reasons we believe the PLA will be unable to 'liberate' Taiwan in the near future simply because it would not be able to control the Taiwan Straits once war erupted. It also seems doubtful that China could successfully blockade Taiwan. Such an action might lead Taiwan to declare independence and would certainly win Taiwan sympathy in the international community. In fact, any Chinese military action which did not 'liberate' Taiwan rapidly could backfire by creating such sympathy for Taiwan that the international community might recognise an independent Republic of Taiwan. A much more logical policy for China would be to renounce the use of force with respect to Taiwan, emphasise 'peaceful reunification' and 'play the economic card' so as to bind the futures of Taiwan and the mainland together.

Notes

1 The authors gratefully acknowledge grants from the Australian Research Council which enabled the preparation of this paper. We have romanised Chinese terms as well as mainland personal and place names according to the pinyin system, but have romanised Taiwan personal and place names in accord with common Taiwan practice.

2 J. Bruce Jacobs, 'Democratisation in Taiwan', *Asian Studies Review*, vol. 17, no. 1, July 1993, pp. 116–26.

3 J. Bruce Jacobs, 'Rip Van Winkle Returns to Taiwan', *Far Eastern Economic Review*, 13 May 1993, p. 36.

4 White Paper, 'Taiwan wenti yu Zhongguo tongyi' (The Taiwan Question and China's Unification), *Renmin ribao* (People's Daily), Beijing (hereafter *RMRB*), 1 September 1993, p. 2; White Paper, 'The Taiwan Question and Reunification of China', *Beijing Review*, vol. 36, no. 36, 6–12 September 1993, p. iv. We have translated the Chinese original because the official English translation (White Paper, 'The Taiwan Question and Reunification of China') does not adequately convey the true meaning of the Chinese original.

5 Yan Jiaqi, '"Yiguo liangzhi" he Zhongguo tongyi de tujing' ('One Nation, Two Systems' and the Road of Chinese Unification), in Yan Jiaqi, *Quanli yu zhenli* (Power and Truth), Guangming ribao chubanshe, Beijing, 1987; reprinted from *Zhengzhixue yanjiu* (Political Science Research), no. 2, 1985. When Yan Jiaqi wrote these words in 1985, he was a senior government adviser. Yan fled China following the 4 June 1989 Beijing massacre.

6 Xu Yan, *Taihai dazhan, Vol. 1: Zhonggong guandian* [War in the Taiwan Straits, vol. 1: The Chinese Communist View], reprinted Tiandi Book Ltd, Hong Kong, 1992, p. 117.

7 ibid., p. 159.

8 ibid., pp. 115–16; Sima Muwen (ed.), *Zhongguo sanjun shili* (The Strength of the Chinese Army, Airforce and Navy), Sichuan daxue chubanshe, Chengdu, 1993, p. 148.

9 Sima Muwen (ed.), *Zhongguo sanjun shili*, p. 149.

10 Thomas E. Stolper, *China, Taiwan and the Offshore Islands*, M.E. Sharpe, Inc., Armonk, N.Y. and London, 1985, p. 35.

11 ibid., p. 39.

12 ibid.

13 ibid., p. 66.
14 ibid., p. 98.
15 Xu Yan, *Taihai dazhan, Vol. 1: Zhonggong guandian*, pp. 181, 183, 186.
16 Du Junyu, Xu Weimin and Zhao Guojian, 'Guo Gong zai Taihai de zhudao yuxue zhan' (The Bloody Island to Island Battles Between the Nationalists and Communists), in Li Yuanping, and others, *Taihai dazhan, vol. 2: Taiwan guandian* (War in the Taiwan Straits, vol. 2: The View from Taiwan), Tiandi Book Ltd, Hong Kong, 1992, pp. 106.
17 ibid., pp. 106–7.
18 Xu Yan, *Taihai dazhan, Vol. 1: Zhonggong guandian*, p. 205.
19 Du Junyu and others, 'Guo Gong zai Taihai de zhudao yuxue zhan', pp. 106–7.
20 Xu Yan, *Taihai dazhan, Vol. 1: Zhonggong guandian*, pp. 230–31.
21 Di Zongheng, 'Jinhou shei jiang kongzhi Taiwan haixia' (Who Will Control the Taiwan Straits in the Future?), in Li Yuanping, and others, *Taihai dazhan, vol. 2: Taiwan guandian*, p. 294.
22 Xu Yan, *Taihai dazhan, Vol. 1: Zhonggong guandian*, pp. 221–22.
23 Sha Li and Min Li (eds), *Jianguo hou Zhongguo guonei shici junshi da xingdong* (Ten Major Military Operations Since the Founding of the People's Republic of China), Sichuan kexue jishu chubanshe, Chengdu, 1992, pp. 90–91; Stolper, *China, Taiwan and the Offshore Islands*, pp. 117–19. Many commentators argue that the Chinese ultimately did not want to occupy Jinmen and Mazu because this would have created a much wider buffer between Communist and Nationalist forces and made an independent Taiwan easier to achieve. The Nationalist control of Jinmen and Mazu meant that the opposing forces could literally see and hear each other. Furthermore, since Jinmen and Mazu both belong to Fujian province, Nationalist control of the offshore islands also meant they also controlled some Chinese territory in addition to Taiwan province.
24 *RMRB*, 1 March 1978, p. 3.
25 ibid., 8 March 1978, p. 1.
26 ibid., 17 December 1978, p. 1.
27 ibid., 24 December 1978, p. 1.
28 ibid., 1 January 1979, p. 1.
29 ibid.
30 Yan Jiaqi, '"Yiguo liangzhi" he Zhongguo tongyi de tujing', p. 185.
31 For example: Hua Guofeng's Government Work Report of 18 June 1979 (*RMRB*, 26 June 1979, pp. 1–4, esp. p. 4; translated in *Beijing Review*, vol. 22, no. 27, 6 July 1979, pp. 5–31, esp. p. 31); Ye Jianying's speech on the 30th anniversary of the People's Republic (*RMRB*, 30 September 1979, pp. 1–4, esp. p. 4; translated in *Beijing Review*, vol. 22, no. 40, 5 October 1979, pp. 7–32, esp. p. 31); Hua Guofeng's speech of 7 September 1980 (*RMRB*, 15 September 1980, pp. 1–3, esp. p. 3; translated in *Beijing Review*, vol. 23, no. 38, 22 September 1980, pp. 12–29, esp. p. 29); and Hu Yaobang's speech on the 60th anniversary of the Chinese Communist Party (*RMRB*, 2 July 1981, p. 3).

32 *RMRB*, 1 March 1980, pp. 1–2; *Beijing Review*, vol. 23, no. 10, 10 March 1980, pp. 7–10.

33 *RMRB*, 1 October 1981, p. 1.

34 We have found only two minor references, both by Taiwan Democratic Self-Government League leaders, using the words 'peaceful' and 'reunification' in the same sentence prior to Ye's statement. At the meeting commemorating the 32nd anniversary of the 28 February Uprising, Taiwan League Chairman Cai Xiao said: 'The Chinese Communist Party and the People's Government have proposed striving peacefully to solve the Taiwan question', but the main speaker, Liao Chengzhi, made no reference to 'peaceful' (*RMRB*, 1 March 1979, p. 2). League Vice-Chairman Li Chunqing actually used the phrase 'peaceful reunification' towards the end of a December 1979 article (*RMRB*, 12 December 1979, p. 3).

35 Yan Jiaqi, '"Yiguo liangzhi" he Zhongguo tongyi de tujing', p. 184.

36 *RMRB*, 1 October 1981, p. 1.

37 Yan Jiaqi, '"Yiguo liangzhi" he Zhongguo tongyi de tujing', p. 185.

38 ibid.

39 'Zhonghua renmin gongheguo xianfa' [Constitution of the People's Republic of China], in *Zhonghua renmin gongheguo falü ji youguan fagui huibian 1979–1984 nian* (Collection of laws and related legal regulations of the People's Republic of China, 1979–1984) Falü chubanshe, Beijing, 1986, pp. 1–33. Emphasis added.

40 Zhao Ziyang, 'Zhengfu gongzuo baogao' (Government Work Report), in *Zhonghua renmin gongheguo di liu jie quanguo renmin daibiao dahui di er ci huiyi wenjian huibian* (Compilation of Documents of the Second Session of the Sixth National People's Congress of the People's Republic of China), Renmin chubanshe, Beijing, 1984, pp. 3–34.

41 Note that Li incorrectly states the Third Plenum 'made the *peaceful reunification* of the motherland a strategic policy'. (Emphasis added.) Li Jiaquan, 'Formula for China's Reunification', *Beijing Review*, vol. 29, no. 5, 3 February 1986, p. 19.

42 Deng Xiaoping, 'Deng Xiaoping On "One Country, Two Systems"', *Beijing Review*, vol. 29, no. 5, 3 February 1986, p. 25.

43 *RMRB*, 12 December 1979, p. 3.

44 Tony Walker, 'Taiwan contemplates a future closer to China', *Age*, 21 August 1993, p. 22.

45 'Tai shang touzi dalu xin taishi' (The Recent Situation of Taiwan Business Investment on the Mainland), *Xin haichao bao* (New Tide News), Melbourne, 14 October 1993, p. 4.

46 ibid.

47 Chen Wenhong, 'Dui liang'an touzi maoyi de zai sikao' [A Reconsideration of Investment and Trade across the (Taiwan) Straits], *Xinbao caijing yuekan* (Hong Kong Economic Journal Monthly), no. 198, September 1993, p. 3.

48 ibid.

49 White Paper, 'Taiwan wenti yu Zhongguo tongyi', p. 2; White Paper, 'The Taiwan Question and Reunification of China', p. vi.

50 ibid.

51 Personal communication.

52 Jacobs, 'Rip Van Winkle Returns to Taiwan'; Jacobs, 'Democratisation in Taiwan', p. 125; Lai Yixiong and Lin Zhengyi, 'Taiwan fangwei zhengce jiantao' (An Examination of Taiwan's Defence Policy), in Xiao Quanzheng (ed.), *Guofang waijiao baipishu* (White Paper on National Defence and Foreign Relations), Guojia zhengce yanjiu ziliao zhongxin, Taibei, p. 222.

53 Edward W. Ross, 'Taiwan's Armed Forces', in Edward A. Olsen and Stephen Jurika, Jr. (eds), *The Armed Forces in Contemporary Asian Societies*, Westview Press, Boulder, Col., 1986, p. 56.

54 *Zhongguo shibao zhoukan* (China Times Weekly), no. 62, 7–13 March 1993, p. 11.

55 *Zhonghua minguo bashi yi nian guofang baogaoshu* (1992 National Defence Report), Liming wenhua gongsi,Taipei, 1992, pp. 202–3.

56 ibid., p. 203.

57 David Lague, 'Chinese Arms Trade Fuels Tension', *Weekend Australian*, 16–17 October 1993, p. 12.

58 Rosita Dellios, *Modern Chinese Defence Strategy, Present Development, Further Directions*, Macmillan, London, 1989, p. 167.

59 Tammy C. Peng, 'Navy launches 1st made-in-Taiwan frigate', *Free China Journal*, vol. 10, no. 34, 11 May 1993, p. 1.

60 According to Ian Pfennigwerth, a naval expert, the above table understates Taiwan's naval strength by neglecting to include the frigate project, the Lafayette corvette project, surveillance aircraft including shipboard helicopters and some thirty coastal patrol vessels. The United States also provides direct military assistance in such areas as intelligence, missiles and technology, which also do not appear in the table (personal communication). The table also does not include the more modern T-90 tank based on German technology which Chinese military officials suggest China is now producing (personal communication).

61 International Institute for Strategic Studies, *The Military Balance 1993–1994*, Brassey's for IISS, London, 1993, pp. 152, 168.

62 Japanese White Paper, Defence of Japan 1992, cited in *Japan's Defence and Security in the 1990s*, Report of the Senate Standing Committee on Foreign Affairs, Defence and Trade, Canberra, pp. 20–21.

63 Glynn L. Wood, 'Civil–Military Relations in Post-Colonial India', in Olsen and Jurika (eds), *The Armed Forces in Contemporary Asian Societies*, pp. 273–74.

64 Di Zongheng, 'Jinhou shei jiang kongzhi Taiwan haixia', p. 302.

13 The PLA's Military Modernisation in the 1990s

You Ji[1]

Under the professional-minded leadership centred around Liu Huaqing and Zhang Zhen, the People's Liberation Army (PLA) has embarked on a new path of development. Indicators include breakthroughs in strategic military thinking, restructuring of force components with the specialised services given priority considerations, greater emphasis on state-of-the-art military hardware, and revised military training programs to enhance the PLA's rapid response capabilities. Reviewing these changes, this chapter argues that the PLA is exploring a new grand strategy to guide its development in the 1990s and beyond. The key to understanding this new strategy is the slogan currently most popular among PLA top brass: 'to fight modern warfare under high-tech conditions', as compared with the slogans of the 1980s: 'to fight a people's war under modern conditions'. However, the significance of this strategic change has transcended military terms. It reflects the changed threat perception of Chinese leaders in the new world order. Logically, the new strategy will make the PLA's defence increasingly forward postured and thus it could affect the regional strategic balance. As China looks set to increase its influence in world affairs, the international community needs to observe carefully the direction of this evolution.[2]

Breaking away from the People's War strategy: A review

A study of any country's military strategy is important, as it reveals the nature of its armed forces — whether defensive or offensive in terms of force structure and power projection. It can tell us what potential threat the country has identified and what measures its military has adopted in dealing with it. Different strategies also create different weapons programs. These are crucial areas of research in the evolution of China's military strategy in the post-Mao era, and can shed light on our understanding of the PLA's defence posture in the years to come.

In the 1960s and 1970s, the threat of a Soviet land attack formed the base of the Maoist people's war strategy. Mao Zedong's mobilisation of the whole nation to defend China was then probably the only option available to the PLA with the country's economy struggling at a subsistence level. In 1979 this strategy was revised to highlight Deng Xiaoping's stress on fighting a war under 'modern conditions'.[3] The essence of the change was an emphasis on a relatively well trained and equipped professional army capable of withholding a Soviet attack, particularly in the major battle directions. This was later formally termed an 'active defence doctrine'. General Yang Dezhi, former chief of general staff, elaborated the doctrine as 'instead of allowing the enemy to move fairly freely into the country, the PLA should stick to positional warfare and wage counter-attacks by a combined army'.[4] Politically, this change reflected the PLA's recognition that by the time the enemy was 'lured' into China's heartland on the premise of a people's war strategy, much of the country's vital industries and transportation nodes would have been destroyed.[5] Militarily, it expressed a measure of confidence in the PLA after it had accumulated more heavy military hardware and achieved a limited second-strike nuclear capability.

In a meeting with party leaders on 2 March 1983, Deng proposed that the PLA's war strategy change further, from the preparation for an early war with the Soviet Union to 'steady development' in an environment of lasting detente. The proposal assumed that the Soviet Union was mainly focused on Europe and dealing with a hard-line United States foreign policy. Thus the PLA enjoyed an historical opportunity to modernise its weaponry, taking a long-term approach. In other words, barring an imminent attack, the PLA was no longer forced to deploy costly but ineffective equipment. Its modernisation could now be based on the general improvement of the country's economy, science and technology, which would provide the PLA with a more solid base for development.[6]

Deng's new policy gave greater emphasis to the upgrading of military hardware under modern conditions than the elements prescribed by the strategy of a people's war. He particularly singled out research and development (R&D) of advanced weapons to be the priority for the PLA. In December 1985, the party's Central Military Commission (CMC) formally adopted Deng's proposal.[7] As the PLA opened a new page of transformation from quantitative to qualitative development, a number of far-reaching military reforms quickly followed. Firstly, in 1985–86, a thorough restructuring of a military that had traditionally drawn its strength from large numbers of soldiers was initiated. To this end, the PLA demobilised one million officers and men, reduced the number of its regional commands from eleven to seven, removed construction and railway units from its structure, transferred the command of the militia to the government, and merged its 36 armies into 25 combined army corps.[8]

Secondly, the PLA's new strategy required a new approach to the study of military strategies and tactics. The diminished Soviet threat allowed PLA strategists to reassess the determinants of the country's security, leading to the conclusion that in the foreseeable future limited regional conflicts were the more likely scenarios that they would have to deal with along and beyond the country's borders.[9] This recognition rectified a visible weakness in its preparation of war — an obsession with all-out war had prevented an in-depth study of limited wars both in theoretical planning and in development of appropriate weaponry.[10] In a limited war caused by territorial disputes, traditional war strategies and tactics would become irrelevant. Nor would positional defence — the core of the active defence doctrine — help in achieving the PLA's objectives.

Thirdly, Deng's strategy gave prominence to the professional training of officers and troops. In the early 1980s, the PLA established a three-tiered system of military educational institutions.[11] The CMC prescribed that by the year 2000 most PLA officers would have tertiary qualifications.[12] It was hoped that, as the quality of officers' education and technological hardware gradually improved, so would the level of professionalism of the PLA.

Overall, the PLA's efforts at modernisation yielded mixed results in the 1980s. On the one hand, groundwork had been laid for future development in terms of force restructuring, military thinking and general training. The war strategies of different services had been rewritten to suit contemporary warfare. Yet the PLA's modernisation advanced slowly. The reason is multifold. The doctrine of active defence against a Soviet land attack seemed to be out of touch both with the reality of international affairs and the PLA's own assessment of security concerns. The term 'people's war under modern conditions' became contradictory in itself — whether to rely on populous power (people's war) or firepower (modern conditions) confused the PLA in determining its basic direction of modernisation.[13]

To a lesser extent, traditional military thinking based on the people's war strategy still exerted a powerful influence. Most top military leaders had been imbued with such a strategy throughout their long professional careers. Moreover, the history of contemporary warfare had proved the salience of the strategy, first in Vietnam and then in Afghanistan. The idea of 'bleeding the invaders' in a protracted war remained attractive to many defence planners in the PLA.

However, the key obstacle to the PLA becoming a 'qualitative army' was lack of financial resources. In the 1980s, the military budget shrank despite robust economic growth. During the period the PLA was repeatedly enjoined by Deng to self-restraint, *rennai*. As a result, it could hardly meet the cost of personnel maintenance and basic training, let alone significant upgrading of its weaponry.[14] Moreover, weak scientific and technological foundations had frustrated a number of key military high-tech projects, such as the development of a new generation of aircraft.

The emergence of a high-tech war strategy

Since 1989, debates on the direction of the PLA's defence strategy have intensified among China's top military officers. During the Gulf War, all PLA services set up special research task forces to study the war. Towards the end of 1991, the CMC convened a series of meetings to analyse the reports with leaders Jiang Zemin, Yang Shangkun and Liu Huaqing present at most of them. Subsequently, the CMC called for a serious study of high-tech warfare. For this, General Zhang Zhen, vice-chairman of the CMC, urged the PLA planners to attain 'five breakthroughs' in the PLA's war strategy.[15]

Although the strategy of people's war under modern conditions has not formally been discarded, its substance has completely changed. General Liu Jingsong, commander of Lanzhou Military Region, stated that 'modern warfare under high-tech conditions has forced us to shift our preparation from an ordinary conventional war to a high-tech war. To this end, all the officers at middle and high command posts must learn earnestly the law of high-tech warfare and breaking new ground of combat for the PLA.'[16] A general consensus seemed to have emerged towards a strategy to prepare for a high-tech war, as demonstrated by the outcome of the Gulf War.[17] The following are several key features of this new strategy.

Rationale and changed perception of threat

The perception of potential threat is a key input in the formulation of a country's defence policy and war strategy. In the case of China, its defence policy is not always in accord with its foreign policy. While the latter is designed to prevent a crisis situation from emerging through diplomatic means, the former is more influenced by a worst case scenario: armed conflicts. The active defence doctrine, the revision of Maoist strategy, was the result of the PLA's review of its strategy against the Soviet Union. The revision of the Dengist strategy (people's war under modern conditions) was followed by the emergence of a high-tech strategy that stemmed from the PLA's assessment of the post-Cold War world order. According to PLA analysts, the protracted peace, as then calculated by Deng, was based on a relative balance of power between the two superpowers. The collapse of the Soviet Union removed one supporting pillar for that kind of peace so that the remaining superpower might be tempted to exercise hegemonic power. In Asia, the unstable elements existing between major players might become confrontational, heralding a long period of uncertainty. China would have to prepare militarily for such a development.[18]

The PLA is particularly concerned that most of the countries with which China may enter into conflicts possess high-tech weaponry more advanced than China's. Russia still represents a potential threat not only because it has territorial disputes with China, and a current pro-West stance, but also because its future is uncertain. As nationalistic tendencies gather force in Russia, the PLA's contingency plans have to deal with a high-tech Russian military.[19]

Japan is set to achieve a status of a political power. This will inevitably dictate an increase in its military capability. China may have seen this as a mixed blessing, as a militaristic Japan may alarm the Americans and Russians as well and thus may increase the weight of the China 'card'.[20] Indeed, the PLA believed that the post-Cold War era could see rising conflicts among Western powers. Prominent among these would be worsening trade ties between Japan and United States.[21] On the other hand, most Chinese analysts believe that Japan will not emerge as a threat before the turn of the century.[22] Beyond that, the PLA is confident that its enhanced capability, which can make an island country vulnerable in a nuclear age, may prevent the Japanese from attempting a repetition of history. This may be the reason China has chosen Japan to be the first country with which to create mechanisms for limited security transparency.[23] As for the PLA, the need to be able to cope with a militarily powerful Japan would provide impetus for a faster modernisation of the PLA.[24]

While the threat posed by Russia and Japan is a long-term one, the independence movement in Taiwan has emerged as a pressing issue. Taiwan's pragmatic foreign policy has increased collisions between the two parties across the Straits, and this may tempt Beijing to consider more military pressure. More importantly, as popular vote decides who rules the island, the mainlanders can no longer count on the unification commitment of the Guomindang. If Taiwan declares independence, it will force China to take action. Whatever the extent of the action, the PLA will encounter Taiwan's armed forces equipped with advanced Western technology. To some military planners, the possibility of a high-tech war is not as remote as it might earlier have seemed.[25]

The fundamental basis for the change in the PLA's strategy is, however, the perception of threat posed by the United States' lethal weaponry and war strategy, as demonstrated by the Gulf War.[26] Politically, this was a logical response to America's post-June 4 sanctions, F-16 sales, the Most Favoured Nation (MFN) debate, obstruction to China's Olympic bid and human rights pressure. The United States-led Western efforts of 'peaceful evolution' to change China's socialist system have been perceived as a grave threat to its security. PLA analysts often cite references to United States nuclear targeting of China as evidence that Washington views Beijing as a potential military adversary.[27] Although the PLA generally does not regard the increased tension in Sino-United States relations to mean any imminent military confrontation, the series of incidents, such as the inspection of the *Yinhe*, have crystallised a downward spiral of bilateral relations,[28] and have stimulated the PLA to prepare for a potential conflict at some time in the future. Some signs appear serious enough to pose a question: would it spark small armed rifts if next time China were not to allow an inspection of a shipment? A punitive surgical strike on China is not likely, but has to be considered as an extreme case. This has made a high-tech defence strategy more relevant than that of people's war.[29]

The United States threat has also been magnified by possible American involvement in regional conflicts that may also involve China. The PLA planners could not have failed to notice that, behind almost every flash-point in Asia and the Pacific, the United States looms large in the background. This may bring to the surface a potential Sino-United States rift in an unexpected incident. The plan for an action against Taiwan, for instance, would have to take United States intervention into consideration. The possible use of airborne warning and control systems to help co-ordinate Taiwan's air defence would greatly increase PRC losses with little threat to American lives.[30] The significance of the PLA's opting for a new strategy is that it has created a realistic defence target against which it can adjust its war tactics, R&D projects and force structure. Now it is increasingly clear that the Gulf War has convinced the PLA that its future lies in high-tech development.[31]

Diplomatically, the PLA's shift to a high-tech strategy has been in keeping with the changed emphasis in China's foreign policy in the 1990s, which aims at improving the country's relations with neighbours. Partly this is designed to alleviate Western pressure. Partly it is the prerequisite to enhancing China's economic security in the emerging G-3 constellation of economic blocs in Europe, North America and East Asia. China is vulnerable in this regionally based trade alignment, since its economic take-off depends heavily on exports to the market outside of the region. Improved relations with its neighbours may enable it to diversify its exports. A military emphasis on limited regional wars is in conflict with this foreign policy orientation, which seeks resolution of territorial disputes through negotiations. The high-tech military strategy seeks to switch the PLA's war preparation away from regional issues to strategic concerns. Yet the enhanced weaponry gained in such a strategy may deliver an enhanced capability for dealing with regional issues. In this sense, the shift away from the people's war strategy will generate far-reaching implications both for the PLA's modernisation and for the Asia-Pacific security landscape.

Some key features of the high-tech strategy

A two-tiered defence strategy and high-tech based tactics

Based on the changing perception of threat to China in the post-Cold War period, a two-tier national defence strategy has been adopted. The first tier is to enhance the PLA's nuclear capability to deter big powers, and particularly the potential threats posed to China by the United States strategy of 'global deterrence and rapid response'. As pointed out by a senior PLA analyst, 'we must have a clear vision of the world's future posture of nuclear powers. Any relaxation of our efforts will put us in a sorry position'.[32] However, even under rising American pressure, the PLA still believes that the pressure will not be translated into confrontation in the near future. Therefore, to augment the PLA's ability to deal with any regional crisis on land and at sea serves as the second tier of national defence strategy. At this level of war preparation, the PLA has made it an urgent task to improve the firepower of its conventional weapons through introducing more high-tech hardware.[33]

With the emergence of the high-tech strategy, the PLA's traditional war tactics have been thoroughly reviewed, and this has strongly affected its campaign theories and training programs. The PLA planners have learned from the Gulf War that a high-tech war entails a complete set of new military tactics. One analyst commented that Iraq had some high-tech weapons but it had not developed appropriate tactics to use them to advantage. It could only stick to a strategy of line defence, waiting to be wiped out by the enemy's superior firepower.[34] This was a profound lesson for the PLA, as its active defence doctrine and associated campaign tactics heavily emphasised positional warfare, a legacy from its earlier war design against a Soviet land attack.

So the study of tactics for use against high-tech warfare has been undertaken, simulating a battle that is launched using electronic warfare, preceded with large-scale air attack and followed by an integrated air and ground invasion. Since 1991, numerous academic papers have been published to explore the counter-measures available to a less well equipped army in such a war. The exercises have focused on how to increase survivability and mobility in high-tech warfare. A debate is continuing as to how much emphasis should be given to traditional combat techniques such as short-distance infantry fighting (grenade throwing or bayonet charge) and attacks at night on an enemy equipped with sophisticated night vision weaponry. One researcher argued:

> It would be better if we set out now to upgrade our C^3I and weapons systems and establish new combat theories of high-tech warfare than waste time and energy repeating those obsolete fighting techniques. Our training programs must aim at enhancing troops' capabilities against [the] enemy's attack of high-tech weaponry.[35]

Restructuring the PLA's force components

Even before the Gulf War, a consensus existed in the PLA high command that modern warfare would elevate the position of specialised services in the military. At a CMC conference in 1989, Yang Shangkun ordered that research on the PLA's force structure be stepped up, stating that the development of the navy and air force should be given priority.[36] The PLA's shift to the high-tech strategy has required it to adjust further the ratio of the four services: the army, navy, air force and the strategic missile force (SMF). While the latter three are to be enhanced and the former restructured, upgrading electronic warfare and the anti-air attack units to the level of independent arms of service has been proposed, with the airborne force to be enlarged.[37] This reflects the PLA's recognition that, in high-tech warfare, victory depends more on the specialised service — particularly, the air force — and that the infantry would play a decreasing role.[38]

The new round of restructuring of the PLA has been unfolding simultaneously on three fronts since the 1990s. The first was to trim the PLA central command. Following Deng's instruction that the scale-down of the PLA must start from its headquarters,[39] major reform was undertaken within the General Staff in September 1992, which saw the commands of the Artillery, Armoured Corps, Anti-Chemical, Telecommunications, Engineering and Army Aviation merged into the Department of Specialised Arms. Similar cuts also took place in other headquarters of the army, such as in the General Political Department and the General Logistics Department. This has reduced the size of the PLA central command by 30 per cent. The second concerns an additional reduction of military personnel by up to 500 000.[40] Since the late 1980s, discussion has been pursued vigorously about whether to reduce further the PLA's regional commands from seven to six, as the Jinian Command stands outside China's traditional strategic regions (*Zhanlüequ*). Although a final decision has not yet been taken, there have been general cuts in personnel in group armies and other army units, and obsolete weaponry has been eliminated. For instance, the replacement of old anti-aircraft artillery by missiles has reduced the size of artillery brigades in the group armies. In addition, over a dozen military tertiary institutions have been merged with many courses cancelled, being regarded as out of touch with the new military evolution. The third front of PLA restructuring occurred in the navy and air force. The central theme was to raise the proportion of units of high-tech weaponry in the overall service structure and put in reserve the equipment regarded as inappropriate for a high-tech war. A large number of obsolete submarines have been moth-balled, for example, and the personnel of submarine units reduced.

The high-tech military R&D

Under the people's war strategy, the hierarchy of importance in R&D was, according to former Defence Minister Zhang Aiping, the second strike capability of the SMF, followed by the hardware of the army, and then the equipment of the air force and navy. In developing conventional weapons, priority was given to anti-tank and anti-air attack weapons, and to long-range artillery. The army was preferred to the air force and the air force to the navy in this priority ranking.[41] This sequence has been reversed since the late 1980s. While the SMF remains a priority, the high-tech weapons needed by the air force and navy have gained importance in the PLA's R&D.[42] Basically, progress in the following areas is deemed to be crucial to uplift the general level of the PLA's weaponry and to narrow the gap with the West.

- C³I is the weakest link in the PLA's preparation for a high-tech war. Currently China's six communication satellites have allocated very limited channels to the PLA. To rectify the situation, it has been proposed that a network of defence satellite communications be created. In this network, in addition to expanding strategic communication channels and reception points, attention would be paid to the development of small mobile stations with an antenna smaller than 3 metres in diameter. These stations should particularly be deployed in the sensitive border areas and in the rapid response units in order to meet the needs for high-tech regional wars.[43]

- More efforts should be devoted to accelerate China's space program. After the initial design for a space shuttle was approved in 1989, the project was launched in 1992. It is suggested that the first human-operated trial in space be set in 2005.[44] It has also been proposed that a space army command be created in the air force. And a system of space monitoring and surveillance, similar to Western Europe's limited space defence program, should become operational around the year 2000.[45]

- More efforts should be devoted to the R&D of equipment for electronic warfare, precision-guided missile technology, high-speed computers, powerful laser facilities and the application of artificial intelligence in military hardware.[46] For instance, the PLA is now able to develop computers with an operating speed of one billion bytes per second. The challenge is that the number of high-speed computers is so small that there is still a long way to go to meet the PLA's needs. And there is an urgent need to reduce the size of the military computers.

- The air force and navy have formulated their own plans to develop high-tech weapons. The air force has specified three crucial technologies as its R&D priorities in the short to medium term — namely airborne early warning and command systems, in-flight refuelling, and an anti-missile defence system.[47] The navy's R&D is centred around the aim to achieve blue water capabilities in the early twenty-first century.[48] To this end, the navy has formulated a three-phased development program, which gives priority to boosting naval aviation capability, particularly that of airborne anti-submarine warfare, and to introducing a new generation of submarines, both conventional and nuclear. It is also campaigning strongly to have aircraft carriers built.

The PLA's high-tech R&D is ambitious. However, the guiding principle for the overall military modernisation as a whole is prudent, reflecting the personality of the current PLA leader Liu Huaqing and his grasp of China's defence realities. Generally speaking, the PLA's weapons program in the 1990s and beyond can be characterised by a middle course between a strategy of steady generational upgrading and a strategy of generational leap. This has been spelled out by the CMC as 'concentrated research on key items, selected production for "fist" units, co-ordinated retrofitting of some current equipment and coexistence of both old and new weapons'.[49]

This middle course policy has been a rational choice by the PLA leaders. Generational development may provide the PLA with a level of technology to cope with the demands of immediate and low-intensity conflict but, as the Soviet experience indicated, such a 'tortoise' strategy was accompanied by an enlarged gap with the West. Nevertheless, this was the base of

Chinese military R&D policy until the late 1980s. In comparison, the generational leap strategy aims at the frontier of world technology. But it involves a great deal of risk for a military whose R&D program rests on a weak industrial base. The long acquisition intervals and less than adequate level of scientific expertise may mean a waste of time and funds. To solve weaknesses in both strategies, the middle course policy is meant to avoid a situation where a war erupts before the desired high-tech weapons can be secured, and the normal generational change of equipment is disrupted. In order to narrow the gap with Western technology, the PLA has selected a number of military technologies for urgent development as well as technologies deemed applicable at the beginning of twenty-first century.[50] The hardware so developed will equip the PLA's elite units. At the same time, generational upgrading of weaponry will continue so as to prevent a vacuum in the transition period. The funding has, however, leaned toward R&D for the high-tech equipment which, again, is a calculated risk that a period of lasting peace will prevail.

Foreign procurement and military budget

A key prerequisite for China's defence modernisation is procurement of advanced weapons from abroad. Deng raised the issue of importing advanced technology as 'being the starting point for our own high-tech development'. In practical terms, the purchase of advanced weapons has several functions. First, it provides hardware for reverse technology, thus reducing the lag time for the PLA's own R&D. In fact, the PLA's buying missions have always had a list of specific items most needed in its services.[51] Second, PLA analysts often quote the United States upgrading of the B-52 bomber as an example of how it is feasible and desirable to upgrade old equipment with improvement of its key parts. This motivated the PLA air force to retrofit several types of its aircraft with Western technologies of the 1970s. From this, we see the third function of buying foreign arms — namely, the prevention of a vacuum in the process in which the obsolete hardware is cancelled before new weaponry becomes available. The fourth function is that foreign procurement may provide the PLA with first-hand operating knowledge about high-tech warfare. A case in point is the PLA's acquisition of Su-27s from Russia. Before the deal, the PLA had never operated heavy, long-range and electronically sophisticated fighter jets. The air force could only theoretically probe how to handle an attack by aircraft of the fourth generation. With the Su-27, it can narrow the gap between theoretical simulation and practical operation. The result is that this has, to some degree, shortened the lag time of the PLA's readiness for a high-tech war.

Despite a fairly balanced R&D program, the PLA has been, and will continue to be, handicapped by a lack of funds to realise its goal of a high-tech strategy. Officially the PLA's budget in 1993 was US$7.33 billion, or $2291 per soldier.[52] If we multiply this by three, a common Western practice, the amount of money per head was still less than $7000, which can do very little in a high-tech era.[53] Although the Chinese economy is likely to sustain a high growth rate well into the early decades of the twenty-first century, a fast-expanding economy will absorb more resources to maintain the developmental vigour. This means that the PLA will be forced for a long time to strike a balance between an increasingly ambitious weapons program (the United States and Soviet Union experience had shown that an ever-rising demand for advanced weapons may create a life of its own) and a limited budget allocation.[54] To overcome this contradiction, the PLA has adopted a number of measures to maintain its priority research.

- The military has been successful in obtaining an enlarged share of the state budget. Each year since 1989 has seen a growth of 12–13 per cent in budget allocation. And it is highly likely that this trend will continue.[55] If sustained for a fairly long period of time, this will effectively help meet the PLA's quest for the status of modern military power, as the military budget will double every six to seven years.
- While the ratio of military outlay in the state budget increases, the share of the equipment expenditure will also increase within the PLA budget. For a long time, the allocation for new equipment remained as low as 10 per cent of the total while personnel expenditure was three times that proportion. After years of readjustment, the equipment budget has now risen to about 20 per cent, while that for personnel has dropped to about 30 per cent.[56]
- To concentrate funds on high-tech weaponry, the PLA has constantly eliminated outdated hardware since the late 1980s. Here China has a vast potential. For instance, if the air force deactivated its 3000 J-6 jets (MiG-17s and MiG-19s), the maintenance fees saved could be used to quicken the development of new aircraft without increasing the current level of funds.
- Various means of 'self-generation' of income are seen as a key supplement to the limited military budget. Three common ones are:
  1 converting military research institutes, and factories that design and make obsolete weaponry, to civilian production;
  2 leasing military facilities such as naval ports or air force airfields to civilian users; and
  3 the export of conventional arms.
  A large proportion of the profits so generated will be transferred to subsidise high-tech R&D.[57]

The development of a high-tech military power

The search for a high-tech military strategy does not mean that the armed forces can become high-tech capable in the near future. In fact, the PLA will have a long way to go before it meets the minimum requirements for a world-class high-tech military. Nevertheless, the shift to the strategy *per se* is important, as it has set the PLA on a new course of advancement. The following section will analyse some of the new developments in China's nuclear forces, air force and navy.

The modernisation of the Strategic Missile Forces

Formally created in 1964 and comprising over 90 000 officers and troops, the SMF is the smallest service in the PLA. Yet, out of proportion to its resources, it assumes a mission of deterrence against the major powers. In the 1960s, General Zhang Aiping and Qian Xuesen, a United States trained missile expert, proposed to the CMC that the first stage of China's nuclear program should be to achieve a level of deterrence by retaliation. Problems of survivability and lack of long-range carrier vehicles therefore had to be solved. To achieve the former, it was deemed essential to acquire Submarine Launched Ballistic Missiles (SLBMs) and MIRV capabilities; to achieve the latter, the PLA had to possess Intercontinental Ballistic Missiles (ICBMs) with a range of over 8000 kilometres.[58]

After 20 years of development, China has basically accomplished the goal. Its first ICBM was launched in 1980 with a range of near 10 000 kilo-metres. This enabled the PLA to target key United States cities. One year later, China demonstrated its MIRV capability by simultaneously sending three satellites into orbit. In 1982 the PLA fired its first sea-based missile. All these efforts gradually turned China, through the SMF, into the third largest nuclear power in the world with a triad system of second strike capability.[59] Yet throughout the 1970s and 1980s the emphasis of the SMF had been placed more on 'force consolidation' (*heliliang de zhunbei* or surviv-ability) than practical operation (*heliliang de yunyong* or the employment of the weaponry).[60]

To be more concrete, the 'force consolidation' was dependent on two cru-cial factors:

1   the survivability of launching sites; and
2   mobility of the launching units.

China's nuclear policy is to use nuclear weapons only after being attacked by nuclear weapons. This has increased the weight necessarily placed on the PLA, as its chance of a second strike hinges upon whether its launching bases can survive a surgical attack. Therefore, the 'consolidation' entails, firstly, maintaining the secrecy of the launching sites, for the design of launching silos for China's DF-4 and DF-5 ICBM is fairly primitive. They are less deep than the silos used by the Russian SS-18 and have low resis-tance against pressure.[61] As the PLA has to rely mainly on such land-based nuclear weapons, the 'consolidation' of the silos becomes the key to the sur-vival of the SMF.

As far as high mobility is concerned, the SMF is required to be able to wage a kind of nuclear 'guerilla warfare' similar to that seen in the Gulf War where United Nations forces engaged the Iraqi Scud missiles in a cat and mouse game. To this end, in the last two decades, the PLA has devoted enormous efforts to improving the mobility and rapid response capabilities of its missile units. Priorities have been given to the development of the solid fuel and miniaturised warheads and to a sophisticated C^3I system. The solid fuel is of particular importance because most of the mobile missiles (mainly DF-3 IRBM) use liquid fuel and need two hours to get ready for launch.[62] In the meantime, the SMF has stepped up its exercises and simulation launches, essentially in remote mountainous areas.[63]

Another priority in the 'force consolidation' period has been the PLA's efforts to boost the number of warheads and carrier vehicles, the crucial factors of survivability. China conducted a series of nuclear tests with large payloads in the 1970s and 1980s. Western analysts believed that these tests were meant to double the number of warheads. They agreed that China had developed a nuclear deterrent.[64] China, too, has openly declared that it has a credible second strike capability.

The shift to a high-tech strategy has greatly affected the PLA's nuclear programs. This may have pushed the SMF to move beyond the stage of 'force consolidation', although the problem of survivability remains pressing. A key to understanding the transition toward 'practical operation' is that the PLA has gradually altered its passive defence of 'hiding missiles and increasing the number of warheads' to a more forward posture. As pointed out by a senior PLA commander, the task of the new era for the SMF is to improve its overall quality, including tactics, launching, targeting, precision, command and control.[65] The following are important features of this strategic shift.

- China's non-first use policy was formulated from a position of weakness. With a capability to strike back, some PLA strategists were tempted, despite the technological gap with other nuclear powers, to contemplate the use of nuclear weapons in an escalation of conventional war, which they believed may place the whole nation at stake.[66] The PLA researchers often cite the example of the Soviet Union's plan for using nuclear weapons against China to illustrate that the use of nuclear weapons was not inconceivable. They have not failed to notice that Russia has discarded the non-first use policy. At the same time, the SMF has tried to grapple with the concept of the theatre nuclear war, while in the past most PLA strategists did not see such a boundary in a nuclear exchange. Li Xuge, the former commander-in-chief of the SMF, was the first to question why the SMF had not developed a campaign (theatre) theory and he opened the way for the SMF to increase theatre nuclear missile exercises,[67] which have become more frequent in the 1990s.
- The modernisation of the SMF has been quickened. In 1988 China detonated a neutron bomb. In the post-Cold War era, China has continued to conduct nuclear tests, which are regarded as essential to miniaturise the warheads. Meanwhile the PLA has been working to improve precision of missile targeting. According to a Russian expert on Chinese missiles,

the CEP of DF-4 and DF-5 is about 1.5 kilometres and 2 kilometres respectively.[68] A computerised measuring and control system in SMF could have improved these.[69]

- The modernisation of the SMF has been stepped up. By the year 2000, all DF-4 and DF-5 ICBMs will be placed in new generation launching silos. DF-3 IRBM will use solid fuel which will substantially reduce the time of preparation for launch. In fact, the PLA has reported that the preparation time for launch has been reduced by 33 per cent due to the improvement of its high-tech level.[70] The SMF still has problems in producing small-sized but powerful missile engines, although its co-operation with Russia in missile technology may help narrow the gap. The series of nuclear tests serve as the proof that the SMF is designing a new generation of ICBMs and IRBMs. In the next decade DF-31 (with a range of 8000 kilometres) and DF-41 (12 000 kilometres and MIRV) will replace DF-5.[71] In addition, early warning, anti-missile-attack and space monitoring systems are being developed.[72]

The PLA will press ahead with its nuclear weapons program, despite opposition from the West. To the PLA, the need to enhance the SMF is based on the fact that the PLA's conventional weaponry is too backward to serve as any meaningful deterrent to major powers. The strengthened second strike capability may provide the PLA with a level of confidence no other weapons can. And the development of nuclear weapons is relatively cheap in this regard. All of this indicates that the PLA will build up its nuclear inventory rather than scale it down in the foreseeable future.

The push for a high-tech air force

The PLA Air Force (PLAAF) is in the midst of a generational change. Despite the scale-down in 1985, the basic structure of 36 fighter divisions, seven bomber divisions, six attack divisions and two transport divisions remains largely unchanged.[73] However, the general technological level of its aircraft is so low by world standards that the bulk of it should be decommissioned. Therefore, the PLAAF has been and will remain the weakest link in China's defence modernisation. Yet it will certainly be a major beneficiary from the PLA's strategic shift to high-tech development. Since the late 1980s, the PLAAF has undergone considerable change in terms of its combat strategy, force structure and weapons programs.

Three new developments are crucial in understanding the changes in the PLAAF's combat strategy. The first is the elevation of the air force to the position of an independent strategic force. One lesson the PLA learned from the Gulf War is that the air will become the decisive battle arena in future high-tech wars.[74] As such, the PLAAF is deemed more than a supporting unit to the operations of the army. The second is the theoretical evolution of the PLAAF from a mainly defensive force to one with a combination of defensive and offensive capabilities. The PLA has now realised that, under high-tech conditions, a defensive air force will be quickly destroyed, especially when it is inferior in equipment.[75] The third is the establishment of air force rapid response strategies, particularly for limited regional wars. This requires the PLAAF to develop a set of combat principles to guide its various operations in different circumstances.[76] Behind these developments is a clearer recognition of the functions of the air force in a high-tech era: it is an important component in a country's power projection and deterrence. For instance, the offensive nature of the air force requires it to be able to launch a surgical attack away from home base. This is also a key guarantee for the country's maritime security.[77]

These theoretical developments have paved the way for the PLAAF to restructure its current force composition. The PLAAF comprises three main elements: the aviation, air defence and airborne forces. In the PLA's strategic plan, each will be reinforced. For instance, the air defence force of the PLAAF has a few dozen surface-air missile brigades.[78] However, the bulk of the missiles deployed are updated versions of the Soviet prototype of the 1950s. Their reliability is in question. Additionally, according to the calculations of the PLAAF, if the density of air-defence coverage is to reach the former Soviet average, the number of batteries has to be increased at least fivefold.[79] The big 'holes' in air defence have made the strategic cities and military facilities extremely vulnerable to a 'Desert Storm' type attack. This was the major reason the PLA included the purchase of 100 S300 surface-to-air missiles in the first Sino-Russian military deal. China has purchased S300PMU-1 (five units have been delivered), said to be the world's most advanced surface-air intercept missile.[80] There is no doubt that air defence will remain a priority in the overall development of the PLAAF.

Army No. 15 of the PLAAF has been China's only airborne unit. In the 1960s Mao Zedong personally allowed it to maintain a force level of over 30 000 soldiers. In the PLA's 1985 restructuring, its three divisions were reduced to three brigades.[81] However, one of the PLA's recent efforts to reinforce the PLAAF has been to restore its former army–division–regiment structure with the overall force level enlarged by 25 per cent. Even so, PLA analysts believe that its current level is still far from adequate for the three million strong military. They calculate that China's airborne force is only about a quarter of that of the United States in terms of its percentage in the total of the armed forces. It should thus be further increased.[82]

The reinforcement of the Airborne Army has been stimulated by the development of the PLA's rapid response strategy. It is one of few army corps coming under the category of 'strategic troops on constant duty'.[83] In the last several years it has increased its exercises in difficult locations to simulate campaigns in regional flashpoint conflicts, including a paradrop in the South China Sea and the Chinese Himalayas. The Army claims to possess a capability for air-dropping at one time more than 10 000 soldiers with light tanks and self-propelled guns.[84] As the Army is crucial to the

PLA's preparation for limited high-tech wars, it will continue to enjoy priority in funds and equipment allocation. One indication is that the PLA has purchased several IL-76 Russian transport planes for Army No. 15, so as to enhance its airlift for rapid response.

As the air defence and airborne troops are not liable to be reduced, the required readjustments will proceed predominantly in the aviation wing of the service. The defensive nature of the PLAAF is reflected by the fact that it has a disproportionate number of fighter divisions in the overall force structure. The PLA analysts have noted that in the last decade the former Soviet Union had reduced the number of its fighter jets by 55 per cent, and the United States by 24 per cent. They concluded that, under high-tech conditions, simple function fighters could establish neither air superiority nor a level of deterrence. So the ongoing restructuring aims at cuts in the number of fighters and the enhancement of the bomber/attack units. It is proposed that the number of J-6s — comprising over 50 per cent of the air force's planes — should be halved. At the same time, in addition to the provision for air defence by jet fighters, more scope will be given to defence by surface-air missiles. Moreover, reinforced air attack and air defence units should be deployed in the 'flashpoint' areas to exercise a function of deterrence and 'containment'.[85]

Another priority in the force restructuring of the PLAAF is the strengthening of the units of specialised aircraft such as the early warning and airborne control, aerial refuelling, electronic warfare, transport, and surveillance and reconnaissance. One proposed ratio is that the fighter jets should constitute 55 per cent, bomber/attack aircraft 35 per cent and others 10 per cent.[86] This proposal was tabled in the late 1980s. It is likely that the percentage of fighter jets is to be further reduced as a long-term development plan, while the specialised units will be strengthened. Many PLA reports of the Gulf War noted that the percentage of supporting aircraft was larger than the percentage directly involved in the attack. This is understood to constitute a feature of high-tech warfare.

The PLA's high-tech strategy has provided a new impetus to the air force's hardware modernisation. In the late 1980s, the PLAAF formulated a weapons program, *The Research and Development of the PLAAF's Weaponry and Equipment to the Year 2000*. It contained six special reports covering the R&D of the new generation of aircraft, air defence and the upgrading of a number of existing weapons systems. The program targeted the Western technological level of the late 1980s and prescribed that the new weapons should become operational at the beginning of the twenty-first century. For instance, the new generation of fighter jets should have multifunctional air superiority capabilities with effective avionics and strong air–ground assault systems.[87]

Since the 1980s, as a transitional measure, China has implemented a program of retrofitting its aircraft such as J-8IIs and A-5s with Western technology. However, the program has not been successful in achieving the PLA's objective to narrow the gap with the third generation of Western aircraft. That the PLAAF is in a risky transition period can be seen precisely in this sense: more and more old aircraft are to be decommissioned before replacements can be produced. Vice-Admiral Li Jing, deputy chief of the General Staff, announced in 1989 that several types of new-generation aircraft would enter service in the late 1990s.[88] But it is unlikely these will be deployed in effective numbers in a short time. Technically, it is in this context that China has turned to the Russians for supply of advanced aircraft. The Su-27 deal is a response to the PLA's efforts for a 'quick fix'.

A number of high-tech projects are currently underway in the PLAAF. The R&D of advanced radar systems, such as pulse doppler and millimetric radars, both airborne and ground-based, has been a priority in the air force's Year 2000 program.[89] The development of in-flight fuelling has been speeded up. Using the B-6 as the tanker and the J-8II as the receiver, the PLAAF has carried out a number of successful trials in recent years. It is believed the technology will become operational soon, although deployment may take more time because the air force is still unsatisfied with the performance of the kits.[90] China's airborne early warning and control systems can also be expected to become operational in the near future. The PLA has indigenously developed a prototype ECW system on board its Yun-8. The purchase of three IL-76 Mainstay AWACS was arranged in 1993.[91] In fact, the military co-operation between China and Russia, and to a lesser extent, between China and other countries such as Israel, may have improved these crucial military technologies.

Naval forward defence strategy and power projection

The PLA Navy (PLAN) relinquished the people's war mentality in the 1980s. This was partly due to the sovereignty dispute in the South China Sea which required the navy to deploy its forces far away from in-shore waters. In part, the navy's switch to high-tech development has been personally sought by Liu Huaqing, who knows more about modern warfare than most other senior PLA leaders due to his training in the Voroshilov Naval Academy in the 1950s. Soon after he assumed office in the navy, Liu put forward an active green water defence strategy (*Jiji de jinhai fangyu zhanlie*).[92] The following are its basic features. Firstly, the strategy stressed long-range manoeuvrability of naval fleets, embracing Chinese waters adjacent to Vladivostok in the north to the Straits of Malacca in the south, and continuing to the first island chain of the West Pacific in the east. Secondly, the strategy gives priority to preparation for regional flashpoint conflicts, which extends the PLAN's power projection in and beyond the Spratly Islands.[93] The navy has been entrusted with missions to capture islands, protect and blockade sea lanes of communication, and pursue other overseas operations. Thirdly, the strategy is aimed at being an ultimate deterrent against the big powers.[94]

The weapons modernisation and rationalisation of force structure are crucial to the navy's search for blue water power. The navy has mothballed a large number of warships not capable of blue water navigation and decreased the number of conventional submarines.[95] On the other hand, according to Rear-Admiral Cheng Ming, the head of the navy's equipment department, the development of new generations of major surface combatants, larger submarines and long-range aircraft will take priority in the 1990s.[96] Special R&D efforts have been devoted to creating aircraft carrier task groups.[97]

The composition of the major surface combatants of the PLAN is seeing a generational change both in terms of ship design and weaponry. Due to many weaknesses, the *Luda* class destroyers, currently the mainstay of the PLAN's ocean-going fleet, do not make the PLAN a blue water navy.[98] Since the late 1980s, a number of new DDGs and FFs have entered service. Similar to the air force's J-8IIs, these serve as transitional ships, pending more sophisticated designs being developed. *Zhanjiang* Class destroyers have an enlarged displacement of 4200 tonnes versus *Luda* class's 3200 tonnes and are an embodiment of many foreign technologies.[99] Meanwhile, at least three types of new frigates joined the service. Since 1985 an additional class of three new missile frigates, Kaifeng, Wuhu and Xiangtan, entered service with a capability of anti-nuclear, chemical and biological warfare.[100] Powered by CODOG and equipped with eight C-801 missiles, this series will gradually replace the *Jianghu* class as China's attack frigates.[101] The *Jiangdong* class FF is equipped with China's first vertical launch system, HQ61 SAM, which is controlled by an indigenous phased-array radar system. *Jiangwei* is the latest series of China's missile frigates with an enlarged displacement of 2250 tonnes. Two ships, 539 and 540, have been commissioned. They also carry the HQ61 SAM system with six canister-launched missiles mounted with a reported effective range of 8000 metres altitude at Mach 3.[102]

These new destroyers and frigates have been designed to provide the navy with more specialised escort ships to cater for different tasks required by deep ocean combat missions, and potentially for the formation of aircraft carrier groups. The PLA's high-tech centred strategy has provided additional push to the construction of aircraft carriers. The 708 Institute began feasibility studies of a carrier in its 600 metre model pool in the early 1980s. Further tests were conducted in Tai Lake in Jiangsu.[103] In April 1987 the Navy Air Force conducted the first take-off and landing trial on a simulated deck at a naval base in North China. According to the information available, officer Li Guoqiang successfully piloted a J-8II to take off on the 70 metre-long deck. Using a catapult, Pilot Li reached 80 km/h at 20 metres, 110 km/h at 30, 160 km/h at 40 and 250 km/h at 60 metres. Then he landed at the second arrester wire of which there were four, and continued another 30 metres before stopping. Since then, several dozen pilots have been trained intensively on the deck.[104]

In November 1990, a model of China's first-generation carrier was displayed at a classified weapons exhibition in Beijing. The carrier had a displacement of 40 000–50 000 tonnes, and carried 20 fixed-wing planes on deck and another 20 in the hangar. The deck was over 70 metres in length and made use of catapults and arrester wires. The navy plans to establish two battle groups centred on such carriers in the early years of the next decade.[105] As far as the design is concerned, it is a generational leap from the navy's initial consideration which envisaged a lighter carrier with only STOVL on board.[106] PLA leaders see the construction of an aircraft carrier as boosting the general level of naval technology, in areas such as effective AA and anti-missile systems, early warning and electronic counter-measure technology, the development of carrier aircraft, and a sophisticated C3I system. One often cited example is the effect of the navy's nuclear submarine project on China's long-range telecommunication technology.[107] Some analysts, however, believe that China's first generation of carrier will be more of symbolic significance than a real threat,[108] given a carrier's vulnerability without a major accompanying air, sea and undersea defence force. To the Chinese, however, a carrier represents a symbol of having achieved blue water naval capability. Acknowledging the deficiencies of the first carrier, and given a policy decision to develop a carrier force, the navy will need to begin planning in the near future if it wants to develop a sophisticated carrier at a later date.[109]

Conclusion

There is no doubt that the PLA's shift to high-tech development will exert a heavy impact on the regional balance of power. Geographically, the strategy dictates a qualitative expansion of defence in depth on land, air and at sea. In terms of hardware, high-tech increasingly blurs the boundaries between offensive and defensive weapons. For instance, when the PLA's aerial refuelling technology becomes operational, it can easily extend the reach of J-8IIs to the Spratlys. One may expect to find the PLA defence posture increasingly forward-deployed. As the PLAN's search for blue water power has shown, over time this posture will influence the regional security landscape.

The current aim of the PLA is to modernise its weapons so as to narrow the gap with the West. China's economic boom seems to make it more affordable than before. A senior PLA officer stated clearly that it was against logic everywhere in the world that a big country should become an economic power of the twenty-first century but leave its military capability behind in the twentieth century.[110] Chi Haotian spelled out the PLA's weapons program as 'we must have whatever other big powers have already had in their inventory'. The question is, what should China have first? Most Western analysts are indifferent to the prediction made by Albert Wohlstetter in 1988 that the PLA would become a world-class military power.[111] Chong-pin Lin explained that this was largely due to a general trend in the West to underestimate the PLA's capabilities. In his opinion, however, the PLA has been successful in achieving a level of 'pockets of excellence'.[112]

It is not easy to make a realistic assessment of the PLA's capabilities. The large numbers of obsolete weaponry such as J-6s and T-59 tanks may fix a stereotype picture in our minds. The PLA's weapons program of 'more research, less production' has enhanced the secrecy of its achievements in military technology. Neither do we know how helpful the foreign technological transfers to the PLA's R&D programs have been. In addition, there is a question of what standards are applicable when evaluating the implications of China's military buildup. By United States standards, the PLA is certainly poorly equipped. Yet, as seen from countries in Asia and the Pacific, it has formidable military strength. This is the reason why the spillover of the PLA's efforts of arms catch-up with the West may galvanise the regional military buildup.

Chinese military strength will grow steadily, not only because of China's economic boom, but also due to new mechanisms that are stimulating the country's development of science and technology. These mechanisms include the state-directed '863' and 'Touch' high-tech programs.[113] More importantly, market-driven civilian high-tech projects have tapped the country's great scientific potential, and will quickly enlarge the technological base of the country.[114] For instance, the Beijing Electronic Development Zone has developed so rapidly that the science adviser to President Clinton dubbed it a potential Silicon Valley. For the first time the PLAAF has purchased and installed in its aircraft the technology of 'black box' — the global satellite positioning equipment FMC-91, developed by a civilian firm.[115] This has shown that the civilian and private sectors can quickly provide the PLA with high-tech facilities that the PLA itself is not able to develop due to its limited research funds and personnel. When this is coupled with the state high-tech projects and the PLA priority R&D programs, military modernisation can be expected to accelerate, as it is now more solidly based. In conclusion, the recent change in China's grand military strategy will promote another revolution in the PLA, but it will take time and a great deal of research to fully appreciate its strategic implications.

Notes

1 You Ji is a lecturer in the Department of Political Science, University of Canterbury. At the time this chapter was written, he was a Visiting Fellow in the Northeast Asia Programme and the Contemporary China Centre of the Australian National University. He would like to thank Helen Wilson for her great help in the research for and writing of this chapter.
2 Gerald Segal, 'A Changing China and Asia/Pacific Security', paper presented at the conference, Security Dimensions of Chinese Regionalism, Hong Kong, 25 June 1993.
3 In the late 1970s, there were heated debates in the PLA which promoted this change. PLA historians agree that the most forceful impetus for the change was the speech by the former chief of general staff, Su Yu, at the PLA Academy of Military Science on 11 January 1979, entitled 'Several Questions on Strategy and Tactics During the Initial Phase of a War against Aggression', *Military Science*, no. 3, 1979.

4 Yang Dezhi, 'Several Questions on Strategy and Tactics During the Initial Phase of the War against Aggression', *Military Science*, no. 11, 1979.

5 June Teufel Dreyer, *China's Political System: Modernization and Tradition*, Paragon House, New York, 1993.

6 Deng Xiaoping, 'Talks after Inspecting Jiangsu and Other Places', *Selected Works of Deng Xiaoping*, vol. 3, Renmin chubanshe, Beijing, 1993.

7 Li Cheng and others, *The 100 Events in the History of the PLA Since 1949*, Zhishi chubanshe, Beijing, 1992.

8 Usually the group armies are numbered at 24. I use the number 25, including the Airborne Army No. 15 under the Air Force, because it is a mini-group army by nature. In the West, airborne troops belong to the army.

9 Huang Yuzhang (ed.), *Limited War: Yesterday, Today and Tomorrow*, PLA National Defence University Press (NDU Press), Beijing, 1988.

10 Mi Zhenyu, 'An Initial Study of the Campaign Theory of Limited Wars', *Military Science*, no. 12, 1986.

11 The National Defence University and a small number of academies directly run by the headquarters of each service were to train officers at the army level or above. A few dozen institutions assumed the task of training officers at the divisional and regiment levels and the rest trained leaders of platoon, company and battalion levels.

12 Lan Shuchen, 'To Widen the Channels of Training for the Officers of Our Army', *Information About Military Studies*, no. 3, 1986.

13 There was a lengthy debate among officers in the 1980s about whether the people's war strategy became obsolete under modern conditions. They argued that if this fundamental question was not resolved, many other key questions could not be answered, such as what weapons programs should be worked out.

14 Zhang Feng, 'On the Overall Policy of Self-Development and Self-Improvement', *Military Economics*, no. 2, 1989.

15 Liang Minglun, 'The Basic Features of the PLA's Combined Campaigns Under Conditions of High-Tech Conventional Regional Wars', *Journal of the NDU*, no. 1, 1993.

16 Liu Jingsong, 'To Enhance the Studies of Guiding Theoretical Principles and Quicken the PLA Modernization and Reforms', *Journal of the NDU*, no. 5, 1993.

17 The shift is reflected in the revision of overall military strategy and tactics for future wars, weapons programs, and the training of the PLA. The CMC has decided that all PLA officers should participate in intensive and regular training to familiarise themselves with high-tech warfare. Chinese Central Television (CCTV), 16 November 1993. However, since this strategic change is just underway, further observation will be needed to gain a better understanding of it.

18 'A General Analysis of the World Strategic Constellation in 1992', *Journal of the NDU*, no. 2, 1993.

19 During the Sino-Russian summit in Beijing in 1992, President Yeltsin advised China, 'do not hurt our feelings by making capital out of our current problems. Russia will stand up again in the not too distant future.' This may have made an impression on the current Chinese leaders, the majority of whom were trained in Russia in the 1950s and were well aware of Russian potential. After Yeltsin's visit, a circular was issued by the party, stating that Russia's weakness was only temporary: Seminar on Sino-Russian Relations at Beijing University, 20 November 1992.

20 Nayan Chanda, 'George Bush, Japan, and the China Card', *Christian Science Monitor*, 15 February 1990. For a more sophisticated academic analysis, see Charles Morrison and Michel Oksenberg, 'Japanese Emperor's Visit to China Sends Important Signals to the United States', *Asia-Pacific Issues*, October 1992.

21 He Fang, 'The Rivalry Among Western Powers is to Become Key Contradiction in Current International Relations', *Journal of the NDU*, no. 1, 1993.

22 B.S. Glaser, 'China's Security Perceptions: Interests and Ambitions', *Asian Survey*, vol. 33, no. 3, March 1993.

23 *Kyodo News Service* and *Japan Economic Newswire*, 21 November 1993.

24 Information gathered from interviews with PLA researchers in Beijing in late 1992.

25 When addressing a meeting on Taiwan affairs in December 1992, Jiang issued a blunt warning as saying that 'China will take drastic counter-measures against a Taiwan attempt at independence': *People's Daily*, 16 December 1992.

26 Several dozen papers and books have been published by the PLA campaigning for a high-tech strategy. Many officers simulated a Gulf War situation where they placed themselves in defence against the allied operations. In so doing they studied the high-tech war and proposed counter-measures.

27 Glaser, 'China's Security Perceptions'.

28 For a good analysis on the consequences of this downward spiral, see Harry Harding's talk to Worldnet (USIS), 26 October 1993.

29 180 key military generals reportedly sent a notice on 8 September 1993 to the party leadership, expressing their displeasure over the inspection and demanded appropriate measures to be taken against 'the hegemonist act'. In response, Jiang Zemin proposed to accelerate the development of sophisticated conventional weapons, as well as strategic nuclear weapons, based on efforts to increase the country's comprehensive national power: *Ching Pao Monthly*, no. 10, 1993.

30 Lasater, Martin, *U.S. Interests in the New Taiwan*, Westview, Boulder, Col., 1993.

31 A senior officer remarked to me during an interview shortly after the Gulf War that 'we should thank the Gulf War which taught us a great deal. Without this learning, were we to be thrown into such a conflict

the damage to the country and the army would be beyond our endurance.'

32 Tang Daoshen, 'On the Qualitative Development of Our Strategic Missile Force', in Academy of Military Science (ed.), *The Study of the Development of the Standing Army in the New Era*, Academy of Military Science Press, Beijing, 1990.

33 Yao Zhenyu, 'Scientific Guidance for Our Army's Weapons Program', *Journal of NDU*, no. 7–8, 1993.

34 Wang Wenpo, 'A Study of the Consumption of Ammunition in a High-Tech War', *Journal of the NDU*, no. 5, 1993.

35 Hu Siyuan, 'On the Counter Measures to Win a High-Tech Regional War', *Journal of the NDU*, no. 5, 1993.

36 Zheng Wenhan, 'Speech at the Conference on the Army-Building', in Academy of Military Science (ed.), *The Study of the Development of the Standing Army in the New Era*.

37 Hu Wenlong, 'To Raise Quality Necessitates Rationalising the Structure of the Services and Arms', in Academy of Military Science (ed.), *The Study of the Development of the Standing Army in the New Era*.

38 Zhang Liangyu, 'Who Will Decide the Victory of the Future Wars — the Role of the Specialised Services', *Journal of the NDU*, no. 6, 1993.

39 Liu Qingzhong, 'The Guiding Principle for the PLA's Reform and Development', *Military Science*, no. 7, 1993.

40 Kayahara Ikuo 'China's Defence Policy as Seen on the Reform and Open-line', *National Defence* (Japan), no. 8, 1992.

41 Zhang Aiping, 'The Weapons Program should be Based on the Principle of Seeking Truth from Facts', *Military Science*, no. 8, 1982.

42 Ye Zhi, 'Come, the Aircraft Carriers', *Military Economics*, no. 1, 1989.

43 Yang Jinhua, 'The C3I Problems in Our Army's Combat Preparedness under High-Tech Conditions', *Journal of the NDU*, no. 7–8, 1993.

44 Shi Fei, *The General Developmental Trend of the Chinese Military*, Sichuan kexue chubanshe, Chengdu, 1993.

45 Bao Zhongxing, 'The Initial Design for the Creation of a Space Army', in National Defence University (ed.), *The Study of the PLA's Modernization Programs*, National Defence University Press, Beijing, 1988.

46 Yao Zhenyu, 'Scientific Guidance for Our Army's Weapons Program'.

47 Li Jiang, 'Weapons Development Strategy to the Year 2000', in National Defence University (ed.), *The Study of the PLA's Modernization Programs*.

48 You Ji, 'Developments in Maritime Forces — China', in Dick Sherwood (ed.), *Maritime Power in the China Sea: Capabilities and Rationale*, Australian Defence Studies Centre, University College of the University of New South Wales, Canberra, 1994.

49 Zheng Wenhan, 'Speech at the Conference on the Army-Building'.

50 Wang Yamin, 'On How to Quicken the Development of our Weaponry and Equipment', *Journal of the NDU*, no. 5, 1993.

51 According to a survey in 1991, the PLA has purchased a number of single pieces of state-of-the-art equipment meant to be disassembled and

duplicated by reverse technology. One example is the Chinese Exocet. See articles by Larry Engelmann, 'China's Arms Business', carried in *Life*, starting in January, 1992.

52 *Bauhinia Magazine*, no. 8, 1993.

53 For instance, the United States military budget per soldier in 1993 was US$156 300; in Japan, $125 800; in Korea, $17 000; and in India, $5424: ibid.

54 The question is whether the post-Deng civilian leadership is strong enough to deny the continuing demands from the military for increased allocations. For instance, the 1991 military budget was 9.1 per cent of the state revenue, or 1.7 per cent of the GNP. The military required that its allocation should be raised to about 15 per cent of the state budget and 2.5–3.0 per cent of GNP which, it believed, would not cause too heavy a burden on the economy. See Ku Guisheng, 'The Socialist Market Economy and the Military Development', *Journal of the NDU*, no. 6, 1993.

55 One of the outcomes of June 4 was that the PLA managed to extract a guarantee from the civilian leaders that the growth of the military outlay should at least keep abreast with the growth of the economy. Before June 4 it was planned that the PLA's budget would remain at its low level until the end of the seventh five-year plan period, which was 1990: Interview with a State Council official in 1992.

56 Li Jingchun, Lizimin and Zhouxie, 'On How to Achieve Maxium Efficiency out of the Limited Military Budget', *Military Economics*, no. 1, 1993.

57 Wang Yamin, 'On How to Quicken the Development of Our Weaponry and Equipment'.

58 Li Cheng et al., *The 100 Events in the History of the PLA since 1949*.

59 Ching-pin Lin, *China's Nuclear Weapons Strategy: Tradition Within Evolution*, Lexington Books, Lexington, Mass., 1988.

60 Zhang Baotang, 'On a Few Questions Concerning the Development of the SMF in the New Era', in *The Study of the PLA's Modernization Programs*.

61 Pin Kefu, 'The CCP is Strengthening its Nuclear Force', *Contemporary China*, 31 October–6 November 1993.

62 ibid.

63 In one such exercise in 1983, four DF-3 and DF-4 were launched one after another to test the rapid response and retaliation capabilities: Sha Li and Min Li, *The PLA's Ten Major Domestic Military Operations*, Sichuang keji chubanshe, Chengdu, 1992.

64 Mark Kramer, comments on Jonathan Pollack, 'China Between the Superpowers: In Search of a Security Strategy', in Michael Ying-Mao Kau and Susan Marsh (eds), *China in the Era of Deng Xiaoping: A Decade of Reform*, M.E. Sharpe, Armonk, 1993.

65 Tang Daoshen, 'The Study of the Quality Improvement of the SMF in the New Era', in Academy of Military Science (ed.), *The Study of the Standing Army in the New Era*.

66 Xu Zhongde and He Lizhu, 'The Nuclear Threat Should Not Be Ruled out in Study of the Future Wars', in Academy of Military Science (ed.), *Military Theory and the Development of National Defence*, Military Science Press, 1988. In private conversations with a senior PLA researcher immediately after the Gulf War, I asked him whether, if the PLA were in Iraq's position and deemed that nothing could stop the enemy's advance, the use of tactical nuclear weapons would be considered as the last resort. He agreed that it would probably be the only option.

67 'The Development of the SMF', in the CCTV Press (ed.), *The Marching Song for the PLA*, Beijing, 1987.

68 Pinkov, 'The CCP is Strengthening its Nuclear Force'.

69 Chong-pin Lin, 'Chinese Military Modernization and its Implications on Taiwan', in *Defence and Foreign Policy White Paper*, Yeqiang Publishing House, Taipei, 1992.

70 *Jiefangjun huabao*, no. 10, 1993.

71 'Chinese Nuclear Forces 1993', supplement (8 November 1993) to *Bulletin of the Atomic Scientists*, vol. 49, no. 9, November 1993; and ISEAS, *Trends, Business Times* (Singapore) supplement, 27–28 November 1993, p. IV.

72 Zhang Baotang, 'On a Few Questions Concerning the Development of the SMF in the New Era'.

73 Li Ke and Hao Shengzhang, *The PLA in the Cultural Revolution*, Zhongyang dangshi zhiliao chubanshe, Beijing, 1989.

74 Wang Pufeng, *The High-Tech War*, NDU Press, Beijing, 1993.

75 Liu Longguang, *The Military World of High-Tech*, NDU Press, Beijing, 1993.

76 Teng Liangfu and Jiang Fusheng, *The Study of Air Force Operations*, NDU Press, Beijing, 1990.

77 Zhang Cangzhi, 'Re-shaping the PLAAF from A Defensive Force to One Combining Defensive and Offensive Capabilities', in Academy of Military Science (ed.), *The Study of the Standing Army in the New Era*.

78 In 1971 the PLAAF already had 55 surface-air missile battalions. See Li Ke and Hao Shengzhang, *The PLA in the Cultural Revolution*.

79 Dong Wenxian, 'On the Size of the Air Force and its Structure of Combat Operations in the New Era', in Academy of Military Science (ed.), *The Study of the Development of the Standing Army in the New Era*.

80 *Lien Ho Pao*, 20 October 1993.

81 Zhang Songshan, 'The Development of the Chinese Airborne Force', *Kunlun*, no. 4, 1992.

82 Dong Wenxian, 'On the Size of the Air Force and its Structure of Combat Operations in the New Era'.

83 There are a number of layers of rapid response units. The CMC commands a few elite units at the army level, such as the 38th Group Army. Each of the seven regional commands and services has its own armies, divisions, air force and naval units designated as rapid response units; and the group armies also assign a few of their best units to be the 'fist formation'.

84 Zhang Songshan, 'The Development of the Chinese Airborne Force'.

85 Zhang Cangzhi, 'Re-shaping the PLAAF from A Defensive Force to One Combining Defensive and Offensive Capabilities'.

86 Dong Wenxian, 'On the Size of the Air Force and its Structure of Combat Operations in the New Era'.

87 Sha Li and Min Li, *The Capability of the PLAAF*, University of Electronic Engineering Press, Beijing, 1993.

88 Huang Caihuang, 'The Evolution of the NAF Entered a New Stage', *Jianchuan zhishi*, no. 2, 1989. Among these new types are F-9s and F-11s. The successful flight test of an F-9 was carried out in October 1991. See Bin Yu, 'Sino-Russian Military Relations: Implications for Asian-Pacific Security', *Asian Survey*, vol. 33, no. 3, 1993. H-8 — a supersonic bomber — is also said to become operational in 1996. Reportedly China and Russia will jointly develop a new fighter jet Super-7, using the improved engine of the MiG-29, RD 33. Its series production is set for 1996 and it is basically intended for export but the PLAAF will deploy a small number. *Yomiuri Shimbun*, 9 November 1993.

89 Sha Li and Min Li, *The Capability of the PLAAF*.

90 Shi Fei, *The General Developmental Trend of the Chinese Military*.

91 Desmond Ball, 'The Post Cold War Maritime Strategic Environment in East Asia', in Dick Sherwood (ed.), *Maritime Power in the China Sea: Capabilities and Rationale*.

92 A proper translation of the Chinese word *Jihai* is the term 'green water'. According to Bradley Hahn, the term is used to express a naval capability somewhere between 'brown water' (coastal defence) and 'blue water' (full open-ocean fleet). See Bradley Hahn, 'Hai Fang', *US Naval Institute Proceedings*, March 1986. This paper argues that a 'green water' power is not the navy's goal. All its efforts point in the direction of its becoming a blue water power.

93 The naval exercises have been conducted beyond the second island chain which lies more than 1000 nautical miles away from continental China. See Lu Rucun et al. (eds), *The Contemporary Chinese Navy*, Zhongguo shehui kexue chupanshe, Beijing, 1987.

94 You Ji and You Xu, 'In Search of Blue Water Power: The PLA Navy's Maritime Strategy in the 1990s', *Pacific Review*, vol. 4, no. 2, 1991.

95 Li Dexin et al., 'The Balanced Development is the Prominent Task for the Navy in the New Era', Academy of Military Science (ed.), *The Study of the Standing Army in the New Era*.

96 *Jianchuan zhishi*, no. 8, 1991.

97 Bai Kemin, 'The Future Development of the PLAN', *Jianchuan zhishi*, no. 12, 1988.

98 G. Jacobs,'Chinese Navy Destroyer Dalian', *Navy International*, no. 9–10, 1992.

99 *Jane's Defence Weekly*, 18 January 1992.

100 *Jianchuan zhishi*, no. 3, 1988.

101 *Wide Angle*, no. 11, 1989.

102 *Jane's Defence Weekly*, 11 April 1992.

103 Ye Zhi, 'Come, the Aircraft Carriers'.

104 Shi Fei, *The General Developmental Trend of the Chinese Military*.

105 ibid.

106 Ye Zhi, 'Come, the Aircraft Carriers'.

107 *Laowang*, no. 43, 1993.

108 For instance, were a carrier to be used in a Spratly conflict, it would be quite vulnerable to attacks by MiG-29s based in East Malaysia. Besides, the shallow waters around the Spratlys are not suitable for a carrier and its supporting vessels. See Sheldon Simon, 'Regional Issues in Southeast Asian Security', paper prepared for the conference Enhancing Security in Southeast Asia, Canberra, 5–6 April 1993.

109 An opinion expressed to me by a naval researcher in Beijing in 1992.

110 supra, note 52.

111 Cited in Chong-pin Lin, 'Chinese Military Modernization and its Implications on Taiwan'.

112 ibid.

113 Over 3800 high-tech projects have been underway in the 'Touch' program. Many of them are military related. *Beijing Review*, 27 September– 3 October 1993.

114 Nationwide, there are 52 centrally approved high-tech industrial development zones where 5569 high-tech enterprises are set up in the fields of electronics, information, biology, new materials and new enegy resources: ibid.

115 CCTV, 12 October 1993.

14 China's Arms Buildup and Regional Security

Gary Klintworth and Des Ball

Introduction

This chapter examines the issue of China's defence modernisation and perceptions of China as a threatening great military power. While it is no longer original to say that the end of the Cold War has created a favourable strategic environment in Pacific-Asia, nonetheless, as a judgment about the region, it remains a valid description. There are several areas where disputes over maritime territory remain unresolved, and change in North Korea has yet to run its course. But the main feature of relations between most countries in the Asia-Pacific community is their increased co-operation on regional security and economic issues. There is, in consequence, pressure on the major powers, as well as smaller ones, to reduce or at least restrain their defence expenditure.

China's co-operative approach to regional security in Korea and Cambodia has contributed to what many observers judge to be a favourable strategic outlook. Paul Wolfowitz, United States Under-Secretary of Defense for Policy, for example, observed that:

> on the whole this region [East Asia] has enjoyed an historically unprecedented period of peace, of relative peace. And the key to that ... has been the willingness of virtually all countries of the region — most of them at least — to work with one another to maintain that peace and security.[1]

When China was weak and disunited, it attracted great power intervention. When it was isolated and radicalised, it supported insurgencies in Southeast Asia. Today China is unified and secure from external military threats. It is market-oriented domestically, outward looking and pragmatic in the conduct of its foreign policy. It is involved in orthodox regional diplomacy, has participated in conflict resolution in Korea and Cambodia and in talks on the South China Sea. Its behaviour as a Permanent Member of the United Nations Security Council has been beyond reproach, certainly as far as the United States is concerned.

The China threat

However, with the end of the Cold War, the collapse of the Soviet Union and a significant reduction in forward-deployed United States air and naval forces in the Pacific, there is a perception that China, Japan and India will inevitably seek to exercise predominant regional influence.[2] Of the two East Asian powers, China is seen to be the state that is most likely to disturb the equilibrium in the region — and, indeed, in the world.[3] The time frame for this prognosis is some time in the twenty-first century.

China is central to the Pacific community in terms of culture, geography and political and economic influence. It is also non-European, non-democratic, avowedly non-capitalist, about to take over Hong Kong, and one can find a record of conflict between China and its neighbours over the last 2000 years. China is also perceived to be the last bastion of communism — that is, it is still ruled by first-generation revolutionaries. It is a large country and large countries, we are reminded, tend to be ambitious, outward-looking and inevitably seek to increase their power and influence.[4]

Ironically, China's strategic and economic circumstances are more favourable than they have been for some time, with China more secure from external threats than at any other time in the last two centuries.[5] The end of European challenges to Chinese integrity will formally end with the handover of Hong Kong to China in 1997 and Macau in 1999. The collapse of the Soviet Union removed the last great power military challenge to China, a circumstance that has lent weight to the view that, unrestrained in the north, China is free to strike in the south.

At the same time, China has made impressive economic progress. Average annual growth in Gross Domestic Product (GDP) of 6 per cent between 1949 and 1978 jumped to an average of 9 per cent after 1978. In 1992–94, China was the fastest growing economy in the world, with a real GDP growth rate of nearly 13 per cent.[6] China's dilemma, however, is growth that is too fast on the one hand and, on the other hand, growth that is too slow.[7] Paul Kennedy argues that, without technological breakthroughs, China may be stuck in a poverty trap that it cannot escape.[8] Assuming China can overcome its many problems, and provided further that it can maintain political stability and its program of incremental reform, it may be able to continue a pattern of sustainable economic growth.[9] Then a stable, relatively prosperous China could spread positive economic benefits throughout the Asia-Pacific.

Yet this stronger, unified China, conscious of its history as the Middle Kingdom, is the great power China that worries many security analysts.

China has disputed territory on the Sino-Indian border, the Sino-Russian border, the Sino-Vietnamese border and in the East and South China Seas. It supported insurgencies in Southeast Asia throughout the 1960s and 1970s and retains ties with overseas Chinese communities throughout Southeast Asia. Traditionally, China has often been the dominant power — the Middle Kingdom — in Pacific-Asia. With its rapid national development, an ambitious China is again perceived to be expansive and outward looking. In China's case, sheer size means its regional political influence will inevitably expand and it could become the biggest player in the Asia-Pacific region in the twenty-first century.[10]

For some security analysts, China's size is enough. In addition, however, concern about China's long-term great power ambitions is felt to be justified on other grounds: China is the only nuclear power that is continuing to conduct nuclear weapons tests. It has what is claimed by some observers to be the fastest growing defence budget in the region.[11] Its defence doctrine has shifted away from fighting a people's war to developing a mobile rapid-reaction, high-technology military force that is able to fight small 'low-intensity' border conflicts. With no credible great power threats imminent for at least 20 years, the PLA has redeployed some of its forces from the north to the south. It is expanding its naval capabilities with a new class of destroyers (the Luhu) and frigates (the Jiangwei) equipped with modern anti-ship and anti-aircraft missile systems.[12] It is training marine and airborne forces in amphibious landings and has increased coastguard and naval activities in the South and East China Seas — that is, China is adopting a more outward-looking defence posture. In this context, China built an airstrip and berthing facilities on Woody Island in the Paracels, followed by a helipad and pier on Fiery Cross Reef in the Spratly Islands further south.[13] It has up to 30 B-6 naval bombers, equipped with Exocet-type C-601 anti-ship missiles (range 95 kilometres) and 130 torpedo-equipped A-5 light bombers that can cover the South China Sea and could stage through Lingshui airfield, on Hainan Island, to Woody Island, 400 kilometres further south.[14] A full-length runway on recently acquired Mischief Reef would give China two key stepping stones in the South China Sea. Meanwhile, China's acquisition of long-range Su-27 fighter aircraft and Il-76 transport aircraft, its interest in inflight refuelling technology, Kilo-class submarines, aircraft carriers and other technology are seen as 'particularly menacing' because they give the People's Liberation Army (PLA) improved mobility, greater lift and longer reach.[15] In this context, a five-year Sino-Russian military co-operation 'pact' signed in Beijing on 8 November 1993 is seen in a negative light.[16]

These trends, and what is perceived to be a heavy handed approach to territorial issues in the South China Sea, are regarded as a Chinese quest for regional dominance.[17] John Garver suggests that an overpopulated China is embarked on a 'slow march south' into the South China Sea to satisfy its need for energy resources.[18] According to the Central Intelligence Agency, in testimony to the United States Congress, China has an interest in building the country 'into a great power'.[19] Confirmation of a belligerent China might be found in *Can the Chinese Army Win the Next War?*, a recently published monograph that lists the United States, Japan, Vietnam, Russia and India as potential Chinese adversaries and discusses the possibility of use of force in the South China Sea.[20] The result has been a considerable degree of nervousness in the region about China and what is perceived to be a growing Chinese capability to project military force into the western Pacific.[21]

Regional wariness about China is justified in terms of prudence. China is large and has a problem with its history. It is regarded, rightly or wrongly, with instinctive apprehension in Southeast Asia, especially in Malaysia and Indonesia: for that China is partly to blame. It has failed to explain the impact of the Gulf War on its recent defence expenditure, or the rationale for its regional defence policies and plans with the degree of diplomacy and transparency that might help reassure neighbouring states, especially in Southeast Asia.

China is a central actor in the Asia-Pacific and its influence will continue to grow. It is destined to loom ever larger in the economic, strategic and environmental affairs of the Asia-Pacific region, whether as a greater China or a China in disarray.[22] But is China expansionist? Will it behave towards smaller neighbours just like any other large dominant power? Is it determined to acquire control of all the islands in the South China Sea? Has China's defence budget increased disproportionately in the past few years and has it embarked on a major program of military modernisation? Are nations in the region engaged in an arms buying spree because they are worried about China's intentions?

To answer these questions, it might be sensible to engage China in dialogue so that we can learn more from China about its defence policy and plans, its strategic interests and its security concerns. A co-operative dialogue, therefore, between leading PLA institutes, such as the National Defence University, the Academy of Military Science and the China Institute of International Strategic Studies, and strategic studies institutes in the region, especially in the Association of Southeast Asian Nation (ASEAN) countries, should be encouraged. As Assistant Secretary of Defence for Regional Security Affairs Charles Freeman said during a recent visit to Beijing, the region wanted to know more about China's defence plans and policy — 'not because we regard China as a threat but because it is an important factor in world politics and the security of East Asia'.[23] At the same time, we can do more to deepen our understanding of China. We can try to view China's defence expenditure, its modernisation and its foreign policy in strategic and historical context and not just from the perspective of the United States Congress or realist theory.

In assessing China's future strategic role, we should not view it in isolation from the rest of the region. We need to bear in mind that Japan is one of China's leading trading partners and a key source of soft loans; that the United States is China's number one source of foreign exchange, a vital market for Chinese exports and that it will remain the strongest military power in the Pacific for the foreseeable future. China, even as a great power, will be forced to work with the more powerful and influential United States which is likely to retain its strategic interests in the affairs of the western Pacific. Japan, and prospectively a united Korea, will fill a balancing role in the region (and, indeed, China may in turn balance them). There will also be a patchwork of interlocking economic interests and military capabilities that will constrain maverick behaviour. An aggressive policy in the region, furthermore, would be contrary to China's self-interest, its regional diplomacy and the kind of stable great power relationship it seeks and needs to maintain with Japan and the United States.

Looking at China

China is often described in the United States in negative terms — for example, that it is 'the world's rogue elephant' with no regard for human rights, missile proliferation or international stability.[24] Such views are heard less often in the Asia-Pacific region, or at least they are more nuanced because, while small Asian nations may fear China, for most the reality is that they must learn to live with their biggest neighbour. Such views, moreover, can easily fan regional concern about China as a great power threat. As Singapore's Senior Minister, Lee Kuan Yew, observed, when Western critics wrote about 'the China threat' they were mining 'a rich lode filled with apprehension and fears'.[25] Lee said the West should try to see China from an Asian perspective and not simply in terms of threats.[26] Malaysia's Defence Minister, Najib Razak, put it more crudely, saying that mainland China was 'being made out to be the new bogeyman' in Asia.[27] Indonesia, Malaysia and the other ASEAN states may fear China to varying degrees and for sometimes subjective reasons, but at the same time they want to ensure that China is engaged in, and not isolated from, regional affairs. Prime Minister Mahathir, who led a delegation of nearly 300 Malaysian businessmen to Beijing in June 1993, claimed that China had changed and its 'past was very much forgotten and, in many ways, it was irrelevant' for the future of the region.[28] For the Japanese, China is as important as the United States, especially if Japan is to become a Permanent Member of the United Nations Security Council. Japan also considers Sino-Japanese relations to be the 'anchor' to a stable East Asia.[29] The Japanese might nudge China on human rights, but they also recognise China's positive achievements and its power. They believe that to control China, it should be further integrated into, and not alienated from, the regional political economy.[30]

Analogous to Paul Dibb's suggestion in looking at the insecurity of the former Soviet Union, we should bear in mind China's history and geography when we analyse its defence posture and defence expenditure.[31] China has long land and sea borders and a deep historical sense of vulnerability to attack from the north and from the sea to the east. Chinese naval commanders often remind the government that China was invaded from the sea several times in its recent history and that, therefore, it needs to strengthen its navy so that 'it could intercept enemy naval forces at sea at great distances from China's coast'.[32]

The almost unrelenting external pressure on China from the early nineteenth century up until the early 1980s (when the Soviet Union began its withdrawal from Indochina) has had a significant impact on China's security thinking — or rather, its sense of insecurity. As Politburo member Yang Baibing remarked, China needed to build 'a powerful army and a firm national defence' because only then could China 'acquire the proper position of a big country in the international community' and only then would other countries 'not look down on us and dare to rashly offend us'.[33] The problem, however, is that China's quest to prevent other countries looking down on it or rashly offending its dignity can easily translate into insecurity for small neighbouring states like Vietnam. This is a problem of perception about which China should be more sensitive. At the same time, countries in the region should, as You Ji suggests, be more understanding and more patient with China.[34]

Defence budget

Part of the problem in assessing whether or not China is likely to become a source of regional disequilibrium stems from debate about the size of its defence budget.

Estimates of China's defence expenditure range up to US$51 billion, which means China would rank as world's third largest in terms of military spending.[35] The Central Intelligence Agency, on the other hand, put China's defence budget somewhere 'in the range of US$16 billion or $17 billion' in 1992.[36] This is twice the amount declared by China but is less than half the amount spent by Japan and still less than that spent by the major nuclear powers.[37]

In fact, China is not spending disproportionately on defence. According to the *World Military Expenditures and Arms Transfers 1991–1992*, as a percentage of Gross National Product (GNP), China's military expenditure declined from 8.2 per cent in 1981 to 3.3 per cent in 1991, which is on a par with the ratio of most ASEAN states.[38] In renminbi terms, there were increases in Chinese defence expenditure (see Table 14.1) of 15 per cent in 1989/90, 12 per cent in 1990/91, 12.5 per cent in 1991/92–1992/93 and 20 per cent in 1994 — or as much as 100 per cent in the last four years. This is much greater than the rate of increase in defence expenditure in most of the ASEAN states over the same period.[39] However, taking into account inflation rates in China of 10 per cent or more per annum, real growth in China's defence expenditure was less than 2 per cent per annum[40] and indeed, according to the United States Arms Control and Disarmament Agency, in real terms there has been almost no increase in China's defence expenditure between 1981 and 1991.[41] Harlan Jencks, an authoritative commentator on the PLA, observes that recent increases have in fact been very meagre.[42] While there have been increases of between 10 and 20 per cent in 1992, 1993 and 1994, most of the increase has been spent on increased salaries and allowances and equipping PLA units for an internal security role. The PLA, in fact, has complained that it is being squeezed for funds.[43]

Table 14.1 Trends in official Chinese defence expenditure

	RMB mn Constant 1994	US$ mn Constant 1994
1981	16 797	4 390
1982	17 635	4 609
1983	17 713	4 569
1984	18 073	4 466
1985	19 153	4 342
1986	20 126	4 357
1987	20 962	4 320
1988	21 796	4 013
1989	25 100	4 243
1990	28 970	4 603
1991	32 510	4 887
1992	37 000	5 292
1993	43 200	5 380
1994	52 400	6 042

Sources: International Financial Statistics (Yearbook) 1992; PRC Government Finance Statistics (Yearbook) 1992, 1993, 1994.

China has avoided buying large quantities of foreign military equipment and has switched around 65 per cent of its defence industries to making civilian goods, such as bicycles, cameras, refrigerators and other consumer goods.[44] The size of the PLA has been trimmed from 4.7 million to three million. Overall, the pace of China's defence modernisation, measured in qualitative terms, has been slow. To become a great power on a par with the United States, the former Soviet Union or Japan, or even just to keep up with Taiwan, China will have to drastically increase its defence expenditure.

Bearing in mind the problems with statistical data on defence expenditure, we have tried to put China's defence budget into comparative perspective in Table 14.2. There it appears that China's defence budget is less than that of Taiwan and is on a par with India's. It is a fraction of America's defence expenditure, whether you use the Chinese figures or inflate them several times using the World Bank's purchasing power parity method of calculation.

Reports that the PLA has access to large amounts of hard currency from foreign arms sales are probably exaggerated. The total earned by China in arms sales over the period 1984–92 was about US$14.4 billion.[45] In 1992, earnings from arms sales dropped to just US$100 million (see Table 14.3). Of the total amount earned from arms sales, about 30 per cent would have been paid

Table 14.2 China: A comparison

	China	Taiwan	India	Japan	Russia	USA	France	UK
Nuclear	Yes	?	?	No	Yes	Yes	Yes	Yes
Defence budget ($US b)	7.5	9.2	8.0	˙34.0	133.7	289.2	34.9	41.2
Armed forces (million)	3	0.36	1.26	0.25	2.7	1.9	0.43	0.29
Principal surface combatants	54	41	28	64	192	188	41	43
Carriers	nil	nil	2	nil	2	12	2	2
Submarines	46	4	15	17	250	110	17	21
SSBNs	1	nil	nil	nil	55	25	4	2
ICBMs	8	nil	nil	nil	1 400	1 000	nil	nil
IRBMs	Yes	?	Yes	nil	Yes	Yes	Yes	Yes
Combat aircraft	4 970	486	674	440	3 700	3 485	808	466
Population (mil)	1 200	21.6	873	124	148	252	57	58
Land area 000 km^2	9 597	36	3 288	378	17 075	9 373	547	245
GDP US$ b2	5 053	173	315	3362	na	5 674	1 212	1 018
GDP growth 1980–90 Constant 1987 (%)	9.81	8.32	5.67	4.11	na	3.35	2.31	3.06
GDP/capita 1990 Constant 1987 US$	328	6 003	371	22 821	na	19 316	17 530	12 853

Notes:

1 Data for Russia and China are estimates. Data for all other countries are for 1992.

2 1991 for all countries except China, which is 1992.

3 The International Monetary Fund, *World Economic Outlook*, May 1993, suggests China's GDP is closer to $1260 billion, using purchasing power parities. Greater China (China and Taiwan and Hong Kong) — US$674 billion.

Source: *World Bank Tables*, International Economic Database, Australian National University, for growth in GNP per capita. IISS, *The Military Balance* for all other data.

to the factories supplying the weapons and another 30 to 40 per cent would go to various State Council Ministries, leaving less than 30 per cent of the earnings available for the PLA. However, assuming that all proceeds went to the PLA, it would mean an average addition to the PLA's defence budget over the period 1984–91 of US$1.8 billion per annum, a relatively modest sum when placed in the comparative context shown in Table 14.1.

Whatever the precise figures may be — and there is room for considerable debate — the United States Department of Defense believes that China's defence spending had started from 'a relatively low base' and while it was being 'carefully watched' it was 'basically moderate'.[46]

China is continuing to modernise and expand its strategic missile forces, as it has been doing since the inception of the Second Artillery Corps (China's missile force), but the pace is slow and the numbers are minimal. We should note (Table 14.2) that China has a tiny fraction of the number of ICBMs possessed by the United States and Russia and that its overall strategic force posture is non-offensive. China's present testing of nuclear weapons, moreover, can be seen as preparatory to signing a comprehensive nuclear test ban treaty in 1996, which it has said it would do. Similarly, the number of Chinese

Table 14.3   Arms transfer agreements with the Third World, by supplier, 1984–92* (current US$ mill.)

	1984	1985	1986	1987	1988	1989	1990	1991	1992	1984–1991
United States	6 407	4 785	3 421	5 231	8 733	7 610	18 209	14 161	13 600	82 157
Soviet Union	21 300	17 100	24 800	20 400	12 500	11 500	11 200	5 000	1 300	125 100
France	6 500	1 500	1 300	3 200	1 300	3 800	3 100	400	3 800	24 900
United Kingdom	700	19 300	900	500	900	1 100	1 700	2 000	2 400	29 500
China	300	1 400	1 800	4 700	2 100	1 600	2 100	300	100	14 400
Germany	800	200	500	800	200	900	300	400	700	4 800
Italy	700	1 300	600	200	200	300	200	0	400	3 900

Source: US Government; and R.F. Grimmett, *Trends in Government Arms Transfers to the Third World by Major Supplier 1984–1992*, Library of Congress, Washington, 1993

* Based on US Department of Defense Price Deflator

conventionally powered submarines that are operational has dropped by more than half, from over 100 in 1984 to around 47 in 1992.[47] The number of China's principal surface combatants has increased marginally, from 52 in 1988 to 55 today. Of these, only the Luhu and the Jiangwei class are comparable to the modern warships in, for example, the Taiwanese navy. China does not have an aircraft carrier — it has a limited air and sea lift capability and its marine force of about 5000 is much less that Taiwan's 31 000 personnel.[48] In fact, Taiwan has a greater amphibious lift capability than China. While China's air force may be the third largest in the world, it is 'essentially a defensive force equipped with obsolete aircraft'.[49] It does not yet have an operational air-to-air refuelling system.

Overall, China's forces are oriented to defence and have little capability for major overseas conflict, especially if the United States were to become involved.[50] Militarily, China lags well behind the kind of precision firepower that the United States demonstrated during the Gulf War. As former United States Navy Admiral Lloyd Vasey observed, 'compared with the West, most of China's current inventory of equipment and weapons systems is remarkably obsolete'.[51] China's military equipment is mostly of 1950s and 1960s vintage. It has quantity but lacks quality, especially in submarines and aircraft.[52] Its technology, especially in aircraft, is a generation or two behind other great powers. China, in short, is the weakest of the great powers, and is not well qualified to assume the role of dominant great power in Asia.

However, China is not weak when its military capabilities are compared with those of its Asian neighbours on a one-by-one basis. It could best Vietnam in a skirmish over islands in the South China Sea. It is more powerful than any of the ASEAN countries, but Japan, Russia, South Korea and Taiwan all have more modern fighter aircraft than China and equally powerful naval platforms.[53] Moreover, several of China's neighbours have treaty or near-equivalent security relationships with the United States (Japan, Korea, the Philippines, Thailand and, increasingly, Taiwan). Most of them together belong to or participate in the United Nations, APECO[54], ASEAN or some other forum in which there is a high premium on regionalism and good neighbour policies. ASEAN is an increasingly cohesive security related association.[55] In any event, China was deterred from attacking India in 1987 and it was unable to give Vietnam 'a second lesson' from 1979 to 1985. It could not invade Taiwan without incurring both huge military losses and risking great domestic social, economic and political instability.

Arms purchases

To make up for the military deficiencies that were highlighted by the lessons of the Gulf War, China bought 'firesale' equipment from Russia, including 26 Su-27 long range fighters for the air force, five SA-10 Grumble anti-missile systems, some Il-76 transport aircraft and several Kilo-class submarines.[56]

The Su-27s are a high performance long-range fighter aircraft, but even with the reported addition of 48 more Su-27s, China's inventory of modern fighter aircraft is relatively modest when compared, for example, to the 150 F-16s and the 60 Mirage 2000s bought by Taiwan, ASEAN's 70 or so recently acquired F-16s and Japan's 160 F-15s.[57] Weaknesses in combat pilot training suggest that China is unlikely to deploy the Su-27s operationally for some years. According to United States Air Force intelligence specialists, China's Su-27s may make a strong political statement, but they have limited operational significance.[58]

In the long term, Russian technology transfers to China, such as the AL-31F jet engine and assistance in upgrading China's F-8 aircraft, rather than specific items like the Su-27s, will prove to be more important for China's capabilities. Even then, Moscow will not be selling China weapons or technology that could create a problem for Russia or the region, despite Moscow's pressing need for foreign exchange.[59] China will also have difficulty in absorbing the technology.

As the United States Defence Department concluded:

China's 1950s vintage force of outmoded T-62 tanks, aging artillery and underpowered MiG-19 and MiG-21 fighters requires modernisation and this should not be misconstrued as hostile activity ... Chinese purchases of Russia [equipment] ... should not incite alarm ... [because] it's a drop in the bucket compared to their aging force. So to say they've become a threatening military force is not true; they have a long way to go [before they] become threatening.[60]

The South China Sea

To illustrate a China threat, many analysts refer to China's use of force against Vietnam in the South China Sea in 1974 and 1988. According to a Malaysian analyst, J.N. Mak, China is intransigent and unco-operative over disputed island claims in the South China Sea.[61] It is building up its navy and buying long-range Russian aircraft, including Su-27 aircraft, so that it can 'take the Spratly Islands by force'.[62] Such views tend to overlook the history of the Chinese claim — whether by Taiwan or China — to islands in the South China Sea, where, at least in the case of the Paracels, the Chinese have a particularly strong claim in international law.[63] Vietnamese leaders, furthermore, including Prime Minister Pham Van Dong, previously acknowledged Chinese claims to the Spratly Islands and when China did use force for 20 minutes or so in March 1988, it is as well to remember the circumstances: the Vietnamese fired first; China had vastly superior force but stopped short of taking all the islands held by the Vietnamese when it could have done so; it did not threaten islands held by other claimants; and, arguably, it simply established a physical presence as a basis to reinforce its claims.[64] Furthermore, many countries thought the Vietnamese only got what they deserved after their invasion and occupation of Cambodia.

Nonetheless, there is no doubt that China has a public relations problem about the way it has asserted its claims to islands in the South China Sea. It subsequently adopted a more flexible approach and participated in several Indonesian-sponsored workshops on co-operation and joint development of seabed resources in the South China Sea with nine other Asian countries (Taiwan, Vietnam, the Philippines, Brunei, Malaysia, Indonesia, Singapore, Laos and Thailand). At the first meeting in Bandung in July 1991, China and the other claimant states (Taiwan, Brunei, Malaysia, Vietnam and the Philippines) agreed as a basic first principle that 'any territorial and jurisdictional dispute in the South China Sea area should be resolved by peaceful means through dialogue and negotiation. Force should not be used.'[65]

China does not like negotiating with small countries over territory that it regards as Chinese. Indeed, some in the PLA would argue that as the islands are all Chinese, there is no such thing as disputed territory in the South China Sea and claimant states were simply using 'the China threat' argument as a way to negate China's sovereignty.[66] Their preference is to simply seize the islands and evict occupiers that they regard as trespassers. But Wang Yingfan, Director of the Asia Department of the Chinese Foreign Ministry, said China was prepared to discuss joint development of seabed resources with other claimant states and would put aside the sovereignty issue for future generations to resolve.[67] He said that, without prejudicing its jurisdictional claims, China proposed joint programs in such areas as safety of navigation, communications, maritime research and meteorological and environmental studies.[68] The same point has been made by Chinese Premier Li Peng and Chinese Foreign Minister Qian Qichen.[69]

China's policy approach to the South China Sea in the future may depend on whether the PLA or the Foreign Ministry predominates in the conduct of Chinese foreign policy. Recently, there have been indications of a growing PLA influence in the conduct of Chinese foreign policy — for example, in Sino-United States relations and on policy towards North Korea, the Spratly Islands, Burma and arms sales.[70] This could cause concern, especially in view of China's 1995 occupation of Mischief Reef.

There is clearly a lot of room for misunderstanding over the South China Sea.[71] However, the fact that the claimant states, including China, are still able to sit down together and discuss their common interests is a significant achievement. The last thing China wants to do is fuel regional fears of a China threat. That sensitivity, and the reasons for it, should be borne in mind when we make threat forecasts about China and its neighbours. Equally, however, China may need to bear the same sensitivities in mind when it passes legislation or makes public announcements about issues or disputes that involve its smaller neighbours. China, in short, may need to be more conscious of its size.

China and regional security

If we analyse the state of China's bilateral relations with neighbours like South Korea, Russia, Taiwan, India, the ASEAN states and Vietnam, there is one thing they all have in common. In each case, tension and even confrontation have been replaced by growing volumes of trade and economic co-operation, leadership exchanges and a variety of confidence-building measures conducive to regional stability. There is residual suspicion, and there will almost inevitably be uncertainty over the next ten years. But for the moment, as Winston Lord observed, the fact is that relationships amongst the great powers are remarkably free of confrontation, 'or freer than they have been for many, many decades'.[72] This has contributed to conflict resolution in Indochina and Korea and a growing sense of opportunity, as was reflected in the Seattle meeting of leaders from the Asia-Pacific community.

With India, China has agreed to promote stability on one of the longest and most sensitive borders in the world, including parity of border forces, transparency in troop movements, a non-aggression clause and acceptance of the line of actual control.[73] Though this *detente* does not guarantee good Sino-Indian relations, the danger of misperception, tension and conflict has receded and the relationship, the best it has been since the 1950s, is a good example of the practice of co-operative security between two big neighbouring powers.[74]

China's relations with Russia have made equally positive progress, with agreement on the demarcation of most of the border, an enormous expansion of cross-border trade, substantial cuts to border forces and the sale of advanced Russian weapons and military technology to Chinese armaments factories.[75]

Even China and Vietnam have improved their relations. The most recent talks on disputed land and sea borders between China and Vietnam produced positive results, according to Vietnamese and Chinese officials.[76] Their relationship, however, is still based on an underlying hostility and distrust, and small incidents on the border or in the South China Sea could easily become the catalyst for increased tension.[77] China regards Vietnam as ungrateful, while Vietnam sees China in historical terms as a grasping great power.

Relations between China and Taiwan have improved dramatically in the last five years. Both sides still view each other with distrust, but their primary focus is on the mutual advantages to be gained from closer economic relations. Taiwanese enterprises are the second largest source of foreign investment in China.

China completed the normalisation of its relations with the ASEAN states in 1990 when it established diplomatic relations with Indonesia and Singapore. China and Indonesia and China and Malaysia have since exchanged military attachés. They hold regular bilateral intelligence exchanges and have made substantial headway in resolving questions about the dual citizenship of ethnic Chinese.[78] China participated in the ASEAN Post Ministerial Conference in Kuala Lumpur in July 1991 for the first time and the ASEAN Regional Forum in July 1994.

Regarding the Sino-Japanese relationship, there are question marks over its future with forecasts of increasing economic rivalry and a competing nationalism that could develop into a great power struggle.[79] On the other hand, relations between China and Japan are presently the best they have been since the mid-nineteenth century and the immediate prospect is for a further strengthening of what is an increasingly complementary and interdependent relationship.[80] Both sides have a vested interest in maintaining regional stability and held their first high-level security talks in Beijing in December 1993.[81]

One consequence of the improvement in relations between China and its neighbours is that countries like Russia, the United States, India and even Vietnam have been able to cut or restrain their defence expenditure because they have been able to reduce deployments on the border with or near China. Vietnam, for example, has cut its defence force by 50 per cent and relaxed its military posture on its northern border. The United States is making 'measured reductions of ground and some air forces' in the Western Pacific'.[82] Japan may be increasing its defence expenditure but it is because of political pressure from the United States and concern about Russia rather than a concern about China. The 1993 Japanese Defence Agency's *The Defence of Japan* pointed out that China's military modernisation was progressing, but very slowly.[83]

India's defence expenditure was cut in 1991/92 by at least 6 per cent in real terms and possibly as much as 20 per cent with devaluation of the rupee.[84] The cuts were attributed to the improved state of Sino-Indian relations.[85] Defence expenditure by Australia, New Zealand and the Philippines declined slightly, while in the case of Indonesia, the increase has not been significant.

Taiwan's defence expenditure in 1993 was US$9.75 billion, or 22.8 per cent of the total government budget (down from 33.5 per cent in 1980). Taiwan's opposition Democratic Progressive Party has demanded a cut of 20 per cent in the budget and 33 per cent in personnel because Taiwan and the mainland 'had entered a new era in which confrontation is giving way to co-operation'.[86]

Generally, China's rapid growth, its raw materials, market potential, human capital and central location make it a natural hinterland and trading partner for Taiwan, South Korea, Japan, Singapore, the United States and other members of the Asia-Pacific economic community. It was the principal engine of economic growth in the Pacific region in 1993, with an import growth rate of 25 per cent per annum over 1992–93.[87] China is the number one export market for Hong Kong, number two and the fastest growing for Taiwan, number three for Singapore, Australia and the United States, number six for South Korea, number five for Canada and Russia, and number two for Japan. If taken together, China and Hong Kong constitute ASEAN's fourth largest trading partner. China's trade with Indonesia doubled after normalisation. China's trade with South Korea is at least ten times its trade with North Korea. Cross-border trade is flourishing between China and Vietnam.

Regional arms race

Despite these trends, there have been reports of a regional arms race in Southeast Asia triggered by fear of China.[88] Closer examination suggests that the term arms race is misleading.[89] United States Under-Secretary of Defense Policy Frank Wisner concluded that what was happening 'was hardly an arms race' and that, in any case, the buildup in military forces in the areas in the South China Sea was a modernisation process which was 'no cause for alarm at this point'.[90] According to a detailed study by Graeme

Cheeseman and Richard Leaver, the pattern of defence expenditure falls 'short of what would be expected in a fully developed regional arms race' and can best be 'explained by the process of force modernisation'. They conclude that 'although real increases in regional military spending have been regularly recorded through the last decade, these merely continue a trend which commenced in the previous decade when the rate of increase was even more rapid'.[91]

More accurately, there has been a sustained buildup in the ASEAN countries for a variety of reasons. China's power projection capabilities represent one factor.[92] A vague notion of threat from China was a convenient rationale, but the main reason has been that the states concerned can afford to spend more and have been encouraged to do so by the United States.[93] Other factors include perceptions of India as an emerging great power, the fact that ASEAN countries have increased economic resources available, the impact of Law of the Sea principles on defence priorities, corruption and prestige factors, and supply-side pressures.[94]

While Malaysia, Thailand and Singapore have significantly increased their defence expenditure over the last decade, the rate of increase has levelled off in recent years. With the exception of Singapore, the level of ASEAN defence expenditure as a proportion of GDP is around 2–3 per cent of GDP, which is not abnormal and is approaching the 2 per cent of GDP that Australia spends on defence. Meanwhile, nearly every country in Pacific-Asia has given a higher national priority to education.[95] Expenditure on education increased significantly in almost every country in Pacific-Asia over the last decade and with a few exceptions (Taiwan, China, Singapore and South Korea), all spent more on education as a proportion of GNP than on defence.[96]

Besides, most ASEAN countries have a need to replace and modernise their defence equipment.[97] Such improvements were regarded by Australia as 'appropriate and expected'.[98] And, one could argue, strong regional defence forces offer the best protection from possible military confrontation.[99] In a sense, the modernisation of ASEAN defence capabilities represents the fruition of American expectations outlined in President Nixon's Guam Doctrine of July 1969. That is, countries in the Asia-Pacific region should increase their defence expenditure and become self-reliant instead of relying on United States military protection.[100] Increased military capabilities of individual states could then be expected to contribute to a co-operative security network that leaves few gaps in the region — or, in the current strategic parlance, no vacuum.[101] This is, in fact, what is happening. It has contributed to regional stability, and in the case of Southeast Asia, the result has been to reduce the opportunity for interference by outside powers, including China.

An additional overlay has been formed by a proliferation of financial, trade, aid and transportation linkages. These linkages present opportunities for co-operative economic endeavours (as opposed to military competition). Progress on concepts of economic regionalism and co-operation is well established within the region — for example, through the ASEAN dialogue process, the roundtables organised by the ASEAN Institutes of Strategic International Studies, the Pacific Economic Co-operation Council, the South China Sea workshops, the South Pacific Forum and Asia Pacific Economic Co-operation (APEC). China participates in all of these forums and supports 'bilateral and regional security dialogues of various forms, at different levels and through various channels in response to the diversity of the region', such as the Council for Security and Cooperation in Asia Pacific (CSCAP).[102]

Additionally, cross-border linkages that were once impossible to imagine are proliferating along China's borders. They have led to emerging economic circles around the Sea of Japan, the Yellow Sea, the East China Sea, and potentially, the South China Sea. Examined on a map, one can see that most of these circles involve China or the Chinese and would not have been possible or held such promise if China were not making its epochal transition from communism to capitalism with Chinese characteristics.[103] Instead of thinking only in terms of the balance of naval and military forces opposing China or some other great power threat, the Asian countries of the Asia-Pacific in particular are focusing on the gains to be made from economic co-operation, the China market and the development of a strategic dialogue.

Conclusion

There is a tendency to view China in stark terms as a strong, ambitious, assertive power. However, China's record and its self-interest do not suggest an ambitious expansionist state. Since the mid-1970s, Beijing has not pulled unorthodox foreign policy levers. It may share more borders with more countries than any other great power, but it has also negotiated by peaceful means the settlement of more disputed territory than any other country. It is sensitive to the norms of good citizenship in the region, internationally and at the United Nations. It is also conscious of the limitations of the PLA and the strong military capabilities of neighbouring states, and especially of the United States. It has been mostly constructive in supporting the United Nations system. Its defence modernisation is proceeding at a slow and measured pace. Its domestic preoccupations call for the avoidance of conflict and tension over ideology, marginal territory or 'matters of principle'. Such a country profile, when taken in the context of China's history and geography, and its essentially defensive force posture, suggests that Chinese foreign policy should be a cause of reassurance and not insecurity. Indeed, unqualified portrayals of China as a threatening military power run the risk of encouraging latent Chinese distrust of the West and its political values. This could then fuel a spiral of misperception and contribute to the start of a new Cold War in the Asia-Pacific.[104]

On the other hand, once China becomes a successfully modernised state, it may well become a formidable military power. It is this possibility that lurks at the back of the minds of many strategic analysts, especially if China seeks to right old wrongs and recover territory it lost during the nineteenth century. A strong China, however, may also be a stabilising force in the region — by balancing Japan and a united Korea, for example, and by providing avenues for investment and a huge consumer market, it is already contributing to regional economic prosperity. We should not automatically assume that China as a great power will be a factor for instability. Nor should we be focusing on possible scenarios ten years in the future, especially when we have difficulty in interpreting events unfolding in China and the region today.

Forecasts about China as a great power overlook its low per capita income and the mismatch of its huge population, poor resources and infrastructure bottlenecks.[105] In per capita terms, China is one of the poorer countries in the world, even if the World Bank figures based on purchasing power parity are used.[106] It is grappling with regionalism, income disparities, uneven development and serious environmental, social and ideological problems. These issues raise serious doubts as to whether China can ever escape from the weight of its population and poverty and develop into a truly great power.[107] Some observers would argue that a successful outcome for China is by no means certain, given its domestic impediments and fissiparous tendencies.[108] This is not to suggest that China can never be a great power, as it may well achieve that status. But to predict that China must become a great power and, *ipso facto*, a threat to regional stability, risks overlooking the inevitable rise of other great powers such as Germany and Japan, and the positive role that China might then play.

China's size is a factor in our strategic analysis, but it is also China's Achilles' heel. An enormous effort will be needed to keep Chinese society intact, lift living standards, satisfy rising political expectations and cope with restive Moslem and Tibetan minorities in the western periphery. For modernisation to succeed — and it will take many decades — China needs peaceful borders and the co-operation of its neighbours. This gives China a vested interest in maintaining a peaceful international environment, avoiding unnecessary conflict situations, co-operating with other members of the United Nations Security Council and contributing to conflict resolution.

Notes

1 Paul Wolfowitz, Under-Secretary of Defense for Policy, transcript of interview, Washington, 3 August 1992, USIS Wireless File, Canberra, 4 August 1992, pp. 8–22.
2 See, for example, 'End of the Cold War: Strategic Trends and Outlook', Appendix 1, in East Asia Analytical Unit, Department of Foreign Affairs and Trade, *Australia and North-East Asia in the 1990s: Accelerating Change*, Australian Government Publishing Service, Canberra, 1992, pp. 95–105.
3 See, for example, Paul Dibb, 'Asia's Security in the 21st Century', *Strategic and Defence Studies Newsletter*, March 1994, p. 1, and his arti-

cle, 'Asia's Simmering Cauldron Could Soon Boil Over', *Australian*, 19 November 1993. Articles with a similarly pessimistic viewpoint, certainly about China, include Denny Roy, 'Hegemon on the Horizon? China's Threat to East Asian Security', *International Security*, vol. 19, no. 1, Summer 1994, p. 140, and Barry Buzan and Gerald Segal, 'Rethinking East Asian Security', *Survival*, vol. 36, no. 2, Summer 1994, pp. 3–21.

4 Richard K. Betts, 'Wealth, Power, and Instability', International Security, vol. 18, no. 3, Winter 1993/94, pp. 34, 37; Christopher Layne, 'The Unipolar Illusion: Why New Great Powers Will Rise', *International Security*, vol. 17, no. 4, Spring 1993, p. 5; and Samuel P. Huntington, 'Why Primacy Matters', *International Security*, vol. 17, no. 4, Spring 1993, pp. 68, 71.

5 Yan Xuetong, 'China's Security After the Cold War', *Contemporary International Relations* (Beijing), vol. 3, no. 5, May 1993, p. 1.

6 *Asia-Pacific Profiles 1993*, Asia-Pacific Economics Group, Research School of Pacific Studies, Australian National University, Canberra, 1993, p. 63.

7 *Asia-Pacific Profiles 1994*, Asia-Pacific Economics Group, Research School of Pacific and Asian Studies, Australian National University, Canberra, 1994, p. 68.

8 Paul Kennedy, *Preparing for the Twenty First Century*, Harper Collins, London, 1993, p. 190, suggests that in the absence of technological breakthroughs, China may be stuck in a poverty trap indefinitely.

9 Peter Harrold, *China's Reform Experience to Date*, World Bank Discussion Papers 180, The World Bank, Washington, 1992, p. 38.

10 Lee Kuan Yew, Singapore's former Prime Minister, observed that 'it is not possible to pretend that [China] is just another big player. This is the biggest player in the history of man'. Quoted by Nicholas Kristof, 'China's rise from dinosaur to dragon', *Australian*, 29 November 1993, p. 11. See also Nicholas D. Kristof, 'The Rise of China', *Foreign Affairs*, vol. 72, no. 5, November/December 1993, p. 59; and William H. Overholt, *China: The Next Economic Superpower*, Weidenfeld and Nicolson, London, 1993.

11 See, for example, the remarks attributed to Derek da Cunha, Institute of Southeast Asian Studies, Singapore, reported in the *Straits Times*, 28 June 1994; and J.N. Mak, *ASEAN Defence Reorientation 1975–1992: The Dynamics of Modernisation and Structural Change*, Canberra Papers no. 103, Strategic and Defence Studies Centre, Research School of Pacific Studies, Australian National University, Canberra, 1993, pp. 45, 170.

12 'New Ships for the PLAN', *Jane's Defence Weekly*, 18 January 1992, p. 88.

13 Chang Pao-min, 'A New Scramble for the South China Sea Islands', *Contemporary Southeast Asia*, vol. 12, no. 1, June 1990, p. 27; and Sheng Lijun, China's Policy Towards the Spratly Islands in the 1990s, draft paper, with *neibu* documents, May 1994.

14 Duncan Lennox and Arthur Rees (eds), *Jane's Air Launched Weapons*, Jane's Information Group, Surrey, 1989, Issue 11; and International

Institute for Strategic Studies, *The Military Balance 1993*, Brassey's for the IISS, London, p. 154.

15 Michael T. Klare, 'The Next Great Arms Race', *Foreign Affairs*, vol. 72, no. 3, Summer 1993, pp. 136, 141. These goals, however, have been long-standing ones for the PLA. See Gary Klintworth, *China's Modernisation and the Strategic Implications for the Asia-Pacific Region*, Australian Government Publishing Service, Canberra, 1989, pp. 41ff.

16 The agreement was signed during the visit to Beijing of Russian Defence Minister Pavel Grachev on 8 November 1993: Reuters textline, 8 November 1993. The two were 'very secretive' and their military establishments were working 'hand in glove' according to James Lilley, a former United States ambassador to China and Director of Asian Studies of the American Enterprise Institute: *Washington Times*, 12 November 1993, p. 16. China was seeking technology in the area of nuclear submarine propulsion, underwater missile launches, muffling technology for diesel submarines, improving the range and accuracy of ICBMs, triggering devices for nuclear weapons, solid rocket fuel and mobile ICBMs: *Washington Times*, 12 November 1993, p. 16.

17 Klare, 'The Next Great Arms Race'.

18 John Garver, 'China's Push Through the South China Sea: The Interaction of Bureaucratic and National Interests', *China Quarterly*, no. 132, December 1992, p. 999.

19 Martin Petersen, Director, Office of East Asian Analysis, CIA, Hearings of the Joint Economic Committee, US Congress, Washington, USIS Wireless File, 30 July 1993.

20 Xiao Bing and Qing Bo, *Can the Chinese Army Win the Next War?*, published in Chongqing, June 1993, in *Foreign Broadcast Information Service* (hereafter *FBIS*), JPRS Report, 5 May 1994.

21 Mak, *ASEAN Defence Reorientation 1975–1992*, p. 170.

22 Gerald Segal, 'China Changes Shape', *Korean Economic Weekly*, 30 May 1994, pp. 11–15.

23 Freeman was on a visit to Beijing for talks with senior Chinese defence officials: reported in USIS Wireless File, 3 November 1993.

24 Remarks reported in the *South China Morning Post*, 16 May and 4 June 1991 and the *Australian*, 12 July 1991.

25 Lee Kuan Yew, quoted in 'A Sense of Insecurity', *Asiaweek*, 1 June 1994, pp. 24–26.

26 See Fareed Zakaria, 'A Conversation with Lee Kuan Yew', *Foreign Affairs*, vol. 73, no. 2, March/April 1994, p. 109. Ironically, the Singaporean perspective on China is often distorted by Singapore's sensitivity about being perceived as a Chinese state in a Malay sea: Singaporean analysts, therefore, are often unusually critical of China as a threat.

27 *China Post* (Taipei), 12 June 1993.

28 ibid.

29 Shi Ding, 'Outlook for Japan in 1994', *Contemporary International Relations*, no. 52, 20 February 1994, pp. 6–10 in FBIS, JPRS Report, 24 May 1994, pp. 1–3.

30 Toshiki Kaifu, 'Japan's Vision', *Foreign Policy*, no. 80, Fall 1990, p. 28; 'Kaifu Nudges China on Human Rights', *Australian*, 14 August 1991. See also Yoshio Okawara, *Evolving Political and Economic Scenes in Asia*, International Institute for Global Peace, Tokyo, no. 201E, June 1993, pp. 8–9.

31 Russia's strategic outlook is shaped by its history of successive invasions from the west and the east, the death of 20 million during the 'Great Patriotic War', a feeling of vulnerability that stems from the number of borders it has with other countries as well as the fact that it has to defend the Far East as well as the European homelands: Paul Dibb, *The Soviet Union, the Incomplete Superpower*, Macmillan, London, 1986, pp. 7, 9, 21.

32 Former Navy Commander Zhang Lianzhang, quoted in *Renmin Ribao*, in *FBIS China*, 4 August 1988, pp. 24–25.

33 Yang Baibing was formerly Director of the PLA's General Political Department and Secretary General of the Military Affairs Commission. Quoted in *Renmin Ribao*, in *FBIS China*, 5 August 1992, p. 29.

34 You Ji, 'Developments in Maritime Forces — China', in Dick Sherwood (ed.), *Maritime Power in the China Seas: Capabilities and Rationale*, Australian Defence Studies Centre, Australian Defence Force Academy, Canberra, 1994, pp. 85, 105.

35 US Arms Control and Disarmament Agency, *World Military Expenditures and Arms Transfers 1991–91*, US Government Printing Office, Washington, 1994, p. 58.

36 Petersen, Hearings of the Joint Economic Committee.

37 Gerald Segal, from the International Institute for Strategic Studies, London, claims that using the World Bank's purchasing power parity (PPP) formula, China's defence budget may be four to eight times as large at between US$32–72 billion, making it the world's second largest after the United States: Gerald Segal, 'A Changing China and Asia-Pacific Security', paper for the Conference on the Security Dimensions of Chinese Regionalism, IISS/CAPS, Hong Kong, 25–27 June 1993. The PPP formula, essentially, is determined by the price of a hamburger in China compared to the price in America. Vaclav Smil, 'How Rich is China?', *Current History*, vol. 92, no. 575, September 1993, p. 265. The US Arms Control and Disarmament Agency estimated China's defence expenditure in 1991 at US$51 billion: *World Military Expenditures and Arms Transfers 1991–1992*, p. 58.

38 ibid.

39 Thailand's budget increased by 50 per cent over the same period. Bilveer Singh, 'Arms Buildup in Southeast Asia not a Race', *Straits Times*, 20 March 1993; the Philippines' defence budget rose by more than 43 per cent in the last four years: IISS, *The Military Balance*, 1988–89 and 1992–93 editions.

40 Shunji Taoka, 'A Shrinking Tiger', *Bulletin/Newsweek*, 16 November 1993, p. 69.

41 US Arms Control and Disarmament Agency, *World Military Expenditures and Arms Transfers 1991–1992*, US Government Printing Office, Washington, 1994, p. 58.

42 Harlan Jencks, 'Civil–Military Relations in China', *Problems of Communism*, vol. 40, no. 3, May–June 1991, pp. 14, 24.

43 Interview, Senior Colonel Pan Zhenqiang, National Defence University, Beijing, November 1992.

44 *South China Morning Post*, 1 May 1991.

45 China's arms sales are fairly modest. China's problem, however, is that it is allegedly prepared to sell nuclear, missile and chemical weapons technology to countries in disfavour in the West such as Iraq, Iran, Pakistan, Algeria and Syria. For an analysis leading to the conclusion that Chinese arms sales 'threaten US interests' and indicate 'China's long term aspirations to become a more dominant and influential regional and continental power', see R. Bates Gill, *The Challenge of Chinese Arms Proliferation: US Policy for the 1990s*, Strategic Studies Institute, US Army War College, 1993.

46 US Under-Secretary of Defense for Policy, Frank Wisner, press conference, US Embassy, Tokyo, 2 August 1993, USIS Wireless File, 4 August 1993.

47 IISS, *The Military Balance*, 1984–85 and 1992–93 editions; and *Jane's Fighting Ships*, Jane's Information Group, Surrey, 1993 edition.

48 *Weyers Rotten Taschenbuch* (Warships of the World, Warship Documentation), Bernard and Graefe, Federal Republic of Germany, 1990/91, pp. 81, 83; and IISS, *The Military Balance 1993–1994*, p. 169.

49 Harlan W. Jencks, *Some Political and Military Implications of Soviet Warplane Sales to the PRC*, SCPS Papers no. 6, National Sun Yat-Sen University, Kaohsiung, Taiwan, April 1991, p. 1.

50 *Defense Monitor*, Center for Defense Information, vol. 22, no. 6, 1993, p. 4.

51 *China's Growing Military Power and Implications for East Asia*, Pacific Forum/CSIS, Honolulu, August 1993, p. 13.

52 ibid.

53 See Desmond Ball, 'The Post Cold War Maritime Strategic Environment in East Asia', in Sherwood (ed.), *Maritime Power in the China Seas*. See also Zhu Chun, 'Security Problems of the ASEAN States and Southeast Asia', *International Strategic Studies* (Beijing), no. 2, 1993, p. 11.

54 APECO, or Asia-Pacific Economic Co-operation Organisation, is the term used by Chinese Minister for Foreign Trade and Economic Co-operation, Wu Yi, to describe APEC: 'Asia Pacific Economic Co-operation Should Be Developed on the Basis of Equality and Mutual Benefit', *Qiushi*, no. 11, 1 June 1994, p. 7, in *FBIS China*, 28 June 1994, p. 1.

55 Sheldon Simon, 'US Strategy and Southeast Asian Security: Issues of Compatibility', *Contemporary Southeast Asia*, vol. 14, no. 4, March 1993, pp. 301, 313.

56 The SA-10 Grumbles, at US$100 million each, with about 80 missiles altogether, are sufficient to defend perhaps one or two cities against missile attack. They are essentially a defensive system.

57 The Su-27s, presently based at Wuhu in central-east China, have medium-range (40 kilometre) Alamo missiles, compared with the short-range AIM-9s (17 kilometre) on the F-16s, but this edge — and the Su-27s were not necessarily intended for the Taiwan Strait — is balanced by Taiwan's Mirage-2000s, which will have the Mica long-range (55 kilometre) air-to-air missile.

58 According to Colonel Richard Latham, formerly USAF attaché in Hong Kong, and Colonel Kenneth Allen, a former USAF attaché in Beijing, 'Defense Reform in China: The PLA Air Force', *Problems of Communism*, vol. 40, no. 3, May–June 1991, pp. 30, 48.

59 Strict rules apply to arms sales to China with 'all policy making departments in Moscow' involved in the decision-making process. Several deals have been rejected, including one from a Russian factory for the sale of the Backfire bomber. Interviews with the Russian Ambassador, Beijing, 21 October 1992 and a Russian Foreign Ministry official, Canberra, 12 July 1993.

60 Pentagon official, 22 April 1993, quoted by Barbara Opall, 'US, Allies Fear Chinese Buildup', *Defense News*, 26 April–2 May 1993, p. 1. In a similar vein, Australian Foreign Minister Senator Gareth Evans concluded that, while the modernisation of China's armed forces was continuing and their reach and effectiveness would inevitably grow, there was no sign that China would become an aggressive power; China's military posture was land-based and essentially defensive, its navy was suited only to coastal operations and its air force was primarily defensive: 'Australia's Regional Security Environment', in Desmond Ball and David Horner (eds), *Strategic Studies in a Changing World: Global, Regional and Australian Perspectives*, Canberra Papers on Strategy and Defence, no. 89, Strategic and Defence Studies Centre, Research School of Pacific Studies, Australian National University, 1992.

61 Mak, *ASEAN Defence Reorientation 1975–1992*, p. 44.

62 J.N. Mak 'The Chinese Navy and the South China Sea: A Malaysian Assessment', *Pacific Review*, vol. 4, no. 2, 1991, pp. 158–59.

63 Greg Austin, Island Claims of the PRC, unpublished Master's thesis, Australian National University, Canberra, 1985.

64 For an excellent overview and analysis of the Chinese perspective on the South China Sea, see Sheng Lijun, 'China's Policy Towards the Spratly Islands in the 1990s'.

65 *South China Morning Post*, 19 July 1991.

66 Sheng Lijun, 'China's Policy Towards the Spratly Islands in the 1990s'.

67 *China Post*, Taipei, 20 July 1991.

68 ibid.

69 Li Peng said China wanted a peaceful solution to the Spratlys issue by proposing joint development while shelving the sovereignty issues. *Far*

Eastern Economic Review, 30 August 1990. Foreign Minister Qian Qichen said China would settle border disputes through 'the process of patient negotiations in a friendly atmosphere' and if 'an agreement cannot be reached in a short period of time, China was willing to put the contradiction aside for the time being' and in the case of the Nanshas, China would consider 'joint exploitation under conditions of Chinese sovereignty': *Xinhua*, Beijing, 28 March 1991.

70 Wo-Lap Lam, 'Senior Generals Involved in Foreign Affairs', *South China Morning Post*, 25 June 1994, pp. 40–41. A similar point is made by You Ji, 'Developments in Maritime Forces — China', pp. 85, 103–4.

71 China, for example, caused mild heartburn in the region in February 1992 by setting out its legal claims to offshore islands in the South and East China Seas, and its right to use military force to prevent violations of its sovereignty. Similar concern arose with China's occupation of Mischief Reef in February 1995: *Straits Times*, 27 February 1992.

72 Winston Lord, Assistant Secretary of State for East Asian and Pacific Affairs, speech in Washington, 13 October 1993, in USIS Wireless File, 14 October 1993.

73 Surjit Mansingh, 'India–China Relations in the Post-Cold War Era', *Asian Survey*, vol. 34, no. 3, March 1994, p. 285.

74 Gary Klintworth, *The Practice of Common Security: China's Borders with Russia and India*, Working Paper no. 1993/1, Department of International Relations, Research School of Pacific Studies, Australian National University, January 1993. However, India still perceives China to be a competitor for regional influence in South Asia. This is reflected in India's suspicions about Chinese arms sales to countries in South Asia, Chinese roadbuilding activities in Yunnan province towards Burma and what might be interpreted as a thrust to the Andaman Sea, and China's alleged naval facilities on Burma's Coco Islands, in the Andaman Sea. See, for example, Rahul Roy Chaudhury, 'The Chinese Navy and Indian Security', *Indian Defence Review*, vol. 9, no. 1, January 1994, pp. 51, 54, and, in this volume, J. Mohan Malik, Chapter 8, 'India's Relations With China Post Soviet Union'.

75 Klintworth, *The Practice of Common Security*.

76 British Broadcasting Corporation, *Summary of World Broadcasts*, FE/1780 G/2, 31 August 1993.

77 There was, for example, an exchange of small arms fire between Vietnamese and a Chinese fishing boat in the Gulf of Tonkin on 2 July 1994: press release, Embassy of Vietnam, Canberra, 7 July 1994.

78 The Asia Society, 'China and the Region', *Williamsburg Conference*, Zhongshan, China, March 1993, p. 21.

79 See Bill Powell, 'Asia's Power Struggle', *Bulletin/Newsweek*, 16 November 1993, p. 60.

80 Michael Oksenberg, President of the East-West Center, Honolulu, quoted in USIS Wireless File, 23 September 1993; and Allen Whiting, *China*

Eyes Japan, University of California Press, Berkeley, 1989 are even more optimistic.

81 Kyodo News Agency, Tokyo, 21 November 1993.

82 US Defence Department, *A Strategic Framework for the Asia-Pacific Rim*, Report to Congress, Washington, 1992.

83 Shunji Taoka, 'A Shrinking Tiger', p. 69. This is not to say that Japan has no concerns about China's defence modernisation. Japanese strategic analysts worry about China's naval capabilities and vetoed the sale of British air-to-air refuelling technology to China in COCOM in January 1989 because of its significance for China's power projection capability: Harlan W. Jencks, 'China's Defence Buildup: A Threat to the Region?' in Richard Yang (ed.), *China's Military: The PLA in 1992/1993*, Chinese Council for Advanced Policy Studies, Taipei, 1993, pp. 95, 106.

84 Defence spending was marginally increased in rupee terms, but taking into account the most recent 18 per cent devaluation, it showed a US$3 billion cut from the US$9.2 billion that India spent on defence in 1990/91: *Canberra Times*, 26 July 1991 and discussions with Dr A. Gordon, Strategic and Defence Studies Centre, Research School of Pacific Studies, Australian National University, Canberra, 9 October 1991.

85 'India Puts Outlays on Army in Mothballs', *Australian*, 12 March 1992, p. 8.

86 *Free China Review*, June 1993, pp. 42–43. President Lien Chan pointed out that the military had started a five-year personnel reduction plan in 1989, cutting the armed forces by 20 000 to 500 000 with further cuts expected.

87 Pacific Economic Co-operation Council, Sixth Economic Forecast, Washington, 8 June 1994, in USIS Wireless File, Canberra, 9 June 1994.

88 See, for example, the remarks attributed to Paul Dibb in a speech to the Institute of Public Affairs and the Heritage Foundation in Canberra on 15 July 1992, reported in the *Canberra Times*, 16 July 1992; and remarks attributed to Ross Babbage at the Chief of General Staff's Land Warfare Conference, Darwin, 7 April 1992, reported in the *Australian*, 8 April 1992.

89 See Mak, *ASEAN Defence Reorientation 1975–1992*, p. 142.

90 Wisner, press conference.

91 Graeme Cheeseman and Richard Leaver, 'Trends in Arms Spending and Conventional Arms Trade in the Asian-Pacific Region', in Gary Kintworth (ed.), *Asia-Pacific Security: Less Uncertainty, New Opportunities*, Longman, Melbourne, 1995.

92 See Paul H. Kreisberg, Daniel Y. Chiu and Jerome H. Kahan, *Threat Perceptions in Asia and the Role of the Major Powers: A Workshop Report*, East West Center, Honolulu, 1993.

93 Wisner, press conference; and Malaysian Prime Minister Mahathir Mohammad claimed that increased arms purchases by Asian countries are a consequence of their improved finances and there was no arms race in the region. Mahathir was speaking at the 27th meeting of PBEC in Kuala Lumpur, 23 May 1994: Reuters Wire Service, 23 May 1994.

94 Desmond Ball 'Arms and Affluence', *International Security*, vol. 18, no. 3, Winter 1993–94, p. 78. The appearance of an arms race has been fuelled by the liberalised arms sales policies of the United States and Russia. Both have surplus equipment and capacity. The United States, for example, reversed its long-standing policy of refusing to sell Harpoon missiles and F-16 aircraft to Taiwan. Russia has been willing to sell sophisticated weapons to China, Malaysia and Thailand. Australia, too, has an active defence sales program in Asia. China, for its part, has been a major arms supplier for Thailand and Burma.

95 Ruth Leger Sivard, *World Military and Social Expenditures 1993*, 15th edition, Publications of World Priorities, Washington, 1993, p. 44.

96 ibid.

97 Malaysia's Deputy Prime Minister, Anwar Ibrahim, reported in the *Nation* (Kuala Lumpur), 7 June 1994.

98 Evans, 'Australia's Regional Security Environment'.

99 Australian Minister for Defence, Robert Ray, quoted in the *Canberra Times*, 19 November 1993.

100 As the Indonesian Ambassador to Australia, Sabam Siagian, observed in Canberra recently, the idea of a power vacuum in the Asia-Pacific as a consequence of a reduced United States presence 'belittles the capacity of the regional countries to manage their own security', not only through alliance formation and the procurement of military equipment but also through 'the strengthening of ... national and regional resilience': Sabam Siagian, National Press Club address, 18 September 1991.

101 Carl Ford, 'Co-operative Vigilance Essential to Asian Security', National Defence University Pacific Symposium, East Asia and Pacific Wireless, File no. 044, 6 March 1991.

102 Chinese Foreign Minister Qian Qichen, 'China Ready to Take Part in Asian Security Dialogues', *Beijing Review*, vol. 36, no. 32, 9–15 August, 1993, pp. 8–9.

103 A condition known in China as socialism with Chinese characteristics.

104 American concerns about a downward spiral in Sino-United States relations are reflected in, for example, Barber B. Conable and David M. Lampton, 'China the Coming Power', *Foreign Affairs*, vol. 71, no. 5, Winter 1992, p. 133.

105 Kennedy, *Preparing for the Twenty First Century*, p. 190.

106 In 1990, China was ranked 115th in the world with per capita income of US$317 compared with Taiwan, in 36th place with US$4780, and Australia, in 21st place with US$12 446: Sivard, *World Military and Social Expenditures*, p. 48.

107 For a pessimistic outlook for China, see Richard Hornik, 'Bursting China's Bubble', *Foreign Affairs*, vol. 73, no. 3, May/June 1994, p. 28. On China's spiritual dilemmas, see Liu Binyan, *China's Crisis, China's Hope* (trans. Howard Goldblat), Harvard University Press, Cambridge, Mass., 1990. On the environment and population issues, see Hu Angang and

Zou Ping, *China's Population Development*, China's Science and Technology Press, Beijing, 1991; Hu Angang et al., *Survival and Development*, Science Press, Beijing, 1992; and Vaclav Smil, *China's Environmental Crisis: An Inquiry Into the Limits of National Development*, M.E. Sharpe, Armonk, NY, 1993.

108 See, for example, Robert Scalapino, 'China in the Late Leninist Era', *China Quarterly*, no. 136, 1993, pp. 949, 963; and Gerald Segal, 'China Changes Shape', *Foreign Affairs*, vol. 73, no. 3, May/June 1994, pp. 43, 56.

15 China and the Regional Economy

Christopher Findlay[1]

Introduction

The patterns and determinants of, along with the prospects for, China's links with the rest of East Asia are the topics of this chapter. The purpose is to provide material for the context in which other strategic issues can be discussed. As Stuart Harris points out in his introduction, China's size and geographical position mean that economic growth in China has great regional and global significance. One question examined here is the sustainability of growth in China. The horizon for this and related questions is the turn of the century.

Size is not the only feature which will matter. Also important is the path, or reform process, taken by China. The reform process will have important internal political implications which are beyond the scope of this chapter. It will also have impacts on China's international economic relations. The key aspects here include the volume of China's trade, its composition and the country patterns involved. Another key aspect is the flows of capital into and out of China. Examination of these aspects of reform and growth make up the bulk of this chapter.

Other aspects of reform are also given attention. One is the regional economic differences within China and how these might affect China's international economic relations. A second is the strategy of pursuing so-called sub-regional development strategies. A third is the environmental impacts of China's growth which will include international impacts. The resolution of environmental issues in East Asia will depend on co-operation with China. While a great deal of attention has been paid to China's trading relationships with East Asia and the rest of the world, less has been given to environmental issues. They could be even more important and even more contentious, as noted in Chapter 17.

It is often observed that analysis of events in China gains more insight if it takes account of regional differences within China and that China is one state made up of many economies. An attempt to capture the flavour of this point is made here. But it is also argued that the external economic boundary of China is becoming less clear compared with the situation a decade ago. Growth in China has had some special features which have made the Chinese economy much more highly integrated with the rest of East Asia than has been the case in the other industrialising economies in the region. This must also have implications for the 'regional and global significance of China's growth'.

Chinese growth

China has grown relatively rapidly over the last decade. Figure 15.1 shows real Chinese GDP growth rates over that period. Compared with real growth in other developing economies, China's growth rate in absolute terms has shown some wild fluctuations — an important feature of its development which has implications for the rest of the region. However, the trend level is much higher than for other developing economies. The average growth rate since the reforms began has been about 9 per cent per year in real terms. The Chinese economy is nearly four times bigger than it was in 1978. If this growth rate were sustained — a question examined below in more detail — then by the year 2000, China would be over seven times bigger than in 1978.

How big is 'big'? According to the World Bank, the Chinese economy in 1991 was about 6.5 per cent of the size of that of the United States and about 11 per cent of that of Japan. It accounted for about 1.7 per cent of world output.[2]

In 1991 dollars, income in China is estimated by the World Bank to be about US$370.[3] With real output growing at over 9 per cent a year and population growing at about 1.5 per cent a year, then real incomes on average would be expected to increase by 7.5 per cent a year. In that case, incomes

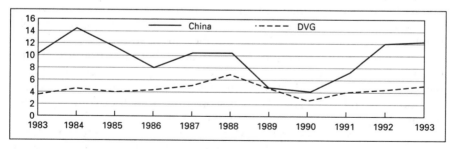

Figure 15.1   Real GDP growth rate, China vs developing economy average, 1983–93 (%)

per person would more than double every decade. The population in China is about 1.15 billion, so this increase in incomes represents a large increment to purchasing power in East Asia.

The size of those real incomes may be understated by the official statistics, even those calculated according to standard national accounting practices. Data such as GNP values are commonly used in analysis of the determinants of military spending for example. Many studies have found a close relationship between military spending and GNP.[4] A recent paper on the connection between defence spending and economic growth in China did not uncover a strong relationship.[5] The lack of relationship may be due to the difficulties in measuring income, and therefore growth, in China.

Ma and Garnaut have sought to revise the estimates of Chinese GDP per head by comparing patterns of consumption in China with those in other developing economies at similar stages of development. On the basis of these comparisons, they estimate that Chinese actual income per head is two to three times higher than is officially reported. Changes in this sort of measurement error over time could also affect reported growth rates and therefore the analysis of the relationship to defence spending.[6] These are topics for further work.

Prospects for growth

These prognoses for the size of the Chinese economy depend on assumptions about the maintenance of relatively high growth rates in China. Are these assumptions warranted? Could growth rates be expected to fall?

Bangs for a buck

There are a number of factors which are associated with a slowdown in growth. One is that the return to investment falls. In the early stages of development, when capital-to-labour ratios in production tend to be relatively low, a dollar of investment has a high output yield. As capital is accumulated, this yield declines and there is a natural constraint on growth. Is this an issue in China? It seems unlikely. China is still operating at relatively low levels of income per head. This number can be interpreted as a reflection of the relative contributions of capital and labour to value added. The low aggregate value added (i.e. GDP) per head (a proxy for the number of workers involved in production) indicates that the capital intensity of production is also relatively low. There is scope, therefore, for a continuing significant 'bang for a buck' of investment in China.

To put this proposition in context, consider some of the other East Asian economies. As the recent World Bank review of the East Asian economies points out, they have maintained relatively high growth rates for a number of decades.[7]

Factor productivity

Other determinants of growth include the productivity with which the factors of production are employed in China. This will be determined by the technology used to combine those inputs and the proximity between actual and potential output from any particular technology. These issues have been subject to intensive empirical investigation and the results are not always clear. However, it could not be argued that Chinese firms are generally at 'the frontier', either in terms of their use of existing technology or their access to technologies available in the rest of the world and which suit their factor endowments.

Within the agriculture sector (which now accounts for about 30 per cent of GDP), it has been argued that there is still scope for productivity growth (e.g. from plot consolidation and changes in land tenure arrangements).[8] The extent of this potential is a topic for further work.

Within the industrial sector, it is important to make a distinction between state-owned enterprises, which still operate to some extent within the planning system and which have relatively soft budget constraints, and those which operate outside the plan. The former now account for only about 52 per cent of industrial output, compared with 31 per cent in the rural enterprise sector and 17 per cent in the category of 'other', which includes joint ventures. To this extent, the Chinese economy could now be described as 'mixed', although the nature of the Chinese ownership of enterprises operating outside the plan is not strictly private (that is, in terms of there being a market in the equity in those enterprises).[9]

Total factor productivity growth in rural industrial enterprises was much higher than that in the state sector (5.5 per cent compared with 1.8 per cent over the reform period). Thus, not only have the input volumes grown rapidly in rural enterprise, but also the productivity with which they are used is high. This outcome is likely to be due to the special structural features of the rural sector enterprises, in particular their ownership, control and market orientation.

Productivity growth is distinguished from efficiency, which can be defined to refer to the difference between the actual output of an enterprise and its potential output. More efficient firms produce closer to their potential output. Assessments of efficiency defined in this way have found that rural enterprises are less efficient than urban enterprises — that is, rural enterprises on average produce a smaller proportion of their potential output than do urban enterprises. However, two other points should be noted. First, the output levels of both rural and urban enterprises have been estimated to lie in the range of 50 to 70 per cent of their potential. Second, the efficiency analysis refers only to output, not sales. Urban enterprises have also been criticised for the production of unsaleable products, the accumulation of stocks and therefore of losses and debts.

While there has been a gap between rural and urban performance in terms of output, the results of the analysis of productivity growth reported above indicate that the gap has been closing. Therefore, while the static picture suggests that rural enterprises are in some dimensions less efficient than urban ones, they are catching up to urban enterprises in terms of their efficiency performance. It should also be stressed that there is significant variation in rural enterprise performance between industrial activities and between regions. This variation qualifies any generalisations.

Given their market orientation, rural enterprises might be expected to be more efficient. This may be the case in terms of producing goods and services in demand, but the efficiency with which they produce those items appears to have been affected by other forces. Some of the factors involved include the age of the firm and the experience and skill levels of the workforce. Another is the location of rural enterprises, since those located in more industrialised areas tend to be more efficient. Some rural enterprises suffer from loss of economies of agglomeration. In some cases, there are also severe constraints on rural enterprises, especially on their access to inputs. Despite their market orientation, markets for inputs may not be well developed. Firms may face shortages and in that situation are, not surprisingly, observed to be less efficient.

Another factor affecting the efficiency of rural enterprises may be the influence of local government in their operations in pursuit of objectives other than profit. While it may be significant in explaining the gap between actual and potential output, it may not explain the difference in performance between rural and urban enterprises since the latter are subject to similar, if not worse, management and ownership incentive problems, given the softer budget constraint of urban sector firms.

In summary, within the industrial sector, both further reforms in the management of state-owned firms and technology transfers (including those from the state to out-of-plan sectors as well as from offshore to either sector) will add to productivity growth.

Other factors

There will be other factors which affect the rate of growth of the Chinese economy. These include various aspects of inter-regional relations and macroeconomic control which are discussed below. The contribution from the external sector to growth is another issue which is discussed in the next section, and which will be the important mechanisms via which China's relationships with the rest of East Asia develop over this time period. There are yet other factors which have been highlighted by the World Bank's review of the East Asian miracle,[10] such as investment in education, which are beyond the scope of this chapter.

Growth and trade

Growth of the Chinese economy has been associated with a rapid growth of exports. Figure 15.2 shows the rate of growth of exports compared to GDP growth. Figure 15.3 shows the ratio of exports to GDP using official data

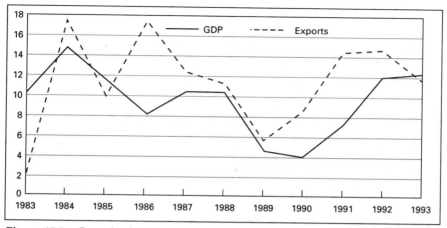

Figure 15.2 Growth of GDP versus exports, China 1983–93 (%)

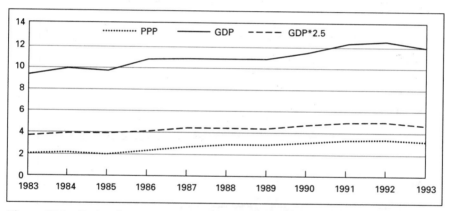

Figure 15.3 Ratio of exports to GDP, China 1983–93 (%)

and using adjusted GDP data. A ratio of exports to GDP of about 16 per cent is relatively large for a big country. The ratio for India is 9 per cent, for example. This is a further indication that the Chinese GDP number is too low. When revised by the Garnaut/Ma factor of 2.5, the exports to GDP ratio falls to the expected number of about 7 per cent.

The exports-to-GDP ratio is an indicator of the extent to which the benefits of trade can contribute to growth. These include the benefits of the exploitation of the gains from specialisation and trade, from the impact of trade on competition and thereby productivity performance in the domestic market and from the access to technologies embodied in imports.

China's direct trade is highly concentrated within the East Asian region. Figure 15.4 illustrates the breakdown of the destinations of exports and Figure 15.5 shows the origin of imports. East Asia (including Australia/New Zealand) accounts for about 48 per cent of exports and 55 per cent of imports. These shares are relatively high compared with those of other East Asian economies.

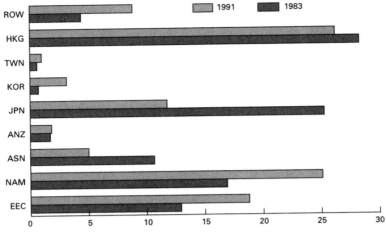

Figure 15.4 Destinations of China's exports, 1983, 1992 (%)

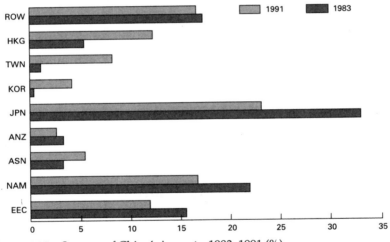

Figure 15.5 Sources of China's imports, 1983, 1991 (%)

One complication in the analysis of China's trade directions is the role of Hong Kong as an entrepôt. In 1991, about 52 per cent of goods exported to Hong Kong were re-exported. The trade data reported in Figures 15.4 and 15.5 have been reallocated to final destinations or origins.

While the relative shares may differ, China has in common with other East Asian economies the important role of the high-income economies in its exports. Japan now accounts for about 12 per cent (half of its share a decade ago). Over the 1980s, the importance of North America and the European Community (EC) in China's exports has risen. North America now accounts for a quarter of its exports. The vital interest that China has in maintaining access to those markets is taken up again in the later section on GATT, APEC and MFN.

China's share of world trade is larger than its GDP share, but that share is still small in absolute terms. It accounts for about 2.2 per cent of world trade and so, at this level of aggregation, China looks like a small country in world trade. What it does will not much affect world markets and its own actions will attract little attention, according to this perspective.

Clearly, however, China is not regarded as a small player. The reason is the difference between its position in aggregate and in particular markets. The point is often made that, even though only a small share of output or consumption of a particular product in China might be traded, those volumes might account for large shares of world trade. Drysdale and Elek,[11] applying a methodology of Findlay, Phillips and Tyers,[12] estimate that by the year 2000 China in one scenario could account for 15 per cent of world clothing exports, about a third of world exports of toys and of cotton fabric and over a quarter of world exports of travel goods.

Policy change in those industries in China will therefore have effects on the rest of the world. The domestic reform process in China, such as the extent to which domestic markets are open to imports, does attract a lot of attention.

There is another source of feedback from the world market into the allocation of resources in and the growth of the Chinese economy. Rapid export growth can, in principle, lead to changes in relative prices of exports and imports. These so-called terms of trade effects reduce the gains from opening up the economy to the rest of the world.

The particular resource endowments of the Chinese economy (relatively large endowment of labour relative to capital and to land) suggest an export specialisation in labour-intensive products. This is not surprising given that China accounts for about 22 per cent of world population and at most 9 per cent of cultivable world land area. This situation is reflected in the indices of revealed comparative advantage for China.[13] These also show that the degree of specialisation of labour intensive products has increased over the reform period. As stressed by other authors, the reform process has shifted China's trade pattern closer to its underlying comparative advantage.[14] This development is driven, to a large extent, by the growth of the out-of-plan sector.

The emergence of China as a supplier of such products has forced adjustments on competitor suppliers. Is there enough space in the markets for labour-intensive products — for example, to accommodate the Chinese exports? Empirical work on this issue puts it into context. It is not sensible to think about the terms of trade problem by assessing the impact of the growth of Chinese exports holding everything else constant. In that case, the terms of trade effects would appear to be startling. The context, in East Asia in particular, is a simultaneous reform process or else a high degree of openness in other economies. Chinese export growth then becomes part of a 'virtuous circle' where the emergence of China forces adjustment on other economies. Their departure from their old markets makes way for Chinese exporters. The growth in demand for importables in China opens up new markets for the other economies.

Export growth, when it is the result of cuts in protection and when it occurs simultaneously in a number of economies, can actually be mutually reinforcing.[15] Increases in exports lead to higher incomes, which lead to higher import demand from other economies. Liberalisation therefore becomes a source of growth in demand within the group of liberalising economies. All economies also gain from access to imports at lower prices. In addition, economies can specialise in the production of particular products which they export and yet at the same time be importers of the items in the same broad commodity group.

The more important constraint on export performance in China is a protectionist response by the high-income economies faced by a surge of imports from China. As noted already, the importance of the EC and North America in China's exports has increased from about 30 per cent to about 44 per cent since 1983. This surge in supply has created some adjustment problems in those markets and led to demands for protectionist responses. Herein lies the significance of the debate in the United States about the application of the MFN principle to China. This is discussed below.

Growth and foreign investment

The inflow of foreign capital is an important source of growth for a number of reasons. It augments the stock of domestic capital. It carries with it technology and management practices which raise the productivity of the factors of production in the host economy. It can also change the political economy of protectionist policy making in the home country of the capital to favour keeping markets open for exports of the host economy.

Capital inflow into China is booming. According to the *China Daily*, contracts were signed in the first nine months of 1993 for a total value of US$83 billion, but of that only US$15 billion has been realised so far. This ratio of 18 per cent is about the same as the rate for 1992 but much lower than earlier years (i.e. before the crash of the economy in 1989). It could simply reflect the lags involved in getting projects underway. It may also reflect current macroeconomic policy, which is making it more difficult for the partners to find finance.

Other sources indicate that up to the end of 1992, there was an accumulated foreign investment in China of US$35 billion so an increment of another US$15 billion or more in 1993 is a significant change.[16] There are some measurement problems involved in the compilation of the DFI data.[17] Zhang and Tracy report an estimate that, while the official inflow in 1992 was about US$11 billion, the actual inflow may have been closer to US$8 billion.

The 70 000 foreign-funded enterprises that existed in China at the end of 1992 are estimated to account for 20 per cent of China's exports, compared with 17 per cent in 1991 and 5 per cent in 1988.

Where is the capital coming from? Zhang and Tracy report the five largest sources of direct foreign investment in China in 1992 were, in order, Hong

Kong/Macau, Taiwan, the United States, Japan and Korea.[18] Taiwan's position jumped from fourth to second compared with 1991 (although in 1991 some of its investment may have been made via Hong Kong). A special feature of capital flows into China is their origins within East Asia, and more importantly from newly industrialising economies in East Asia. At least 70 per cent of the capital inflow comes from these economies.[19]

Another feature of this capital flow, according to Zhang and Tracy, is that it is predominantly managed by overseas Chinese. By country of origin, their contribution to capital inflow into China is about three times that of the United States and Japan. Their role is obvious in the cases of other East Asian industrialising economies. In addition, overseas Chinese families and companies from Southeast Asia are increasing their rate of investment (or 'accelerating'), but since much of this is routed through Hong Kong, their precise contributions are hard to quantify. The same may apply to investments from North America. However, Zhang and Tracy also note that, in 1992, investments in China by larger firms and well-known multinationals increased more rapidly. The average size of projects also increased.

The role of Japan is interesting. Japan accounts for about 13 per cent of the total capital inflow into China. This is smaller than its share of capital inflow into some other East Asian economies, where Japan has accounted for a third to a half of the capital inflow.[20]

In summary, these data indicate a rapid integration of China with the world economy through investment flows, and more recently a greater degree of integration of Chinese manufacturing into regional patterns of intra-industry trade. This process has been led by overseas Chinese communities in the newly industrialising economies with a relatively smaller role for Japanese investors, traditionally a much more important source of funds for East Asian industrialisation. There are signs of an increasing role being played by the traditional multinational corporations.

One state — many economies

The Chinese economy has so far been treated as one economy whereas there are significant regional variations. One aspect is the differences between rural and urban China which were discussed earlier in relation to industrial growth. Depending on the issue, it is useful to take various cross-sections of the Chinese state and consider the possible economic relationships that might emerge and which might affect China's relations with the rest of the world.

Another aspect of regional variations is the differing degrees of international orientation of the various regions of China. About 40 per cent of the foreign capital inflow goes to Guangdong province. Other major destinations are Fujian, Jiangsu, Shandong, Liaoning and Shanghai. Investments in Jiangsu and Shandong are led by projects involving rural enterprises.

A simple indicator of the differences between regions is the differing degrees of export orientation of China's provinces. Figure 15.6 shows the provincial

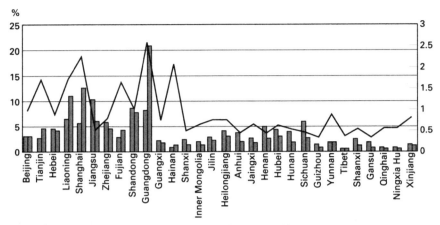

Figure 15.6 Provincial shares of GVO and exports, China, 1989

shares of output (as indicated by the gross value of output), exports and the ratio of the export share to the output share (on the right-hand scale) in 1989.

The export data suffers from the same problem as that of Hong Kong, since the coastal provinces (the first eleven categories in the chart) may simply be providing entrepôt services for the centre and the west. However, their shares of exports are generally much higher relative to their output shares than in the central or western regions. The outliers are Tianjin, Liaoning, Shanghai, Fujian, Guangdong and Hainan.[21]

Watson and Wu also discuss some important variations in the reform and development process between regions of China. An important aspect of the variation in the growth of rural enterprises has been their role as a source of disparities in rural incomes. The overall effect has been to improve the position of the countryside in absolute terms, but inter-regional disparities have also tended to increase. Policies which compensate for some of the problems of the interior regions are likely to receive more attention in China so as to reduce the potential for worsening economic disparities to worsen political conflicts.[22]

Regional differences are important for a number of other reasons. First, the pattern of specialisation and trade within China will affect China's international trade flows. One issue is, for example, whether the development of the coastal region and a movement of population towards coastal China will shift the relative factor endowments to such an extent that the western regions of China will tend to specialise in resource-intensive products which they supply to the coastal provinces. This shift is accelerated by the transfer of rural land into industrial and other urban uses in the coastal provinces.

It might be the case, on the other hand, that even if the population movements are large in absolute terms, the relationship between coastal China and the hinterland is closer to that between two resource-poor economies, one of which has relatively more capital than the other. Even if the first scenario did emerge, it is not clear how long it would be before the accumulation of capital in the hinterland of China would see a shift on to a similar pattern of specialisation to that of the coastal regions. There are some uncertainties, therefore, in how the pattern of China's international trade will be affected by the developments within China.

Regional differences in development can also create some problems for the reform process, which has involved a devolution of power to lower levels. Regional governments have sought to protect their own industrial sectors and to compete for the available investment funds, including foreign funds. The former was more important in the period of relatively large distortions in prices in the planning system, particularly between prices of raw materials and processed products.[23] The latter has since become more important — for example, the creation of special development zones which offer concessional terms for infrastructure services to investors.

The World Bank has stressed the connection between regional governments' autonomy and the national macroeconomic problems in China. Apart from the fiscal implications of funding the losses of enterprises in the state sector, the expenditure patterns of governments with local autonomy (either their own spending or their contributions to investment in their areas) have been identified as major contributors to swings in the macroeconomic performance of the economy. The links between reform, decentralisation and macro stability are the subject of continuing research.

In summary, these regional differences will affect China's economic relations with the rest of the world, either directly through impacts on trade patterns, and through their indirect effects on policy-making in China on issues such as positions on trade, protection policy and foreign investment. Some parts of China are already highly integrated with the rest of the world, especially the nearby economies in East Asia. Their attitudes to policy issues may differ from regions which are less internationalised. There are also important links between regional autonomy and the macroeconomic performance of the Chinese economy which affect its cyclical behaviour and can also affect long-run growth.

Growth triangles

The emergence of the so-called growth triangles in East Asia has been matched by the boom in the literature on the topic.[24] The main sub-regional area within China has been called the Greater South China Economic Zone, which includes southern coastal China (mainly Guangdong and Fujian provinces), Hong Kong and Taiwan. As already illustrated, there are relatively intense flows of capital and trade within this area.

Chia and Lee argue that the development of the growth triangles like that observed in southern China is driven by factors such as economic complementarity, the availability of uncongested infrastructure, the policy framework and the encouragement it gives (via ownership, tax and foreign exchange arrangements) to capital inflow and market access (either to a large home market or unrestricted access to export markets).[25] Such items would be part of the checklist of any multinational corporation based in a high-income economy and looking for a new production site, whether they were considering an investment in Guangdong or in Uruguay.

All the items on this checklist are relevant in southern China, but some other force must explain the regional concentration of capital flows. There must be extra benefits of proximity. This is not immediately obvious in these days of rapid change in communications and transport technologies — which, it has been argued, is one of the factors contributing to the global boom in direct foreign investment flows from the second half of the 1980s.[26]

Chia and Lee highlight some important aspects of proximity in the case of southern China.[27] Proximity can still lower transport costs, either for management personnel or for the products of the process. Proximity means less time is involved in transport, which also lowers costs. The value of the savings in time and/or from proximity, they argue, is even greater in the era of so-called flexible production systems. Flexible systems (compared with mass production) are characterised by low inventories, short lead times, low prices and wide product choice.

Secondly, proximity may also mean that the areas involved have greater cultural affinity and important kinship ties (the latter was stressed in the discussion of direct foreign investment flows). These lower the costs of doing business.

Thirdly, there are some special features in the case of Hong Kong and Taiwan which bring benefits from integration with the mainland. Their economic relationships will condition their future political relationships with the mainland. In addition, they will have established alliances with regional political interests within China who can help argue their case in Beijing. Chia and Lee regard the southern China economic zone as being 'market driven' since the main actors are the enterprises involved. However, there are side-effects with regard to long-term political relations which are of interest to governments. Superficially, though, according to policy on matters such as capital flows, the Hong Kong government has been more supportive of the development of the regional economy than has Taiwan.

One feature of the relationship with Hong Kong which it is important to stress here is consistent with the theme of the fuzzy boundaries between China and the rest of the region. The shift to an open door policy in China and the scope for greater contact between China and the rest of the world might be expected to lead to less of a role for an intermediary like Hong Kong. In fact, the share of China's exports which were re-exported via Hong Kong rose from 8.3 per cent in 1981 to 38 per cent in 1991. If goods which are transhipped via Hong Kong are included, then this share rises to about 56 per cent (1990). About half of China's imports are re-exported or transhipped via Hong Kong. Also, the share of China as an origin in Hong Kong's total re-exports rose from 28 per cent in 1980 to 59 per cent in 1991.[28] As Sung explains, the proliferation of trading channels actually increased the demand for intermediation channels.[29]

MFN, GATT and APEC

The picture presented so far is of a Chinese economy which is highly integrated with the rest of East Asia. This is because of the concentration of trade flows and, more recently, of capital flows. The latter is especially important in southern China.

Despite this regional concentration of trade, it is still the case that a large proportion of China's exports in absolute terms goes to the United States in particular. As explained above, these exports tend to be dominated by labour-intensive products, a surge of which into a high income economy creates substantial pressures for adjustments in industries which traditionally are powerful actors in protectionist politics. China has a greater interest in obtaining Most Favoured Nation (MFN) treatment for its products into markets like the United States. Various United States political interests have also taken a great interest in the extension of MFN rules to China and the debate has been joined with other items, such as the pursuit of the United States' human rights agenda.

China will therefore benefit from a reduction in the uncertainties surrounding its access to markets for exports. It will also benefit from the assurances in markets for its imports, which are likely to include resource-based products, especially food,[30] but also steel.[31]

Drysdale and Elek discuss the role of APEC and of GATT membership for China in dealing with these issues. Membership of the General Agreement on Tariffs and Trade (GATT), they argue, will provide China with a firmer commitment that it will be treated by its trading partners according to the non-discriminatory rules of the trading system. It will also give China access to a rules-based system of dispute resolution. It could appeal, for example, against the sorts of measures that might be taken by its trading partners to protect local interests against the surge of Chinese exports. The application process will also accelerate and reinforce the reform process within China. Finally, a deeper integration of China into world markets will not only benefit China, but also its trading partners.[32]

As Drysdale and Elek explain, GATT membership will not necessarily solve the MFN issue with the United States.[33] A combination of United States legislation and GATT rules (especially for qualified membership) still makes it possible to deny MFN status to new GATT members.

Asia-Pacific Economic Co-operation (APEC) can play a complementary role, Drysdale and Elek argue. About 80 per cent of China's trade is with APEC members. They are affected by and can gain by China's openness to trade and investment. APEC can serve a role of increasing the regional awareness of the likely impacts of Chinese growth. In more detail, it can generate some specific proposals for dealing with the technical issues associated with GATT membership for China. It can also discuss a formula for timing the entry of both China and Taiwan, both of whom are APEC members. APEC can serve other functions as well, for example, anticipating then dealing with other potential bottlenecks to trade in the region, such as the transport infrastructure required to accommodate Chinese exports and imports. Another important potential role of APEC in relation to China is discussed in the next section.

Environmental constraints[34]

Some of the most heavily polluted cities in the world include Beijing and Shenyang. Groundwater quality is falling in parts of China. Toxic wastes are being dumped in rivers in the region, a special issue in China. Land degradation rates are very high in some parts of East Asia, especially Vietnam but also China.

Many environmental issues are associated with energy consumption in China where the energy intensity of output is among the highest in the world. Per capita energy consumption is only about 40 per cent of the world average and 6 per cent of that of the United States.[35] But the energy consumption per unit of GDP is about twice the level of the OECD countries. China is the third largest energy consumer in the world after the United States and the former Soviet Union. The state of the technology available for processing energy raw materials contributes not only to the volumes of materials consumed but also high rates of emissions of gases like CO_2 and other atmospheric pollutants.[36]

The environmental effects of development will attract increasing domestic and international attention. While environmental issues may not appear to be high on the Chinese agenda at present, it is likely that they will become more important over the next decade. This will occur for both domestic and international reasons. Rising incomes in China will, it is expected, lead to increasing demand for environmental quality. Radetski provides empirical evidence that increasing levels of economic activity are linked to improved environmental conditions. He identifies the high income elasticity of demand for environmental quality, compositional shifts towards cleaner economic activities at higher income levels and the extension of property rights combined with the development of policies to deal with global common externalities in more developed economies as key factors explaining this relationship.[37] Empirical research also supports a positive relationship between economic growth and environmental quality, beyond a threshold income level.[38] There will, as a consequence, be internal pressure within China for change towards 'cleaner' manufacturing processes.

There is also international interest in the environmental impacts of industrialisation in China. Acid rain is one of the major pollution problems in Asia. Severe environmental impacts from local acid deposition have been registered in many areas of Asia, most notably northeast and southwest China, the Korean peninsula, Japan, northern and possibly southern Thailand and western Java.[39] Long-range transboundary transport of SO_2 and NO_X is expected to take place from northeast China to Korea, from southeast China to Vietnam, and across mainland Southeast Asia. The Asian Development Bank (ADB) concluded that, with the projected increase in fossil fuel consumption, increased and in some cases severe damage from long-range transport of acid precipitation is expected to affect vegetation, aquatic systems and human-made structures across many of the developing countries of Asia. Other air pollutants like particulate matter, tropospheric ozone and trace metals are also probably carried across national borders in Asia.

These impacts of industrialisation need to be anticipated if the Chinese industry is to make choices which in hindsight it will not regret. There is also an important interaction between environmental policy and trade and investment flows. The argument can be made that trade and foreign investment flows are consistent with the objective of reducing the environmental impacts of industrialisation.

If environmental and other resources are priced appropriately, trade may actually enhance environmental quality.[40] This is because free trade encourages a more efficient allocation of the world's resources, labour, capital and natural resources. Scarce environmental resources and highly polluting resources will be more costly to use in production processes. Increased efficiency means that more production can be achieved for the same material input and, therefore, output of waste.

Environmental standards, along with standards in numerous other social and economic areas, will differ across countries depending on assimilative capacity and social preferences, which will, among other things, depend on the state of economic development. There is, therefore, no case for equalisation of environmental standards across countries by any policy instrument. The imposition of uniform standards would be to the detriment of environmental quality from a global perspective because it would hinder the allocation of pollution-intensive activities to locations where the cost of pollution is lowest — for example, in areas of low population density and less sensitive ecological systems. It could even result in the relocation of industrial activity to heavily populated areas with already serious pollution problems.

Crowley and Findlay observe that in the last few years, there has been a merging of interests of the protectionist, environmental and labour lobbies in Europe and the United States in relation to trade policy.[41] This powerful coalition of interests presents a major threat to the maintenance of an open international trading regime and in particular a threat to China because of its size and the extent of the environmental impacts of its growth.

The contribution that trade liberalisation can make to improved environmental standards is even more apparent if it is accompanied by liberalisation of controls on foreign investment.

Direct foreign investment in China may itself be a force for improved environmental standards. There are a number of positive incentives for multinational firms to transfer their environmental practices and technology from developed to developing countries. Many of these factors stem from the integration of economies and the tendency for this to increase the channels of influence that interest groups are able to exert on production decisions in other countries.

Much environmental technology is embodied in capital and production processes. Equipment has been designed not only to meet stricter environmental standards, but to produce efficiently. In many cases, the most efficient equipment has been developed in industrial countries and is designed to meet stricter environmental standards. This factor will be present in the case of both direct foreign investment and in the case of imported capital equipment used by local firms. To the extent that trade results in increased competition, there will be increased pressure on local industry to reduce costs by scrapping outdated and often highly polluting equipment, with new equipment embodying the latest technology. As this equipment is most likely manufactured in developed economies, it will also incorporate advanced economy environmental standards.

Multinational companies may find it costly to vary their production processes and capital equipment to take advantage of variations in environmental standards. The meeting of product standards in export markets may require the use of the same technology, regardless of the location of the plant.

There are also costs associated with retrofitting plant and equipment which may induce firms in their choice of capital equipment and production processes to anticipate increasing environmental standards in developing countries. The least-cost way for the industrial sector to respond is to urge the government to adopt a mutually negotiated set of standards: this is particularly attractive to the larger, cleaner firms as it would permit them to eliminate local cost competition from dirtier firms. For multinational firms, the least-cost way to meet the threat is to adopt the standards they employ in their developed country plants. Another factor is that it may be more costly to alter production processes and retrofit capital equipment after it has been installed. It may be more efficient to adopt cleaner technology at the outset. This would certainly be the case if changing environmental standards forced the closure of plants unable to comply.

Shareholders in developed countries are also able to exert considerable pressure on multinational companies operating in developing countries. Apart from the value that these shareholders — and management for that matter — place on the environment, there are more pragmatic reasons for this. The legally enforceable liability of the firm for environmental damages caused now, in the future and in the past by the operations of the firm to those affected provides a powerful constraint on the choices of firms.[42] The prospect of future development in environmental law and enforcement in developing countries is, or should be, a concern to shareholders of both multinational and local firms in developing countries. It should also be a concern to companies providing finance and environmental liability insurance to projects in developing countries. Environmental standards may be lax now, but damage currently being caused could be the subject of future litigation under stricter environmental laws.

Moreover, courts in developed countries have shown an increasing willingness to prosecute domestic multinational firms operating outside of their jurisdiction, therefore extending the extraterritorial application of their environmental liability law.[43]

In summary, industrialisation in China will consume increasing amounts of environmental resources. This process will have both domestic and international impacts which will lead to reactions within China and in East Asia. It will also lead to increasing pressure to reduce the environmental costs of industrialisation. Trade and foreign investment will play a key role. However, there is still scope for conflict over the issue. The environmental impacts of immediate interest are concentrated within East Asia and regional groupings like APEC can play a key role in defining the appropriate principles for responding to these issues. An important element of any response will be to recognise the role that can be played by trade and capital flows.

See Chapter 17 for a further discussion of environmental issues.

Conclusion

China is already a large economy, according to the official statistics. In 'real' terms it may be even larger. Its recent growth rates imply that its size may quadruple at the end of the century compared to when the reforms began. Maybe a decade later, again in 'real' terms, it may be the biggest economy in the world, bigger than the United States.

The international economic impacts of this growth are substantial. In aggregate terms, even in the early 1990s, China still appears to be a small player in world trade. The attention that trade issues involving China receive suggests that the reality is different. China is already a big actor in many markets, especially in a number of high-income countries which are more likely to be subject to protectionist political pressures.

China can benefit from a reduction in the uncertainties surrounding its trading relationships, both as an exporter and — again because of the scale of its demands — as an importer. Institutional developments such as GATT membership and the development of APEC are significant in this context. GATT membership alone, however, may not be enough to resolve some of the uncertainties in China's relationship with the United States.

China has also become one of the biggest recipients in the world of capital inflows. There are some differences to the experience of other developing economies, such as the concentration of the origins of the inflows from within East Asia, especially from the newly industrialising economies, and the role of the overseas Chinese community. This feature serves to blur the economic boundary of China compared with the pre-reform period.

Not only is there some uncertainty now about where the external boundary of China lies in economic terms, there are also marked internal differences within China which are affecting China's international economic relations. These effects work through economic factors and policy-making processes. The national response to policy issues reflects the interaction of views of different sub-economies in China. Policy towards Hong Kong and Taiwan, for example, will reflect the influence of their allies among the local 'warlords' on the mainland.

A great deal of attention has been paid to trade and direct foreign investment issues involving China. Likely to be equally as important over the rest of the 1990s will be environmental issues. Industrialisation in China is already having significant spillovers on to the rest of East Asia. Responding to these environmental problems will be more contentious than trade policy within the region since, in contrast, the East Asian community tends to have common interests in the design of the world trading system. Managing environmental issues will be an even greater challenge for the emerging institutions of the Pacific region.

Notes

1 Huang Yiping helped collect some data, all of which, unless otherwise noted, was obtained from the Australian National University's International Economic Data Bank.

2 World Bank, *World Development Report 1993: Investing in Health*, Oxford University Press for the World Bank, Washington, DC, 1993.

3 ibid.

4 For comments, see Desmond Ball, 'Economics and Security: Towards Greater Cooperation in the Asia/Pacific Region', paper prepared for the Institute on Global Conflict and Co-operation (IGCC) at the University of California, San Diego, December 1993.

5 Chen Chien-Hsun, 'Causality between Defence Spending and Economic Growth: The Case of Mainland China', *Journal of Economic Studies*, vol. 20, no. 6, pp. 37–43.

6 Guonan Ma and Ross Garnaut, 'How Rich is China: Evidence from the Food Economy', *Working Paper* 92/4, Department of Economics, Research School of Pacific Studies, Australian National University, 1992.

7 World Bank, *The East Asian Miracle: Economic Growth and Public Policy*, Oxford University Press for the World Bank, Oxford, 1993.

8 C. Findlay, W. Martin and A. Watson, *Policy Reform, Economic Growth and China's Agriculture*, OECD Development Centre, Paris, 1993.

9 These ownership issues are discussed in more detail in Chen Chunlai, C. Findlay, A. Watson and Zhang Xiaohe, 'Rural Enterprise Growth in a Partially Reformed Chinese Economy' in C. Findlay, A. Watson and H. Wu (eds), *Rural Enterprises in China*, Macmillan, London, forthcoming. The following review of results of studies of the productivity performance of rural and urban industry is based on H. Wu and Wu Yanrui,

'Rural Enterprise Productivity and Efficiency', in Findlay et al., *Rural Enterprises in China*.

10 World Bank, *The East Asian Miracle*.

11 Peter Drysdale and Andrew Elek, 'China and the International Trading System', *Pacific Economic Papers*, 214, Australia–Japan Research Centre, Australian National University, 1992.

12 C. Findlay, P. Phillips and R. Tyers, 'ASEAN and China Exports of Labour-Intensive Manufactures: Performance and Prospects', *ASEAN Economic Bulletin*, vol. 3, no. 3, 1987.

13 Peter Drysdale and Andrew Elek, 'China and the International Trading System'.

14 See, for example, Zhang Xiaohe, 'Rural–Urban Isolation and its Impact on China's Production and Trade Pattern', *China Economic Review*, vol. 3, no. 10, 1992.

15 W. Martin, 'What Would Happen if all Developing Countries Expanded Their Manufactured Exports?' *Working Papers*, WPS 1110, International Economics Department, World Bank, 1993.

16 X. Zhang and N. Tracy, 'The Third Foreign Investment Wave in Mainland China: Origins, Features and Implications', mimeo, Flinders University, Adelaide, 1993.

17 Zhang and Tracy note that reported direct foreign investment (dfi) data in China may be exaggerated because of the process of the collection of the data from local governments who have incentives to overstate capital inflows. They also note that many apparent foreign investments are actually investments by Chinese enterprises registered offshore. (*Newsweek*, 15 November 1993, reported an estimate that the flow of capital from China to Hong Kong was about the same as that in the opposite direction in cumulative terms and was of the order of US$10–15 billion.) The motive is to gain access to some preferential policies. They report one estimate that 28 per cent of Hong Kong and Macau investment in China is by the 'false foreign devils'. Other measurement issues noted by Zhang and Tracy arise from real estate investments where the initial investment involves nothing more than the establishment of a land holding or investment via the transfer of equipment, the value of which may be overstated: Zhang and Tracy, 'The Third Foreign Investment Wave in Mainland China'.

18 According to Jetro's *China Newsletter*, no. 104, May–June 1993, the implementation rate for projects involving Japanese investors is by far the highest at 64 per cent compared with 48 per cent for Hong Kong and Macau, 45 per cent for the United States and 25 per cent for Taiwan.

19 ibid.

20 UNCTAD, *World Investment Report 1993: Transnational Corporations and Integrated International Production*, United Nations, New York, 1993.

21 Data for Figure 15.6 were provided by Harry Wu, using Chinese sources such as the *Statistical Yearbook*.

22 A. Watson and H. Wu, 'Regional Disparities in Rural Enterprise Growth' in Findlay et al., *Rural Enterprises in China*.

23 A. Watson, C. Findlay and Du Yintang, 'Who Won the Wool War? A Case Study of Rural Product Marketing in China', *China Quarterly*, no. 118, June, pp. 213–41.

24 For example, Lee Tsao Yuan, *Growth Triangle: The Johor–Singapore– Riau Experience*, Institute for Southeast Asian Studies and Institute for Policy Studies, Singapore, 1992; Toh Mun Heng and Linda Low, *Regional Cooperation and Growth Triangles in ASEAN*, Times Academic Press, Singapore, 1993; and a review by Chia Siow Yue and Lee Tsao Yuan, 'Subregional Economic Zones: A New Motive Force in Asia-Pacific Development', in F. Bergsten and M. Noland (eds), *Pacific Dynamism and the International Economic System*, Institute for International Economics and PAFTAD Secretariat, Australian National University, Washington, DC, and Canberra, 1993.

25 Chia and Lee, 'Subregional Economic Zones'.

26 UNCTAD, *World Investment Report 1993*.

27 Chia and Lee, 'Subregional Economic Zones'.

28 Data in this paragraph are reported by Chia and Lee, 'Subregional Economic Zones', but sourced to a conference paper by Sung Yunwing dated 1992.

29 Sung Yunwing, 'A Theoretical and Empirical Analysis of Entrepot Trade: Hong Kong and Singapore and Their Roles in China's Trade' in C. Findlay and L. Castles (eds), *Pacific Trade in Services*, Allen & Unwin in conjunction with the PAFTAD Secretariat, Sydney and Canberra, 1988.

30 Ross Garnaut and Ma Guonan, *Grain in China*, East Asia Analytical Unit, Department of Foreign Affairs and Trade, Canberra, 1992.

31 For example, see P. Crowley and C. Findlay (eds), 'Steel in East Asia in the 1990s: Towards an East Asian Steel Agreement', PECC Minerals and Energy Forum, Canberra, 1993.

32 Drysdale and Elek, 'China and the International Trading System'.

33 ibid., pp. 20–21.

34 This section is based on Crowley and Findlay (eds), 'Steel in East Asia in the 1990s'.

35 World Energy Council (WEC), *Energy for Tomorrow's World — The Realities, the Real Options and Agenda for Achievement: Pacific Regional Report*, WEC, London, 1992.

36 ibid.

37 M. Radetski, 'Economic Growth and Environment', in P. Low (ed.), 'International Trade and the Environment', *World Bank Discussion Paper*, no. 159, World Bank, Washington DC, 1993.

38 Grossman and Krueger is one of many studies whose results reject the hypothesis that economic growth results in increased environmental degradation. Grossman and Krueger use a cross-country sample of comparable measures of pollution in various urban areas to test the rela-

tionship between economic growth and air quality. They find that ambient levels of both sulphur dioxide and dark matter suspended in the air increase with per capita income at low levels of national income, but decline with per capita GDP at higher levels of income. The turning point comes between income levels of US$4000 to US$5000: G.M. Grossman and A.B. Krueger, 'Environmental Impacts of a North American Free Trade Agreement', *Discussion Papers in Economics*, no. 158, Woodrow Wilson School, Princeton, NJ, 1991.

39 Asian Development Bank, *Environmental Constraints in Energy Development*, ADB, Manila, 1991.

40 Stuart Harris, 'International Trade, Ecologically Sustainable Development and the GATT', *Australian Journal of International Affairs*, vol. 45, no. 2, November 1991, pp. 196–212; K. Anderson, 'Economic Growth, Environmental Issues and Trade', in Bergsten and Noland (eds), *Pacific Dynamism*.

41 P. Crowley and C. Findlay, 'Trade and the Environment: Power and Steel in East Asia', paper presented to the conference of economists, Perth, September, 1993.

42 T. Walde, 'Environmental Policies Towards Mining in Developing Countries', *Journal of Energy and Natural Resources Law*, vol. 10, no. 4, 1992, pp. 327–57.

43 ibid.

16 Integrating China into East Asia: Cross-border Regions and Infrastructure Networks

*Peter J. Rimmer**

Looking outwards

The decentralisation of economic management and decision-making in post-Mao China provides the key to understanding the emergence of contemporary cross-border regions and the demand for new infrastructure networks involving China and East Asia. The foreign and defence policies of the People's Republic of China (PRC) have become increasingly subservient to national industrial policy and managerial efficiency in guiding the economy. Under this new regime, the government's efforts are directed at competing and co-operating with rival states, and co-operating with multinational enterprises to attract capital and technology.[1]

Several issues are raised by the elimination of economic barriers between China and the rest of the world. How successful have China's multidirectional efforts at cross-border regional economic integration been? How have China's transport and communications infrastructure networks become more deeply enmeshed in the international economy to meet this need, and how has this change been reflected in traffic trends? More specifically, given the size of China (5000 kilometres in both length and breadth, 9.6 million square kilometres and 1.2 billion people), how far can existing international sea, air and telecommunications networks meet the accelerated demand for goods, personal travel and information triggered by economic restructuring and geopolitical change? Finally, how has the creation of cross-border regions and connections with the international infrastructure network affected China's political actions?

These questions are addressed by identifying those border areas whose position and potential have been affected by transnational integration. Then the need to develop adequate cross-border infrastructure networks is discussed in relation to China's international sea–land transport, air transport and telecommunications linkages. Attention is then directed to the way in which the PRC's obligations and responsibilities in transport and communications restrain its political actions.

Cross-border regions

Post-Mao China has actively sought economic integration with adjacent nations in order to improve its efficiency and competitiveness by breaking down its former trade barriers.[2] Essentially, China's efforts at economic reform and policy devolution have been in response to past government failures which have led to inertia in the nation's overall economic performance and that of specific regions. The government's policies have focused economic development on three contiguities: the border, the coast and along the Yangzi.

The peripheral land-border regions between China and the independent nation-states of Korea, Russia, Mongolia, Pakistan, Nepal, India, Thailand, Laos and Vietnam have been marked by differences in language, culture and economy, and in administrative, legal and welfare systems. Similarly, the large national minority areas of Tibet, Xinjiang and Inner Mongolia within China's borders are characterised by different histories and traditions of independence. Development of both sides of the land border has been restricted by their isolated location and orientation towards national core regions rather than to their back-to-back neighbours.[3] The inadequate economic performance of these border regions has been compounded by separation from natural hubs and hinterlands, their poor natural endowment, and peripheral locations in transport and communications systems. Stronger economic relationships have been forged between the land-locked Xinjiang province and the Turkic Republics of the former Soviet Union (i.e. as part of a Great Islamic Circle with new Central Asian states). Belatedly, Beijing has recognised the importance of these connections as a counterbalance to the strong priority it has given to the coastal provinces.

The latter constitute an 18 000-kilometre, relatively ice-free, maritime crescent which integrates more closely with the international economy than with the interior. Although Chinese policy continues to highlight the paramount importance of the domestic over the international market, 'there is increasing stress on the future importance of continuous economic development along the southeast China coast and its relation to regional and world markets'.[4] Coastal China, stretching from the Russian border to Vietnam and inland via the city of Wuhan, has been the focus of efforts to build a modern, industrialised economy. Moving in tandem with the maritime crescent have been the other 'Chinas' — Hong Kong, Macau and Taiwan — together with Japan, Korea and the resource-rich, but underdeveloped, Russian Far East.

The fresh orientation towards cross-border contact has led to the emergence of new economic zones 'in which mutually supportive economic relations reach across national borders and have grown in tandem with the crumbling of the Cold War structure'.[5] These zones have produced new opportunities for international trade and the movement of goods, people and information. A wide variety of zones has been identified which involve China (Figure 16.1). The most prominent is the South China zone which includes two sub-zones: the Pearl River Delta based on an integration of part of Guangdong province and Hong Kong; and the Cross Straits area involving indirect interactions between Fujian province and Taiwan. Another key zone is focused on Shanghai (including Pudong's Jinqiao Export Processing Zone) and its Jiangsu and Zhejiang environs in the Lower Yangzi. Also well established is the Yellow Sea economic zone, which comprises the Shandong and Liaoning peninsulas, and Korea. An emerging zone covers the 'growth square' involving Yunnan province with Laos, Myanmar and Thailand. Looking to the future, Guangxi province could be involved in the Tonking economic zone. Even more speculative is the Japan Sea zone, which would include China's Jilin province along with Russia, North and South Korea and Japan.

Many see these local economic zones as offering a more practical approach to regional development than free trade associations promoted by national governments. Nevertheless, their development potential is not always realised because bottlenecks still persist in international transport and communications. Integration benefits from higher production possibilities hinge on the development of an efficient network infrastructure as cross-border development is being accompanied by a strong growth in goods and passenger flows and a marked increase in information traffic. However, it is not sufficient to note international connections because trade facilitation depends on connections to domestic networks which, in China, have been heavily dependent upon the railway, Yangzi River navigation and coastal shipping.

Infrastructure networks

China and adjacent neighbouring states are developing towards an open — if not yet integrated — network economy in which trade barriers are progressively being removed and spatial interactions involving goods, people and information are increasing. The network economy comprises both tangible and intangible components, including Electronic Data Interchange (EDI) and business networks. As the maximisation of economic growth is dependent upon exploiting the country's competitive advantage in an open international system, the existence of an accessible and coherent network infrastructure is critical for the further development and integration of China into the East Asian economy. Thus an examination of the strategic inter-

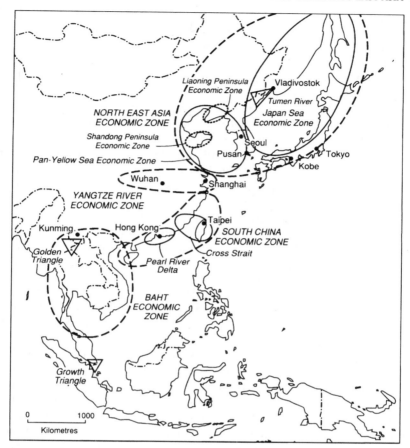

Figure 16.1 China's economic zones

Source: Adapted from H. Takano, *Joho Sekai Chizu*, Kokusai Chigaku Kyokai, Tokyo, 1993, pp. 42–53.

connectivity of all relevant modes — sea–land–water, air and telecommunications — is a necessary precondition for regional development and competitiveness.

Sea–land–water transport

Attention in discussing sea–land–water transport is focused on container movements, as they offer a sensitive indicator of the degree to which China's market economy has been integrated into the international economy.[6] In 1992 only 10 per cent of China's 25 million tonnes of general cargo was containerised. Annual container throughput at major ports, however, is growing at 25 per cent.[7] Most containers originating and terminating in China are handled by feeder services (200–1000 TEUs) connecting mainline trans-Suez and trans-Pacific services (2000–5000 TEUs) concentrated on external hub ports or load centres.[8] Typically, trans-Suez containers are transhipped at Singapore, and trans-Pacific containers are transhipped at Hong Kong, Kaohsiung and Pusan. An intra-Asian route links these load centres in Northeast Asia and Southeast Asia, and an intra-Central Asian route links Hong Kong and Kaohsiung.

Political barriers prevent direct shipping between China and Taiwan. Consequently, links between Taiwanese ports and Fuzhou, Xiamen, Shanghai, Dapeng Bay and the Pearl River Delta ports are serviced by feeder ships through Hong Kong. A mainline-container shipowner moving containers from Guangzhou to Los Angeles would minimise door-to-door costs if they were loaded on to a small feeder vessel at the Port of Huangpu and transhipped to the mainline service at Kaohsiung. As this is precluded by Taiwanese regulations, it may be advisable to ship from Yantian in a medium-size feeder vessel and tranship to the mother ship in the Port of Kobe.

The Chinese market affects four major container load centres (see Table 16.1). At best, Singapore is marginally involved. Hong Kong is already the undisputed gateway to Guangdong as its annual 25 per cent growth rate in container movements reflects manufacturing growth in the Pearl River Delta. Kaohsiung's ambitions to become Central Asia's hub port between Xiamen and Shanghai hinge on a rapprochement between Taipei and Beijing and the resumption of direct trade.[9] Pusan and the new Korean port of Kwangyang Bay are expected to become the hub centres for Northeast Asia, transhipping cargo from China and North Korea.[10]

Parallelling the activities of these load centres has been the development of China's own ports stretching from the Siberian border to Vietnam. Collectively, they handled almost 1 551 000 TEUs in 1991 compared with Hong Kong's 6 162 000 TEUs (Table 16.1). Joint venture projects with foreign companies are being pursued with funds from international lending agencies on Hainan Island, along the Pearl and Yangzi Rivers, on the Gulf of Bohai and in the Japan Sea. These have been boosted by China's booming economy and export drive, and the delegation of more authority from the central government to the ports. New container facilities are being built at Dalian, Tianjin, Qingdao, Shanghai and Guangzhou. These ports are unable to accommodate deep draught container vessels because of shallow depths. This has led to plans to develop a deepwater port at Ningbo.

Already these container ports are the focus of China's own shipping enterprises, including the Chinese Ocean Shipping Company (COSCO) and China National Foreign Trade Transportation Corporation (known as Sinotrans), which offer no-frills, port-to-port services (i.e. they do not own a network of terminals and trucking depots overseas).[11] Since 1984, they have had to compete with each other and the feeder operations of shipping companies owned by coastal provinces. Both COSCO and Sinotrans have used their links with foreign companies and have ordered new container ships. When COSCO's vessels are delivered, it intends to introduce a pendulum service linking Europe, the Far East and the United States and an

Table 16.1 Containers handled by major offshore load centres and China's ports, 1982 and 1990–92 (TEUs)

Port	1982	1990	1991	1992	1993
Load centres					
Singapore	1 116 288	5 223 500	6 354 000	7 161 600	n.a.
Hong Kong	1 659 943	5 100 637	6 161 912	7 972 235	n.a.
Kaohsiung	1 193 998	3 494 631	3 913 108	3 960 518	4 249 520
Keelung	702 922	1 840 796	2 007 752	1 940 587	n.a.
Pusan	786 653	2 348 475	2 570 734	2 751 006	2 942 597
Kobe	1 504 374	2 595 940	2 635 425	2 608 272	2 681 000
China's ports					
Dalian	12 258	131 259	172 536	217 464	250 000
Qinhuangdao	-	4 031	7 421	(20 000)	n.a.
Tianjin	40 909	286 000	339 000	n.a.	n.a.
Yantai	-	11 922	14 132	(18 000)	n.a.
Qingdao	-	135 419	184 340	222 306	264 384
Lianyungang	-	8 590	14 415	(20 000)	n.a.
Nanjing	-	41 826	52 260	73 301	89 000
Shanghai	66 095	456 123	576 000	730 000	n.a.
Fuzhou	1 500	n.a.	n.a.	n.a.	n.a.
Xiamen	-	45 337	74 668	104 422	n.a.
Guangzhou (Huangpu)	6 815	80 744	116 003	118 161	n.a.
Yantian	-	n.a.	14 132	18 000	n.a.
China total	127 577	1 201 251	1 564 907	n.a.	n.a.

Source: M. Lambert (ed.), Containerisation International Yearbook, London, National Magazine Company Ltd, various years.

upgraded service linking Shanghai, Hong Kong, Ho Chi Minh City, Singapore and Bangkok. Sinotrans has used its new vessels to strengthen its services to Europe. COSCO has maintained 50 per cent of China's general cargo trade and Sinotrans 10 per cent, with the balance being handled by provincial and foreign carriers.[12]

Since the Ministry of Communications relaxed regulations governing activities of United States shipping companies in 1992, China's ports have been incorporated in the feeder services of the mainline-container operators in the trans-Pacific trade. For instance, Sea-Land Asia offers 35 sailings per week between China, Hong Kong and Japan. These feeders from China's ports of Dalian, Nanjing, Nantong, Ningbo, Qingdao, Shanghai and Tianjin link mother ships at major load centres (e.g. Hong Kong, Kaohsiung, Kobe and Pusan).[13] There has also been an increase in direct services from China. The American President Line has introduced a service from north China to Los Angeles; Maersk, a Danish company, has an agreement with Sinotrans to provide a service between Shanghai and Kobe; Singapore's Neptune Orient Line has a similar arrangement with Sinotrans to link Fujian province and Japan; Britain's P&O Containers has a share in the terminal facilities at Shekou, northeast of Hong Kong, which could become a port on the Europe-Far East service; and the Hong Kong-based Orient Overseas Container Line

(OOCL) has set up territorial headquarters in Shanghai to service China (except Guangdong) and Mongolia.[14] Compagnie Maritime d'Affretment (CMA), a French shipowner and operator, has also established a company in Shanghai.[15] As carriers take advantage of China's economic boom, there is a pressing need for new deepwater berths and modern handling facilities to alleviate congestion and to speed up cargo flows.[16]

In China, containers are moved by truck, barge, intercoastal vessel or junks and sampans, which sail up key rivers. As most containers only travel an average distance of 70 kilometres inland in China, road is generally preferred by foreign mainline-container operators. The line haul companies are intent, however, on extending their multimodal transport networks further inland from China's ports by road. For example, a joint venture, Guangdong Orient Trucking, has been formed between Orient Trucking, Sea-Land's wholly owned Hong Kong container trucking subsidiary, and the Guangdong branch of Sinotrans.[17]

Such joint venture intermodal activities are prompted by the limited capacity and capability of China's railways to handle cross-border movements of international standard containers across ten direct railway routes connected with Korea, Russia, Mongolia, Kazahkstan, Vietnam and Hong Kong.[18] A line between Urumchi and the Alatau Pass has been completed to connect China and Kazahstan railways to form a second Asian landbridge to Europe which allows an integrated sea–rail system. Most major rail routes, however, are grossly overloaded because of the excessive burden of coal traffic and under-pricing. They can only cope with 70 per cent of current demand.[19] Their capacity to handle international-standard containers is extremely limited.

These difficulties are compounded by the virtual absence of a conventional highway network.[20] In 1992 there was 652 kilometres of expressway. Only 52 700 kilometres out of one million kilometres was graded as Class 1 or 2 (i.e. properly paved and consisting of more than one lane in each direction). Traffic speed on arterial roads does not exceed 45 kilometres per hour. Other roads are experiencing rapid deterioration of their pavements as they are too thin to support modern trucks carrying international standard containers. Economic reform has been slow to permeate the planning and management of the rail and road sectors. There are, however, ambitious national plans to construct new railways centred on six corridors connecting major economic zones. Similarly, priority has been given to roads which can serve as the backbone of high-quality arterial corridors to meet the anticipated 6–8 per cent increase in demand stemming from economic growth, population growth and a marked increase in vehicle ownership.

As part of an ambitious program to improve the poor coverage and low quality of China's road network, there is a US$190 billion construction program between 1990 and 2010 (though improving the condition of existing roads must also be addressed).[21] In particular, two east–west and two north–south trunk highways have been designed to connect China's main port cities. Although no detailed costings are available for planned rail and road programs, they will be heavily dependent on multi-channel financing derived from provincial and municipal governments, domestic and foreign loans, surcharges and tolls. Until the new roads are completed, much could be achieved through demand management by increasing petrol prices and introducing telecommunications and computerised freight information to reduce one-way loading trips. Given the focus on China's external connections, it is more pertinent to consider regional sea–land–water developments. As the major national minority areas — Inner Mongolia, Tibet and Xinjiang — have experienced less economic development, they are excluded from further consideration. Interest is centred on the cross-border regions (sometimes referred to as 'natural economic territories').

South China

South China is an appropriate place to start because it has been at the forefront of providing new sea–land–water infrastructure as a step towards an integrated multimodal transport system. Apart from the joint venture development of the freeport of Yangpu on Hainan Island, led by the Japanese firm Kumagai Gumi (Hong Kong) Ltd, most activity in South China has been heavily focused on buttressing the economic triangle between Hong Kong, Shanghai and Taiwan.

Pearl River Delta

In the Pearl River Delta sea–land links have already been established between China's Guangdong province and Hong Kong (sometimes referred to as Greater Hong Kong).[22] China, however, has surrounded Hong Kong with numerous similar, more accessible and lower-cost port facilities, notably Huangpu, Shekou and Chiwan.[23] The container terminal at Shekou is a joint venture with Swire and Britain's P&O shipping line in conjunction with Chinese interests. Wrangling over Hong Kong's New Container Terminals (CT9 and CT10) may lead to Kwai Chung being omitted from the schedules of some shipping companies as they develop direct services from Pearl River Delta ports and undermine the colony's agglomeration economies.[24] In 1994, Shekou's effectiveness will be enhanced by the completion of the 120 kilometre Shenzhen–Guangzhou–Zhuhai superhighway — a pacesetting, three-lane, dual carriageway being financed through Hong Kong's Hopewell Holdings. Once rail and road links are completed, a joint venture involving Hong Kong International Terminal (a subsidiary of Hutchison Whampoa Ltd) will be able to develop container facilities at the deepwater port of Yantian which, like Gaolan Island, had been originally earmarked for bulk cargoes. Hutchison Whampoa also have interests in new container facilities at Zhuhai, north of Macau, and Gaolan Island, south of Zhuhai.

Cross-Strait

Much of the indirect Taiwanese investment has flowed into the capital-starved Fujian province. As Xiamen port is congested, goods are often exported through Shenzhen. Negotiating an agreement on direct services between China and Taiwan is difficult because China's shipping companies are unlikely to give up their rights to cargo to compete with highly efficient Taiwanese shipping companies such as Wan Hai and Evergreen.[25] When an agreement is reached, up to 30 per cent of Hong Kong's export, import and re-export trade would be diverted to Taiwan.[26] Kaohsiung is likely to be the main beneficiary of direct port-to-port ties with the mainland, since stacking room for containers at the other Taiwanese port of Keelung is too limited for it to become a major transhipment centre for Southeast and Northeast Asia. Not only does the port of Kaohsiung offer potentially lower operating costs to users than Hong Kong, but it leases dedicated facilities to some of the world's largest shipping lines, notably the American President Line, Sea-Land, OOCL (Orient Overseas Container Line) and Evergreen. Kaohsiung's position as a hub port will be consolidated by Terminal 5 — a new state-of-the-art facility — and the decision to permit foreign mainline operators to manage their own off-dock container yards and trucking fleets.

In the longer term, Kaohsiung could become a major transhipment point for central and northern China, when barriers to the flow of goods, people and information are removed. China, however, has problems in making a bilateral shipping agreement with Taiwan. As both governments claim to be the sole domestic authority, it is difficult to create cabotage. Questions about which is the legitimate government, which of the flags should be used, and the nature of customs arrangements will have to be settled before direct services can develop. Resolving these political matters is becoming more pressing because Taiwan's option of going through third party Hong Kong to China will disappear in 1997.

Shanghai and the Yangzi River

Unlike the other regions, it has no dominant connection to a country outside China. Generally, the Yangzi River economic zone is seen as the weakest leg of the Hong Kong–Taipei–Shanghai triangle. Without an adjacent cross-border region, Shanghai was neglected by the central government during the 1980s. This oversight was reversed in the early 1990s and Shanghai has since attracted a wide range of trading partners and investment. They include Hong Kong's Hutchison Whampoa Ltd, which is engaged in a joint venture with Shanghai Port Authority and Shanghai Container Terminals Ltd to manage the three existing container terminals. Owing to shallow draught, however, Shanghai's terminals are unable to service the newer generations of mainline services. Plans are therefore afoot to develop new deepwater terminals, including those serving Pudong New Area — an export zone and bonded area. Other major container terminal developments are also being considered in the Shanghai area: Daxie Island, opposite Ningbo Island, has been targeted by China International Trust and Investment Co.; Zhangjigang, 90 kilometres upstream from Shanghai, has attracted the interest of P&O; and Beilun, south of Shanghai, has enticed the China–Singapore International consortium. Beilun is the main port for the inland city of Wuhan, 1200 kilometres from the coast, and also the site of port services of the Hong Kong-based Wharf Group.

Wuhan, with Hong Kong and Shanghai, is seen by the Wharf Group, headed by Li Ka-shing, as the fulcrum of an inland 'economic tripod' and an alternative to the Hong Kong–Shanghai–Taiwan triangle.[27] With a population of seven million, Wuhan is strategically located at the junction between the Yangzi River corridor running from Shanghai to Chongqing and the main trunk railway connecting Beijing and Guangzhou. The city has long been promoted as the base for a river terminal and distribution centre linked by shallow-draught container vessels which can negotiate winter depths and link Sichuan's inland city of Chongqing. Wuhan's pivotal position would be confirmed by a 'containerised' rail link with Hong Kong. It would be further enhanced with the realisation of Hopewell Holdings' plan to extend the Hong Kong–Guangzhou road 500 kilometres north through Hunan province to Hengyang because a barge system could be instituted on the Xiang River to connect Yueyang on the Yangzi River. With access to both Hunan and Hubei provinces, Wuhan could become a major hub of foreign investment. More importantly, the 'inland triangle' of Wuhan, Hong Kong and Shanghai would allay Beijing's concern over regional imbalance arising from Guangdong's greater affluence and the concentration of investment from Hong Kong and Taiwan in coastal areas.

North and Northeast China

Yellow Sea Rimland

The hub ports serving the Yellow Sea Rimland encompassing Shandong and Liaoning provinces are Pusan, Kobe and Yokohama. Feeder services link Dalian and Tianjin Xingang with Kobe and Yokohama, which are hubs of both trans-Pacific and intra-Asian services.[28] Since 1989, Tianjin and Dalian have enjoyed direct liner services with Pusan and Inchon. The enhanced prospects for Sino-Korean trade have led to complementary port developments in Asan Bay, Kunsan Port and Taebul on Korea's west coast. China's ports in the Yellow Sea economic zone, notably Dalian, Lianyungang, Qingdao and Tianjin Xingang, have been upgrading their container facilities and improving their links to inland centres.

A container pier is being built at the port of Lianyungang, which is the eastern terminus of the Trans-China Railway (TCR).[29] The TCR commenced operation in 1992 and connects Lianyungang to Rotterdam via the Trans-Siberian Railway (TSR). Trains at the Chinese border have to change their wheels because the TCR has a standard gauge (1435 mm) and the TSR a wider gauge (1502 mm).[30] Management of TCR cargo tracking, cargo collecting and operating facilities is inferior to that offered by competing shipping companies. These problems are aggravated by substandard roads in Lianyungang's hinterland. Other potential Eurasian landbridges in the Yellow Sea area include the link between the TCR and the Trans-Korean Railway (TKR), which would connect Pusan to Rotterdam if the Koreas were unified; the Trans-Manchurian Railway (TMR) from Dalian via Harbin with the TSR; and the Trans-Mongolian Railway (TMGR) from Tianjin via Beijing and Ulan Bator to link up with the TSR.[31] As both the TMR and the

TMGR are overloaded, attention is focused on the TCR, TKR and TSR. As shown in Table 16.2, the TCR offers the hub ports of Pusan and Kobe the shortest distance and cheapest freight rate to Rotterdam.

Table 16.2 Comparison of distance, freight rate and time between Northeast Asia and Rotterdam, 1991

Mode	Pusan	Kobe
Distance (km)		
Trans-China Railway	10 370	11 000
Trans-Korean Railway	13 023	12 230
Trans-Siberian Railway	12 230	12 820
Sea	20 024	20 352
Freight rate (US$)		
Trans-China Railway	1 464	1 541
Trans-Korean Railway	1 388	1 859
Trans-Siberian Railway	1 700	1 764
Sea	1 845	1 629
Time (days)		
Trans-China Railway	24–32	24–32
Trans-Korean Railway	24–35	24–35
Trans-Siberian Railway	25–35	25–35
Sea	26–32	25–32

Source: Seok-Hyong Yoo, 'The Implication and Prospects for the Eurasia Land Bridges in Northeast Asia', in Far East–US Symposium on Maritime Development of the Northeast Asian Pacific Rim, The 4th KMI International Symposium Proceedings August 1992 Seoul Korea, Korea Maritime Institute, Seoul, p. 253.

Japan Sea

At present, Jilin and Heilongjiang provinces rely on the single gateway port of Dalian in the Yellow Sea zone (Heilongjiang has a strong orientation towards Russia). If the proposed hub port at Hunchun near the mouth of the Tumen Delta is reconstructed and linked by rail to Jilin, the province would be connected to alternative, international container feeder services. Already container links have been established between the hub port of Pusan and the Siberian port of Vostochny, which offers overland connections to China. However, it is Nakhodka which has the potential to serve both Siberia and China, to offer a landbridge between Moscow, Berlin and Rotterdam, and to provide sea links to the Japanese ports of Muroran and Niigata. Few of the other ports in the Golden Delta comprising Russia, China and North Korea are given much prospect of gaining international container port status.[32] The US$23 billion plan for the Tumen River Development Area, however, is designed to establish a load centre container port and can be seen as a starting point for another landbridge to Europe using wide-gauge trains — the proposed Mongolia–Jilin Trunk railway being seen as an important addition to the Eurasian railway system.[33] As existing local roads are inadequate for moving containers, an urban expressway network is envisaged.

Southwest China

The landlocked Yunnan province has developed strong trading and commercial relationships with Burma and Thailand, but these could be extended to its other shared borders with Laos and Vietnam. Already Yunnan, like Thailand, is prospering from double-digit growth rates. Trade and commerce, however, are limited by inadequate infrastructure. The most urgent requirement is to improve the land-based transport so that Yunnan can be connected to major seaports.[34] Its closest major facility is Haiphong Harbour in Vietnam.[35] An ambitious plan to link Yunnan to the Thai railway system via Laos is contemplated. As there are 2130 kilometres of Mekong waterway in China, ferrying cargo between Yunnan and Laos has been trialled — though commercial viability is dependent upon dredging and other improvements. Until these experiments succeed, Yunnan will be heavily dependent on upgrading its airport connections.

Air transport

China has not been part of the large upsurge in international air traffic in East Asia.[36] Anticipating East Asia's continuing expansion, large airport projects are planned for Hong Kong (Chek Lap Kok), Taipei, Seoul and Kansai. Although China has 98 main airports open to civil aviation, only 47 are capable of accommodating Boeing 737 series. Statistics on international passenger origin and destination are sparse and unreliable. They are only available for Beijing and Shanghai, and for a limited number of origins and destinations (Table 16.3). There are no records of flights to and from Hong Kong. Origins and destinations not serviced by direct international flights from Beijing and Shanghai are concentrated on the larger Hong Kong and Tokyo hubs — Osaka, Taipei and Seoul also have aspirations to

Table 16.3   Number of international passengers departing from China's airports and offshore hubs, 1983 and 1989–91

Airport	1983	1989	1990	1991
Beijing				
Bangkok	—	—	9 988	11 492
Bombay	585	457	298	—
Karachi	3 092	5 013	3 521	4 947
Singapore	—	—	—	12 366
Tokyo	29 423	156 429	47 676	81 500
Total	33 100	161 899	61 483	110 305
Shanghai				
Osaka,	—	—	27 272	41 994
Tokyo	23 785	50 161	16 911	33 284
Total	23 785	50 161	44 183	75 278

Note: These statistics are incomplete.
Source: On-Flight Origin and Destination Year and Quarter Ending 31 March 1983, No. 301, Montreal, International Civil Aviation Organization. Also for 1989, 1990 and 1991.

become hubs for China (Table 16.3). Multiple Chinese carriers are only allowed on the Shanghai–Tokyo and Beijing–Hong Kong routes.

Since 1987, seven major government-owned airlines have operated China's 49 international routes to 46 cities in 33 countries.[37] Although Air China is the main international flag carrier, the other five major airlines — China Northwest, China Northern, China Eastern, China Southern and China Southwest — have also provided international services, though their main task is domestic. There are more than twelve domestic airlines which are owned by provincial governments and private sources. Collectively, they have to meet the phenomenal domestic growth in air passenger and air freight which has led to predictions that China will need 800 more aircraft between 1990 and 2005.[38] There is a temporary ban on new local airlines but the major carriers are undergoing corporatisation and part-privatisation preparatory to an expansion of their international schedules. Once 100 000 passengers are attained on a route and load factors exceed 68 per cent, a new carrier can be introduced to that route.

Most airport construction activity has been concentrated in the Pearl River Delta (Table 16.4). Five airports costing US$24 billion are under construction or have been opened recently, with a combined capacity of 76 million passengers. They include Shenzhen, Macau, Chek Lap Kok, Hong Kong, Zhuhai and Guangzhou Huaxian.[39] Apart from the conversion of the Second World War airstrip at Zhuhai, which is restricted to domestic traffic, all of the other airports are seeking a major international role. Given the planned design capacity of Chek Lap Kok and Guangzhou, the future of Shenzhen as an international airport is problematical (though it could become a major cargo base for Federal Express, United Parcel Services and Nippon Express). Macau, however, can claim it is the only international airport on the Pearl River's west bank.[40]

Table 16.4   Airports in the Pearl River Delta, 1993

Airport	Cost US$ mill	Design capacity mill pax	Opening
Chek Lap Kok	21 000	35	Mid-1997
Guangzhou	1 760	30	Oct–1997
Macau	913	4	Mid-1995
Zhuhai	36	2	1997
Shenzhen	184	6	Oct–1991

Note: pax = passengers
Source: D. Knibb, 'Pearls of the Orient', Airline Business, January 1994, p. 39.

Outside the Pearl River Delta ten new airports were completed in 1992 and 1993 (including Yining in Xinjiang province, Wuhan, Wujaiba Airport in Kunming, Jinan and Tacheng).[41] Another 40 airports will be commissioned by the year 2000. Twenty-two of them will be located in the coastal belt. Most of the funds, however, will be concentrated on the new Shanghai

Airport in Pudong New Area (Table 16.5). Apart from these national investments, provincial governments have become involved in airport construction with the aid of foreign loans (e.g. Xiamen Airport and Wuhan Airport). China's air force has also opened up 51 military airports in various parts of the country to civil aviation.[42] More speculative plans are afoot for a world-class Tumen River Airport at Jingxin on China's border with Russia which lies on the polar route between Europe and Japan.[43] Already international flights have been inaugurated between Changchun in Jilin province and Khaborovsk in the Russian Federation.[44]

Table 16.5 Major airport developments in China, 1993–98

Year	Airport	Notes
1993	Zhuhai	US$140 million upgrade — a second runway should be completed in 1997
1995	Guangzhou	Y49 million upgrade
1995	Guilin	Y500 million upgrade to B-747 standard
1995	Shijizahuang	2600m runway, 8000 sq.m. terminal building for 960 000 pax p.a.
1995	Xiamen	Kuwaiti funds — 60 000 sq.m. apron, 27 000 sq. m. terminal for 5 million pax p.a.
1995	Shanghai	Runway completed; airport opening before 2005.
1996	Beijing	New 120 000 pax terminal (Y2 bil.) to handle 20 million pax p.a.
1996	Nanjing	New airport, 6–6.5 pax p.a.
1997	Guangdong	New airport Y6 bil. project
1998	Shenzhen	US$500 million development for new pax and cargo terminals

Note: Y = Yuan; pax = passengers.
Source: P. Butterworth-Hayes, 'Airlines Seek Take-off Points', *Jane's Airport Review*, vol. 5, no. 8, 1993, p. 23.

Telecommunications

Since the early 1950s, the Ministry of Posts and Telecommunications (MPT) has been the sole controller of international telecommunications connections. All international voice communications are switched and routed through MPT exchanges and international ports in Beijing, Shanghai and Guangzhou. Since 1978, satellite communications through five earth stations (three in Beijing and two in Shanghai; another is planned for Guangzhou) and optical fibre transmission structures have made it easier for the Ministry to develop China's external telecommunications linkages rather than its domestic infrastructure. INTELSAT satellites provide direct access to 48 countries and through transit networks to 198 countries.[45] In 1992, International Direct Dialling calls could be made to them from 876 of

China's cities. The expansion of domestic satellites, terrestrial microwave and optical-fibre systems has also enabled China's public switched-telephone network to boost domestic *telephonic services*. A marked increase from 4.1 million telephones in 1980 to 19.5 million telephones in 1992, however, still only represented an increase in the penetration rate by population from a density of 0.40 per cent to 1.63 per cent.[46] Subscriber waiting lists continue to grow and internal long-distance telephone circuits are overloaded and therefore completion rates are low.[47] Even if the target of 68 million telephones is reached in 2000, the penetration rate by population will still be only 5 per cent (though it will be greater than 20 per cent in Beijing, Shanghai, Tianjin and Guangzhou).

In 1991 and 1992, Hong Kong was the leader in the 'Top 10' destinations for international traffic from China (Table 16.6). If Macau and Taiwan were included, these three destinations accounted for more than two-thirds of the traffic in 1991 and three-quarters in 1992. Japan was the major destination outside the 'Greater Chinese Economic Circle'. When other intra-Asian destinations are added — South Korea and Singapore — it is evident that China's outgoing traffic was heavily concentrated within Asia. The other destinations were the United States, Canada, Germany and Australia.

Table 16.6 China's 'Top 10' telecommunications routes, 1991 and 1992

Destination	1991 MiTT	%	Destination	1992 MiTT	%
1 Hong Kong	340.0	57.2	1 Hong Kong	412.0	64.9
2 Japan	40.0	6.7	2 Japan	56.9	9.0
3 Macau	30.0	5.1	3 Taiwan	47.1	7.4
4 Taiwan	25.0	4.2	4 United States	30.3	4.8
5 United States	17.0	2.9	5 Macau	24.8	3.9
6 South Korea	5.0	0.8	6 South Korea	9.3	1.5
7 Singapore	4.0	0.7	7 Singapore	7.3	1.2
8 Australia	3.0	0.5	8 Australia	6.2	1.0
9 Germany	3.0	0.5	9 Germany	5.2	0.8
10 Canada	2.0	0.3	10 Canada	4.9	0.8
Other	125.0	21.0		31.1	4.8
Total	594.0	100.0		635.1	100.0

Note: MiTT is Minutes of Telecommunications Traffic.
Source: G.C. Staple (ed.), *Telegeography: Global Telecommunications Traffic Statistics & Commentary*, International Institute of Communications, London, 1992; Telegeography Inc., Washington, 1993, p. 125.

Since 1993, international non-voice *data services* have been handled by a new Public Switched Packet Data Network with one gateway port for Hong Kong and Macau and two other international gateways with links to 5500 ports within China.[48] Indicative of the nature of *telegraphic services* in China, international telexes are expected to decline in numbers but, contrary to experience elsewhere, domestic telexes are expected to increase. International *telematic services* are being provided, albeit with restricted coverage, as enhancements to telephone, data and telegraphic services. As detailed in Table 16.7, they include TELETEX for exchanging office correspondence, TELEFAX, VIDEOTEXT for the transmission of text or pictorial information, the electronic mail system (E-mail), Electronic Data Interchange (EDI) for the paperless transaction of all aspects of commercial data, and voice mail. Future developments include directory services (incorporating a telephone directory inquiry system) and information services databases which, increasingly, will provide network services.

Table 16.7   China's telecommunications services, networks and coverage, 1992

Service	Network	Coverage	Notes
TELETEXT	PSTN	n.a.	TELEX/TELETEX terminal still being developed
	PSPDN		
TELEFAX	PSTN	200 000 FAX machines in China	In 1992 Fax traffic volume increased to 1.7 million pieces — an annual increase of 76 per cent.
VIDEOTEX	PSTN	Beijing, Shanghai	
	PSPDN	Shenzhen, Guangdong	
Electronic	PSTN	Beijing, Shanghai	
Mail (E-mail)	PSPDN	Guangzhou, Jiangmen, Shenzhen, Qingdao	
Electronic Data Interchange (EDI)	n.a.	n.a.	n.a.
Voice Mail	PSTN	Shenzhen (50 000 boxes), smaller system in Guangzhou, Nanhai, Chengde, Nanning, Shanghai, Chengdu and Changsha	Expected to increase demand for PTSN services

Note: PSTN Public Switched Telephone Network; PSPDN Public Switched Packet Data Network.
Source: Based on She Qijang and Yu Renlin, 'Telecommunications Services in China', *IEEE Communications Magazine*, July 1993, pp. 30–33.

China relies heavily on importing leading-edge technologies from overseas and has benefited from the availability of Hong Kong as an international switching centre. Rivalling Singapore as a location for telecommunications-intensive business, Hong Kong not only possesses a satellite station and subterranean optical fibre network, but provides cheaper international direct-dial rates.[49] Besides functioning as an international teleport, Hong Kong offers a solid base for China's telecommunications system and could become its long-distance switching centre. Also, Hong Kong Telecommunications offers a model of operational efficiency for local telephone organisations. Already Guangdong province has a cellular network provided by Sweden's L.M. Ericsson which allows access via microwave systems to Hong Kong's international switching centre — an exemplar for the rest of China.[50] Indeed, Hong Kong has the potential to be the central hub serving all China. Although international linkages have stimulated economic and social progress, they expose China's domestic network to international competition and may raise issues of trans-border data flows.

Conclusion

This survey of cross-border regions and infrastructure networks has raised a series of issues concerning China's integration into East Asia. How dependent is China on the global market economy; how integrated is China into East Asia; and how far can we say that China is so enmeshed in the region that it has to be on good terms with its Pacific Community neighbours?

Dependence

As China's competing regional economies are increasingly determined by the global market economy, the country's independent options have been narrowed by structural changes in the international economy which have increased the country's reliance on bilateral and multilateral transport and communications agreements, and trading associations. Without adherence to these agreements, China would be in a weak position to attract investment from multinational firms. These firms are engaged in creating systems of economic activity across borders and in concentrating on those territories offering the best returns. A key element in their decision is the efficiency of transport and communications connections.

Integration

China's coastal provinces and those along the Yangzi are more closely integrated with the international economy than the interior. Given the inadequate statistics on international movements of goods, people and information, it is not possible to quantify China's degree of integration into the international economy in any meaningful way. Past policy bias in socialist planning against non- or semi-productive international transport and communications activities was evident in Mao's China.[51] Predictions that China's lack of integration into the international economy would smother the post-Mao growth spurt have not eventuated. The problem has been mitigated by the state confining itself to macroeconomic control and allowing regional governments and entrepreneurs to follow more independent market-oriented strategies. These strategies have involved regions capitalising on their competitive advantages in the world economic system since the 'open door' policy was introduced to attract economic activities and direct foreign investment.

Much emphasis in this study has been on the infrastructure, equipment and technology required for China's international transport and communications connections. These are designed to promote accessibility and contribute to an innovative climate and a skilled labour force. The next step is to extend international linkages and foreign investments beyond the coastal provinces (e.g. Sichuan) — the longer-term foreign investment targets being the national minority areas of Tibet, Xinjiang and Inner Mongolia. A widely held view, however, is that the most intransigent problems are software not hardware in origin.[52] These software problems include investment decision-making, planning and administration, management and organisation, and pricing. As these now involve the inter-connectivity of cross-border regions and infrastructure networks, the issue of transnational integration moves attention from domestic policies to foreign affairs.

Political implications

Optimists argue that Beijing will be bound by the ties of economic interdependence to avoid aggressive action.[53] They maintain that China will continue to need direct foreign investment and access to foreign markets — so as to create wealth within its territory — and therefore will not seek power over more territory.[54] Rather than put international trade at risk, optimists contend China will adopt a more 'tolerant' stance on human rights to maintain its Most Favoured Nation (MFN) status with the United States and not pursue territorial disputes (e.g. South China Sea and the Sino-Japanese conflict over the Senkaku Islands). In particular, Japanese policy-makers favour China's economic interdependence but want to deter Chinese nationalism and militarism. Given that China was its second largest trading partner in 1993 after the United States, the critical question for Japan is if, when and how it will confront China.[55] Southeast Asian states are more constrained because improved economic relations with China have not reduced its claims over disputed territories.

Assuming China's economic boom based on export-led strategies continues — and this is by no means certain — further direct foreign investment will be attracted to generate the surpluses to buy the production, transport and communications infrastructure, and technology required. The new transport systems will have to accommodate an increase in both raw material movements and exports, and the resultant shift in regional and global patterns of trade. Of course, Japanese entrepreneurs and other interests may welcome increased exports from China's cross-border regions, provided they can exploit rival regional supply and distribution systems in order to lower export prices (inter-regional competition, therefore, can be fierce). There is no sign, however, that these interests would want to proceed to the political dismemberment of China because the ensuing transport and communications dislocation and chaos would interfere with regional growth.

Notes

* Christine Tabart is thanked for library searches on this topic. Barbara Banks made some helpful editorial comments on the text. The figure was drawn by Nigel Duffey, Cartographic Section, Research School of Pacific and Asian Studies, The Australian National University.

1 J.M. Stopford and S. Strange with J. Henley, *Rival States, Rival Firms: Competition for World Market Shares*, Cambridge University Press, Cambridge, 1991.

2 Cf. P. Nijkamp, 'Border Regions and Infrastructure Networks in the European Integration Process', *Environment and Planning C: Government and Policy*, vol. 11, 1993, pp. 431–46.

3 ibid., pp. 435–37.

4 R.C. Keith, 'The Asia-Pacific Area and the "New International Political Order": the View from Beijing', *China Report*, vol. 25, 1989, p. 348.

5 T. Aoki and H. Ohashi, 'Asia: Integration of the World's Most Dynamic Economies', *Tokyo Business*, vol. 60, no. 6, 1992, pp. 26–29.

6 A review of the situation in the mid-1980s is provided by the Asian Development Bank, 'People's Republic of China: Port Sector Review', *Staff Working Paper*, Infrastructure Department, Ports, Railways & Telecommunications Division, Manila, 1988.

7 T. Carding, 'Carriers Open Gateway to China', *Intermodal Container News*, November 1993, pp. 17–20.

8 International standard containers are measured in terms of Twenty-Foot Equivalent Units (TEUs). A 40-foot container would count as two TEUs.

9 J.E. Ricklefs, 'A Hub Port Policy for Taiwan', unpublished paper presented at the Hub Port Seminar, sponsored by the European Council of Commerce and Trade, Taipei, Taiwan, 1 December 1993.

10 Pil-Soo Jung, 'Logistics System in the Northeast Asian Area for the 21st Century', in *Far East–US Symposium on Maritime Development of the Northeast Asian Pacific Rim, The 4th KMI International Symposium Proceedings August 1992 Seoul Korea*, Korea Maritime Institute, Seoul, 1992, pp. 223–42.

11 H. Wan, 'Organization and Management of Chinese Deep-sea Shipping Companies: With Special Reference to the Impact of China's Reforms', *Transport Reviews*, vol. 10, no. 1, 1990, pp. 1–27.

12 Carding, 'Carriers Open Gateway to China', p. 19.

13 K. Chinnery, 'More Pain than Gain?', *Lloyd's List Maritime Asia*, July 1993, pp. 31–34.

14 K. Kishore, 'Foreign Lines' Increasing Presence in China Reflects Market Importance', *Box Carriers*, no. 3, May 1994, pp. 18–21.

15 Nippon Yusen Kaisha (NYK Line), Mitsui O.S.K. and Kawasaki Kisen Kaisha ('K' Line), three Japanese carriers, have all applied to China's Ministry of Communications to establish subsidiaries. See 'Japanese shipping firms converge on China to set up operational bases', *Box Carriers*, no. 3, May 1994, pp. 14–18.

16 LSE, 'How Long will the Chinese Boom Last?', *Lloyd's Shipping Economist*, July 1993, pp. 6–9.
17 J. Fossey, 'Sea–Land Asia Looks Inward', *Containerisation International*, June 1993, pp. 47–51. This joint venture stemmed from pressure on China from United States' Federal Maritime Commission. It had threatened to act under the *Foreign Shipping Practices Act* 1988 unless China liberalised its business rights for United States carriers. The freeing-up process has led Sea-Land Service (China) to establish offices in Tianjin, Dalian, Nanjing, Guangzhou, Shenzhen, Qingdao and Xiamen.
18 Small 1 to 5-tonne containers have been used for many years on China Railways.
19 T. Plafker, 'Rails Still Fail', *China Trade Report*, no. 31, April, 1993, p. 2.
20 L. Song, B. Zhao and B. Shi, 'Road Transport Demand and Constraints in China by 2010', *Australasian Road Transport Research Forum*, vol. 18, no. 2, 1993, pp. 654–63.
21 ibid.
22 CBR, 'A Transportation Transformation', *China Business Review*, July–August 1993, pp. 24–29.
23 P.J. Rimmer, *Hong Kong's Future as a Regional Transport Hub*, Canberra Papers on Strategy and Defence no. 87, Strategic and Defence Studies Centre, Research School of Pacific Studies, Australian National University, Canberra, 1992.
24 D. Thomas, 'Pearl River Delta: Reckoning Forces', *Lloyd's List Maritime Asia*, March 1992, pp. 27–31; D. Griffiths, 'The China Syndrome', *Port Development International*, October 1992, pp. 29–36; and K. Chinnery, 'Big, Rich and Cornered', *Lloyd's List Maritime Asia*, October 1993, pp. 33–35.
25 Chinnery, 'More Pain than Gain?'.
26 Rimmer, *Hong Kong's Future as a Regional Transport Hub*.
27 C. Goldstein, 'Projects: Ties that Bind — Hong Kong Firms Seek Closer China Links', *Far Eastern Economic Review*, 30 July 1992, pp. 61–62.
28 R. Selwitz, 'Expanding the Pacific Basin: Ocean Links to China and Russia are Growing', *Intermodal Container News*, November 1993, pp. 22–27.
29 Dai Yannian, 'Large Asian Harbour under Construction', *Beijing Review*, vol. 35, no. 40, 1992, pp. 19–21.
30 Dai Yannian, '"Oriental Express" Will Start Here', *Beijing Review*, vol. 35, no. 40, 1992, pp. 16–18.
31 Seok-Hyong Yoo, 'The Implications and Prospects for the Eurasia Land Bridges in Northeast Asia', in *Far East–US Symposium on Maritime Development of the Northeast Asian Pacific Rim, The 4th KMI International Symposium Proceedings August 1992 Seoul Korea*, Korea Maritime Institute, Seoul, 1992, pp. 243–54.
32 Z. Wada, 'Summary of Regional Infrastructure: Ports and Harbors', in W.B. Kim and B.O. Campbell (eds), *Proceedings of the Conference on Economic Development in the Coastal Area of Northeast Asia*, East-West Center, Honolulu, 1992, pp. 111–21.

326 CHINA AS A GREAT POWER

33 UNDP, Master Plan for the Transportation Sector: Tumen River Area Development Programme, A.R. Holm & Associates, San Francisco, 1993.

34 Asian Development Bank, *Conference on Subregional Economic Cooperation, Manila, 21–22 October 1992*, Asian Development Bank, Manila, 1992, pp. 12–13.

35 'Liner Service Analysis: Japan/Vietnam Trade', *Box Carriers*, no. 2, April 1994, pp. 38–44.

36 W.M. Chen, 'Transport in China — The Development of Civil Aviation in New China', *Transport Reviews*, vol. 8, no. 2, 1988, pp. 88–99.

37 'Presentation by the Chinese Delegation', APEC Third Transport Working Group Meeting, 8–10 December 1992.

38 D. Knibb, 'New Orders in China — Government Clamps Down on New Orders', *Airline Business*, December 1993, pp. 34–37.

39 D. Knibb, 'Pearls of the Orient', *Airline Business*, January 1994, pp. 36–39.

40 UNDP, *Master Plan for the Transportation Sector*, p. 60.

41 P. Butterworth-Hayes, 'Airlines Seek Take-off Points', *Jane's Airport Review*, vol. 5, no. 8, 1993, pp. 21–24.

42 'Airforces Contribution to Civil Aviation', *Jiefangjun Bao*, Beijing (Item 23), *Summary of World Broadcasts: Weekly Economic Report, Part 3 Asia-Pacific*, FEW/0304 WG/4, 20 October 1993.

43 UNDP, *Master Plan for the Transportation Sector*, pp. 106–17.

44 'Russia–Jilin Province Inaugurates International Flights', *Jilin Ribao*, Changchun, (Item 9), *Summary of World Broadcasts: Weekly Economic Report, Part 3 Asia-Pacific*, FEW/0306 WG/2, 3 November 1993.

45 Liu Shen, 'Satellite and Terrestrial Microwave Communications in China', *IEEE Communications Magazine*, July 1993, pp. 38–40; She Qijong and Yu Renlin, 'Telecommunications services in China', *IEEE Communications Magazine*, July 1993, pp. 30–33.

46 In 1990, average telephone penetration in provincial capitals reached 8.9 per cent and there were 11.5 million telephone subscribers in the network. See Wan Siding, 'An Overview of Telecommunications in China', *IEEE Communications Magazine*, July 1993, pp. 18–19.

47 The cost of wiring a new subscriber in China is US$2000. This high figure is attributed to difficult terrain, long local loops and the constant need for repairs. Upgrading the conventional network would cost US$25 million between 1993 and 2000. As wireless technology could cut this figure by half, there have been a large number of cellular projects established in China. See P. Haynes, 'Telecommunications: The End of the Line', *Economist*, 23 October 1993, p. 13.

48 Originally, public data services in China were provided by the SESA company, established in 1989. It now has 800 users with more than one-third of its traffic comprising electronic mail and international information retrieval services. Of the total users, 23 per cent were foreign companies, 12 per cent foreign residents, 18 per cent foreign trade enterprises, 21 per cent scientific institutes and universities and 26 per cent

domestic companies. The network, however, was inadequate to meet growing demands and led to the installation of the Public Switched Packet\Data Network.

49 W.H. Davidson, Wang Dong-min and S.C. Hom, 'Telecommunications Policy and Economic Development: Models for the People's Republic of China', *China Economic Review*, vol. 1, no. 1, 1989, pp. 93–108.

50 S. Gorham and A.M. Chadran, 'Communicating on the Go', *China Business Review*, March–April 1993, pp. 6–30.

51 J. Yenny, 'China', in Tsuneo Akaha (ed.), *International Handbook of Transport Policy*, Greenwood Press, Westport, 1992.

52 Sang Heng-kang, *Zhongguo de Jiaotong Yunshu Wenti* [China's Transport Problems], University of Aviation and Aeronautics Press, Beijing, 1991; J.H.E. Taplin, 'Economic Reform and Transport Policy in China', *Journal of Transport Economics and Policy*, January 1993, pp. 75–86.

53 G. Segal, 'The Coming Confrontation Between China and Japan?', *World Policy Journal*, vol. 10, no. 2, 1993, pp. 27–32.

54 Stopford and Strange, *Rival States, Rival Firms*, p. 1.

55 See 'Another Record Set in China Trade: Now Japan's No. 2 Partner after U.S.', *Box Carriers*, no. 3 May 1994, pp. 12–14.

17 China's Environmental Issues
Hu Angang

Introduction

China is the most populous country in the world. It has a total population nearing 1.2 billion, which accounts for about one-fifth of the world's total. The population is expected to reach 1.5 billion by 2020.[1] China is also a big developing country, facing the pressing task of industrialisation. It is now at the stage of becoming a middle-income country. In the 1980–90 period, China's Gross Domestic Product (GDP) increased at an average annual rate of 9.5 per cent.[2] By 2020, China's Gross National Product (GNP) is expected to increase tenfold. On the basis of these expectation, the energy consumption would increase from 990 million tonnes of standard coal in 1990 to 2.5 billion tonnes in terms of standard coal by 2020. Coal consumption would increase from the current 1.06 billion tonnes to 2.6 billion tonnes, making China one of the largest energy consumers in the world.[3] The growth in population and economy places a tremendous and lasting pressure on China's eco-environment. Such pressure is aggravated by ineffective marketing and policy blunders during the period of transition to a market economy.

China's current and future eco-environmental problems will mainly manifest themselves in the following three ways:

1 large-scale destruction of the ecology in rural areas, such as water loss and soil erosion, a sharp reduction in forests, degradation of the grassland, a worsening of natural disasters and the dwindling of lake surfaces;
2 very serious environmental pollution, first in the cities and then in economically developed rural areas, such as water pollution, air pollution and pollution by solid wastes; and
3 global environmental problems, which can be expected to have a substantially unfavourable impact on China's environment, such as rising sea levels, which will affect the coastal areas of China, global warming which will destabilise China's agricultural production, the damage to the ozone layer, which will affect China's eco-system, and global environmental changes, which will affect the biodiversity of the country.

This chapter is divided into five sections. The first is an introduction to the principal environmental problems in China; the second section deals with the mutual influence of environmental problems in China and the whole world; section three is an analysis of the main causes of China's environmental problems; section four explores principal ways for solving environmental problems in China; and section five considers China's response to the global environmental agenda.

Ten major environmental problems in China

China's official policy of industrialisation began in the 1950s, when the population of the country — already the world's largest — was experiencing the highest rate of growth and fastest increase it had ever known. The consequence has been a large-scale destruction of ecological systems and serious environmental pollution. A basic appraisal of China's eco-environment is that it is generally worsening. While there is improvement in part, the capability for environmental control lags far behind the speed of destruction, with the ecological deficits increasing day by day.[4]

Serious water loss and soil erosion

The area suffering from water loss and soil erosion was 1.16 million square kilometres in the post-liberation days (1950s). But the total area suffering from water loss and soil erosion was enlarged to 1.8 million square kilometres, accounting for 18.7 per cent of the country's land area, according to a 1992 satellite remote-sensing survey. The areas suffering the most serious water loss and soil erosion include (from north to south) the upper reaches of the western Liaohe River, the Loess Plateau, the middle and lower reaches of the Jialing River, the lower reaches of the Jinsha River, the Hengduan mountain range and part of the southern hilly areas. They are mainly distributed west of the Daxingan Ling–Taihang Mountains–Xuefeng Mountains line and east of the arid areas of the Qinghai–Tibet Plateau and Inner Mongolia and Xinjiang, which is the second platform of the general stairs of the terrain and the ecotons of China.

China's rivers wash about two billion tonnes of silt down to the sea, accounting for 13.3 per cent of the total in the world. The major silt-laden river is the Yellow River, whose total silt accounts for 60 per cent of the total. The total water loss and soil erosion is estimated at about five billion tonnes every year, washing away a large amount of nitrogenous fertiliser, phosphate and other soil nutrients.

Sharp reduction in forest resources

The forest areas in many of China's major forest zones have been reduced sharply. Gone are the days when there were seas of verdant forests. At the current consumption level, the overwhelming majority of state-owned forest enterprises will have no mature forests to log by the end of the century. The output of timber has been falling.

Statistics show that timber output was 65.02 million cubic metres in 1986, the record year. But it dropped to 58.07 million cubic metres in 1991.[5] The forest cover in China is 13.4 per cent, far lower than the world's average (31.3 per cent),[6] making China a very forest-poor country in world terms.

The accelerated extinction of biospecies

It has been estimated that about 15–20 per cent of the plant species in China are on the verge of extinction. Estimates of the number of plant species of higher order on the verge of extinction range up to 5000. Statistics of the past three decades show that the areas where such precious wild animals as high-nosed gazelle, giant panda and Manchurian tiger are distributed have been markedly reduced and the number of species and groups has been reduced sharply. The number of precious animals and plants native to China on the verge of extinction which have been listed for priority protection by the state comes to 312. The first group of plants listed in the catalogue of plants on the verge of extinction numbers 354.[7]

Degradation of pastures

The degradation rate was 15 per cent in the 1970s and reached over 30 per cent by the mid-1980s. The area of pastures degraded in the country has reached 66 million hectares and is on the increase at an annual rate of 1.33 million hectares. The main causes are the destruction of pastures to grow crops, and over-grazing. The output of grazing grass has dropped significantly and the eco-system of the pastures has been threatened by plagues of rats and other rodents.

Rapid desertification

China suffers some of the worst desertification in the world. In northern China, the desertified land has reached 1.49 million square kilometres, accounting for 15.5 per cent of the total territory. In the 1980s, the desertified land increased at an annual rate of 2100 square kilometres. In the past 25 years, China has lost 39 000 square kilometres of land. Under threat at present are about four million hectares of farmland, about five million hectares of pastures, more than 2000 kilometres of railway line and many cities, towns, factories and villages.

Frequent natural disasters

Statistics show that, in the 1950s, the areas afflicted by natural disasters averaged 22.26 million hectares a year and the area falling victim to disasters was 9.26 million hectares. The figures rose to 37.6 million hectares and 17.73 million hectares, respectively, in the 1960s (figures for 1967–69 are lacking), 37.67 million hectares and 11.58 million hectares in the 1970s, and to 41.55 million hectares and 20.38 million hectares in the 1980s (see Table 17.1).

Table 17.1 Crop acreage and areas stricken by disasters

Year	Areas stricken by disasters	Areas affected by natural disasters (Mil. ha/yr)	Rate of disaster-stricken areas (%) (Mil. ha/yr)	Rate of disaster-affected areas %
1950–59	22.26	9.26	15.4	41.6
1960–66	37.60	17.73	26.0	47.2
1970–79	37.67	11.58	25.3	30.8
1980–89	41.55	20.38	28.6	49.0

Note: Areas affected by natural disasters refer to areas whose crop output is reduced by 30 per cent compared with a normal year.
Disaster-stricken areas = areas stricken by disasters/sown areas of farm crops.
Disaster-affected areas = areas affected by natural disasters/areas stricken by natural disasters.
Source: China Statistical Yearbook, 1993, p. 391.

Worsening pollution of water bodies

This pollution is mainly caused by the discharge of industrial waste water. The principal pollutants are ammonia, nitrogen, oxygen-consuming organic matters and volatile phenol. The most harmful are toxic chemicals and heavy metals. At present, about 80 per cent of industrial waste water is discharged into rivers, lakes and other water bodies without being treated. The monitoring of 532 rivers in 1988 showed that 436 of them were polluted to varying degrees.[8] At present, the discharge of industrial waste water has been brought under control. The amount of industrial waste water discharged was 23.4 billion tonnes in 1980 and reached 26.8 billion tonnes in 1988, but dropped to 23.4 billion tonnes in 1992.[9]

Viewing the country as a whole, water quality along most of the coastlines is good. But near the cities and port towns, river mouths and bays have been polluted to varying degrees due to discharge of pollutants on land and dumping of waste matters into the sea. The main pollutants are hydrocarbon, organic matters and heavy metals. Due to eutrophication of sea water, disasters of equatorial tides have increased. Such tides occurred on 26 occasions in 1990, ten times the average before 1980. This poses a serious threat to offshore aquaculture.[10]

Serious air pollution

Burning coal is the fundamental cause of air pollution in China. Air pollution in China is mainly found in cities, with the main pollutants being sulphur dioxides and soot. The average daily value of the total suspending particles in the air is 432 micrograms/m^3, 526 micrograms/m^3 in northern cities, and 318 micrograms/m^3 in southern cities. In 43 per cent of northern cities and 29 per cent of southern cities, the average daily value of the density of sulphur dioxide has exceeded the standards set by the state.[11] Statistics show that the total amount of discharge of waste gas in the country was 7397 billion standard m^3 in 1985, but this rose to 10 478.7 billion m^3 in 1992. In the same period, the discharge of sulphur dioxide rose from 13.25 million tonnes to 16.85 million tonnes.[12]

Acid rain in China is confined to some local areas. According to statistics from 58 cities, the average pH value of rainfall ranged from 3.85 to 7.43, and over 52 per cent of them had an average pH value of lower than 5.6. Most of these cities are in southern China, but the frequency of acid rain has reached over 90 per cent in Ganzhou, Changsha and Xiamen, and over 70 per cent in Nonchong, Yichang, Nanchang, Huaihua, Baise, Nanjing, Chongqing and Guangzhou.[13] Acid rains over large areas of southern China have formed a serious threat to forests, soil and farm crops.

China is very concerned over the possibility of long-distance transmission of acid air caused by sulphur dioxide discharged as the result of coal burning. But, up to now and despite years of monitoring, no trace has been found of acid rain being transmitted to neighbouring countries. Acid rain is confined to the mountains and basins in southwest China, but China has still made it a major task to monitor and control rains and their transmission.

Extensive pollution by solid wastes

According to statistics, China produced 530 million tonnes of solid wastes in 1985 and the amount rose to 620 million tonnes by 1992.[14] At present, the refuse from daily life comes to 60 million tonnes a year on average, double the amount ten years ago. For about 200 cities in China, the disposal of solid wastes is a major unresolved problem.[15]

Toxic wastes have also caused serious environmental pollution. For instance, a factory producing chrome-containing wastes in northeast China was found to have polluted the underground water with chrome-containing liquid leaked from the wastes, resulting in the forced abandonment of drinking water wells for more than 1800 local residents.[16] It was estimated that China discharged 16.97 million tonnes of waste matters from the chemical industry and 900 000 tonnes of radioactive wastes in 1989. At present, apart from the ten dumps for radioactive wastes which provide safe disposal of such matters, most of the toxic and hazardous solids are left to pollute the environment, without being treated or rendered non-hazardous.[17]

Extension of environmental pollution to rural areas

The causes of rural pollution include the application of chemical fertilisers and pesticides and rural industries. In 1990, China ranked number three in the world in terms of the production of chemical fertilisers. The country uses 16.384 million tonnes of nitrogenous fertiliser, 4.624 million tonnes of phosphate and 1.479 million tonnes of potash fertiliser a year. On a per hectare basis, China applies 148 kilograms of nitrogenous fertiliser (four times the world average, but lower than in Britain and Germany), 169 kilograms of phosphate (14 kilograms more than the world average) and 10.2 kilograms of potash (lower than the world average of 19 kilograms).[18] Studies show that the effective utilisation rate of chemical fertiliser in China is only 30 per cent and the rest vanishes into the air or is lost in soil or waterways, causing pollution of the soil, eutrophication of water and an excessive amount of nitrate in drinking water. At the same time, irrational application of fertilisers has caused hardening and infertility of the soil. Rural industries are the chief way to rural industrialisation and the main prop of the rural economy, but the rapid development of such industries has caused heavy pollution. According to a joint survey by the State Environmental Protection Agency, the Ministry of Agriculture and the State Statistical Bureau, the percentage total discharge of industrial waste water by rural industries accounted for 5 per cent of the national total in 1989, with the proportion of industrial waste gas being 13 per cent, of carbon dioxide 12.4 per cent, of soot 18 per cent, and of solid wastes 17 per cent of the national total. Taking rural industry as a whole, it has not caused extensive pollution to the rural environment. But in some localities, especially the southeastern coastal regions, where the rural industries have developed especially fast, with the total output value accounting for two-thirds of the rural industries of the whole country, pollution is very serious and there is a trend for industrial pollution to spread from urban to rural areas. It should be noted that the increase in the discharge of waste water, gas and solids shows a trend towards slowing down, but far more slowly than the rate of growth of GNP. Statistics show that GNP in 1992 was 2.87 times that of 1980, but the discharge of waste water was only 1.14 times, while the discharge of waste gas doubled, with sulphate dioxide up 1.05 times, and industrial solids, 1.27 times. This shows that the fast increase in the discharge of industrial wastes was held in check in the latter half of the 1980s. Further declines are expected in the 1990s.

The mutual influence between the environmental problems of the world and China

Environmental issues in China are an integral part of the global environmental crisis. This problem has two main aspects. The first is that global environmental issues will have a serious, and unpredictable, effect on China.

Any rise in sea levels would seriously affect the economically developed and densely populated areas in China, especially the coastal plains, such as the Yangzi River Delta, the Pearl River Delta and the Yellow River Delta. For instance, half of the area in the Pearl River Delta rises less than 0.3 millimetres above sea level and the land sinks 0.78 millimetres a year. If the sea level should rise by 15 centimetres, it would submerge 20–30 per cent of the delta; if the sea level should rise by 30 centimetres, it would inundate half of the delta.

In such large cities as Shanghai, Guangzhou and Tianjin, the flood threat is real. Added to the threat is the sinking of the land as the result of the excessive tapping of underground water. It is estimated that the land will sink by 0.4 metres by the year 2030, thus making it more susceptible to flooding. Furthermore, the rise in the sea level will make it more difficult for some coastal areas such as the Taihu Lake plain area on the Yangzi River Delta to drain flood water and by then these areas might become lakes or marshes.

Global warming is making China's agricultural production increasingly unstable. Since the beginning of the 1960s, the rise in temperature in the Northern Hemisphere basically conforms to the trend of rising surface temperature in China. The rise in the temperature in the Northern Hemisphere has markedly reduced the rainfall in northern China, resulting in a big rise in the evaporation of surface water and frequent high temperature and drought. Influenced by the hot monsoon climate, southern China is suffering more from rainstorms, floods and waterlogging. The warm winters have also caused more crop pests.[19]

The impact of ozone depletion will be exacerbated. Monitoring results shows that the ozone layer has been reduced by 3.1 per cent over southern China, by 1.7 per cent over eastern and northern China, and by 3 per cent over northeast China.[20] This will lead to changes in the aquatic ecological system, the lowering of the natural infiltration capacity of water bodies and the destruction of biological resources of the sea and fresh water. It will also affect the health of the people, stimulating a rise in the incidence of skin cancer, cataract and other diseases.

The changes in the global environment will also have a long-term effect on biodiversity in China, such as changes in the distribution of biological belts and biological groups, and the mutation, extinction or disappearance of biospecies, thus putting some animals and plants on the verge of extinction.

The second main aspect of environmental issues in China as an integral part of the global environmental crisis is that environmental problems in China will have a substantial impact on the global environment. The population of China is the largest in the world, accounting for 22 per cent of the world's total. It is expected to grow to 1.3 billion by the year 2000, or about one-fifth of the world's total, and to 1.5 billion by the year 2020, or 20 per cent of the world's total. This means that China will remain the most populous country in the world until the period from 2040 through 2050, before being overtaken by India.

China is also the largest producer and consumer of coal in the world, thus becoming a principal contributor to global warming. In 1986, China produced 894 million tonnes of coal, or 20.2 per cent of the world's total coal production. Of the total energy consumed, three-quarters is coal. This energy consumption structure will remain for a long time to come. According to statistics, China emitted 12 million tonnes of sulphur dioxide in 1980, ranking third in the world after the former Soviet Union and the United States, and discharged 440 million tonnes of carbon dioxide to the air in 1983, accounting for 9.2 per cent of the world's total discharge or ranking third after the United States and the former Soviet Union.[21]

In a word, China is part of the world. Not only is it subject to the impact of world environmental problems, but it also has its impact on the global environment. Such relationships determine that China has to place efforts to tackle environmental problems high in strategic importance, and should join hands immediately with other countries of the world to protect the environment.

Causes of environmental problems

There are many reasons accounting for the daily deterioration of the eco-system and environment in China, which are the inevitable result of the interaction of both natural and human factors, and the historical legacy of modern development.

First, the eco-system and the environment in China themselves are vulnerable and unbalanced. Low in the east and high in the west, the great differences in topography make the land prone to water loss and soil erosion. The monsoon climate with rains and heat in most parts of the country does both good and harm to agricultural production. The shifting, force, duration and abnormalities of the East Asia monsoon are the basic dynamic mechanism for the widespread drought and flooding in most parts of the country.[22] Besides, China is sandwiched by two main geologically active zones, with the creation of new geological structures being more active than anywhere else.

This accounts for the frequent natural hazards, such as earthquakes, landslides and mud-rock flows, which pose a major threat to the survival of humans, biospecies and rare animals. There are also widespread, diversified and fast-changing ecotons. These are mostly in the economically backward areas of China, where ecological degradation is very serious.

Second, coal is the main form of energy consumed in China and is the chief cause of air pollution. Of the energy consumed in China, coal accounts for three-quarters. Coal provides 75 per cent of industrial fuel and power, 65 per cent of chemical raw materials and 85 per cent of fuel for civilian use.[23] But in OECD countries, coal accounted for only 22.5 per cent of energy consumption in 1985, and in other developing countries, coal consumption accounts for 21.6 per cent of energy consumption. Coal consumption in the former Soviet Union accounts for 26.5 per cent.[24] But coal consumption in China is much higher than those countries. This trend is expected to continue into the 2020s. The demand for coal will be around 1.5 billion to 1.6 billion tonnes by the year 2000 and up to 2.5 billion to 2.7 billion tonnes by the year 2020 (see Table 17.2). Coal is regarded as a form of 'dirty energy'. If there should be no major breakthrough in burning technology and in coal conversion (into electricity), it is going to be hard to redress the serious air pollution situation.

Table 17.2 Projection of waste, demand and supply of energy, coal and petroleum

		Low scheme		Middle scheme		High scheme	
Years 1990		2000	2020	2000	2020	2000	2020
Energy	(D)990	1450	2400	1500	2500	1550	2600
	(S)960	1350	2300	1400	2400	1450	2500
Coal	(D)1060	1500	2500	1550	2600	1600	2700
	(S)1020	1400	2400	1450	2500	1500	2600
Petroleum	(D)120	170	270	180	280	190	290
	(S)120	160	250	170	260	180	270

Source: Figures for 1990 are from the China Statistical Yearbook, 1993. Other figures are from National Conditions Investigation Group, Chinese Academy of Sciences, Opening Up Sources and Conservation — Development of China's Natural and Human Resources and Counter Measures.

It needs to be explained here that, in China, the increase in coal consumption after 1980 has been slower than the growth of GNP. The energy elasticity coefficiency dropped from 1.42 in 1980 to 0.57 in the period 1980–89, within the low range of growth elasticity. This is a result of the rise in the price of coal, the spread of energy conservation technology and changes in the industrial structure.[25]

Thirdly, the large scale and steady growth of the population has exerted a huge pressure and has had a persistent impact on the eco-system and environment in China. In post-liberation days, the total population on China's mainland was 542 million, but it rose to 1.172 billion by 1992.[26] The total population will continue to increase, to about 1.3 billion by 2000, about 1.5 billion by 2020 and 1.6 billion by 2030.[27] Population growth is a major factor contributing to the changes in environment. Due to population growth, arable land is dwindling and people in rural areas have to reclaim land from lakes or fell trees to grow crops in order to survive, thus destroying the vegetation. In urban areas, growth of population has caused severe housing shortages, a sharp increase in garbage and serious air pollution. Besides, population growth has a direct bearing on the demand for energy, which in turn puts intense pressure on the environment.

Fourth, there is the pressure of industrialisation. Industrialisation is an important mark and foundation of the modernisation of a country. Any country has to industrialise in order to achieve modernisation. China was very late in launching its industrialisation and started from a very low point. In order to catch up with and overtake developed countries, China has to put the emphasis of its development on heavy industry, which is energy consuming and heavily polluting. At the same time, it has to sustain its high rate of economic growth by way of high input and high consumption of resources. This also increases pressure on the environment. As well, the development of rural industrialisation and the rapid rise of the township enterprises have stimulated the spread of industrial pollution from cities to small townships and, further, to rural areas overall.

The fifth factor is pressure of the market. China is in transition to a market economy. The market itself may produce many external economic or external non-economic effects. Environmental pollution is the most obvious example. The supply of the environment as a public good, such as clean water and air, is good for all and it will not cost much if more people enjoy the benefits. However, without this public good, everybody's interests are in peril. The characteristics of public goods determine that neither individuals nor the market can provide the cost and service for controlling the environment. It is only the government which can be the provider of public goods. In the transition to a market economy, if government lags behind in the changes of its functions and fails to withdraw from the production area in a timely way in order to provide the necessary public goods, it can cause environmental pollution on a large scale or delay the control of pollution.

Major policies and measures for environmental protection

With the constant growth of population, the doubling and redoubling of the economic aggregate and the intensified development of resources and energy, China has adopted a series of positive measures to control environmental pollution and prevent degradation of the eco-system. These include:

- Making environmental protection a basic state policy. The Constitution of the People's Republic of China clearly stipulates: 'The state protects and improves the living environment and eco-system, prevents and controls pollution and other hazards', and 'the state ensures that the natural resources are rationally utilised and rare animals and plants are protected'.
- Incorporating environmental protection into the national economic and social development program. The state has adopted economic and technical policies favourable to environmental protection in a bid to well co-ordinate environmental protection with economic and social development.
- Carrying out land development and control. The state has organised surveys and a comprehensive evaluation of farm land, water bodies, forests, grassland, wasteland and lakes, and has compiled data and maps about the land resources. It has also formulated programs for controlling the Yangzi and Yellow River basins, carried out control of water loss and soil erosion on the Loess Highland, built the shelter belt that extends from northeast China through north China to northwest China, the shelter belt

along the upper and middle reaches of the Yangzi River and the shelter belt along the coasts, and planted trees on the plain areas. It has also carried out large-scale water control projects, built more than 200 000 dikes along various rivers, expanded the irrigated farmland in more than 5300 places, bringing more than 4800 hectares of farmland under irrigation, and ameliorated 1870 hectares of low-lying and water-logged land. The irrigated farmland produces over 70 per cent of grain and cash crops.

- Enforcing family planning programs, to ease the pressure of population on the environment. The total fertility rate dropped from 5.8 in 1970 to 2.2 ten years ago. The fertility level is far lower than other large developing countries with populations of over 100 million.

- Developing eco-agriculture. At present, the country has designated more than 2000 places to try out eco-agriculture of different types and scales. The country has extended widely the comprehensive method of combining chemical, biological and physical means in preventing and controlling plant diseases and pests. In the vast pasture areas, land used for growing grain has been returned to grassland and artificial pastures have been created. Efforts are being made to control rodents.

- Launching pollution control projects in the process of technical transformation of enterprises. Strict measures have been taken to control the use of small industrial boilers and replace them with central heating systems so as to reduce the discharge of pollutants into the air. The state also encourages the building of regional sewage treatment plants to improve the quality of water bodies and the building of centres for treating solid wastes (especially toxic and harmful wastes).

- Improving the urban infrastructure facilities and urban living environment. Efforts have been made to spread the use of tap water, the treatment of sewage water and the use of gas, expand the urban sewage system and increase green areas. Cities are making efforts to dredge river beds and have adopted strict measures to prevent the occupation of land on the city fringes.

- Introducing environmental protection policies based on the market economy. The state has imposed fees for discharging wastes and collected fees for developing natural resources. It has also raised the prices of coal and water and abolished price subsidies for fuel to smooth out distortions in the prices of resources.

- Strengthening education among the people to make them more environment-conscious. The state has tried to use the mass media to spread knowledge about ecology and environment and to encourage the public to take action to protect the environment.

- Inventing and adopting new technology for reducing pollution. The state has encouraged the development of new technologies and technological processes to reduce the energy consumption for per unit output and the discharge of pollutants. It has also made efforts to readjust the industrial structure, with emphasis on developing high value-added industries that cause little or no pollution, and to reduce heavily polluting industries.

China's response to the global environmental agenda

China is working hard to solve global environmental problems. In the 30 years from 1990 to 2020, China's GNP can be expected to grow eight to ten times and energy consumption to increase by two to three times. China has not only to raise the per capita income of its people, but also to improve the quality of life, including environmental quality. This conforms to the interests not only of the Chinese people, but also to the interests of the whole of humankind. For this, China is deeply aware of its responsibilities and the role it must play in solving global environmental problems, and has been actively participating in international co-operation for protection of the environment.

China has become a signatory to the Basle Convention for controlling trans-border movement and disposal of dangerous and waste matters, the Vienna Convention for protecting the ozone layer, and the Montreal Protocol on matters that deplete the ozone layer.

In June 1992, Chinese Premier Li Peng attended the United Nations Conference on Environment and Development in Rio de Janeiro, Brazil. At the conference, the Chinese Premier made clear China's stand on international co-operation in solving global environmental problems. He made the following points:

- Economic development must be well co-ordinated with environmental protection. To many developing countries, the main task is to develop the economy and eliminate poverty. This burning desire of developing countries should be taken into full account in solving global environmental problems.
- It is the common task of the whole of humankind to protect the environment, but economically developed countries should bear greater responsibilities. Developed countries should provide extra funds to developing countries and transfer environmental protection technology on preferential terms.
- It is essential to respect state sovereignties in strengthening international co-operation.
- Environmental protection and development depend on peace and stability in the world.
- In handling environmental problems, it is necessary to take into account both the practical interests of all countries concerned, and the long-term interests of the world. While focusing attention on climatic changes, biodiversity and other global environmental problems, priority should be given to problems of environmental pollution, water loss and soil erosion, desertification, denudation of vegetation, floods and drought and other ecological problems now facing the developing countries.

At the Rio conference, China signed two conventions — the United Nations Framework Convention on Climatic Change and the Bio-Diversity

Convention. This shows that China is willing to accept its obligations and responsibilities according to the provisions of the two conventions.

China has pursued effective and fruitful co-operation with United Nations Environmental Program (UNEP), United Nations Development Program (UNDP), the World Bank, the Asian Development Bank and other international organisations, and many other countries in respect of environmental protection. It is receiving financial aid and low-interest loans from these organisations and countries, for improving environmental quality. At the same time, it has taken an active part in international conferences and in making international laws concerning the environment.

On 23 March 1994, China's State Council officially approved China's Agenda 21. The country is making unremitting efforts to control population growth, improve the living conditions of the people, gradually eliminate poverty and protect the ecological balance of the environment. It has set the following environmental goals for the year 2000:

- to control the total population within 1.3 billion and the natural growth rate at 12.5 per thousand;
- to control the discharge of industrial waste water at about 32 billion tonnes, the discharge of sulphur chloride at 20 million tonnes; to bring the industrial waste water treatment rate up to 84 per cent, the industrial waste gas treatment rate to 82 per cent, and the rate of comprehensive utilisation of solid industrial wastes to 37 per cent;
- to afforest 3093 million hectares and seal off 8.98 million hectares of mountains for protecting forests, and to bring the forest coverage up to 17 per cent, the land protected from soil erosion up to 200 000 square kilometres and the area of nature reserves to more than 50 million hectares.

Notes

1 Hu Angang and Zou Ping, *China's Population Development*, China's Science and Technology Press, Beijing, 1991, p. 182.
2 World Bank, *World Development Report 1992*, Oxford University Press, New York, 1992, p. 220.
3 The National Conditions Investigation Group of the Chinese Academy of Sciences, *Opening Up Resources and Conservation — Development of the Natural and Human Resources in China and Countermeasures*, Science Press, Beijing, 1992.
4 The National Conditions Investigation Group of the Chinese Academy of Sciences, *Survival and Development — A Study of China's Long-Term Development*, Science Press, Beijing, 1992; Angang Hu, Yi Wang and Wenyuan Niu, 'Ecological Deficit is the Biggest Crisis of National Survival in the Future', *China Science and Technology Review* (Beijing), vol. 2, 1990, pp. 60–64, and vol. 3, 1990, pp. 60–64.

5 The State Statistical Bureau of the People's Republic of China, *China Statistical Yearbook, 1993*, China Statistical Publishing House, Beijing, 1993, p. 447.

6 ibid.

7 *The Environment and Development Report of the People's Republic of China*, China Environmental Sciences Press, Beijing, 1992.

8 ibid.

9 *China Statistical Yearbook, 1993*, p. 822.

10 *The Environment and Development Report of the People's Republic of China.*

11 ibid.

12 *China Statistical Yearbook, 1993*, p. 822.

13 China State Environmental Protection Agency, 'Bulletin of China's Environment for 1992', *China Environment News*, 15 June 1993.

14 *China Statistical Yearbook, 1993*, p. 822.

15 The State Planning Commission, the State Science and Technology Commission, China's Agenda 21 (draft), Beijing, October 1993, pp. 19–21.

16 ibid.

17 *The Environment and Development Report of the People's Republic of China.*

18 United Nations Food and Agricultural Organization (FAO), *Chemical Fertilizer Yearbook*, 1989, 1991, cited in *China Statistical Yearbook, 1993*, p. 897.

19 *The Environment and Development Report of the People's Republic of China.*

20 ibid.

21 World Resources Institute/International Institute for Environment and Development, *World Resources: A Report*, Basic Books, New York, 1986.

22 *Introduction to China's Agricultural Geography*, Department of Economic Geography of the Institute of Geography, Chinese Academy of Sciences, Beijing, 1980.

23 *The Environment and Development Report of the People's Republic of China.*

24 British Petroleum (BP), *BP Statistical Review of World Energy*, BP, London, 1986, pp. 31–32.

25 Angang Hu, 'Population Growth, Economic Growth, Technological Change and Environmental–1990)', *Advances in Environmental Sciences*, vol. 1, no. 5, 1993, pp. 1–17.

26 *China Statistical Yearbook, 1993*, p. 81.

27 Hu Angang and Zou Ping, *China's Population Development.*

18 The Domestic Political Environment

David Goodman

Since the middle of 1992, economists have predicted that within a relatively short period of time — perhaps even within 20 years — the People's Republic of China (PRC) will have the world's largest aggregate economy: it is already considered the third largest when the purchasing-power parity of GDP is calculated.[1] As the rest of the world starts to come to grips with the prospect of China as Number One, it will also have to recognise that economic growth is likely to lead to fundamental political change. China's domestic politics are unlikely to stay the same: change — and even possibly revolution — is already well underway.

One obvious example is the emergence of an intense regionalism since the early 1980s. The rapid economic growth of the 1980s and 1990s — when China's GDP has grown at an annual average of 9.1 per cent since 1978 — has been based on an unbalanced growth strategy that encouraged the coastal provinces to build on their more obvious comparative advantages and develop export-oriented industry. First, in South China and more recently in East China and elsewhere, local authorities have been granted, and to some extent have taken, degrees of autonomy that would have been inconceivable before 1978. For economic growth to be sustained nationally at current levels it seems likely that such practices will have to become even more widespread.

Change may be inevitable, but the precise political consequences of economic development and their impact in turn on China's international relations and foreign policy environment are less certain. Regionalism, after all, need not lead to either disunity or political disintegration, nor for that matter must it necessarily alter China's foreign policy or international relations. The long-term possibilities for change are suggested not only by the reform process within China, but also by three historical experiences elsewhere, which seem likely at first sight — because of shared characteristics — to offer pointers to China's future: the collapse of communism in the Soviet Union and Eastern Europe; the emergence of capitalism and democracy in Western Europe; and the transformation of authoritarian regimes in East Asia. In the shorter term, China faces the challenges brought by central government's lack of macro-economic control, particularly inflation; the changing role of the military, the People's Liberation Army (PLA), in a modernising regime; and the need for leadership and organisation during a period of rapid and intense social, political and economic change.

The collapse of communism and political disintegration

The experience of Eastern Europe and the then Soviet Union in and after 1989 suggests that reform may not only be a necessary process in Communist Party states, but that it leads eventually to the end of Communist Party rule, and ultimately to the dangers of political disintegration. This fairly common series of assumptions — though apparently borne out by the examples of the Soviet Union and Yugoslavia and even to some extent Czechoslovakia — is neither universally applicable nor particularly accurate. Reform has certainly challenged the position of the Chinese Communist Party (CCP), but at least in the immediate future there appears no necessary incompatibility between the two. Communist party rule may come to an end in China, and there may be forms of political disintegration, but these are unlikely to occur under the same conditions or for the same reasons as in Eastern Europe.

Communist Party rule undoubtedly created similar political and economic structures in all the countries of the postwar socialist bloc. However, Communist Party rule in the PRC has several notable features which it does not share with the former Soviet Union and states of Eastern Europe. The most obvious is that it came about as the result of an indigenous communist movement, struggling for power through popular mobilisation for some 28 years, two civil wars, and war with a foreign invader. One result is that the CCP's nationalist and popular base of support has always been greater than that enjoyed in the Soviet Union. This does not mean that the Chinese are not alienated from the CCP but it does mean that disenchantment is a slower process and the party's support less ephemeral.

Popular support for the CCP might in any case have been strengthened rather than weakened by the performance of the Chinese economy, particularly since the late 1970s. During 1979–82, the CCP presided over a major reorientation of industrial policy. This reform, perhaps more than any other single factor, explains why the events of 1989 represent different kinds of turning points for communism in China and Eastern Europe. A major limiting factor to reform in Communist Party states was always going to be the power, politically as well as economically, of the heavy industrial sector that lay at the heart of the Stalinist command economy. The effective start of the reform era in China was the successful attempt that immediately followed the Third Plenum to divert additional investment into the development of light and consumer industries. In the event the amount of additional investment was not phenomenally large — only about 3 or 4 per cent of GNP on most current estimates — but it was enough to substantially alter the structure and growth pattern of the economy. Essentially through the exercise of political will, a small net transfer of resources broke the nexus of power that in other Communist Party states bound cadres, planners and state enterprises together in a situation of mutual dependency, all seeing the need for reform, but unable to bring it about. Quite apart from the effect of this change on economic development, it has resulted in the emergence of a genuinely consumer-oriented consumer goods market and hence general social and political support not only for reform but also the CCP.[2]

Economic reform has led to social problems and even political protest in the 1980s and 1990s, but these have resulted from a rapid increase in the standard of living and are largely a consequent and unsatisfiable revolution of rising expectations. Basically such problems are the side-effects of economic growth and development rather than the economic stagnation and decline characteristic of the Soviet Union. Even before the Beijing demonstrations of April–June 1989, such manifestations had become — if not commonplace — certainly not unknown on the streets of the capital.

Economic regionalism certainly has been a major result of the reform process in China. The development of the southern provinces, Guangdong and Fujian, bordering Hong Kong and facing Taiwan respectively, has been quite spectacular through the 1980s and into the 1990s and has caught the international public imagination. It is an example which other regions — notably the East China provinces of Jiangsu, Zhejiang, and Shandong and Liaoning in the Northeast — are rapidly emulating, and indeed China's growth into the world's largest economy sometime early next century will be based on the development of such additional regional economic bases. However, a necessary corollary of this development is that all provinces, and not just the highest economic performers, now have more control over their own activities.

Nonetheless, there is little reason to believe that the borders of provinces, or for that matter the new economic regions, do in general represent the fault lines in China's political system. The PRC's regional politics are not, and have not been, the same as those of the former Soviet Union or Yugoslavia. The disintegration of the Soviet Union was essentially determined by Stalin's constitution and its creation of constituent republics, all of which were based on a dominant or sizeable nationality grouping with a separate identity to that of dominant Russia. Racial, ethnic, religious and political divisions — some of them with extremely long and violent histories — within the Soviet Union were to some considerable extent institutionalised in its political structure. Once central control weakened, unity almost necessarily began to be threatened.

The ethnic composition of the PRC in contrast is approximately 92 per cent Han Chinese, and with notable exceptions, the PRC's division into provincial-level units is not based on a nationality principle. The exceptions are the Autonomous Regions of Tibet, Xinjiang, Inner Mongolia, Guangxi and Ningxia. Regardless of the CCP's ability to maintain a firm central control, the conditions for a Soviet Union-style political disintegration to occur generally in the PRC do not exist. Though there are clear and important provincial differences in China, for the most part the dominant 'state idea' remains that of China. There may, as in South China generally, and Guangdong in particular, be fierce local pride and an attitude of resisting interference from the capital, but these are necessary folk myths and not as yet a coherent desire for political separation.

On the other hand, it is entirely possible to see that movements for political separation in both Tibet and Xinjiang (and possibly, but less likely, Inner Mongolia) may well develop. The crucial difference is that there is, and has been for some time, a separate consciousness and political identity, which in both Tibet and Turkic Xinjiang has developed movements for independence in various ways. The demonstration effect of political disintegration in the Soviet Union is far from just an imaginary threat to the PRC, something to which the repeated upheavals of the early 1990s in Xinjiang bear ample witness.

The political economy of modernisation

At first sight, China's economy certainly seems to have developed some significant capitalist features. The introduction of the market has dramatically altered both economic management and the business of government. Slowly but surely, China appears to be developing institutions that are usually considered necessary parts of the infrastructure of capitalism. Moreover, the impact of reform seems to have shifted economic wealth out of the state sector and into private hands. The 1980s and 1990s have seen the relative decline of the state sector's share of the economy, and dramatic increases in the collective, private and foreign-involved sectors of the economy.[3]

State sector involvement in service, retail and commercial activities (except for financial services) is minimal and even the state sector's share of industrial output has fallen. For example, in 1980 the state sector produced 76 per cent of the gross value of industrial output. By 1991 this had fallen to 53 per cent, and according to official estimates is likely to drop still further to 27 per cent by the year 2000. In contrast, the collective sector of the economy has grown from 24 per cent of the gross value of industrial output in 1980 to 36 per cent in 1991, and is targeted at 48 per cent for the end of the century. The private sector, which was virtually nonexistent in 1980, was responsible for 6 per cent of the gross value of industrial output in 1991, and is expected to reach 13 per cent by the year 2000.[4]

Of course, there are some senses in which China's economic development can and should be described in terms of capitalism. Perhaps the most important of these is that, whatever the form and content of economic development in China, it is clearly the process of modernisation that occurred in Western Europe and North America during the nineteenth century that provides its mobilisatory idea and motivation. Not just technology, but also ideas on management and economic organisation, have been copied and adopted in a variety of ways.

Certainly, the problems and difficulties experienced by governments, employers and the workforce are often very reminiscent of the experience of capitalist development elsewhere. Rapid urbanisation has accompanied economic growth and industrialisation with much rural land being switched from agricultural to industrial and other uses. Less than half the rural workforce is now officially estimated to be engaged in agricultural production, and there is said to have been the transformation of about 100 million people off the land into a permanent migratory and transient workforce in the cities. Enterprises in the richer East China and in the south recruit their workforces from the young in the poorer parts of West and North China, pay them low wages and provide little if any health and welfare support.

China's new rich — the new social categories enriched by economic growth in the 1980s and 1990s — can be very rich indeed, with annual incomes of 10 million yuan Renminbi (RMB) and assets in excess of some RMB100 million. By comparison, the average annual income for the country remains under RMB2000, though the average urban worker's wage will be about RMB250–300 a month, or as much as RMB4000 a year with bonus payments and other emoluments. An established industrialist or manager with a few hundred employees in an enterprise can expect to have an annual income of about RMB20 000.

However, wealth alone is not a sufficient indicator of either capitalism or a capitalist class. The separation of state and society, and particularly the independence of capitalists from the state, is usually held to be a key characteristic of capitalism, especially in its European and American manifestations, and an important factor in the development of democracy. Whilst it seems reasonable to regard China's recent economic development as a form of capitalism, it is clear that China's new capitalists — and indeed, the processes of capitalism — are anything but separate from the state. On the contrary, and despite the evidence that the state sector's importance has declined, the state has played a central and continuing role in China's capitalist revolution.

Official descriptions of the structure of China's economy in terms of the state, collective, private and foreign-involved sectors can be misleading. The collective sector is and has always been part of the state economy. Though it is surrounded by an ideological justification that relates to its ownership either by a locality or by the workers in the enterprise, it is more accurate to regard the collective sector as that part of the state economy run by or associated with local government and not governed by the state plan, as opposed to the state sector which is governed by the state plan.

Since the early 1980s, the distinctions between the state, collective, private and foreign-involved sectors, which theoretically relate to systems of ownership, have become extremely attenuated. The collective sector in particular has become home to all kinds of activity. Under the imperative of reform, state sector enterprises have decentralised their activities and established subsidiary companies, but the latter are registered as collective enterprises. Private enterprises, once they become larger, more technologically sophisticate and economically successful, almost invariably become collective enterprises, not least because the financial and tax environment is so superior. Even smaller less successful private companies want to register as collectives for similar reasons. Local government accepts approaches and suggestions for a degree of co-operation and collective registration because it too is becoming market-oriented, and can make money through the 'collectivisation' of enterprises.

The result of all these trends is a very heterogeneous collective sector, but one which nonetheless maintains strong links with both the state economy and the party-state system. On all the available evidence, a large proportion of the private economy 'piggybacks' the state economy. The patterns of economic interaction, notably supplies and distribution, remain those established by the state economy. Entrepreneurs are often state employees who pay for the privilege of being allowed unpaid leave and to maintain their pension and other welfare entitlements not available outside the state sector. Moreover, as is only to be expected, the CCP has made a determined and successful effort to recruit the new entrepreneurs to party membership, with only a short hiatus in that process during the second half of 1989 and into 1990.

The transformation of authoritarianism

Although the Western European experience of capitalist development may be of limited assistance in providing lessons for China's political future, the East Asian example may be more relevant. East Asian economic development can be regarded as a form of late capitalist development in which — as with Germany and Japan in the nineteenth century — the state plays a leading role. Late developers have the obvious added advantages of being able to draw on the earlier examples and experiences of their predecessors. They do not need initially to develop their own technologies, for these can be imported, particularly if their economies are sufficiently internationalised. In addition, development strategies focus on production for the export market with appropriate measures of protectionism.

Economic growth is linked inextricably with an authoritarian political system which is able to direct the mobilised resources to the national goal of modernisation. As the economy develops and social complexity increases, the state has to adapt to internalise the new social forces it creates. However, the experience of South Korea, Taiwan and even Japan within the last twelve months suggest that such transformations of regime can occur peacefully, in contrast to the violent nineteenth century revolutions that marked the political economy of change in Western Europe. It is even arguable in South Korea, Taiwan and Japan that regime change has occurred without fundamentally threatening the state and leaving its authoritarianism intact.

The usefulness of regarding China as an example of East Asian late capitalism is relatively obvious, not least to the leadership of the CCP. Since the late 1980, the CCP has promoted an image of China precisely in that mould, with an emphasis on successful economic modernisation and authoritarianism as somehow more 'Chinese' than the chaos and lack of social harmony that is bound to result from Western-imported democracy. Newspaper and journal articles, as well as films and television programs, have internalised the message to a high degree, and there can be little doubt that such instinctively reactive nationalism strikes strong popular resonances.

From the perspective of East Asian late capitalism, it seems possible that the PRC's political future might involve a slow and gradual transformation in a similar fashion to the development of politics in Taiwan and South Korea. Certainly this was a common view of China's political future among Western commentators before June 1989,[5] and there has been some evidence since of the kinds of processes that might be expected. For example, the decentralisation of both economic management and government has been matched to some extent by the evolution of the CCP's activities. CCP organisation is now extremely localised, though it is a moot point whether its real strength locally is as much political as social. One reason the new industrialists are keen to join is the function of the local CCP as a meeting point, much in the same way that Rotary and Lions Clubs operate elsewhere.

However, China's experience is significantly different to those of its East Asian late capitalist neighbours in ways that may well influence the political consequences of social and economic change, and particularly its foreign policy environment. Its size is a relatively obvious but frequently underestimated difference. China is massively larger than elsewhere and this has always created different problems for political control and economic direction. Even during the period of greatest Soviet influence, China had a higher degree of decentralisation: policies were rarely set centrally with no room for local adaptation. Economic regionalism, entailing a high degree of local variation in national policy and even local regulation, is well developed in the south and east and will increase with economic growth.

China's size and regionalism are also significant because of the role it comes to play consequently in East Asia. China is so big that only a relatively little growth, such as occurred during the 1980s, has created a huge magnet of attraction for investment in the region that adds an extra dimension to international relations in East Asia. Moreover, the economic regions that have developed within the PRC are also becoming increasingly economically integrated with other specific parts of the East Asia region. Thus Guangdong should perhaps for some time have been regarded as Greater

Hong Kong; Fujian's industrial development is almost three-quarters sourced from Taiwan; Japan and Taiwan investors are particularly active in Shanghai, Zhejiang and Jiangsu provinces; and Korean involvement is significant in both Shandong and northeast China.

The ethnic Chinese are the major vehicle for the PRC's economic integration with East Asia and the existence of that diaspora also marks a further significant difference from East Asian late capitalism. There are some 55 million ethnic Chinese throughout the Asia Pacific region, with an additional unknown number of people of Chinese descent. The existence of Taiwan and Hong Kong has clearly influenced the way the PRC's economy has developed, and both are likely to play a central role in the future of domestic as well as international politics. Of course, Hong Kong will become part of the PRC in 1997, but in the meantime the process of adaptation continues as much from the PRC side as from the Hong Kong side. In addition, meeting the challenge presented by both Hong Kong and Taiwan is something that concerns the CCP and generally has driven change in the PRC since the late 1980s. An obvious example is the way the popular music scene has been drastically liberalised through the introduction of Hong Kong 'Canto-pop' and Taiwanese popular music.

One of the great ironies after June 1989 was that at a time when the CCP was protesting loudly about 'harmful' Western cultural influences fomenting rebellion in China, it was permitting an influx of the kinds of popular music it would previously have not permitted. In fact 1989 marked a turning point in the PRC's policies towards East and Southeast Asia, which further increased the involvement in China of ethnic Chinese from those communities. In the aftermath of Western reaction to its suppression of the demonstrations in Tiananmen Square, the PRC quickly moved to resolve its outstanding diplomatic problems in the region, enabling the not inconsiderable Chinese business communities of Thailand, Malaysia, Indonesia and Singapore to invest in and trade with China.

Although Taiwan and South Korea can look back on the period since the 1960s as a virtually single process of modernisation, the PRC since the late 1970s has experienced a period of growth based on economic restructuring. Economic modernisation had already started in the PRC in the early 1950s. There was not inconsiderable growth between 1952 and 1978, but the problem was that the economy had driven itself into a Stalinist dead-end. This economic difference is important because of its political consequences. By the mid-1950s, the PRC had already created the structures of a modernising state, including bureaucracies and bureaucrats and an educational infrastructure. There are thus two generations of modernisers with different traditions to be found in China, rather than just one. The social categories created during the 1950s have one tradition, based on the structures of the state. The other rests with the new rich of the 1980s and the 1990s and the power of market forces. These two social forces may find it generally easier to co-operate than to be in conflict, but they may also moderate each other's influence.

Agents of change

Consideration of the long-term trends in China's development, particularly in comparative perspective, may provide a somewhat misleading image of stability. Modernisation has rarely if ever proved an even or planned process, and already as a result of its boom–bust cycles during the 1980s, and the political consequences, China has proved that it is to be no exception. Rapid economic transformation has been accompanied by social dislocation and political uncertainty, the influence of which, particularly in the short term, may be disproportionate in China's emergent politics.

A basic uncertainty in China's current politics is the transition to the post-Deng era. Deng Xiaoping may hold no formal position of power in the structures of the CCP or the state, but he has been the undisputed 'paramount leader' from the start of the reform era. Even in highly institutionalised political systems, uncertainties about leadership may destabilise politics. In political systems such as that of the PRC, where politics seem determined by personalities, the illness or ageing of the current leadership imposes fairly obvious strains on political stability. There are concerns not only for Deng's health, but for the health of others in the post-Mao leadership generation who, together with Deng, have been responsible for the reform era.

There are those who argue that neither the CCP nor the PRC can survive long after the deaths of Deng Xiaoping and the post-Mao leadership generation. The direst predictions range from the collapse of the state along Yugoslav and Soviet Union lines to the replacement of the PRC by a dozen or more autonomous regions within five years.[6] Such forecasts are usually based on a number of arguments that outline many of the dynamics of change already identified, and in the light of the events of 1989–91 in the communist world the possibilities cannot be categorically denied. However, their sensationalism is more than a little suspect, not least because of the failure to identify agents of change.

The example of a developing regionalism may prove instructive. Often from a perspective of cultural determinism, it is common to suggest that China's new economic regions build on the traditions of provincialism to threaten political unity.[7] China's provinces are well-established economic, social and political units. They have their own languages (which are frequently not intelligible to other Chinese), cuisine and customs. They are large in their own right, with populations averaging 35–40 million and economies equivalent to many countries elsewhere in the world.

Lack of political unity has been a major recurrent theme in China's history. However, the tradition of provincialism is not that the regions always instinctively opposed the centre. The establishment of separate regional government only occurred when the centre had collapsed, and under the condition that it was the duty of the regional authority to reunify the whole country. One reason that such a belief system was articulated and translated into action was that there was no separate or distinctively local leadership, or rather that there was a community of interest and close interrelationship between the local ruling class and the imperial government.

Leadership and organisation are key factors in political change. The local leaders of China's provinces and new economic regions remain as they have been since the establishment of the PRC — not simply members of the CCP, but its specifically chosen appointees. It may be that for various reasons a higher proportion of natives have served as leaders in their home provinces during the 1980s and 1990s than in earlier decades of the PRC, but they remain appointed from above with the process directed by the CCP. In terms of the localisation of interests, at least at provincial level, the most that can be said is that they have to be the agents of the centre in the locality and the representative of the locality to the centre. If they vary from that prescription they are virtually assured of failure. The cadres of the party–state system apart, there remains as yet no independent articulation of a provincial interest.

More generally, those who populate the party–state system remain the key (if not the only) organised agents of political change. Without exaggerating their abilities, they both see the need to accommodate China's new social forces and to learn from the lessons of the collapse of communist rule in the former Soviet Union and Eastern Europe. The communist officials in Eastern Europe who placed themselves at the head of movements for radical change were third or fourth generation revolutionaries, facing major economic problems and surrounded by the apparent attractions of democracy. The current CCP leadership, in contrast, with the original revolutionaries and their successor generation at its head, faces different socio-economic circumstances and is surrounded by a political discourse in East and Southeast Asia that stresses the synergy between economic growth and authoritarianism.

As elsewhere in East and Southeast Asia, the military may come to play a crucial role in the transformation of China's politics. However, here too there is uncertainty. It might be imagined that, with the reform era and the depoliticisation of other aspects of state activity, the PLA would follow suit, concentrate on becoming a more professionalised, standing army and withdraw from civilian affairs, yet remain as the final arbiter and guarantor of state power.

It is certainly the case that the PLA has lobbied hard for its increased professionalisation since the mid-1970s and a concomitant modernisation of its weaponry. However, it is far from clear that the PLA has completely withdrawn from civilian affairs, though its involvement has changed. Charged with existing in a market-oriented economy, the PLA — or rather its various constituent units — has established a large number of enterprises, many of which have only a very tenuous relationship to military activities. PLA unit budgets are now drafted on the assumption that a certain percentage of funds and resources will be generated by commercial and economic activities.[8]

The extent to which the PLA's economic activities may jeopardise or otherwise influence its role as a major organisational support of the state is far from clear. The possibility exists that the PLA will still not be able to stand outside any possible civilian conflict or dispute and may, to the contrary, be forced to intervene either partially or in its own interests. Thus, for example, it would appear that military units have been mobilised to almost purely economic ends during the various 'commodity wars' that have developed since the mid-1980s.[9] Economic competition with other non-military enterprises has already led PLA units in Guangdong — where roughly half of all the PLA's non-military economic enterprises are physically located — into more direct forms of confrontation.

Outside the formal party-state system — which includes the PLA — there is opposition to the CCP and its policies, but accommodation is an inherent part of political life, for businesspeople and even for those in opposition. The events of 1989 alienated intellectuals and drove many into exile, where they remain. Those who were involved in the movement for reform at the time saw themselves as within the system rather than opposed to it root and branch, and that position remains an unreconciled matter of some debate amongst those now in exile. It is possible that the opposition in exile may develop new ideas and even the organisation to represent a significant threat to the CCP at some point in the future. However, at present they face enormous structural problems. They are divided, physically separate and disparate. They are fundamentally a movement of intellectuals, and whilst that leads to a certain influence it also remains a check on their development as a mass movement. Moreover, they are outside China and thus somewhat tainted in terms of their need to appeal to reactive nationalism.

Chinese intellectuals have flirted with Western ideas of democracy since the end of the nineteenth century, but it could not be said that notions of democracy or even civil society have ever developed strong foundations. For the most part, when democracy was spoken of in the PRC before 1989, the meaning was either that of 'socialist democracy' — perfecting state socialism — or the 'small democracies' — freedom of choice in work, home and marriage. Despite such symbolism as the 'Goddess of Democracy', modelled on the Statue of Liberty, which appeared in Tiananmen Square in May, the demonstrations of 1989 did little, directly or contemporaneously, to develop a new discourse or build towards civil society. However, the 1989 movement could now develop its own mythology which may well play a role in China's political future. There is a foundation for consciousness of democracy that did not exist before and which may develop, particularly with increased exposure to the rest of the world.

Given the role of the party–state in the genesis of new patterns of economic development, it would be remarkable to find the new entrepreneurs generated by China's growth since the late 1970s articulating any demand for regime change of any kind, let alone a Western-style democracy, and there is no evidence to suggest that is the case. On the contrary, at this stage — as one might expect with a continually rising market — most of the energy of the new entrepreneurs is concentrated on making money. Moreover, the attraction of Western ideas, even of capitalism, must be kept in perspective. Throughout the twentieth century, those seeking change in China have articulated a common love–hate relationship with the West. The fruits of Western capitalism are attractive, but for the Chinese political nation the goal is a fundamentally Chinese modernisation, and for many the CCP still represents the best hope of achieving that nationalist goal.

Prolonged economic crisis — which to date has been avoided — and decline have the potential to threaten the infrastructure that brings the party–state system and China's new rich together. However, at present, though the latter may prefer on an individual basis to exclude the CCP from their enterprises, they have no problem with working with it on a larger scale and there is certainly no motive for them to actively organise political change let alone revolution. For similar reasons, ethnic Chinese businesspeople located overseas, who may well be anti-communist in their domestic environments in East and Southeast Asia, are attracted by profits in China.

Nonetheless, the economic problems China faces and the potential dislocations that may result should not be minimised. The PRC has committed itself to abandon the last vestiges of the command economy in favour of indirect economic controls, yet its macro-economic structures remain woefully inadequate. By the end of the first half of 1993, when inflation in urban China threatened once again to get out of hand, the solution was to fall back on administrative measures to crack down on credit facilities. Yet it is precisely the dual-track economic system — part market oriented and part planned economy — and the lack of macro-economic controls that cause both economic problems and subsequent social dislocations.

China's GNP growth rates for 1992 and 1993, in excess of 13 per cent per annum, are clearly both unsustainable and highly inflationary. Particularly during 1993 there appears to have been a higher incidence of strikes amongst the urban workforce and rural unrest. Though it seems likely that the increased incidence of such manifestations is a direct function of rapid economic growth, the relationship between growth, inflation and protest is far from simple. For example, where urban workers may strike because the value of their wages appears to have declined quite rapidly, peasants seem to have protested for greater structural reforms — in particular, the deregulation of prices for agricultural products. The problem here is, of course, that there is at least a short-term direct conflict between the interests of peasants and workers — where the wages of the latter have effectively been subsidised through regulated food prices. The deregulation of food prices has, since 1986, led to urban unrest; the reluctance to deregulate prices has, on the other hand, led to rural protest.

Influences on foreign policy

China's likely future, then, would appear to be that of an authoritarian and modernising regime, similar in many respects to those that developed in Japan, Taiwan or South Korea. The key characteristics of its political economy remain the state's dominance of society and its leading position in the economy. Its political institutions are likely to be dominated by versions of Djilas's New Class,whose access to wealth, power and status results from its positions in the nexus of relationships described by business, bureaucracy and politicians. In those terms, it hardly matters how many political parties compete electorally. The formal political system would thus remain dominated either by the CCP or some successor institution which provides the essential framework for the exercise of economic as well as political power.

On the other hand, a high degree of regionalism is likely to characterise China's future — to a degree not experienced elsewhere in East Asia nor since 1949 in China — as a result of its size and growing economic complexity. If China's economy continues to grow as it has since 1978, it seems reasonable to assume that this will result from regions having considerable autonomy, particularly with respect to their own economic development. China's unity will be affected, but not necessarily adversely. A stronger unity based on economic interaction and a domestic division of labour is also a definite possibility.

The future of the CCP is less certain, if also not predetermined to disappear, even given high rates of economic growth. There can be little doubt that the CCP — at least outside its leadership ranks — is currently undergoing considerable change. The new economic elites who have been recruited in the era of reform have radically different perspectives on life, as well as politics, from those of their predecessors. Though they may be only too willing to reach accommodations with the current party–state, they are also part of a process which is changing it from within. At the local level, this means that the party is much less an organisation for ideological activity and more concerned with economic development and providing opportunities for networking. Though the CCP is not particularly popular, and may even be actively unpopular among certain sectors of the vocal and educated, the strongest argument for its continued hold on power is the lack of an organised alternative.

Stability depends to a large extent on the CCP's capacity to keep its nerve and to mediate economic and political problems and social conflict. For the most part the evidence of the 1980s and 1990s would seem to suggest such exercise of its power is not wildly impossible. The events of mid-1989, when the leadership of the CCP did appear more than a little bewildered and to have at least temporarily lost its nerve, were clearly an exception. However, an understanding and interpretation of those events are now integral parts of the environment in which the leadership must operate and they limit its room for manoeuvre. Civilian and military reaction to the events of 1989 both contemporaneously and since probably makes it difficult for the CCP leadership to repeat its actions, but at the same time provides instructive lessons so that preventive action might be taken to avoid such conflicts and crises in future.

International relations and the foreign policy arena will be of increasing importance to the PRC as it becomes a great power and not just because of that particular self-perception. The PRC's economic growth has been driven by the international economy in a number of different ways. Production for the export market, though likely to be less significant in the future with the growth of the domestic market, was the foundation of high growth rates during the 1980s. A significant proportion of that export-oriented production, as well as much of its international trade and investment, has resulted from the involvement of overseas Chinese in the economic development of the PRC.

The potential for a united PRC as a great power to become involved in an international conflict should not be minimised. The PRC has long signalled its desire to develop a 'blue-water' navy; and states which have pacifist agendas are unlikely to test nuclear weapons. Conflict with Japan is not inevitable, but there are clearly grounds for concern,[10] not the least of which are the nationalist foundations of Communist Party rule in the PRC. The CCP's basic perspectives on international relations have the potential to turn into an extremely aggressive nationalism and have done so several times since 1949. Moreover, a more tolerant politics domestically does not necessarily transfer into more tolerant international perspectives.

Clearly, at the other extreme, there can be little doubt that a disintegrated China would probably be a major threat to regional security. However, a united China is not necessarily a single China, even ignoring the complications of Hong Kong and Taiwan. China's new economic regionalism suggests that there will be no single PRC foreign policy. There is a distinct possibility that different regions of China will relate in specific ways to particular parts of East Asia and the world beyond. Indeed, taken to its logical extremes, such an argument suggests that the rest of the world will have to deal increasingly — as it already does to some extent —with the several governments of the PRC and not just Beijing in international relations.

Notes

1 See, for example, Guonan Ma and Ross Garnaut, *How Rich is China: Evidence from the Food Economy*, Department of Economics and National Centre for Development Studies, Working Paper 92/4, July 1992, Research School of Pacific Studies, Australian National University, Canberra.

2 D.J. Solinger, *From Lathes to Looms: China's Industrial Policy in Comparative Perspective, 1979–1982*, Stanford University Press, Stanford, 1991.

3 Chinese statistics are notoriously unreliable. Unless otherwise indicated, all statistics are derived from the State Statistical Bureau's official publications, notably its annual *Zhongguo tongji nianjian* (Statistical Yearbook of China).

4 1991 figures are from State Statistical Bureau, *Zhongguo tongji nianjian* 1992, p. 23; estimates for the year 2000 from *Wen Wei Po*, 13 July 1992, p. 5.

5 See, for example, Harry Harding, *China's Second Revolution: Reform after Mao*, Allen & Unwin, Sydney, 1989, p. 300.

6 See, for example, 'Perception International', 25 June 1993, in PR Newswire, 6 July 1993.
7 The fullest and most recent example of such an argument is presented in W.J.F. Jenner, *The Tyranny of History: the Roots of China's Crisis*, Allen Lane, London, 1992.
8 See for example, Tai Ming-cheung, 'Profits over Professionalism: The People's Liberation Army and its Impact on Military Unity', paper delivered at Conference organised by the International Institute for Strategic Studies and CAPS, Taipei, in Hong Kong, June 1993.
9 For an example from the rice war that developed between Guangdong and Human provinces, see Chao Chien-min, 'T'iao-t'iao vs k'uai-uai: A Perennial Dispute Between the Central and Local Governments in Mainland China', in *Issues and Studies*, vol. 27, no. 8, 1991, p. 31.
10 See, for example, Gerald Segal 'The Coming Confrontation between China and Japan?', *World Policy Journal*, vol. 10, no. 2, Summer 1993, pp. 27–32.

19 Conclusion: China and the Region After Deng

Stuart Harris and Gary Klintworth

Developments in China that will have the greatest impact on the region in the post-Deng era are already in train. Although the passing of the Deng Xiaoping era is bound to lead to major domestic policy changes within China, some with important impacts on the Asia-Pacific region, it is unlikely that China's assumption of a more central economic, political and strategic role in the Asia-Pacific region — and on the global stage — will be affected by post-Deng domestic changes.

Rapid economic growth in the region has already changed the basic security structure in the Asia-Pacific region. The balance among the various regional powers, particularly the four large powers (or five with India) — the United States, Japan, Russia and China — has shifted, with China growing rapidly in relative importance. Although the removal of major external security threats has given it greater international freedom of action, the growth in China's regional influence has come about basically through its economic growth and that is a consequence of its pragmatic 'open door' growth and interaction with the region.

None of the contributors to this volume argues against the view that China's economic development and growth will continue, although the normal cautions are expressed given the difficulties that China faces in its economic and social development. Certainly, the various major interests within the Chinese leadership do not differ sufficiently on the objectives of policy to vary the general direction of post-Deng economic reform. Indeed, Chinese rulers have few options with respect to economic reform. Consequently, the degree of interdependence with the countries of the region, and more widely, is likely to increase.

To the question of how these developments will affect the region in the decades ahead, the answer is that no one can be entirely sure. Answers can only be guessed at in the broadest of terms about any country, let alone one with China's complexity and given the opaque character of its political and social system.

Because of the scanty information about China's world views and limited experience of its responses to rapid changes domestically and internationally, addressing these questions is very much a case of reading such signs as are available — or the Chinese tea leaves, as one of us termed it in the introductory chapter. The problem is that what is read into those signs will commonly depend on the reader's cultural and other attitudes towards China. In particular, given that there are plusses and minuses in the international record of any country, which of their actions attracts emphasis at a particular moment in time is a matter of judgment.

In the case of China, critics often cite its catalogue of conflict with neighbouring states to support a somewhat antagonistic approach. Since 1949, China has been engaged in war or has threatened to resort to force in the Taiwan Straits, in Korea, in Tibet, on the Sino-Indian border, on the Sino-Russian border, in Vietnam and in the South China Sea. China has also supported insurgencies in Southeast Asia in the 1960s and in Cambodia in the 1980s.

This record would appear to confirm the view that China is a dissatisfied, instinctively expansionist state and that it is ready to resort to 'old-fashioned methods' to pursue its national interests. One critic has claimed that China 'has violated every non-proliferation pledge it has ever made'.[1]

On the other hand, it can be argued that China is becoming an integral part of the Asia-Pacific region with a strong interest in the smooth functioning of regional and international mechanisms like the ARF, APEC and the United Nations. As a member of such forums, China is behaving generally in line with the consensus of the majority of member states.

China's relations with states in the Asia-Pacific region, including countries previously hostile towards China, such as Russia, South Korea, Vietnam and Taiwan, can be interpreted as indicating that tension and confrontation have been widely replaced by increased trade and economic co-operation, leadership exchanges and a variety of initiatives conducive to peace and regional stability. Arguably, it has negotiated by peaceful means the settlement of more disputed territory or borders than any other country. Some would put this down as a consequence of the end of great power attempts to contain China.

Whether this is so or not, it is crucial to analyse China in terms that correspond to criteria applied to other countries of comparable size and importance. Perhaps more than for most countries, at the present stage of its development, much will depend upon the influence — for good or ill — of those interacting with China in the region or globally and how policies towards China, and what China sees as its needs, are developed and implemented. Those policies will depend upon getting the basic attitudes and understandings right in the first place. The preceding chapters in this volume have attempted to give the inevitable tea leaf reading process some context and balance.

Given that the apparent stability of the Cold War period has passed, and given the major changes in regional structures already experienced or in train, there are genuine grounds for acknowledging uncertainty in the region that it would be unwise to overlook.

Uncertainties about security relations stem primarily from perceptions of China's inevitable ascendancy and the fear that China's subjugation and humiliation at the hands of Japan and the Western powers will stimulate China to stand up and settle old scores when it becomes a sufficiently strong power some time in the next century. There is already a small cottage industry predicated on forecasts of growing regional insecurity leading to an apprehension — at times stridently expressed — about future strategic relations in particular but also about the economic influence of China, especially when encompassing as well the influence of the ethnic Chinese throughout the region. For those casting about to find a new source of great power threat, Russia is in disarray and avowedly democratic, India is still too weak and Japan has, to a degree, been Westernised. The obvious remaining candidate is a big, strong, nuclear-armed and nationalistic China.

A cautionary note was struck by Singapore's Senior Minister, Lee Kuan Yew, who observed that when Western commentators write about the China threat they are indirectly fuelling 'a rich lode of apprehension and fear'. Or, as the Malaysian Defence Minister Najib Razak observed, China was being made out to be 'the new bogeyman in Asia'. Of course, there is often a difference between what is seen as appropriate to say publicly and the beliefs that are held — and at times expressed — privately.

Nevertheless, the question of whether particular apprehensions about China's role in the future are justified is exercising many minds in the region. In our view, however, the important point is not just that the answer to that question remains open, but that China's future regional posture and policies are not and have not yet been determined, but are open, at least in substantial part, to the influence of the international community, a point to which we return.

A prior consideration of China's future international posture is whether China will remain intact politically. Rafe de Crespigny, in his chapter, suggests that we should not underestimate the pressure for disunity in the country. Assuming that it is viable as a modern state, China still faces formidable problems.

If one considers China's poverty, its huge population and its limited resources, one could conclude that, despite its rapid economic growth, it will have to strive hard and long just to avoid falling into the black hole of internal disarray, let alone catch up and overtake other great powers to become one of the world's leading economies. As well as the standard problems of inflation, corruption and unequal income distribution, other problems have emerged. Among China's growing problems are those of the environment — in his chapter, Hu Angang discusses ten major environmental problems confronting China's hopes of modernisation.

If these and other hurdles can be overcome, then, as Christopher Findlay concludes, China should be able to squeeze more productivity growth out of its rural and industrial sectors and, with growth stimulated by exports and inflows of foreign capital, it should be able to continue to grow rapidly in terms of overall GNP. Moreover, as he notes, China's dynamic growth is fuelling much of the prosperity of the Asia-Pacific region, being a major market for most economies in the region.

Assuming it can satisfy the expectations of hundreds of millions of people who live on or below the poverty line, a more developed China could perhaps follow the Taiwanese path to political reform and democratisation. Such a China could contribute to regional peace and stability. Even without democratisation, a modernising China that remains intact politically could be less threatening, with fewer adverse impacts on the region, than a China in which central authority has broken down, which is in internal disarray and which faces uncontrolled refugee flows out of the country.

As well as its general economic integration in the region, China's modernisation, moreover, will deepen its integration into the regional and global economy in ways that go beyond trade and investment forms. An example — not without its own economic and security implications — is Peter Rimmer's consideration of the growing pattern of infrastructure and communications networks linking China with the region and the rest of the world.

An important question about China's impact on the region is how far China will continue to develop as a more or less co-operative member of the regional and global community. China has already shown a growing interest in working with, rather than against, international and regional groups like the United Nations, GATT and the IMF, as well as ASEAN, PECC, APEC and the ARF.

Discussions on security co-operation, in particular, have progressed from low-key second-track diplomacy to more formally constituted regional forums. These developments, and the growth of regional co-operation in economic matters that is spilling over into the security sphere provide some counter to pessimistic views about China's future role in the region.

Sha Zukang, not surprisingly, is optimistic about the region and China's future good neighbour policies. He stresses his government's desire for a new world order which he says China would base on the principles of peace, stability, justice and rationality. He insists, however, that China has its own 'national interests to protect'. Clearly, there is room for differences as to whose world order we are talking about and the nature and limits of China's national interests. Samuel Kim concludes that China is likely to behave like any other self-interested great power, though in China's particular case, power lies with the state, not individuals.

For Kim, China's rise as a great economic and military power will need to be matched by political reform, as in Taiwan. Major political reform is by no means inevitable, but Hong Lijian and Bruce Jacobs judge it to be possible, not least because of the PLA's inability to use force successfully against

Taiwan, which they see as the source of strong cultural and economic influences that are gradually transforming communism in mainland China and contributing to the decentralisation of Beijing's political authority. More change, perhaps along the lines of the Taiwan model, and more regionalism may be linked to China's modernisation, but as David Goodman points out, disunity or political disintegration will not necessarily follow. On the contrary, good economic management could strengthen popular support for the central government, at least in the Han-dominated heartland of China.

The chapters by the area specialists reflect a mixture of scepticism, fear and cautious optimism as to how change in China will impact on Chinese foreign policy. As Ian Wilson points out in his chapter on Japan, it is difficult to project ahead the nature of the Sino-Japanese relationship in simple terms because of its great complexity. Subject to a range of variables, however, he concludes that the relationship is likely to be generally friendly without being too effusive. Klintworth and McLean make a similar point about the Sino-United States relationship, perhaps the most critical relationship in the Asia-Pacific region after that between the United States and Japan.

As well as the many concerns held within the region about China's growth, for non-Asian countries outside of the region in particular, the focus on China is likely to increase to the extent that the Korean peninsula loses its prime role as the major regional flashpoint. Yet, on the Koreas, as James Cotton observes, China has played a positive role over the last few years — for example, by opening up relations with South Korea while helping defuse the nuclear issue and while trying to ensure a safe landing for North Korea's Stalinist regime. This he sees as likely to continue.

Mohan Malik believes China and India could become great power rivals, but for the forseeable future he judges their relationship will be typified by bilateral co-operation and peaceful competition. While Russia will inevitably remain one of China's long-term security concerns, Greg Austin concludes that there are good prospects for a continuation of the present co-operative relationship between China and Russia, although this could fade in the longer term. Moreover, there is also a possibility of some form of Sino-Russian entente — should China judge the United States' policy towards China to be ill-intentioned, and especially if this is seen to be so in concert with the West as a whole.

While these chapters reflect a degree of optimism about major power relationships, with China's policy built around the notion that Austin attributes to Deng Xiaoping of 'offend nobody', Leszek Buszynski urges caution. He concludes that, although ASEAN–China relations have improved markedly since the 1960s, the ASEAN states still feel the weight of China's proximity and history, in particular, its earlier support for revolutionary movements in Southeast Asia and its claims to islands and waters in the South China Sea. For the future, the relationship will depend on the nature of the regime that emerges in Beijing and how well it handles regional fears of its size and influence.

A similar scenario exists for China's relations with Vietnam. As Carlyle Thayer remarks, there is a tyranny of geography imposed on small states that are close to China: they have to learn to live with their neighbour and yet devise means to remain at arm's length without giving offence. Thayer suggests that Vietnam, having been reminded that alliance with an external power hostile to China is a recipe for war, may at last have now evolved the right formula for coping with China.

While the extent of potential regional insecurity stemming from China's development and modernisation may have been exaggerated, the region is more fluid and therefore more uncertain and, as many analysts argue, we need to avoid the trap of complacency. Historical experience suggests that the time of greatest risk of strategic conflict is when there are significant shifts in the balance of power and influence among major powers. Such transformations are clearly in process in the Asia-Pacific region and will continue in the coming decade or so.

China, already a major regional power, will become a major global power. China's outward pattern of response to international developments or issues can at times seem peremptory and assertive. Although China claims, like most countries, to have a moral basis to its foreign policy, it can be argued that it departs from that approach when its interests require it to do so.

Particular concern is often expressed that China is embarking on a modernisation of its military capabilities. China's modernising of its armed forces, its doctrine and its equipment is discussed in You Ji's chapter. China is seeking to narrow the technical gap between its mainly old equipment and the firepower and technology that was displayed during the Gulf War. This modernisation may speed up, as You Ji suggests, but even so, this will be a long and slow process, as Desmond Ball and Gary Klintworth point out. China will have to commit resources many times larger than at present — whether measured in terms of renminbi, US dollars or purchasing power parity — to achieve a military force with great strategic significance. At the same time, countries in the region will not be standing still. In concert with other countries, the member states of the Asia-Pacific community have made considerable progress economically and in terms of regional organisation and alliance building.

These trends, together with the conclusions of the chapters on China's military capabilities and its defence modernisation plans, suggest that China's military modernisation should not be a cause for undue concern. Above all, there is unlikely to be a vacuum into which China can expand — the United States can be expected to retain a powerful presence in the Pacific so that there is unlikely to be a sudden shift in the balance of power in favour of China. Thus military power in the Asia-Pacific region has to be weighed in the context of the regional political economy, the diplomacy of regional economic and security dialogue processes, the fact that the United States will remain engaged as the number one power in the Pacific region for the foreseeable future, and that Japan and Taiwan will be two of the few countries in the world with surplus capital and, along with the United States, the major sources of technology.

Nevertheless, the introductory chapter to this volume suggested that, barring massive upheavals in China, it will become one of the world's great powers with enhanced economic and strategic influence in the region and globally. This is reflected generally by the contributors, as is the uncertainty this generates in the region.

In a sense, the region as a whole faces an economic security dilemma. It wants China to continue growing in economic terms. This is seen not just as economically rewarding to the region but also as leading China to peaceful international relations and to domestic economic and social stability. Both are seen as important to China's neighbours. But it is that economic growth, which gives rise to the concerns about China's future dominance and to a reading of China's complexity, its history, its geography and its size, that leads to fears that an expansionist China will convert its growing economic strength into military power and strategic influence.

While, as Samuel Kim's chapter notes, the notion of China's need for 'living space' beyond its borders retains some currency,[2] China has to look beyond its borders in a more important sense. China has a major interest in maintaining co-operative relations with the United States and Japan, both of which have strong interests in Taiwan and Hong Kong. China shares their interest in preserving the financial well-being of Hong Kong and Taiwan, so that this will contribute to pragmatism in China's approach to Taiwan and Hong Kong. As Chinese commentators often reaffirm, China needs a long period of peace in order to concentrate on its domestic priorities undistracted by conflict with powers like Japan or the United States, because it needs their overseas markets, capital and technology. It also needs to operate without border tension with large neighbours like India and Russia.

There is little reason to doubt, in the short run, China's statements that it should not be regarded as a threat to its neighbours — unless, that is, China sees itself pushed to respond to the actions of others, whether with respect to Taiwan, the Spratlys, or elsewhere. However, the latter situation is one it almost certainly wants to avoid. It is possible to interpret its seemingly aggressive position on Taiwan or the Spratlys, for example, as a means of warding off actions to which it might be forced to respond unwillingly, particularly in the jockeying for position in the early post-Deng years.[3]

The important question of uncertainty, however, concerns the long run. There can be no guarantee that one day China will not seek to expand its territory and behave as in the past, when it was the dominant power in Asia. How long it might be before that option is reasonably open to China is a moot point. It might be ten or 20 years or, given China's problems and population, it might be considerably longer.

In practice, China is likely to behave like any other great power at an earlier stage, without necessarily doing so in the same way as great powers have acted in the past. China might at some stage in the future have the military capability to be territorially expansive. One constraint on whether it would be in China's interests to do so is that it is not just the growth in economic power that is relevant. In projecting power, the traditional economic objectives of power projection — one-off acquisitions of natural resources, population and territory — have become less important than continuing access to technology and capital. Thus economic interdependence remains a major strategic factor, but in a way that differentiates it from the economic interdependence that was experienced elsewhere earlier in history, and on which judgments about its influence have been made.

An added qualification is that there is now less value in the traditional military approach because it is also much more costly. Influence that is useful is more likely to come through cultural reach, or economic or political pressure. Such pressure might, of course, be buttressed by military threat and provide a motive for further military modernisation.

More generally, if we accept that in the light of those and other factors, China is capable of being influenced for good or ill in terms of its foreign relations, the question arises as to how the international community can respond in a manner that encourages co-operative behaviour globally as well as regionally. While the contributors to this volume were not asked to address this particular question, some conclusions are possible.

Co-operative relationships will not be easy to achieve. China will increasingly impinge on areas where the United States in particular, and the West in general, have been dominant. Considerable suspicion exists on both sides as to the intentions or interests of the other. Yet the international community will have to make room for China not just as an economic competitor but in the political and strategic arenas. The question is not whether, but how, that adjustment is to be made.

While national history will not be the determining factor for Chinese responses any more than it would be for those of any other country, historical experience is generally influential. China's particular history is likely to play a part in determining how it interprets its need to meet legitimate national objectives, the obvious ones being security and economic welfare.

China's security concerns — it has over 20 land and sea borders, many with actual or potential problems — are often underestimated, as is the Chinese fear of internal disintegration. In particular, China believes the rules applied to it in meeting its security needs differ from those of the West. Criticisms of China's arms sales come uneasily from the United States and the United Kingdom, given their large arms exports; even criticisms of sales of sensitive nuclear technologies come uneasily given the West's past experience with the transfer of sensitive technologies to countries such as Egypt, Iraq and Iran. In China's eyes, sales of F16 strike aircraft to Taiwan are just as dangerous as its missile technology sales to Pakistan and it is not unreasonable for them to suggest that exports of both and not just missile technology should be controlled.[4] It also suspects that the expressed concerns about its military modernisation are attempts to maintain China in a weak position.

China's history has also made its political need to protect its sovereignty especially significant. Yet the international developments covered by the term 'globalisation', which are especially important in meeting its economic needs, will involve a continually increasing intrusion into domestic — particularly economic — matters. Earlier this century, tariff autonomy was an important element of Chinese nationalism since China's tariff rates were set by the foreign powers until 1930. This not only puts a particular gloss on China's GATT/WTO membership, but it could imply a greater sensitivity to international concerns with domestic industry or other policies affecting trade competitiveness. Such intrusions are inevitable, but there will be a need for those involved to comprehend the sensitivities involved.

International relationships are not just concerned with the distribution of economic, political or military power. Status and prestige are also important, often critically so, as is likely to be the case for China given its history. China's status and prestige as the most important great power in continental Asia has been recognised implicitly if belatedly by most of its regional neighbours, but considerably less so by the West despite its UN Security Council membership.

Broader issues are involved, and bring into play questions of cultural values, including the often-held belief that Chinese and Western societies hold incompatible political and moral values and that Western values are unquestionably superior. Some of the key issues of international relations will centre on such issues in the future as Asia enters more directly into global consideration. There are reasons for confidence, however, in a growing cultural interdependence based on universal civilisational values, provided China's legitimate needs for security, development and identity are met.[5] Problems are less likely to arise from the values themselves than from questions of the West's motives and, indeed, its moral authority in pursuing selectively some but not all of those values.

A continued implication that the Chinese need not be treated in the same way as other Western or at least friendly countries also offends the concern for prestige and status. The United States policy linking human rights and trade was notable for its lack of consistency with United States policy towards other human rights offenders such as Saudi Arabia. That it was changed was helpful but the reason for change was less a concern to develop a more balanced policy than domestic political concerns about economic exchanges. The aggressive pursuit of its political and economic models has led many Chinese, including reform-minded intellectuals, to conclude 'that American pressure on human rights is a way to keep China frail and divided'.[6]

China wants to change the international system, claiming that, like other developing countries, it has been obliged to follow rules made by the developed countries in their own interests. As its power grows, it wants to be involved in making the rules. History might suggest that that may not in fact involve major changes but China will need to feel that its new power is reflected in an enhanced international role regionally as well as globally.

The region is increasingly groping for a coherent policy approach towards a more influential China. That has not been easy, despite a degree of common understanding of Asian political and economic models. The West still seems hesitant to respond constructively to the growth in the self-confidence that China is sharing with Asian countries. Disagreements will undoubtedly continue, but the lack of a Western policy that reflects an understanding of and sensitivity to the factors that motivate Chinese policies and responses, and can come to grips with a China that would be a major power, and should be expected to be treated as one, remains a critical gap.

Notes

1 A US Senate staffer, William Triplett, cited in Thomas McNaugher, 'A Strong China: Is the United States Ready?', *Brookings Review*, Fall 1994, p. 18.

2 See also John Garver, 'China's Push Through the South China Sea: The Interaction of Bureaucratic and National Interests', *China Quarterly*, vol. 132, December 1992, p. 999.

3 This point has also been made by Ralph Cossa, 'The PRC's National Security Objectives in the Post-Cold War Era and the Role of the PLA', *Issues and Studies*, vol. 30, no. 9, September 1994, pp. 1–28.

4 See McNaugher, *work cited*, p. 19.

5 See Akira Iriye, *China and Japan in the Global Setting*, Harvard University Press, Cambridge, 1992, pp. 139–42.

6 Harry Harding, 'Asia Policy to the Brink', *Foreign Policy*, vol. 96, Fall 1994, p. 71.

Index